POLITICS AND 'POLITIQUES' IN SIXTEENTH-CENTURY FRANCE

During the French Wars of Religion, the nature and identity of politics was the subject of passionate debate and controversy. The word *politique*, in both sixteenth-century and contemporary French, refers to the theory and practice of politics – *la politique* – and the statesman or politician – *le politique* – who theorised and practised this art. The term became invested with significance and danger in early modern France. Its mobilisation in dialogues, treatises, debates, and polemics of the French Wars of Religion was a crucial feature of sixteenth-century experiences of the political. Emma Claussen investigates questions of language and power over the course of a tumultuous century, when politics, emerging as a discipline in its own right, seemed to offer a solution to civil discord but could be fatally dangerous in the wrong hands. By placing this important term in the context of early modern political, doctrinal, and intellectual debates, Emma Claussen demonstrates how politics can be understood in relation to the wider linguistic and conceptual struggles of the age, and in turn influenced them.

EMMA CLAUSSEN is a British Academy Postdoctoral Fellow in French at the University of Cambridge.

IDEAS IN CONTEXT

Edited by David Armitage, Richard Bourke and Jennifer Pitts

The books in this series will discuss the emergence of intellectual traditions and of related new disciplines. The procedures, aims and vocabularies that were generated will be set in the context of the alternatives available within the contemporary frameworks of ideas and institutions. Through detailed studies of the evolution of such traditions, and their modification by different audiences, it is hoped that a new picture will form of the development of ideas in their concrete contexts. By this means, artificial distinctions between the history of philosophy, of the various sciences, of society and politics, and of literature may be seen to dissolve.

The series is published with the support of the Exxon Foundation.

A full list of titles in the series can be found at:
www.cambridge.org/IdeasContext

POLITICS AND 'POLITIQUES' IN SIXTEENTH-CENTURY FRANCE

A Conceptual History

EMMA CLAUSSEN

University of Cambridge

CAMBRIDGE
UNIVERSITY PRESS

CAMBRIDGE
UNIVERSITY PRESS

University Printing House, Cambridge CB2 8BS, United Kingdom

One Liberty Plaza, 20th Floor, New York, NY 10006, USA

477 Williamstown Road, Port Melbourne, VIC 3207, Australia

314–321, 3rd Floor, Plot 3, Splendor Forum, Jasola District Centre, New Delhi – 110025, India

79 Anson Road, #06–04/06, Singapore 079906

Cambridge University Press is part of the University of Cambridge.

It furthers the University's mission by disseminating knowledge in the pursuit of education, learning, and research at the highest international levels of excellence.

www.cambridge.org
Information on this title: www.cambridge.org/9781108844178
DOI: 10.1017/9781108933582

First published 2021

A catalogue record for this publication is available from the British Library.

Library of Congress Cataloging-in-Publication Data
NAMES: Claussen, Emma, 1989- author.
TITLE: Politics and 'politiques' in sixteenth-century France : a conceptual history / Emma Claussen, University of Cambridge.
DESCRIPTION: New York, NY : Cambridge University Press, 2021. | Series: Ideas in context | Includes bibliographical references and index.
IDENTIFIERS: LCCN 2020055289 (print) | LCCN 2020055290 (ebook) | ISBN 9781108844178 (hardback) | ISBN 9781108928335 (paperback) | ISBN 9781108928335 (epub)
SUBJECTS: LCSH: Political science–France–History–16th century. | Political science–France–Philosophy.
CLASSIFICATION: LCC JA84.F8 C62 2021 (print) | LCC JA84.F8 (ebook) | DDC 320.0944/09031–dc23
LC record available at https://lccn.loc.gov/2020055289
LC ebook record available at https://lccn.loc.gov/2020055290

ISBN 978-1-108-84417-8 Hardback

For Bissie, Brian, and Jennifer

Contents

Figures

Preface

This book asks how people understood the concept of politics in sixteenth-century France, and how those who practised it were characterised. Both concept and practitioners were referred to by the same word, *politique*. I trace written uses of this word as a means of studying shifts in the meaning of the concept and the figure. As much as this is a conceptual history, therefore, it is a textual and a literary one. Part of the book's argument is that sixteenth-century literary ideas and processes influenced developments in political thought and practice. It also argues that the word *politique* and the idea of politics hold a specific place in the literature of the period. The book is about the representation of politics and political actors in writing, the writing of politics, and writing *as* politics. It treats a diverse corpus, including polemical pamphlets, high political thought, and works strongly associated with the literary canon such as Montaigne's *Essais* and the *Satyre ménippée*.

This period of European history has been described as foundational for modern politics. I consider the case of France, mostly during the civil wars known as the Wars of Religion. France is at once typical and unusual within the sixteenth-century history of politics and *politiques*. It experienced the renewal in the study of politics and political theory, and the political turbulence, that characterised Europe during the Renaissance and the Reformation. However, in French (as compared to English, for example) there is an especially strong overlap between noun and adjective, and between abstract 'politics' and the somewhat more concrete figure of the political actor, partly because they are all expressed by the same word, *politique*. It is not always easy to identify which part of speech is being employed. There is a complex connection between the idealised or demonised *politique* figure and abstract notions of politics. Moreover, the masculine substantive *politique* attracted controversy during the French

Wars of Religion. The term came to describe a loose party of those who favoured peace and negotiation over violence and intransigence, and who therefore made the pragmatic choice to support Henri de Navarre in the later stages of the conflict and to sponsor his second tactical conversion to Catholicism. So-called *politiques* were castigated in polemic for their willingness to compromise religious uniformity (and authenticity) for civic peace. The question of the nature and identity of real *politiques* is some-what vexed; in this book the *politique* figure is as much a construct as [he] is an identifiable historical actor, if not more so.

The issue of the *Politique* party and the particularity of the *politique* persona represent a unique case in the broader history of political language and ideas in the sixteenth century. This is not an argument for French exceptionalism, but rather for specificity within the larger context. Post-Reformation religiously inflected civil conflict was widespread in the sixteenth and seventeenth centuries, not only in France but also in Germany, the Netherlands, and England. France was intimately connected with the affairs of its neighbours, and foreign powers intervened in the French conflict; many of the writers discussed in this book look abroad, to Spain, Germany, England, or further afield, as sources both of inspiration and of threat. France was also connected to territories beyond Europe, especially the Ottoman Empire and the Americas. Indeed, the category of 'France' itself is very much a permeable one in the sixteenth century.

European writers of the period also drew on the shared heritage of antiquity, and in this France, again, was no exception. The French language of politics comes from Ancient Greece in its very vocabulary, as does the word 'politics' in many other modern vernaculars. In the twen-tieth century, Hannah Arendt wrote that 'the Greek *polis* will continue to exist at the bottom of our political existence – that is, at the bottom of the sea – for as long as we use the word *politics*'.[1] The reason we use the word politics in the way that we do, in both French and English, is in part a sixteenth-century story, the result of early modern attention to classical thought. Today, it may be that sixteenth-century texts have joined their classical predecessors beneath the sea. The sea as symbolic of political existence – and of the historical depth of the present – is part of Arendt's image, in her essay on Walter Benjamin, of the thinker as a pearl diver who finds the 'rich and strange' detritus of history on the seabed. The

[1] Hannah Arendt, 'Walter Benjamin: 1892–1940', in Walter Benjamin, *Illuminations*, tr. by Harry Zorn (London: Random House, 1999), pp. 7–61 (pp. 53–55).

story of politics and *politiques* in sixteenth-century France is not exactly a string of pearls, but it is both rich and strange, and Arendt's suggestion of the word for politics itself as a potential pearl does in some ways express the spirit of this study.

I attempt to connect the French words for politics and political actors with discernible political reality – to trace the impact of language on events, and vice versa, as well as arguing that the changing use of the word *was* a literary-historical event, both material and immaterial, like Arendt's pearls. But the connection between the written and the real is hardly straightforward. The history of politics and *politiques* involves doubt, propaganda, fiction, and all kinds of wishful thinking; it involves political writing marked by desire – desire for freedom, or for uniformity, or for control, and so on. It is marked, too, by thwarted desire for an impossible conformity between words and deeds. Another particular feature of uses of *politique* in sixteenth-century France is self-consciousness concerning the gap between the name and the thing. In the later decades of the century, writers refer frequently to the so-called *politiques* (the Huguenot writer Simon Goulart, for example, mentions 'les politiques qu'on appelle'). The implication is that calling someone *politique* doesn't necessarily make them so; it just gives them the name. Modern historians also often refer to 'so-called' *politiques*, emphasising the act of naming, the speech act. Speech acts, or acts of language, are foregrounded both in the period and in criticism; thus, they are a central focus of analysis in this book.

This is not a study of *all* political language, nor of all instances of the word *politique*. For reasons elaborated in Chapter 1, it focuses on printed text, and especially on political treatises and polemical writing (there being considerable overlap between the two). These were new kinds of text, facilitated by the advent of printing; in particular, the polemical pamphlets printed during the troubles of the League (*c.* 1584–94; especially after 1588) had a critical impact. I consider the kinds of politics imagined, and created, in a new print world that was not entirely institutionalised, even if, for instance, a new translation of Aristotle, dedicated to the Queen Mother, was associated with the newly founded *Collège royal*, and radical Catholic pamphlets with the Sorbonne. This is not, then, directly a book about diplomacy, courtly intrigue, particular factions, peace negotiations, regional *parlements*, or *états généraux* – although these were crucial forms and spaces of political action in the period, familiar to all the figures discussed in the book, many of whom were active in some or all of these arenas. It is, rather, about political imagination expressed in text and especially in the use of a particular keyword, *politique*.

Part I addresses the *'politique* problem', which I treat as a problem of language and of definition. Chapter 1 introduces the historiographical and theoretical frames of the study. I outline the methods I have employed to analyse politics and *politiques*, and consider the relationship between the two. I discuss word-historical and keywords approaches and their use in intellectual history, and demonstrate that within the established overlapping fields of *Begriffsgeschichte*, history of ideas, and word histories, this book takes a specifically literary-critical approach to politics and *politiques*.

I show in Chapter 1 that politics was increasingly prominent and important in the period, that the term *politique* could not easily be defined; at the same time, the people known as *politiques* were themselves hard to identify or to associate with particular ideas. This gave politics and *politiques* considerable possibilities for certain writers and interest groups, but it also made them dangerous. These controversies have also made parsing uses of the term *politique* a historiographical problem: what was the *Politique* party, did it exist, when did it exist, with which ideologies was it associated, and what, if anything, was a typical *politique* attitude? Is this a useful historical category or a misleading one? I suggest that this confusion is indicative of the *politique* problem, that is, of the particular power of *politique* in sixteenth-century discourse, and of the emergence of politics as a distinct object of knowledge.

Chapter 2 is an overview of sixteenth-century literary-political writing, and of the semantic field that produced the *politique* problem, which was influenced by Renaissance humanist thought, the situation of the French monarchy in the run-up to the civil wars, and the Reformation. The semantic field was also shaped by developments in the use of and attitudes to the French language. Just as modern linguistic theories refer to semantic fields, so too sixteenth-century French writers used field, garden, and plant metaphors to describe the flourishing of the vernacular. An early example is Geoffroy Tory's *Champ fleury* ('Field of Flowers', 1519). Not all fields were flowered, however. Later writers complained of overgrown gardens and dangerous offshoots: and one such offshoot was the partisan use of *politique* in the late stage of the civil wars. Chapter 2 charts the development of the *politique* 'plant' (or 'weed') in the garden of French letters, in texts by authors as varied as Rabelais, Etienne Pasquier, Guillaume Budé, Loys Le Caron, Michel de L'Hospital, Montaigne, and François de la Noue. Their writings span the century and are generically diverse, with dialogue the most prominent form. Most of these authors were lawyers or connected to the rising literary-legal elite known as the *noblesse de robe*. Many rework the figure of the adviser to a prince, imbuing that adviser with *politique* skills that characterise an emerging class of experts in and agents of power. They comment on the difficult nature of politics and suggest what good political action could look like. Politics in the sixteenth century has often been understood as being defined by what it was *not*: that is, that it was not religion, or theology, and that under pressure from Reformation conflict it became increasingly incompatible with religious rules. By contrast, I suggest in this chapter that fractured connections between theological and political discourses are only part of the story of how politics came to represent such a problem, and such an opportunity, in the sixteenth century.

Chapter 2 has a wide range of examples. Its purpose is to offer a broad context for the more sustained close reading carried out in the rest of the book, serving as a pre-history within the word history. Guillaume Budé's image of a usefully 'mixed man' who combines political acumen with other kinds of learning for the benefit of both ruler and ruled is not especially prominent in his own text; later writers during the civil wars are, by contrast, obsessed with and haunted by the boundaries of the 'mixed' *politique*'s flexibility. Chapters 3–6, organised chronologically, represent the core narrative of the book, in which the problematic flexibility of the *politique* is a central problem to be resolved, mitigated, or condemned. Part II (Chapters 3 and 4) treats works published *c.* 1568–78; Part III (Chapters 5 and 6) covers *c.* 1588–95. Each period experienced a structuring crisis: in the first case, the Saint Bartholomew's Day massacres of 1572; in the second, Henri de Navarre's final struggle for France and for Paris following the assassinations of the Guise brothers and of Henri III in 1588–89. The texts analysed in these four chapters are different to those that feature in Chapter 2 in that *politique* is an important keyword in all of them; each group of texts made an especially significant intervention in the history of the term *politique*.

Chapter 3 is a comparison of Jean Bodin's *Six livres de la République* (1576) with the paratexts of Loys Le Roy's translation of Aristotle's *Politics* (1568). If, as Arendt wrote, the Greek *polis* is at the bottom of our collective 'sea', by translating the *Politics* and updating Aristotelian precepts with his extensive commentary, Le Roy's work is a diving mission, a work of salvage and transformation. Among the theorists of antiquity, Aristotle held an especially important place in early modern political thinking, both as inspiration and as something to work against. His dictum that 'man is a political animal' informs the period sensitivity to the idea that politics not only exists in the world but is also incarnated by, and is to greater or lesser extents inherent to, the human subject. As such, debates about what behaviour characterises a *politique* person were always a matter of political theory as well as of polemic. Bodin's *République*, one of the most significant interventions in French political theory under the *Ancien régime*, attempts to reimagine the purpose and practice of politics, enacted by a wise *politique* figure who could stand alongside the great *politiques* of antiquity. It is also a kind of salvage of the principles of classical thought, written in French to serve an immediate political purpose and later translated into Latin to make it more accessible to a wider European audience. The word *politique* appears frequently in these texts as title or as generic marker, and both authors work to amplify the significance of politics within the disciplines. Thus the abstract term experiences a moment of positive construction in these works, embodied in the masculine substantive, *le politique*, who is the agent of a particularly powerful kind of knowledge (of politics, *la politique*).

Bodin and Le Roy write about politics as Catholics; in Chapter 4, I analyse Huguenot political writings. Huguenot writers reinforce and appropriate positive, powerful uses of the word *politique* circulating in erudite discourse to argue for an alternative vision of how society should operate, and what politics should be. The key sources in this chapter are the anonymous *Le reveille-matin des françois* (1574) and extracts from Simon Goulart's *Mémoires de l'estat de France sous Charles neufiesme* (1576–78). The *Reveille-matin* was one of the best-known and widely read polemical texts of the war period. It is a pair of dialogues between exiled French citizens, among whom we find a character called Le Politique. The characters analyse recent history and develop a political mission, imaging new 'political laws' for France and ultimately arguing for rebellion against tyrants who suppress the Reformed faith. The main excerpt from Goulart's *Mémoires* analysed is a philosophical dialogue entitled 'Le Politique'. The dialogue is prefaced by a briefer exchange between an uncle and nephew seeking consolation in the wake of atrocities; this exemplifies the spirit of the works in question, which combine energetic desire for change with melancholy at the present situation. An enormous range of references and textual appropriations are embedded in these writings. Alongside classical *exempla*, contemporary authors such as Ronsard appear, and plagiarised anonymous versions and extracts of Etienne de la Boétie's *Discours de la servitude volontaire* are pivotal. Another important contemporary reference in both Chapters 3 and 4 is Machiavelli, whom Bodin names in the preface to the *République* as having been sorely mistaken, and whose nefarious image was forged in Protestant writings in the wake of the Saint Bartholomew's Day massacres – but I argue that the association between

'Machiavel' and *politique* is not the straightforward transfer of moral iniquity that one might expect.

Bodin's *République*, Le Roy's translation, and Huguenot resistance texts all have an established place in the history of political thought – more than analysing their political programmes, though, I am interested in how they define politics and *politiques*, and in the qualities of the texts. These are also important aspects of the politics of these texts. What is clear is that, as well as paying attention to this abstract question of what politics is and the practical question of what it ought to do, they raise the issue of *who* ought to be doing it. These texts imagine visions of a *politique* person or character who might fulfil abstract principles.

In Chapter 5 this previously powerful and often positive, if sometimes ambiguous, *politique* character turns bad. This occurs in the febrile period that saw the expulsion of Henri III from the capital, the assassination of the Guise brothers who led the Catholic League opposing the monarchy, and the retaliatory murder of the king. The aftermath of these events was crucial in the history of the term *politique*. Previously the noun *politique* was an object of knowledge, and a knowing subject; from *c.* 1588 the *politique* person becomes an object to be known and reviled, while retaining some of the qualities of the knowing *politique* subject. Catholic polemicists writing in support of the League seized on the figure of the *politique* as a quasi-fictional enemy who sought compromise, a manifestation of everything they hated and feared about contemporary politics. The pamphlets they wrote attacking *politiques* advertise their attempts to define and otherwise pin down these usefully shadowy figures, and in so doing demonstrate just how difficult they were to define.

Moreover, thanks to the survival of Pierre de L'Estoile's collection of broadsheets and other printed ephemera, we know that this moment produced one of the only remaining images of a *politique* character: the half-woman, half-fish monster with a gorgon's hair that you see on the cover of this book. This extraordinary image and the accompanying verse that condemns the mixed, indecisive, and yet somehow seductive *politique* figure is at once the inheritor and a distortion of the 'mixed man' Guillaume Budé wrote about decades previously; the existence of this image and other pamphlets condemning 'mixed' politics make the figure briefly described by Budé so striking in hindsight. Indeed, the *politiques* of these pamphlets were central in making *politique* a keyword of the war period and of its historiography.

The final chapter, Chapter 6, deals with two longer works that respond to the pro-League pamphlets of 1588–92 and to the political crises of

1593: the *Dialogue d'entre le Maheustre et le Manant* and the *Satyre ménippée*. In 1593, the future king Henri IV was encamped outside Paris, while inside the city, after several years of rule by zealous Catholics, an unofficial meeting of the Estates General was held as an attempt to elect an alternative monarch. This meeting ended in failure, Henri embraced Catholicism, and several months later he was finally able to enter the capital. The *Dialogue d'entre le Maheustre et le Manant* was written by a diehard Catholic, and stages a fractious meeting between a supporter of the Catholic League (Le Manant) and a foot soldier of Henri IV (Le Maheustre). Over the course of their long disagreement they recount the recent political history of Paris in considerable depth, with the Manant consistently blaming 'your friends, who they call *Politiques*' for the ruin of the city. Modern criticism and histories of the period typically refer to the *Politique* party in inverted commas, or to the 'so-called *Politiques*', as I mentioned above; Chapter 6 in particular shows that this highlighting of the speech act began before the end of the wars. The Manant's emphasis on naming, quoted above, is a case in point. This self-consciousness is reproduced in the more famous *Satyre ménippée*, a rambunctious satirical fictionalisation of the disastrous Estates General of 1593. In this closing chapter, I argue that the *Dialogue* and the *Satyre* engage in and block attempts at redescribing the meaning of *politique* as a means of inviting a final reckoning as the wars concluded, and as a way of attempting to shape the historical narrative already being constructed about the word *politique* and what, or who, it referred to.

This is a book about politics and *politiques* in the sixteenth century, and the narrative ends in the 1590s. This makes sense in that there was a particular *politique* problem in the run-up to, and during, the Wars of Religion, reaching a high point around the crisis of 1588–89. This said, ending with the end of a century may give a false impression of closure. In the seventeenth century, politics and *politiques* were still a problem, but differently so. In the Conclusion, I consider ways in which seventeenth-century France and England inherited the *politique* problem, and how modern and indeed contemporary politics might still be shaped by early modern political writing, for instance in the differentiation between feminine and masculine substantives in French, and the association between performance and politics deepened by the creation of a performer, the *politique*, who incarnates political action for better or for worse. My emphasis on performance and fictionality does not mean that there were no political moderates in early modern France, nor that these moderates shouldn't be referred to as *politiques*. But I aim to show that the people and principles identified as *politique* during the Wars of Religion went far beyond a particular group of literary-legal associates or moderate Catholics. The politics and *politiques* of sixteenth-century France indicate both the turmoil and the promise of political writing in the period. None of them are the singular, true, or real *politiques*: they all represent textual interventions in the complex dynamic that was (and perhaps still is) politics.

Acknowledgements

This book is based on my DPhil thesis, completed at St John's College, Oxford. My thanks to that institution, and also to Richard Scholar, a highly engaged and supportive supervisor; to Wes Williams, who gave invaluable feedback on interim versions of the thesis; and to Neil Kenny and Tim Chesters, who examined it and made incisive comments and suggestions that have informed this revised version. I'd like also to thank Kate Tunstall – a continual source of wit, wisdom, and perspective – and Emma Herdman, who introduced me to sixteenth-century literature. It was exceptional luck to have Kate and Emma as my undergraduate tutors in French. Thanks, too, to colleagues in early modern French, especially Emily Butterworth, Vittoria Fallanca, Raphaële Garrod, Jess Goodman, Katherine Ibbett, Thibaut Maus de Rolley, Jennifer Oliver, John O'Brien, Luke O'Sullivan, Jonathan Patterson, Marc Schachter, Helena Taylor, Gemma Tidman, Alain Viala, and Caroline Warman. Particular thanks to Rowan Tomlinson for her help with Chapter 2. During my time as a student and then as a fellow in Oxford, my work benefitted enormously from the Early Modern French Seminar there. I am forever grateful to those who organise and participate in it with energy and curiosity. Thanks to the organisers of the Oxford–Fribourg graduate workshops, and the Early Modern Keywords group run by Ita Mac Carthy and Richard Scholar; these were also formative. I revised this book during a Career Development Fellowship at New College, Oxford. Thanks to the staff, fellows, and students of New College, above all to Andrew Counter, mentor and friend, and also to Julia Nicholls, Ros Temple, and Liz Frazer. Rachel Benoit has to have a special mention for all the coffees and existential discussion: see you at the Missing Bean (thanks also to their staff). After New College I moved to Cambridge, where I made the final changes to the book. I am grateful to the British Academy for awarding me a postdoctoral fellowship, to Michael Moriarty for the mentorship and support, and to Leah Astbury, Anton Bruder, Tim Chesters, Nick

Hammond, Emma Gilby, Lisa Nicolson, Marina Perkins, Emily Kate Price, and Rebecca Sugden for the warm welcome.

This book would have been poorer without conversations with Sophie Nicholls, who also very kindly shared unpublished work. It would have taken much longer to complete without Tom Hamilton, a helpful interlocutor since I started the project, who shared his archival research with me when libraries were under lockdown, and who, along with Mark Greengrass, responded generously to my queries during the final stages of writing up. I would also like to thank the librarians at the Bodleian, the Bibliothèque nationale de France, the British Library, and Cambridge University Library (especially for their efforts during the pandemic). Sophie Smith invited me to speak at her Quentin Skinner Colloquium in 2017, which was the beginning of the path to publishing with the Ideas in Context series. I owe her a debt of gratitude not only for that opportunity but also for her thinking about politics with poetics. I am also grateful to John Robertson, who encouraged me to approach Cambridge University Press, to Richard Bourke, to Elizabeth Friend-Smith and Atifa Jiwa at Cambridge University Press, to the project manager Shaheer Husanne, and finally to the anonymous readers for their engagement with my work and constructive suggestions. Any remaining errors are mine.

Thanks also to my friends for their support during the long process of writing this book. Simon Park, who is an ideal person to talk to about anything, has been the best friend and ally in academia or anywhere that anyone could wish for. Lots of love to Helen Billingham, Stella Dilke, Hannah Jenner, Emily Kay, Flora Kennedy-McConnell, Charlie Mckenna, Laurianne Mons, Olivia Motyer, Rumaysa Patel, Rakhee Radia, Emma Segal, Natalie Southcott, Lidiya Sriyoheswaran, and Katherine Watson. Bissie Braund, who died in February 2020, always made me see that the world is bigger than it can sometimes feel. I am grateful to my family: Fiona Symon, Ian Claussen, Alice Claussen, Yvette Marsh-Feiley and Laura Marsh-Feiley Bowles, the Hetheringtons, Fraser and Mariko Symon, and the Jacquier-Claussens. Thank you to Pauline and Lindsay Symon, who didn't live to see this in print but whose interest in my education meant so much. Last but not least, thanks to Ari Haber and his family: Ben Laura, and Ava Haber, and Dani and Rick Maitland. I can't ever thank Ari sufficiently: he has been there through everything and also read the manuscript an impressive number of times, for which I offer sincere gratitude and semi-sincere commiserations.

This book is dedicated with love to Bissie and to my Dad's parents, my first and best teachers: Brian and Jennifer Claussen.

Note on the Text

I refer to all titles using the MHRA system. Direct short references to one text are usually indicated in parentheses within the text; all others are placed in footnotes. Dates placed after the titles of books in the main text refer to their first publication in printed form. I have used modern English translations of early modern French to preserve consistency, since early modern English translations are available for only some of the primary sources. I have used the same spelling conventions as the editions used, except that when quoting early modern texts I distinguish between 'i' and 'j' and 'u' and 'v', and resolve abbreviations. Any suggested emendation (of spelling or punctuation, place or date of publication, name of author, etc.) is placed in square brackets. In general I italicise *politique* in my text, and capitalise the noun when it refers to the supposed (largely fictional) *Politique* faction or party. When the term refers to a named character in a dialogue, I capitalise but don't italicise. Practice in primary material, with respect to both spelling and capitalisation of *politique*, is entirely inconsistent, and I preserve these inconsistencies when quoting.

PART I

The Politique *Problem*

CHAPTER I

Politics and Politiques

Throughout the sixteenth century in Europe, the possibilities of politics in theory and practice were uncertain, and in the intellectual sphere politics was gaining new prominence as a discipline in its own right. During the French Wars of Religion, politics was sometimes offered as a solution to civil discord, sometimes presented as fatally corrupted, itself the source of strife. Politics was a problem, in the sense both of intellectual or cognitive challenge, and of conflict or unhappiness. The figure of the *politique* person, a kind of proto-politician, emerged in political imagination and in altered socio-political structures as a key character in the transformation of France's fortunes. The noun *politique* was strikingly flexible, invested with significance and danger; language used by the *politique* was considered powerful, and suspect. The problem of politics was in large part a problem of language. Towards the end of the Wars of Religion, writers were especially conscious that the term *politique* had changed, now carrying – for some – a strongly negative charge:

> This name, *Politique*, was a name of honour,
> It was the just name of a just Governor;
> Of a prudent Magistrate, who by civil reason,
> Knew well how to rule ['policer'] the constituents of a town,
> And who, wise and agreeable, harmonising discord,
> Drew good agreements between diverse Citizens,
> Just as Edinthon calls forth harmony from different notes,
> When playing his lute; and so directs our minds,
> and with conquering sound,
> Ravishes our ears and steals our hearts.
> Today this good name, sullied by a thousand vices,
> Is no more than a name of horror, which destroys polities;
> A name filled with filth, and which is disdained,
> Thanks to the crime of those who misused it.[1]

---

[1] 'Ce nom de Politique estoit un nom d'honneur, / C'estoit le juste nom, d'un juste Gouverneur. / D'un prudent Magistrat, qui par raison civille / Sçavoit bien policer les membres d'une ville, / Et qui saige & accord, par accordans discords, / De Citoyens divers tireroit de bons accords. / Comme fait

This is the opening of a pamphlet written in verse and printed in 1588, entitled *Description de l'homme politique de ce temps* ('Description of the *politique* man of this time'), composed in support of the radical Catholic faction known as the League. The author regrets the degradation of 'this name, *Politique*': once honorific, now horrific. The first ten lines are devoted to what this term formerly referred to: a special kind of person – a 'just Governor', a 'prudent Magistrate' – able to employ their powers of reason to create harmony among a diverse population; who could, then, fully activate the potential of the verb 'to rule' ('policer'). The author draws an analogy with Edinthon, a lute player who creates musical harmonies of different tones, and in so doing is master of the ears, hearts, and minds of listeners.[2] From François I's reign onwards, musicians were courtiers with formal offices, and lute players, considered to play with particular finesse, had high status among them; musicians, in other words, held political positions, none more so than lutenists.[3] Music is therefore only partially analogous and metaphorical here. The harmonies of the lute player, and of the *politique* as [he] formerly existed, are figured as a kind of conquest of the crowd, with the images of the 'ravished' ears and stolen hearts perhaps anticipating the negative turn to come.[4] The majority of rhymes in lines 1–10 of the French version are rich, and the lines often tied together by internal rhymes and repetitions, aligning form and content. The last four lines mark a change in tone: today, the poet announces, the word *politique* is sullied by a thousand vices. The noun itself ('a name of horror') is the destroyer of civic harmony. Here, the poetic harmony also suffers a slight decline in standards; the rhymes of lines 11–12 are *suffisantes*, mirroring the moral decline in the meaning of *politique*, which has been degraded ('mesprisé') through misuse ('abusé').[5]

Edinthon, quand son Luth il manie / Qui de tons differends fait naistre une armonie, / Dont il pointe nos esprits, & par un son vainqueur / Des-robbe nostre aureille & nous pille le cœur. / Aujourd'huy ce beau nom, souillé de mille vices / N'est plus qu'un nom d'horreur, qui destruit les polices, / Un nom rempli d'ordure, & qui est mesprisé / Par le crime de ceux qui en ont abusé.' *Description de l'homme politique de ce temps avec sa foy et religion qui est un catalogue de plusieurs hérésies et athéismes, où tombent ceux qui préfèrent l'estat humain à la religion catholique* (Paris: G. Bichon, 1588), p. 3.

[2] The Edinthons were royal musicians of Scottish origin: the first, Charles, joined the musicians of the Royal Chamber late in the reign of François I. His son Jacques played for Charles IX and Henri III. The present tense here implies that the poem is referring to the latter. See Christelle Cazaux, *La musique à la cour de François Ier* (Paris: Ecole nationale de Chartres, 2002), p. 139.

[3] Jeanice Brooks, *Courtly Song in Late Sixteenth-Century France* (Chicago, IL and London: University of Chicago Press, 2000), p. 34.

[4] See Kate van Orden, *Music, Discipline, and Arms in Early Modern France* (Chicago, IL: University of Chicago Press, 2005).

[5] According to conventional French versification (which was being formalised in the sixteenth century), rhymes can be 'riche' (rich), 'suffisant' (sufficient), or 'pauvre' (poor), depending on the

The verse gives a highly polarised sense of what *politique* could mean: 'honour' on the one hand and 'horror' on the other. The rest of the poem describes how *politique* became degraded, and extends the musical metaphor, portraying French society as a grotesque chorus following the wrong conductors. In the view of the poet, toleration of religious difference strikes a fatally false note, and *politique* has become a problem precisely because it has come to mean endless negotiation, and endless quarrelling, between different groups who ought instead to have had religious harmony imposed upon them. Bemoaning this lack of accord, the poem is the expression of an angry stalemate. What it offers beyond the immediate argument about how and why *politique* went wrong is precisely this evocation of perpetual quarrelling and degradation of meaning through misuse of language. The opening line creates an analogy between harmonious government and clearly defined meaning; the dissonance caused by bad politics is equally analogous to an uncontrollable proliferation of negative associations.

The close connection between government and music in this poem, as well as the poetic form, demonstrates the important role of creative and liberal arts in thinking about politics in this period. With its alexandrine verse (its fourteen lines recall a sonnet, even if it doesn't follow Petrarchan or *Pléiade* convention), the poem shows cultural practices put to use in a text that serves ideological functions somewhat removed from concerns traditionally associated with lute music, the *Pléiade*, or innovation in the sonnet form. The violence of confessional disputes in the sixteenth century is more often associated with baser human drives and expressions; Donald Kelley called the Reformation a 'primal scream', expressed in a traumatic complex of human experiences.[6] This book explores uses of *politique* that belong to discursive traditions of both Renaissance and Reformation, and of both high and low culture.

Attention to writing about politics, and uses of the word *politique*, provides insight into politics as a discursive experience and literature as a political phenomenon. As a discursive experience, that is, mediated by discourse and to an extent created by it, politics is always on a dialogic spectrum, from convivial conversation to quarrel, to violent hostility and

---

number of syllables that rhyme. It does not follow that a sufficient rhyme is less poetically desirable than a rich one, but it does mean that the lines (and sounds) are less tightly tied together.

[6] Donald R. Kelley, *The Beginnings of Ideology: Consciousness and Society in the French Reformation* (Cambridge: Cambridge University Press, 1981), p. 7.

vituperative condemnation of the other.[7] As a political phenomenon, literature is a location for these friendly or hostile conversations, exposing, articulating, and adjusting the balance of power between ideas and inter- locutors. The connection between politics and language use, particularly the literary kind, has been fundamental to Western definitions of the political since Plato apparently banned poets from the Republic (*Republic*, 595a5) and Aristotle declared man a political animal distinct from all others because of [his] capacity for complex linguistic interaction (*Politics*, 1253a2). An idealistic view of literature as a privileged form of linguistic communication is that it can enable a more convivial experience of politics. Humanism as expressed in France and Italy *c.* 1400–1550 is sometimes thought to have espoused precisely this kind of optimism about the beneficial effects of the rhetorical upon the real.[8] One argument, which I explore in Chapter 2, is that this was precisely the vision inherited from Erasmus and developed in the politico-poetic circle around Michel de L'Hospital. This was an age that promoted civil conversation (epitomised by Castiglione's *Book of the Courtier*) that developed, however, into an age of civil war. The links between so-called 'civility' and violence, along with the violent, destructive potential of language, have been extensively probed.[9]

---

[7] Charles Taylor has argued for the primacy of the dialogic and conversational in language itself and in the construction of all meaning. See Charles Taylor, *The Language Animal: The Full Shape of the Human Linguistic Capacity* (Cambridge, MA and London: Harvard University Press, 2016), esp. pp. 49–50.

[8] Victoria Kahn writes that 'early' humanism evinced faith in the potential of rhetoric to achieve moral good, but that in the later Renaissance, this faith gave way to intense scepticism; she writes that the works of Erasmus, Montaigne, and Hobbes 'reveal an awareness of the ideal alliance of rhetoric and prudence, [but] their rhetorical strategies prove to be symptomatic of an increasing anxiety or skepticism about the power of rhetoric to persuade to right action'. See Victoria Kahn, *Rhetoric, Prudence, and Skepticism in the Renaissance* (Ithaca, NY and London: Cornell University Press, 1985), p. 27. J. H. M. Salmon and Jan Miernowski also refer to a crisis of faith in the humanist project in the context of the civil wars. See J. H. M. Salmon, 'Cicero and Tacitus in Sixteenth-Century France', *The American Historical Review*, 85.2 (1980), 307–31; Jan Miernowski, '"Politique" comme injure dans les pamphlets au temps des guerres de Religion', in *De Michel de L'Hospital à L'Edit de Nantes: Politique et religion face aux Eglises*, ed. by Thierry Wanegffelen (Clermont-Ferrand: Presses universitaires Blaise Pascal, 2002), pp. 337–56.

[9] As Teresa Bejan points out, 'polemic' derives from the Greek word for war. See Teresa M. Bejan, *Mere Civility: Disagreement and the Limits of Toleration* (Cambridge, MA and London, England: Harvard University Press, 2017), p. 4. On civil war and the connection between civil wars and wars of words, see David Armitage, *Civil Wars: A History in Ideas* (New Haven, CT: Yale University Press, 2017), esp. pp. 232–40. See also Denis Crouzet, *Les guerriers de Dieu. La violence au temps des troubles de religion (vers 1525–vers 1610)*, 2 vols. (Paris: Champ Vallon, 1990); *Civil Histories: Essays Presented to Keith Thomas*, ed. by Peter Burke, Brian Harrison, and Paul Slack (Oxford: Oxford University Press, 2000); Stuart Carroll, *Blood and Violence in Early Modern France* (Oxford: Oxford University Press, 2006), pp. 83–108 and 264–84, and his chapter 'Violence, Civil Society, and European Civilisation' in *The Cambridge World History of Violence Volume III*, ed. by Robert Antony, Stuart Carroll, and Caroline Dodds Pennock (Cambridge: Cambridge University Press, 2020),

This book, while subscribing in part to the view that literature can or could be a non-violent space for political conversation, shows that literary forms are just as much a space for quarrels, vituperation, and virtual violence that in some cases can be quite concretely tied to real acts of violence on real bodies.[10] The poem just quoted, which ultimately attempts to incite murderous action, calling for *politiques* to be burnt at the stake, is a case in point.[11]

In this study of politics and *politiques*, I give an account of the political struggles acted out in uses of *politique*. In this first chapter, I explore the historiographical and theoretical contexts to the enquiry and describe the methods employed. Specifically, this investigation of politics and *politiques* is conducted with a focus on language that is indebted to word history and keywords studies, and also to literary and historical studies that emphasise the connections between the imaginative and the real. I have already indicated that sixteenth-century writers were conscious of the controversy and flexibility associated with the word *politique*, especially the noun; what follows is a discussion of the particularities of the sixteenth-century in histories of early modern political thought and the place of France in those histories, as well as the special place of the so-called *Politique* party or tendency in accounts of the French civil wars. All these contexts point to *politique* being an especially unstable and dynamic term, associated with conceptual shifts and socio-political conflict.

Histories of Politics

Politics, and political thought, occur in every era and every inhabited place. Modern political theory sometimes supposes a timeless aspect to such concerns:

> We are all concerned with our relationship to authority, with notions of good social arrangements, with hierarchies of urgency and significance in deciding whether to support or resist public policies, with ways of asserting our will over others, and with the need to succeed or defend ourselves when faced with competing views in those areas.[12]

pp. 660–78; and Emily Butterworth, *Poisoned Words: Slander and Satire in Early Modern France* (London: Legenda, 2006).

[10] On the nexus of cultural, social, and political causes of violence in early modern France, see Natalie Zemon Davis, 'The Rites of Violence: Religious Riot in Sixteenth-Century France', *Past and Present*, 59 (1973), 51–91, and *Ritual and Violence: Natalie Zemon Davis and Early Modern France*, ed. by Graeme Murdock, Penny Roberts, and Andrew Spicer (Oxford: Oxford University Press, 2012).

[11] 'Description de l'homme politique', p. 11.

[12] Michael Freeden, 'Thinking Politically and Thinking about Politics: Language, Interpretation, and Ideology', in *Political Theory: Methods and Approaches*, ed. by David Leopold and Marc Steers (Oxford: Oxford University Press, 2008), pp. 196–215 (p. 196).

We generally identify early modern experience as 'political' and certain textual production as 'political thought' if it can be categorised as treating these concerns. Thinking historically about early modern politics, then, relies on acknowledgement of the particularity of institutions, representations, and vocabularies that express and facilitate this eternal and eternally flexible concept, politics: contingencies that provide its variations. Many historians view the early modern period as a time of cultural and socio-political changes – and developments in practices of politics and habits of political thought – that were the seeds of the modernity we know today: hence 'early' modernity.[13] Histories that focus on French political ideas (largely written in French) see this period as a transition from constitutional monarchy to more centralised forms of monarchic power (sometimes referred to as absolutism, though this term has been extensively problematised).[14] Meanwhile, this moment in French history is sometimes treated by Anglophone historians of modern political thought looking at politics from a supranational perspective as a transitional phase between Machiavelli, where everything begins, and either Hobbes, or the American and French Revolutions, which represent points of culmination.[15] Writing on politics during the Wars of Religion more specifically has tended to focus on socio-political structures, or on religion and community, although at the time of writing Sophie Nicholls's history of political thought during the wars was forthcoming.[16] This book by contrast is about how politics itself was understood, and represented in language.

---

[13] For reflections on the definition of early modernity, see Terence Cave, 'Locating the Early Modern', *Paragraph*, 29.1 (2006), 12–26.

[14] *L'absolutisme en France*, ed. by Fanny Cosandey and Robert Descimon (Paris: Seuil, 2002); Arlette Jouanna, *Le pouvoir absolu: Naissance de l'imaginaire politique de la royauté* (Paris: Gallimard, 2013).

[15] See Quentin Skinner, *The Foundations of Modern Political Thought*, 2 vols. (Cambridge: Cambridge University Press, 1978), *Hobbes and Republican Liberty* (Cambridge: Cambridge University Press, 2008), and *From Humanism to Hobbes* (Cambridge: Cambridge University Press, 2018); Richard Tuck, *Philosophy and Government 1572–1651* (Cambridge: Cambridge University Press, 1993); J. G. A. Pocock, *The Machiavellian Moment: Florentine Political Thought and the Atlantic Republican Tradition* (Princeton, NJ: Princeton University Press, 1975). Two recent historical studies of political thought pay close attention to the early modern period but mention France only briefly and comparatively: David Runciman's *Political Hypocrisy: The Mask of Power, from Hobbes to Orwell and Beyond* (Princeton, NJ and Oxford: Princeton University Press, 2008), and Armitage, *Civil Wars*.

[16] Natalie Zemon Davis, *Society and Culture in Early Modern France. Eight Essays* (Stanford, CA: Stanford University Press, 1975); Robin Briggs, *Communities of Belief: Cultural and Social Tensions in Early Modern France* (Oxford: Clarendon, 1989); Crouzet, *Guerriers de Dieu*; Mark Greengrass, *Governing Passions: Peace and Authority in the French Kingdom* (Oxford: Oxford University Press, 2007); Joseph Bergin, *The Politics of Religion in Early Modern France* (New Haven, CT: Yale University Press, 2014); Sophie Nicholls, *Political Thought in the French Wars of Religion* (Cambridge: Cambridge University Press, forthcoming); see also Sophie Nicholls, 'Political and

Within their *longue durée* accounts of how social change was wedded to intellectual tendencies and processes, intellectual historians have long seen language use as a key indicator of socio-political experience, and of change; *Begriffsgeschichte*, as Reinhart Koselleck makes clear, is a form of conceptual history that depends to greater or lesser degrees on semantics.[17] Quentin Skinner's analysis of rhetoric has also been highly influential, as has his emphasis on the agency of language users in the construction of new institutions and ideologies. He argues in the second volume of his *Foundations of Modern Political Thought* that the crisis and conflict of the fifteenth and sixteenth centuries fundamentally destabilised political categories and led to the establishment or recalibration of alternatives both conceptual and practical: his examples are the sovereign, the city, and particularly the various vernacular words for the state (*l'état, lo stato,* the state, etc.).[18] Viroli, meanwhile, refers to a 'forgotten revolution' in early modern conceptions of politics, which he sees as being articulated through change in language, from 'art of government' to 'reason of state' (a process started, for Viroli, by Machiavelli, and inaugurated by Botero with *The Reason of State* in 1589).[19] In a different way, Viroli makes a similar argument to the anonymous author of the sonnet quoted above – that 'the word politics' became somehow degraded over the course of the sixteenth century:

Legal Thought', in *The Cambridge History of French Thought*, ed. by Michael Moriarty and Jeremy Jennings (Cambridge: Cambridge University Press, 2019), pp. 90–96.

[17] Koselleck goes as far as saying that there is no such thing as society without common concepts and, above all, no field of political action; he differs from Skinner in placing more emphasis on 'the autonomous power of words', whereas Skinner sees the centre of power as those who use words and is more careful to acknowledge socio-political experience beyond particular or specialised linguistic frameworks. See Reinhart Koselleck, 'Begriffsgeschichte and Social History', in *Futures Past: On the Semantics of Historical Time* (New York, NY: Columbia University Press, 2004), pp. 77–92 (p. 81). For a comprehensive account of the place of linguistic analysis in intellectual history, and its possibilities, see Annabel Brett, 'What Is Intellectual History Now?', in *What Is History Now?*, ed. by David Cannadine (London: Palgrave Macmillan, 2002), pp. 113–31.

[18] Skinner writes, 'The surest sign that a society has entered into the secure possession of a new concept is that a new vocabulary will be developed, in terms of which the concept can be articulated and discussed', in *The Foundations of Modern Political Thought*, II, p. 352. Harro Höpfl, in his analysis of Justus Lipsius, has commented that 'Much of the most valuable historiography of political thought has resulted from treating terms like *jus, virtù, arête, respublica, polis, state, civitas, commonwealth, politique, libertas,* etc. as requiring historical exegesis, rather than casual modernization.' See Harro Höpfl, 'History and Exemplarity in the Work of Lipsius', in *(Un)masking the Realities of Power: Justus Lipsius and the Dynamics of Political Writing in Early Modern Europe*, ed. by Erik de Bom (Leiden & Boston, MA: Brill, 2011), pp. 43–72 (p. 44).

[19] Maurizio Viroli, 'The Revolution in the Concept of Politics', *Political Theory*, 20.3 (1992), 473–95. See also *From Politics to Reason of State: The Acquisition and Transformation of the Language of Politics, 1250–1600* (Cambridge: Cambridge University Press, 1992).

Before the revolution, the word politics had only a positive connotation. Afterwards, it acquired, for the most part, only a negative connotation. Having enjoyed for three centuries the status of the noblest human science, politics emerged from the revolution as an ignoble, depraved, and sordid activity: it was no longer the most powerful means of fighting oppression and corruption but the art of perpetuating them.[20]

Skinner and Viroli tell the history of politics in sixteenth-century Europe as a narrative of progress towards something new (the modern state; reason of state) if not necessarily towards something good. Hiding in plain sight within these arguments is a network of terms – politics, *politique*, *politica*, *politicus*; the 'word politics' that Viroli refers to in the quotation above, in much of his source material, was not 'politics', for example, but a neo-Latin or vernacular equivalent. Skinner shows how new ways of thinking about politics emerged; Viroli tells a story of ethical deterioration; Ian Maclean has argued that the terminology of politics, between 'prudence' and 'policy', underwent significant shifts in the early modern period.[21] In this book I show that such shifts were staged and argued over in uses of the term *politique* itself. If the concept of politics was changing, and if it was generating a new set of vocabulary around figures and institutions (the sovereign; the state), what might 'the word politics' have meant for the people who used it? How did these words and their meanings operate in debates about the nature of political community, how it should be formed, and who should direct it?

This book focuses on the French contribution to the network of terms that roughly align to 'the word politics'. I have followed the historicising approach prevalent in early modern literary studies, focusing on endogenous uses of the term *politique* and excavating its meanings in sixteenth-century terms rather than proceeding from the various definitions of politics and power current in my own moment of writing, even as these inform my understanding of the political dimensions of literature. The focus is on *politique* because – as we shall see, and as the poem *Description de l'homme politique* has already shown – the meaning of the French vernacular term was the object of particularly active and self-conscious contestation. I rarely translate the term *politique* when citing primary texts, because it maps so imperfectly onto either modern or early modern English and is, in

<hr>

[20] Viroli, 'The Revolution in the Concept of Politics', p. 477.
[21] Ian Maclean, 'From Prudence to Policy: Some Notes on the Pre-History of Policy Science', *Guest Lectures* (Nijmegen: Katholieke universiteit, 1993), pp. 5–27. See especially Maclean's gloss on the semantic field and associated concepts around *politeia* in the early modern period, p. 8.

a sense, untranslatable.[22] It could mean, among other things, 'the intellectual discipline of politics', 'monarchic order', 'authoritarian politics', 'non-spiritual authority', 'justice', and 'toleration'; it meant 'politician', 'political actor', 'leader', 'administrator', 'lawyer', 'hack', 'hypocritical enemy', and 'atheist'. *Politique* was the name given to a powerful character in narratives, treatises, and dialogues written about politics at the time, as well as being a term that historians have used to define attitudes and allegiances during the chaotic civil war period. French texts are therefore especially productive for interrogating the connection between the literary and the political present in uses of 'the word politics' (or in fact, *politique*), and the boundaries and possibilities of verbal communication encapsulated in the history of this one crucial term.

The focus is on France, but English, Latin, and Italian terms that all correspond in some way to the idea and practice of 'politics' and the figure of the 'political actor' were mutually influential.[23] Chapter 2 points out the deep influence of Italian works of the previous century on sixteenth-century French conceptions of the political prior to the Wars of Religion. Indeed, Italian political writing was highly influential throughout the period, certainly on Loys Le Roy and Jean Bodin, as is clear in Chapter 3; the reception of Machiavelli is discussed extensively in Chapters 3 and 4. English connections with and responses to French *politiques* are also highlighted; Thomas More's *Utopia* and other political writings are significant intertexts in Chapters 2 and 4 (though only briefly discussed), while the final chapter opens with a reference to *Hamlet*. The Conclusion discusses the web of connections between French politics, *politiques*, and English drama at the turn of the seventeenth century. Future work could consider further Machiavelli's reworking of the 'vivere politico' in his *Discorsi* and the way in which the Italian term *politico* was part of what is now known as civic humanism.[24] It could also usefully explore how the French term *politique* was taken as a marker of allegiance in England

[22] On untranslatability, see *Vocabulaire européen des philosophes: Dictionnaire des intraduisibles*, ed. by Barbara Cassin (Paris: Seuil, 2004). Cassin defines 'untranslatable' terms as those of irreducible multiplicity, such that the act of translating them is never complete, p. xvii.

[23] A more comprehensive approach would not only require more time but also wider linguistic expertise, and perhaps more than one author; the recent study of the 'ingenium/ingenuity' word group demonstrates the success of collaborative word history. See Alexander Marr, Raphaële Garrod, José Ramón Marcaida, and Richard J. Oosterhoff, *Logodaedalus: Word Histories of Ingenuity in Early Modern Europe* (Pittsburgh, PA: Pittsburgh University Press, 2018).

[24] See, for example, Niccolò Machiavelli, *Opere*, ed. by Corrado Vivanti, 3 vols. (Turin: Einaudi-Gallimard, 1997), I, p. 216: as part of an oft-quoted comparison between Sparta and Venice, Machiavelli suggests that the balance those states achieved between conflicting interest groups represented 'la vera vita politica' ('the true political life'). Hans Baron coined the phrase 'civic

and in the English expatriate community, leading to other ways of understanding and using a term of French origin beyond national boundaries.[25]
Beyond Europe, the Ottomans in particular were important allies of the
French at various points in the sixteenth century, and are referenced in
complex ways in some of the texts analysed in this book; encounters with
and colonisation of non-European peoples are also significant contexts to
ideas about the function of politics and *politiques*, as is clear from the
discussion of Montaigne's 'Of Cannibals' in Chapter 2.[26]

Histories of *Politiques*

A study of the term *politique* on its own is necessary here, owing to the
enormous mass of textual material that uses and contests it during this forty-
year period. 'Our disputes are purely verbal', wrote Montaigne.[27] The
Reformation, indeed, can be described as both the product and the cause
of wholesale disruptions of the terms by which early modern people defined
ethical, religious, and social categories, accompanied by extensive printed
production in which many of these definitions and disruptions occurred.
Accordingly, the French Wars of Religion were accompanied, and spurred
on, by a war of words facilitated by printing practices: as Luc Racaut has it,
the wars were 'lost and won by the ability of Catholics and Huguenots to
create and block competing narratives and representations of each other'.[28]

humanism' in *The Crisis of the Early Italian Renaissance: Civic Humanism and Republican Liberty in an Age of Classicism and Tyranny*, 2 vols. (Princeton, NJ: Princeton University Press, 1955). See also Eugenio Garin, *Italian Humanism: Philosophy and the Civic Life in the Renaissance* (Oxford: Blackwell, 1965), and *Renaissance Civic Humanism: Reappraisals and Reflections*, ed. by James Hankins (Cambridge: Cambridge University Press, 1995).

[25] Jan Machielsen gives an interesting account of *politique* being used in this way in the Netherlands, in 'The Lion, the Witch, and the King: Thomas Stapleton's "Apologia pro Rege Catholico Philippo II" (1592)', *English Historical Review*, 129 (2014), 19–46. Maclean treats this more briefly in 'From Prudence to Policy', pp. 14–15.

[26] Noel Malcolm calls the French-Ottoman alliance that arose under François I, lapsed somewhat during the civil wars, and was rekindled by Henri IV, the 'greatest practical example of Christian-Muslim confederacy in early modern Europe'. Noel Malcolm, *Useful Enemies: Islam and the Ottoman Empire in Western Political Thought, 1450–1750* (Oxford: Oxford University Press, 2018), p. 110.

[27] Michel de Montaigne, *The Complete Works*, tr. by Donald Frame (London: Everyman, 2003), p. 997 ('Nostre contestation est verbale', *Essais*, ed. by Jean Balsamo, Michel Magnien, and Catherine Magnien-Simonin [Paris: Gallimard, 2007], p. 1116). All further references to the *Essais* will be to these editions, with the English reference given in the text. This famous phrase has sometimes been extracted, maxim-like, to express an essential quality of the chaotic conflicts of early modern Europe. See, for example, Brian Cummings, *The Literary Culture of the Reformation: Grammar and Grace*, 2nd ed. (Oxford: Oxford University Press, 2007), p. 15.

[28] Luc Racaut, *Hatred in Print: Catholic Propaganda and Protestant Identity during the French Wars of Religion* (Aldershot: Ashgate, 2002), p. 5.

Between radical Catholics and their Huguenot opponents, historians and critics have traditionally located a nebulous group of people called *Politiques*: those moderate Catholics who, according to one definition, prioritised the welfare of the nation above religious principle, and thus were concerned with bringing the devastating wars to a close, no matter that the theological debates raged on.[29] These so-called *Politiques* supposedly played their part, too, in such competing narratives and representations. Their successes in this arena were thought to have facilitated the victory of Henri de Navarre, crowned Henri IV of France in 1594 after his (re)conversion from Protestantism to Catholicism.[30] There is no consensus, however, as to when such a party was formed or how it operated: some suggest it emerged in court circles as early as the 1560s, the 'moderate' or 'self-interested' Catholics known as *politiques* emerging around 1568 with the hardening of radical Catholic factions; others point to the early 1570s, to those who fought in 1575–76 and were appeased by the Peace of Monsieur in 1576, or to Catholics who opposed the League after 1584 or who supported Henri de Navarre from 1589 – most recently, Joseph Bergin has suggested that the closest thing to a *Politique* party only existed between 1589 and 1593.[31]

The historiographical narrative that constructed a *Politique* 'party' has its roots in the work of sixteenth-century writers who harnessed the power of *politique* as a tool of negotiation. One of the reasons why this term has been so compelling, and so tricky, for historians, is the fact that it was thus mobilised and contested, both during and immediately after the Wars of Religion. Even as the poem *Description du politique* was being written, printed, and reprinted, others were spreading counterarguments and alternative uses. If he is to be believed, one such 'other' was the Parisian diarist

[29] The definition is Terence Cave's, from *Thomas More's Utopia in Early Modern Europe: Paratexts and Contexts* (Manchester: Manchester University Press, 2012), p. 81.

[30] See Charles Labitte, *De la démocratie chez les prédicateurs de la Ligue*, 2nd ed. (Paris: Durand, 1865); Francis de Crue, *Le Parti des Politiques au lendemain de la Saint-Barthélemy: La Molle et Coconat* (Paris: Plon, 1892). This view is reprised in literary studies, particularly concerning the *Satyre ménippée*. Lestringant and Ménager write: 'the nationalist attitude with which the *Politique* party identified, of which the *Satyre ménippée* was the triumphant expression, campaigned for a monarchy more inaugurated than restored' ('l'esprit national auquel s'identifie le parti des Politiques, et dont la *Satyre ménippée* est l'expression triomphante, milite en faveur d'une monarchie instaurée plutôt que restaurée'), in 'Introduction', in *Etudes sur la Satyre ménippée*, ed. by Frank Lestringant and Daniel Ménager (Geneva: Droz, 1987), pp. 7–18 (p. 17).

[31] Bergin, p. 31. See Christopher Bettinson, 'The *Politiques* and the *Politique* Party: A Reappraisal', in *From Valois to Bourbon: Dynasty, State and Society in Early Modern France*, ed. by Keith Cameron (Exeter: University of Exeter Press, 1989), pp. 35–49; for an account of this historiography, see Arlette Jouanna, 'Politiques', in Arlette Jouanna, Jacqueline Boucher, Dominique Biloghi, and Guy Le Thiec, *Histoire et dictionnaire des Guerres de Religion* (Paris: Laffont, 1998), pp. 1210–13.

Pierre de L'Estoile, a recurrent supporting actor in the cast of figures who might in some way be *politique*.[32] As well as recording many instances of insulting uses of the term, he describes himself as having a hand in engineering alternative meanings for the word. This hand is quite literal; he writes how he copied by hand and bravely passed around one poem responding to anti-*politique* propaganda of the kind expressed in *Description du politique*, including the following verse:

> But you, who call yourselves Catholics,
> Without having been wronged,
> Wage war against your fellow citizens,
> Whom you name as Royal[ists] and Politiques.[33]

When exactly L'Estoile wrote this has some bearing on what kind of use of *politique* this is, but more than this, it shows a struggle being played out over the words *royal* and *politique*.[34] L'Estoile's part in this is to pass on the message that these words describe loyal citizens, who show loyalty by supporting the heir to the throne. This message was reinforced by contemporary historians – De Thou, La Popelinière, Pasquier – who all lived through the wars, all wrote versions of recent history during and after the wars, and refer to certain people as *Politiques*, either because they refused to take sides between Protestant and Catholic factions or because they were the enemies of the Catholic League and supported the victorious Henri IV.[35] One Catholic polemicist, writing as the wars drew to a close, referred to La Popelinière as the *Politique* Herodotus.[36] It is a truism that history is written by the victors, a view seemingly confirmed by these early historians who have been described as *Politique*, and whose writing – corroborated by

[32] On L'Estoile as *politique*, see Tom Hamilton, *Pierre de L'Estoile and His World in the Wars of Religion* (Oxford: Oxford University Press, 2017), pp. 13–14. Hamilton argues that L'Estoile was not just an observer of his times but active in shaping his moment and collective memories thereof, p. 5.

[33] 'Mais vous, qui tant vous dites Catholiques / Sans qu'on vous ait fait tort en vos moiens, Courez la guerre à vos concitoiens / Que vous nommez Roiaux et Politiques.' Pierre De L'Estoile, *Mémoires-Journaux*, ed. by Gustave Brunet et al., 11 vols. (Paris: Librairie des bibliophiles), v, pp. 261 and 267.

[34] This could have been written any time during the final decade of the sixteenth century, although it is from his journal for 1592. On Pierre de L'Estoile's writing and the composition of his *Mémoires-Journaux*, see Hamilton, esp. pp. 97–165.

[35] La Popelinière began publishing his *Histoire de France* in 1581: in his account of the election of Michel de L'Hospital as chancellor in 1560, he describes him as *politique* in the first sense. See Lancelot Voisin de la Popelinière, *L'histoire de France, t. II 1558–60*, ed. by Jean-Claude Laborie, Benoist Pierre, and Pierre-Jean Souriac, under the direction of Denise Turrel (Geneva: Droz, 2016), p. 331.

[36] [Louis d'Orléans], *Banquet et apresdinee du Comte d'Arête* (Paris: Bichon, 1594), n.p.

the complaints of their Leaguer opponents – gave fodder to the idea that a victorious *Politique* party heralded a new politics for post-war France.

This idea of a moderate anti-League group known as the *Politiques* had a long afterlife. In the early modern period, it partially survives in definitions of *politique* in Furetière's dictionary (1690), and in a different way in the eighteenth-century *Encyclopédie*. Furetière defines the feminine substantive as 'The first part of Moral Philosophy, which consists of the art of government and of policing States to maintain security, tranquillity, and moral integrity in behaviour'.[37] He also notes that *politique* can categorise books, and across the entry he cites a number of prominent authors, with a fairly broad linguistic and geographical range and emphasis on sixteenth-century political writing: Aristotle, Bacon, Cardano, Lipsius, La Noue, Machiavelli. When he comes to the other substantive form, denoting a knowledgeable or discriminating person whose field of expertise is government, the emphasis on sixteenth-century contexts for understanding this term is clear from the references to the Catholic League and to Machiavelli:

> POLITIQUE (masc. or fem. substantive).
>
> He who knows the art of government, or who judges it according to the knowledge ['lumières'] he has acquired. The greatest *politiques* have been fooled by events and have met an unhappy end. During the troubles of the League there were the *Politiques*, who were of the King's party against the Leaguers. The *Nouvellistes* are all *politiques*, and judge wrongly and askance everything that happens in the state. Machiavelli was a great and dangerous *politique*.[38]

The ethical status of the person named *politique* is in doubt, despite the tight connection he has established between 'la politique' and morality and

---

[37] 'La premiere partie de la Morale, qui consiste en l'art de gouverner et de policer les Estats pour y entretenir la seureté, la tranquillité, et l'honnesteté des mœurs'.

[38] 'Celuy qui sçait l'art de gouverner, ou qui en juge suivant les lumieres qu'il a acquises. Les plus grands *politiques* ont été trompez par les evenements, ont eu une fin malheureuse. Dans les troubles de la Ligue il y avoit les *Politiques*, qui estoient du party du Roy contre les Ligueurs. Les Nouvellistes sont tous *politiques*, et jugent à tort et à travers de tout ce qu'ils voyent arriver dans les Estats. Machiavel étoit un grand et dangereux *politique*.' Furetière's definition of the adjective is also interesting - 'this man's conduct is very *politique* and covert' ('cet homme a une conduite fort politique et cachée'). 'Politique', in Antoine Furetière, *Dictionnaire Universel* (La Haye & Rotterdam, 1690) www.classiques-garnier .com/numerique-bases/index.php?module=App&action=FrameMain [accessed 30 July 2020]. The *Nouvellistes* were a group of editors led by Donneau de Visé (1638–1710) who published a regular magazine that contained a mixture of gossip, news, and fiction. Richelet's definition of *politique* is along similar lines but has different examples; two quotations from Pascal indicate that writer's suspicion of the duplicity of the *politique* person. This would be interesting to explore in an account of seventeenth-century uses of *politique* or in a longer discussion of the afterlives of the sixteenth-century keyword than the one offered in the Conclusion to this book. See 'Politique', in Pierre Richelet, *Dictionnaire françois* [1680] (Geneva: Widerhold, 2007) http://ezproxy-prd.bodleian.ox.ac .uk:2242/numerique-bases/index.php?module=App&action=FrameMain [accessed 3 August 2018].

security, and many of the examples are negatively framed: the best *politiques* have been defeated by circumstance; the *nouvellistes* err in judgement; Machiavelli was a significant and dangerous *politique*. The *Politiques* of the Wars of Religion are also negatively framed in a different way, defined by their opposition to the League. They are described as being of the 'King's party', which is slightly ambiguous – it could imply that they helped to form a party in support of the king, but also simply that they took his part in the conflict.

Several decades later, in an unsigned *Encyclopédie* entry, the plural substantive *Politiques* shows a crystallisation of the so-called *Politiques* into an identifiable party:

> POLITIQUES (masc. substantive plural) (*Modern History*). Name of a party formed in France during the League in 1574. They were unhappy Catholics who, without meddling in religion, protested that they would only take up arms for the public good, for the relief of the people, and to reform the disorder that had slipped into the state owing to the too-great power of those who abused royal authority; they were also known as *royalists*, although fundamentally they were not overly submissive to the sovereign.[39]

This is a different 'party' to that which might have sided with the king against the League, in Furetière's definition (although it reproduces L'Estoile's connection between *politique* and *royal*): this group of *Politiques* developed from 1574 and supposedly stood on the side of the king but against the abuse of royal authority. The *Politiques* have frequently been understood as moderates or mediators: the *Encyclopédie* has them adopting a potentially contradictory position in order both to support and to contain royal power. The *Encyclopédie*'s general entry on *Politique*, like seventeenth-century dictionaries, defines it as the art of government and emphasises its importance within philosophy. It goes further, however, in its statement of the ethical doubt associated with politics, calling it 'that science which is so useful and so dangerous' ('cette science si utile & si dangereuse').[40] The *Encyclopédie* also puts sixteenth-century authors at the heart of discussions of what *la politique* could and should facilitate; in this

---

[39] '(*Hist. mod.*) nom d'un parti qui se forma en France pendant la ligue en 1574. C'étoient des catholiques mécontens, qui sans toucher à la religion, protestoient qu'ils ne prenoient les armes que pour le bien public, pour le soulagement du peuple, & pour réformer les désordres qui s'étoient glissés dans l'état par la trop grande puissance de ceux qui abusoient de l'autorité royale; on les nomma aussi *royalistes*, quoique dans le fond ils ne fussent pas trop soumis au souverain.' 'Politiques', in Denis Diderot, Jean d'Alembert, et al., *Encyclopédie ou Dictionnaire raisonné des sciences, des arts et des métiers, par une Société de gens de lettres* (1751–72), ed. by Robert Morrissey and Glen Roe http://artflx .uchicago.edu/cgi-bin/philologic/getobject.pl?c.11:2093.encyclopedie0113 [accessed 3 August 2020].
[40] 'Politique', in *Encyclopédie* [accessed 30 July 2020].

case the authors are Bodin (relying heavily on the portrayal of Bodin in De Thou's *Historia*) and Machiavelli. Several paragraphs are then devoted to anti-machiavellism, concluding with enthusiastic praise of Frederick the Great's *Antimachiavel* (1740). Frederick wrote this work at the height of his relationship with Voltaire, who had written to him in 1739 urging him to see politics as friendship (using the Virgilian friendship topos around the figures of Nisus and Euryalus) and to defeat pernicious Machiavellianism, thereby restoring the term *politique* to its 'true meaning':

> I dare yet to exhort your great genius to honour Virgil's Nisus and Euryalus, and to confound Machiavelli. You must sing the praise of friendship, and destroy the infamous *politique* who makes crime into virtue.[41] The word *politique* means, in its original form, *citizen*: and today, thanks to our perversity, it means *deceiver of citizens*. Return it, my lord, to its true meaning.[42]

This alternative definition of *politique* as, alternately, 'citizen' and 'deceiver of citizens', is another formulation of the continuum between harmony and discord – and between virtue and infamy – presented, in an entirely different context, in *Description de l'homme politique*. What we can infer from this brief tour of early modern definitions of the term *politique* in the centuries following the Wars of Religion is that the sixteenth century provided a crucial frame of reference (possibly because authors risked the wrath of censors, and worse, if they referred in a critical way to the politics of their own time); that there was a sense that some kind of partial group or party had existed during the Wars of Religion known as the *Politiques*; and that as both noun and adjective the term *politique* had dubious ethical connotations, the darkest of which centred around that apparent paradigm of political deviousness and deviance, Machiavelli.

In the late nineteenth century, liberal historians searching for the origins of their nascent democratic state refashioned the vaguely defined *Politique* group as the expression of a particularly French kind of heroism, moderate

---

[41] 'l'infâme politique' could also mean 'the infamous politics', but owing to the context I have opted for the concrete substantive.

[42] 'J'ose exhorter toujours votre grand génie à honorer Virgile dans Nisus et dans Euryalus, et à confondre Machiavel. C'est à vous à faire l'éloge de l'amitié. C'est à vous de détruire l'infâme politique qui érige le crime en vertu. Le mot *politique* signifie, dans son origine primitive, *citoyen;* et aujourd'hui, grâce à notre perversité, il signifie *trompeur de citoyens*. Rendez lui, monseigneur, sa vraie signification.' Voltaire, Letter to Frederick, Crown Prince of Russia, 25 April 1739, in *Correspondence*, ed. by Theodore Bestermann, 107 vols. (Geneva: Institut et musée Voltaire, 1953–65), XLV, p. 111. Thanks to Kelsey Rubin-Detlev for this reference.

and moderating, who, in the spirit of Erasmus and following the example of Michel de L'Hospital, navigated the tempestuous passions of the war period and emerged triumphant, heralding the nationalist, semi-secular liberalism of the post-revolutionary age.[43] The most influential of these studies was probably Francis de Crue's *Le Parti des Politiques au lendemain de la Saint-Barthélemy* (1892). This study reprises in many ways the definition of the substantive plural given in the *Encyclopédie* – according to la Crue, the *Politiques* formed in the aftermath of the terrible massacres of 1572, driven by patriotic duty: a group of noblemen compelled to lobby for peace and temper the rage of the Guise faction and the inconsistency of the monarchy; their values were later adopted by the Parisian bourgeoisie who supported Henri de Navarre.[44] In these accounts, the *Politiques* embodied good political action, and were themselves the resolution to the problems presented by the negative potential of the word *politique* and the concepts to which it was attached. Thus *politique* as epithet partici- pated in the construction of an origin story about particular secular and moderate national characteristics, and indeed in the construction of one version of French nationalism, since unity within 'the nation' was cast as the ultimate ethical value. These narratives seem to find echoes today in French debates about cultural assimilation.

    Later historians of the Wars of Religion largely accepted the 'moderate [proto-]nationalist' understanding of what *politique* meant, even if they were not so fulsome in their praise of that outlook; some use it as an umbrella term to cover opposition to the monarchy from 1572 to 1584, and/or opposition to the League and support for the monarchy from 1584 to 1598.[45] Over the past two decades, though, historical conceptions of the meaning of *politique* have undergone a shift, born of the

---

[43] 'Le bon sens d'Erasme, la probité de L'Hospital, ce fut là le double programme de ces Politiques d'abord raillés par tout le monde ... Mais laissez faire le temps; laissez les passions s'amortir, laissez l'esprit français avec sa logique droite se retrouver dans ce pêle-mêle, et ce parti grandira', wrote Labitte, pp. 180–81; de Crue writes that the *Politiques* sacrificed themselves for the eternal principles of 'libertés religieuses et publiques', p. 349.

[44] See la Crue, pp. 1–22; pp. 345–48. La Crue acknowledges that the term changed meaning over the course of the wars (pp. 347–48). In his conclusion, he writes: 'Henri IV triomphe des Lorrains et de l'Espagne. Avec lui, le parti national est au pouvoir, et avec le parti national, le parti de la tolérance religieuse, autrement dit les Politiques', p. 348. This triad of *partis* is striking in that, even in this triumphalist narrative, 'le parti des politiques' is analogous with other parties and so still plural.

[45] See Frederic Baumgartner, *Radical Reactionaries: The Political Thought of the French Catholic League* (Geneva: Droz, 1976); and Jean-Marie Constant, *La Ligue* (Paris: Fayard, 1996); Robert J. Knecht, *The Rise and Fall of Renaissance France* (Oxford: Oxford University Press, 2001); J. M. H. Salmon, *Society in Crisis: France in the Sixteenth Century* (London: Methuen, 1979). Mack Holt goes as far as identifying a *politique* struggle around the youngest Valois prince, the Duc d'Anjou, until his death in 1584 when the Catholic League was formed, after which point the historians I have just

abandonment of the idea that there was a coherent *Politique* party with any consistent political ideology, and increasing awareness of the lack of evidence of anyone directly referring to themselves as *politique*.[46] This shift is rooted in the linguistic turn in history, from which emerged a stronger focus on language use and the growing realisation that *politique*, when applied to any particular person or group, was often an insult during the Wars of Religion; this has had the consequence of unseating De Thou's history as the key account of what the *Politique* party was.[47] The figure of the *Politique*, previously so useful in delineating the political arena of the civil wars, thus becomes – as Edmond Beame and Marie-Luce Demonet have shown – a myth, a cipher, a propaganda tool in which the *Politique* is either hero or villain, and actually, possibly nothing at all.[48] Thus, the *politique* problem has also proved a problem for historians. Mark Greengrass suggests that to discuss the success of Henri IV as a *politique* triumph is to 'misconstrue rhetoric and reality'.[49]

Should historians and critics use the term *politique* at all when describing early modern politics, since corrupted modern uses do not reflect early modern socio-political experience? If modern writers continue to place

mentioned tend to refer more to a *politique* party or attitude. See Mack P. Holt, *The Duke of Anjou and the* Politique *Struggle during the Wars of Religion* (Cambridge: Cambridge University Press, 1986). Barbara Diefendorf refers to the '*politique*, or pragmatic, resolution to the conflict', in *Beneath the Cross: Catholics and Huguenots in Sixteenth-Century Paris* (Oxford: Oxford University Press, 1991), p. 7. On political thought in the League period, see also Cornel Zwierlein, *The Political Thought of the French League and Rome (1585–89)* (Geneva: Droz, 2016). Sophie Nicholls reassesses Leaguer thought, showing that many intellectuals associated with the movement held 'royalist' views more commonly associated with so-called *politiques*, in *Political Thought in the French Wars of Religion*.

[46] Mark Greengrass, 'Epilogue: Régime Change, Restoration, Reconstruction and Reformation', in *Politics and Religion in Early Bourbon France*, ed. by Alison Forrestal and Elizabeth Nelson (Basingstoke: Palgrave Macmillan, 2009), pp. 246–57 (p. 247). Baumgartner commented in 1976 that 'an adequate study of 'Politique' thought has yet to be written', *Radical Reactionaries*, p. 18. Since then, Beame and Bettinson have both written article-length studies analysing the inconsistencies in historical uses of the term *politique*: see Bettinson, 'The Politiques and the Political Party: A Reappraisal', and Edmond Beame, 'The Politique and the Historians', *Journal of the History of Ideas*, 54.3 (1993), 355–79. French legal historian Julien Broch has attempted to answer Baumgartner's challenge in *L'école des 'Politiques' (1559–98): La contribution des juristes et publicistes français à la construction de l'Etat royal* (Marseille: Presses universitaires d'Aix-Marseille, 2012), in which he defines a *politique* school as a particular trend in legal thought. The best recent accounts of how *politique* was applied and sometimes misapplied are found in *De Michel de L'Hospital à L'Edit de Nantes*, ed. by Thierry Wanegffelen, and Marie-Luce Demonet, 'Quelques avatars du mot "politique" (XIVe–XVIIe siècles)', *Langage et société*, 113.3 (2005), 33–62.

[47] See Miernowski, '"Politique" comme injure', and Mark Greengrass, *France in the Age of Henri IV: The Struggle for Stability*, 2nd ed. (London: Longman, 1995), p. 14.

[48] Beame, 'The Politique and the Historians', pp. 362–63; Demonet, 'Quelques avatars du mot "politique"', p. 54.

[49] Greengrass, 'Epilogue', p. 248.

importance on this term, either they apply their own definition, generally based on period uses that mean 'moderate' or 'civic-minded' Catholic, or they focus on the endogenous uses that indicate troubled, ambiguous, and often overwhelmingly negative meanings. An instructive example of the latter is Jan Miernowski's study of *politique* as insult.[50] Those who opt for the former suggest, like Beame, that the term can be used to indicate an 'attitudinal terrain'.[51] Mario Turchetti, Arlette Jouanna, and Myriam Yardeni have argued that the term *politique* may indicate a certain mentality, united within what Jouanna refers to as 'a family of like minds' ('une famille d'esprits').[52] They have argued that the term unites those who lobbied for peace towards the end of the wars, drawn predominantly from one of two groups: either rootless or dissatisfied nobles who were Catholic but did not align themselves with the League and often had personal connections with Protestants; or members of the rapidly growing *noblesse de robe* who represented a late Renaissance French formulation of civic humanist attention to the life and well-being of the city and the nascent nation.[53] Adjacent to this trend, Julien Broch has traced the influence of what he calls the *politique* school of legal thought from 1559 to 1598 and their contribution to the architecture of the post-war proto-modern state.[54] The analysis offered here, as I have indicated, focuses by contrast on a broader range of endogenous uses of *politique*, rather than applying the term post hoc to a group of similar (but actually rather different) writers and political actors.

And yet, the *noblesse de robe* is important to this book. It was made up of lawyers and parliamentarians who wrote and published discussions of

---

[50] Miernowski, '"Politique" comme injure'.   [51] Beame, p. 379.

[52] See Mario Turchetti, 'Une question mal-posée: l'origine et l'identité des Politiques au temps des guerres de Religion', pp. 357–90 (p. 390), Arlette Jouanna, 'Les ambiguïtés des Politiques face à la Sainte Ligue', pp. 475–93, and Myriam Yardeni, 'La pensée politique des "Politiques": Etienne Pasquier et Jacques-Auguste De Thou', pp. 495–510, esp. p. 509, all in *De Michel de L'Hospital à L'Edit de Nantes*.

[53] On the dissatisfied nobility and the rising *noblesse de robe*, see Arlette Jouanna, *Le devoir de révolte: La noblesse française et la gestation de l'état moderne, 1559–1661* (Paris: Fayard, 1989), Robert Descimon, 'L'invention de la noblesse de robe. La jurisprudence du Parlement de Paris aux XVIe et XVIIe siècles', in *Les parlements de province: Pouvoirs, justice et société du XVe au XVIIIe siècle*, ed. by Jacques Poumarède and Jack Thomas (Toulouse: fraMespa, 1996), pp. 677–90, and Robert Descimon and Elie Haddad, *Epreuves de noblesse. L'expérience nobiliaire de la haute robe parisienne (XVIe–XVIIIe siècles)* (Paris: Belles lettres, 2010). In his introduction to a recent study of Pierre de L'Estoile, Henri-Jean Martin associates this group with the erudite *libertins* described by René Pintard in *Libertins érudits* (Paris: Jammes, 1970). See 'Préface', in Florence Greffe and José Lothe, *La vie, les livres et les lectures de Pierre de L'Estoile: Nouvelles recherches* (Paris: Champion, 2004), pp. 9–15 (pp. 9–11). The idea of an identifiable *libertin* group has been problematised as much as that of a *Politique* party; see n. 65.

[54] Broch's approach, indeed, is to see the 'Politiques' as lawyers who ultimately came to favour strongly centralised state power (see Broch, *L'école des Politiques*).

philosophy and politics, who knew each other, who read each other's work, and who used – and argued over – the word *politique*. The *Parlements* were central to the activities of these figures.[55] The group overlaps closely with those identified by Jotham Parsons as 'erudite gallicans'.[56] Warren Boutcher has noted this overlap; he gives a compelling account of the literary and political motivations of *robins* writing *politique* histories.[57] They contributed to the creation, and manipulation, of the *politique* problem. This points to overlap between the evocation of 'mentalities' and analysis of uses of the term in context: attention to word use offers a productive way of examining how the writing of literature participates in the creation and the remembering of political attitudes, in which the line separating rhetoric from reality is necessarily, even deliberately, blurred. After all, the purpose of rhetoric is to construct persuasive perceptions of reality, and if the term *politique* has engendered centuries of apparent misconstruing, or mis-construction, it would be useful to restore a sense of this being partially the deliberate intention of those who used the term – with consequent, or concomitant, ambiguity and plurality.

The starting point of my analysis is thus the word *politique* itself, given its significance and flexibility in the period – and all the works discussed have *politique* in their title, feature a character called Politique, or make particularly unusual or compelling use of the term. I have also included discussion of authors and texts given prominence in critical and historical discussions to date. Part of my aim is to revise a putative *politique* canon (already being formed in the seventeenth and eighteenth centuries, as Furetière and the *Encyclopédie* demonstrate) in which authors such as Bodin, Montaigne, and Machiavelli have traditionally featured. While these authors are central to critical accounts of literature, politics, and their connections in the sixteenth century, they find a central place in this book only in so far as focus on endogenous uses of the term *politique* allows. This approach has different results for the three figures just mentioned. I look in detail at Bodin's *Six livres de la République* both because his text is an instance of positive construction of *politique* on a linguistic and conceptual level and because his name consistently appears in lists of *Politiques* compiled during the period and after. Montaigne, whose *Essais* are highly politically engaged and who is the pre-eminent canonical literary

[55] Sylvie Daubresse, *Le Parlement de Paris ou la voix de la raison (1559–1589)* (Geneva: Droz, 2005).
[56] Jotham Parsons, *The Church in the Republic: Gallicanism and Political Ideology in Renaissance France* (Washington, DC: Catholic University of America Press, 2004), p. 9.
[57] Warren Boutcher, *The School of Montaigne in Early Modern Europe: Volume Two: The Reader Writer* (Oxford: Oxford University Press, 2017), pp. 20–28.

(and perhaps also literary-political) figure of his age, appears in nearly every chapter of the book, but more often as commentator or counterexample because of the way he uses (and seems to avoid) the term *politique*. Machiavelli, meanwhile, is a key recurrent figure, but marginal in that – contrary to what much of the existing scholarship might give one to expect – neither his name nor his works are a focal point for the negative associations made in the later part of the wars.

Another element of the present critical attitude to the term *politique* and its various referents, real or imaginary, is to draw a line between the abstract noun on the one hand, and the person either named *politique* or qualified as such by an adjectival use of the term on the other. The majority of criticism I discuss above is concerned with the latter kind of word use. Demonet makes precisely this distinction, arguing that there was a stable, neutral understanding of the abstract term *politique* as 'concerned with government', and that it was the concrete substantive that experienced the degradation in ethical status described by sixteenth-century polemicists and twentieth-century historians.[58] The abstract *politique*, in fact, had something like the opposite trajectory – it was increasingly present as a generic marker and as an important form of knowledge and expertise, as I discuss in Chapter 2; we might think more in terms of its rise to prominence rather than of its stability. I consider distinctions made between abstract and concrete iterations of *politique*, and suggest that there is an important connection of mutual influence between them so that the abstract *politique* might be more stable, in a way, but is never neutral. In his study of 'five words' that he sees as crucial to the early modern period ('invention', 'language', 'blood', 'resistance', and 'world'), Roland Greene writes that although they seem neutral they are 'complex semantic events', and become particularly complex owing to the mixing generated by their use both in technical disciplinary contexts and in more everyday contexts.[59] The term *politique* seems to operate in this way, with its 'mixing' occurring partly because the term can function in the abstract, or concretely, or adjectivally, and it is not always clear which is which.

Writing on the political dimension of aesthetic (and specifically literary) production, Jacques Rancière defines politics as regulating both perception and possibility: 'Politics revolves around what is seen and what can be said

---

[58] Demonet, 'Quelques avatars du mot "politique"', p. 34.
[59] Roland Greene, *Five Words: Critical Semantics in the Age of Shakespeare and Cervantes* (Chicago, IL and London: University of Chicago Press, 2013), pp. 5–6.

about it, around who has the ability to see and the talent to speak, around the properties of space and the possibilities of time.'[60] The sense that *la politique* regulates communal experience is very much in tune with sixteenth-century definitions and so seems to prove in a way the stability of the abstract term (unsurprising, since Rancière's major references here are, as they were for sixteenth-century writers, Aristotle and Plato). But the point he makes is that the abstract concept is channelled into speech, sight, space, and time; into subjects who speak, see, and exist in space and time and who are not and cannot be politically neutral. I argue that *la politique* and *le politique* operate in this kind of dialectical relationship and explore that relationship in this book, looking at the subjective substantive *politique* as a character who negotiates between the abstract and the concrete, and who figures as an imagined hero or villain whose virtue or vice is contingent upon specific circumstances and allegiances in the civil wars.

These specific circumstances and allegiances are described in detail in later chapters. The close readings of Chapters 3–6 are gathered around two key periods, when *politique* was an especially prominent and contested term. The first is *c.* 1568–78, a period of intense violence, in which the animosities and factionalism of the wars became more entrenched, and in which one weak king gave way to another. The late 1560s and early 1570s see the first uses of *politique* with meanings specific to the Wars of Religion. With the publication of Le Roy's translation of Aristotle's *Politics* and Bodin's *République*, they also represent a moment in which high political thought was appearing in the vernacular. The massacres of Saint Bartholomew's Day in 1572 and reactions to this intense violence also created a situation of particular urgency; Huguenot writers in particular responded by mobilising their own versions of what politics and *politiques* should be.

The second period in focus is *c.* 1588–94, with a narrower regional focus on Paris, although other cities, particularly Lyon, are important too. In 1588, Henri III was forced out of Paris; the following year he was assassinated, and the Protestant Henri de Navarre became heir apparent but could not claim the throne due to the intense resistance of radical Catholic factions centred in the capital. This is the period that, as discussed above, Joseph Bergin considers as having been the only moment in which there may have been a *politique* party of sorts at once attempting to bolster support for the future Henri IV and to make him more palatable by persuading him to convert. Certainly, a plethora of texts debated the

---

[60] Jacques Rancière, *The Politics of Aesthetics*, tr. by Gabriel Rockill (Paris: La fabrique, 2000), p. 13.

definition of *politique*, and condemned so-called *politiques*, or tacitly defended them. These works had a significant impact on historical under-standings of *politique*; critics who focus on insulting aspects of the term *politique* and who debunk the apparent myth of a coherent *politique* party tend to focus on this corpus. It is important, however, to look beyond their immediate context and to connect them with earlier works of politics and polemic that mobilise a *politique* figure. These writings, like the others discussed in the book, were influenced both by immediate circumstances and by political ideas that had been developing for many decades.

The title of this book is 'Politics and *Politiques*': the word order here follows the rhythm of the English language. However, the order of analysis proceeds from *politiques* to politics. The decision to focus on the term *politique* rather than on texts written by figures considered to be *politiques* or works thought to evince *politique* attitudes is a means of giving a new account of this contested term. It is also a way of moving beyond the issue of whether or not any sixteenth-century person can or should be identified as *politique*. The *politiques* I am primarily concerned with are words in texts. With this focus on text, I show that literature, in its broadest sense, was consciously used to influence the way political reality was perceived for good and for ill; and I also expand the literary-critical discussion of sixteenth-century politics, which, in the field of French Studies, has so far focused on single-author studies, on particular metaphors, on national identity, on rhetoric, and on humanism and its discontents.[61] The empha-sis on the word *politique* itself has consequences for the selection of texts analysed. Firstly, as already discussed, almost all works discussed are in the vernacular, despite the large number of political texts written in Latin in this period. Secondly, I have selected texts that make particular, repeated

---

[61] Studies of the relation between literature and politics that focus on a single author are mainly about Montaigne: see, for example, *Montaigne politique*, ed. by Phillipe Desan (Paris: Champion, 2006), and Biancamaria Fontana, *Montaigne's Politics: Authority and Governance in the* Essais (Princeton, NJ: Princeton University Press, 2008). For descriptions of Montaigne as *politique* see, for instance, David Quint, in *Montaigne and the Quality of Mercy: Ethical and Political Themes in the* Essais (Princeton, NJ: Princeton University Press, 1998), p. 103; for suggestions that he shouldn't be described as such, see Marie-Luce Demonet, 'Le politique 'nécessaire' de Montaigne', in *Montaigne Politique*', pp. 17–37. On an especially rich political metaphor, see Wes Williams, *Monsters and Their Meanings in Early Modern Culture: Mighty Magic* (Oxford: Oxford University Press, 2011); see also Jennifer H. Oliver, *Shipwreck in French Renaissance Writing: The Direful Spectacle* (Oxford: Oxford University Press, 2019), pp. 101–39. On nation and identity, see Timothy Hampton, *Literature and Nation in the Sixteenth Century: Inventing Renaissance France* (Ithaca, NY, and London: Cornell University Press, 2001). All these studies deal with rhetoric and with the humanist legacy, but on this topic see especially Kahn, *Rhetoric, Prudence, and Skepticism in the Renaissance*.

use of the term *politique*, generally in both nominal and adjectival form. Thirdly, I have almost exclusively considered printed works; I explain this decision in more detail below, in a discussion of methodology and source selection.

Approaches

Methods

The study of words and concepts as a means of tracking socio-political and cultural changes, debates, and trends is increasingly established in early modern studies, in the disciplines of literary and cultural analysis, and in intellectual history.[62] In the wake of the linguistic turn that recognised an essential, if variable, gap between signifier and signified, I take the instability of meaning in all forms of language use as read, but suggest that, in a time of considerable linguistic change, the term *politique* is especially visible, and unstable, and that this is spurred on by writers who use the word to argue for and against different interpretations of what its meaning might be. This argument is influenced by Richard Scholar's proposition for a 'new philology' in which particular 'keywords' are considered as 'sites of encounter and conflict between *different* ways of seeing culture and society': a proposition that itself draws on Raymond Williams's study, *Keywords*.[63] In *Keywords*, Williams argued that studies of this kind can demonstrate social and historical processes occurring *within* language.[64] As such, my argument hinges less on a passive relation between text and politics, in which the text is evidence for particular events or thoughts,

---

[62] Neil Kenny, *The Uses of Curiosity in Early Modern France and Germany* (Oxford: Oxford University Press, 2004); Richard Scholar, *The Je-Ne-Sais-Quoi in Early Modern Europe: Encounters with a Certain Something* (Oxford: Oxford University Press, 2005); Wes Williams, *Monsters and Their Meanings in Early Modern Culture*; Jonathan Patterson, *Representing Avarice in Late Renaissance France* (Oxford: Oxford University Press, 2015); Ita Mac Carthy, *The Grace of the Italian Renaissance* (Princeton, NJ: Princeton University Press, 2020). These generally focus on one or two languages. Two critical works that explore particular words across multiple European languages were published in 2013: *Renaissance Keywords*, ed. by Ita Mac Carthy (Oxford: Legenda, 2013), and Greene, *Five Words*. See also Marr et al., *Logodaedalus* (2018). On this approach in intellectual history, besides Skinner and the Cambridge School, and Koselleck, see Kari Palonen, *Politics and Conceptual Histories: Rhetorical and Temporal Perspectives* (Baden-Baden: Nomos Verlagsgesellschaft, 2014), and Cornel Zwierlein, *Discorso und Lex. Die Entstehung neuer Denkrahmen im 16. Jahrhundert und die Wahrnehmung der französischen Religionskriege in Italien und Deutschland*, Schriftenreihe der Historischen Kommission bei der Bayerischen Akademie der Wissenschaften (Munich: Vendoeck und Reprecht, 2006). Zwierlein considers that the word group around 'Discourse'/'Discorsi' loosely indicates a way of thinking the political that marked sixteenth-century Europe.
[63] Richard Scholar, 'The New Philologists', in *Renaissance Keywords*, pp. 1–10.
[64] Raymond Williams, *Keywords: A Vocabulary of Society and Culture* (London: Fontana, 1988), p. 22.

than on a dynamic relation in which the text, via the engineering of 'keywords' such as *politique*, participates in the construction of 'real' socio-political experience.

The term *politique* is contested by reference to other words. I therefore show this keyword encountering other terms with histories of their own: *liberté/libertin*, *heretique*, *royal/royaliste*, and *prudent/prudence* are some of the most significant.[65] Another crucial term associated with *politique* is *police* (that can mean 'polis' or 'polity', but most often 'rule' or 'administration'). This term recurs in this book, but I do not track it with the same attention I pay to *politique*, because it operates rather differently and does not attract the same controversy.[66] A critic wishing to follow Raymond Williams more closely than I have might compile a sixteenth-century political lexicon including the terms just listed as well as *politique*, perhaps with separate entries for regional variants of the term *politique* in the sense of 'pragmatic Catholic who opposes the League'; indeed, these variants are discussed throughout the book, including 'bigarré' ('varied', or 'motley'), 'malcontent', and 'maheustre' (a term used to describe Henri de Navarre's supporters, especially foot soldiers in the Paris region, used in the title of the *Dialogue* analysed in Chapter 6).[67] *Moyenneur* was also a term commonly used to describe political moderation, though it is not used particularly in most of the sources analysed in this book.[68] The diversity of sixteenth-century political terminology is clear. But this book is not about multiple keywords that express something identifiable (or indeed translatable) as '[the] political'; it is a study of one word with a textual history that is exceptional, if not unique. Among the political keywords of sixteenth-century France, *politique* is the only one to appear in high abstract discourse (both the abstract 'politics' and the figure of the *politique* person) as well as having everyday valency as insult or political identifier – rather like *libertin* the following century – and to have become in turn a contested historiographical marker. It is singular within the political vocabulary of sixteenth-century France.

[65] On *libertinage*, see Louise Godard de Donville, *Le libertin des origines à 1665: Un produit des apologètes* (Paris: Biblio 17, 1989). Godard de Donville argues that *libertinage* and *libertins* were defined partially by people who sought to condemn certain attitudes and practices, and partially by those wishing to exonerate them, rather than by people who identified as *libertin*, and in this respect the histories of *politique* and *libertin* share some similarities.

[66] See Sophie Nicholls's illuminating analysis of the concept of *police*, in *Political Thought in the French Wars of Religion*.

[67] See Philippe Papin, 'Duplicité et traîtrise: l'image des "Politiques" durant la Ligue', *Revue d'histoire moderne et contemporaine*, 38.1 (1991), 3–21, p. 4.

[68] On 'moyenneur' see, for example, Bergin, p. 22.

The contestation of *politique* led not only to change in its meaning over time, but also to its meaning different things at the same time. A keywords approach accounts for changes in meaning, treating variation not as aberration but as an inevitable consequence of the variation within society. How exactly meaning is conveyed, and how terms relate to concepts, has been a matter for much debate.[69] In exploring how *politique* gains and loses different meanings, I take inspiration from the model offered by Neil Kenny, who emphasises the inconsistency and permeability of words denoting in his study of curiosity in early modern France and Germany. He argues that '"concepts" exist through a continuous process of being constructed and undone, not only from century to century, but from text to text, and even from sentence to sentence'.[70] Kenny's approach allows for readers who misconstrue, and indeed for authors who engage in deliberate manipulations of language. His discussion of curiosity, both influenced by postmodern accounts of the impossibility of fixed meaning and sympathetic to early modern confidence in the referential capacities of language, explores 'clusters' of meaning that refer in ever-shifting and imperfect ways to concepts and objects.[71] Part of the crisis that the word *politique* represented for its early modern users, I argue, is that at certain moments of particular contestation it tested and undermined confidence in language and its referential capacities.

A strength of this method is to counter teleological claims about 'progress' towards absolutism, or modernity, or secularism, by including the also-rans and might-have-beens in the history of the word *politique*; I emphasise competing uses, some of which have faded more than others from historical memory. Kenny shows that this kind of approach, which Skinner worries could become a kind of 'linguistic fetishism', is necessary to show that the attempts people make to engineer meaning (attempts that make a term 'key') are messy and compromised.[72] If meaning is endlessly compromised, it is not wholly inaccessible. A charge laid at the door of postmodernists and the critics inspired by them is that they emphasise undecidability to the detriment of what Edward Said calls 'the actuality of

---

[69] Indeed, Quentin Skinner criticises Williams for glossing over the difficult relation between words and concepts in 'The Idea of a Cultural Lexicon', *Essays in Criticism*, XXIX (1979), pp. 207–24. The tension between Williams and Skinner is also one of priority – Skinner seeks a vocabulary that historians can use to explain and understand social experience, and to categorise trends, whereas Williams prioritises language users without the same concern for categorising them after the fact.

[70] Neil Kenny, *Curiosity in Early Modern Europe: Word Histories* (Wiesbaden: Harrassowitz, 1998), p. 20.

[71] Ibid., pp. 28–32.   [72] Kenny, *Curiosity in Early Modern Europe*, pp. 29–31.

reading', resulting in 'reductiveness, cynicism, or fruitless standing aside'; Kenny overcomes this by referring to moments of construction as well as deconstruction.[73] Indeed, a balance must be found between undecidability and decision if, in line with a keywords approach, words are thought to *do* things, even if not to *be* things in a relation of direct equivalence.[74] Pragmatic linguistics offers a means of compromise here, and a way of suggesting how meaning might be constructed, if not fixed; broadly speaking, pragmatics accounts for context-dependent meaning, that is meaning acquired relationally as a result of the cognitive effort of language users and interpreters – so that language, and any resulting meaning, is fundamentally cooperative.[75] Essentially, this model is useful because it allows me to make the point that words mean things and do things because people think they do, and want them to, and because the success or failure of social organisation depends, to an extent, on people being able to agree (or not) over what they all might mean when using key terms like *politique*.[76]

This approach to literature and meaning is sympathetic to Rita Felski's call for greater critical sensitivity to the participation of literature in real social, political, and affective experience, not just despite but indeed *because* of the limits of referentiality. I treat representations of politics as literary phenomena that incorporate 'a vast terrain of practices, expectations, emotions, hopes, dreams, and interpretations'.[77] The 'plurality, the

---

[73] Edward W. Said, *Humanism and Democratic Criticism* (Basingstoke & New York, NY: Palgrave Macmillan, 2004), pp. 60–61.

[74] J. L. Austin, *How to Do Things with Words* (Oxford: Clarendon Press, 1962). For a provocative use of speech act theory in literary analysis, see Shoshana Felman, *The Scandal of the Speaking Body: Dom Juan with J. L. Austin, or Seduction in Two Languages* (Stanford, CA: Stanford University Press, 2002). See also Quentin Skinner, 'Interpretation and the Understanding of Speech Acts', in *Visions of Politics I: Regarding Method* (Cambridge: Cambridge University Press, 2002), pp. 121–145.

[75] Laurence Horn and Gregory Ward, 'Introduction', in *The Handbook of Pragmatics*, ed. by Laurence R. Horn and Gregory Ward (Oxford: Blackwell, 2004), pp. xi–xviii. See also Quentin Skinner, 'Interpretation and the Understanding of Speech Acts', in *Visions of Politics I: Regarding Method* (Cambridge: Cambridge University Press, 2002), pp. 121–145.

[76] I am also influenced by relevance theory in my understanding of how meaning is communicated. While acknowledging that some decoding work occurs in communication, relevance theory treats meaning as a cognitive effect that is largely dependent on the relevance assigned to inferences made by association, and therefore determined to a considerable extent by context. relevance theory is not limited to verbal or textual communicative acts; further work, with a slightly altered methodology, could consider the scope for non-verbal communication of the political. See Dan Sperber and Deirdre Wilson, 'Relevance Theory', in *The Handbook of Pragmatics*, pp. 607–32, esp. p. 607, for the relation between 'code' and 'inference'; *Relevance: Communication and Cognition* (Oxford: Oxford University Press, 1986); and *Meaning and Relevance* (Cambridge: Cambridge University Press, 2012). The uses of this theory in literary enquiry have recently been explored at length for the first time, in *Reading Beyond the Code: Literature and Relevance Theory*, ed. by Terence Cave and Deirdre Wilson (Oxford: Oxford University Press, 2018).

[77] Rita Felski, *The Uses of Literature* (Oxford: Blackwell, 2008), p. 8.

instability and promiscuity of text' is not only linguistic play, or an endlessly receding horizon in which meaning figures in a kind of Petrarchan poetics as an ultimately intangible object of desire: it is also, as Annabel Brett describes, a sign of how particular language users have the potential to change conversations, and thus to change history.[78] Sophie Smith has recently addressed the importance of poetic creativity – of 'making' the state – in early modern political thought.[79] Emphasising human creativity in historical change is also a way of seeing a different kind of poetics at work in language acts and in representations of thought, where 'poetics' are understood in terms of creative 'making', or poesis, refiguring the real.[80]

Sources

A very large number of sixteenth-century texts – literary, legal, juridical, polemical, theoretical, historical, and so on – contain at least one or two uses of the term *politique*. Online catalogues and databases such as *Frantext* have been helpful in establishing a sense of this vastness; searchable digitised texts (the online Montaigne provided by the University of Chicago; many of the early printed texts available through the Bibliothèque nationale de France's online library, Gallica) have been invaluable, and without them this study would probably have been different and would certainly have taken longer. The 'keywords' approach I have followed has involved selecting those texts in which the term *politique* is especially 'key'. By no means all of the texts analysed in the book were available in searchable form at the time the research was carried out, but digital searches revealed whether and how certain texts used the term. That said, however useful digital methods have been, they have not been the primary means of establishing the corpus. Owing to the already considerable interest in *politique* as an appellation, existing scholarship provides a series of corpora (pamphlets; vernacular political thought; political literature) that are juxtaposed here in a book-length study for the first time. In this way, I work both with and against literary, political, and *politique* canons.[81]

---

[78] Brett, 'Intellectual History Now', pp. 123–24.
[79] Sophie Smith, 'Making the State: Poetry and the Origins of Political Theory', Quentin Skinner Lecture 2017, University of Cambridge, 7 July 2017. See also Sophie Smith, 'The Language of Political Science in Early Modern Europe', *Journal of the History of Ideas*, 80.2 (2019), 203–26.
[80] Brett, p. 127.
[81] I have been guided in my sense of this canon particularly by Jouanna, 'Politiques', and Demonet, 'Quelques avatars du mot "politique"'.

The key works, as I indicated in the Preface, are Bodin's *République*; Le Roy's introduction, commentary, and translation of Aristotle's *Politics*; vernacular Huguenot texts published 1574–78; Catholic pamphlets c. 1589; the *Dialogue d'entre le Maheustre et le Manant*; and the *Satyre ménippée*. Before I analyse these in detail, in Chapter 2 I establish a semantic field for the term *politique* across the century as a whole.

As well as being appropriate to a keywords approach, the decision to foreground those texts with compelling, repeated uses of *politique* as both noun and adjective is a pragmatic limitation, given the potentially inexhaustible corpus. The majority of the texts studied use *politique* both adjectivally and as a noun (although some of the examples in Chapter 2, which is more of a survey, do not conform to this rule). The noun receives more attention overall than the adjective; this arises in part from the nature of the *politique* problem, with its emphasis on the identity and virtues of the *politique* figure. There are a number of printed texts that would provide useful case studies for mobilisations of the political that are not considered. One group of sources would be the edicts of pacification: Bergin points out, for example, that the Edict of Saint-Germain (1562) affirmed toleration for Huguenots and insisted that they nonetheless had to follow 'political' (*politic*) laws.[82] This text and others like it do not meet the criteria for inclusion in this study because they do not, as far as I have seen, explicitly problematise the noun; they recount and manage political events, but not so much *politiques*, at least not in the way that interests me in this book. Being selective in this way, rather than trying to give a broader sense of the huge number of printed and manuscript documents that contribute to the semantic field around *politique* with one or two uses, also has the advantage of enabling sustained close readings, comparisons between texts, and consideration of issues such as narrative structure, form, genre, and style that might not always be accounted for if the focus were purely semantic.

Printed uses of *politique* emerge in association with key institutions – the royal court; the *Parlement*; even (in a revisionist kind of way) the Faculty of Theology at the Sorbonne, which did much to shape the political lives of those who used and abused the term *politique*. These institutions are part of the story, present in the way that other keywords are present. But they do not provide a framework. I analyse uses of *politique* at a time when institutions had diminishing or conflicted authority, and when, even as the courts and *parlements* were gaining power, the nascent

[82] Bergin, p. 24.

'French state' whose key pillars they formed was in some ways as chimerical as the contested concept of politics itself.[83] My emphasis on the literary, theoretical, and polemical rewritings of the meaning of *politique* is a way of exploring this unstable situation, and of assessing how different kinds of writing participate therein. I have highlighted instances of the term *politique* when it refers to a text, a character in various texts, and a fictional or theoretical persona operating either within or beyond institutions, a means of navigating or explaining late sixteenth-century France, that can be used centuries later to examine the dangerous, porous boundaries between words and deeds.

The focus on printed texts is, in some ways, another pragmatic limitation. The textual world of the sixteenth century was certainly broader than that of the surviving print works, and recent accounts of, for example, the fortunes of Etienne de la Boétie's *Discours de la servitude volontaire* demonstrate not only an enduring manuscript culture but complex interaction between manuscript and print; the annotations Montaigne made to the Bordeaux Copy of his *Essais* on which most print editions are now based are another example of this.[84] However, print culture was vital to the social group with which this book is generally concerned: the *noblesse de robe*, which did so much to create and manipulate the *politique* problem. Henri-Jean Martin explicitly associates the advent of printing with the development of this class, describing it as a new 'aristocracy of knowledge' ('aristocratie du savoir') in his introduction to Florence Greffe and José Lothe's study of Pierre de L'Estoile and his library. As an avid collector of books and pamphlets, a signer of privileges, the grandson of a legal professor, and a lawyer in the Paris *parlement*, L'Estoile could not be a clearer example of the *robin* relationship with print, even as his manuscript journal and methods of collating print ephemera further demonstrate the complex connections between writing by hand and in print.[85]

Moreover, the *politique* problem was exacerbated by print.[86] Printing meant broader, faster dissemination of political texts; *politique* was imbued

---

[83] The collapse of authority should not be exaggerated, however: Penny Roberts argues that the collapse of monarchic authority was not total, in *Peace and Authority during the French Religious Wars c. 1560–1600* (Basingstoke: Palgrave Macmillan, 2013), p. 12.

[84] On the fortunes of La Boétie's text, see *La première circulation de la* Servitude volontaire *en France et au-delà*, ed. by John O'Brien and Marc Schachter (Paris: Champion, 2019).

[85] Henri-Jean Martin, 'Préface', in Florence Greffe and José Lothe, *La vie, les livres et les lectures de Pierre de L'Estoile: Nouvelles recherches* (Paris: Champion, 2004), pp. 9–15 (pp. 9–11).

[86] Elizabeth Eisenstein's classic study of the printing press as 'an agent of change' in early modern Europe stands as a persuasive argument for the socio-political impact of print, even if its claims have been nuanced by later scholars, as does Denis Pallier's work on printing in France during the period

with new power through its appearances in print and new controversy –
especially in printed pamphlets. La Boétie's *Discours* is a case in point. In
1574 the anonymous authors of the Huguenot *Reveille-matin des françois*
brought an unacknowledged extract of that work into print for the first
time, spoken by a character called Politique; a few years later the *Discours*
was reproduced almost in full in Simon Goulart's *Mémoires*. La Boétie's
work that had previously had a more controlled audience was now accessible to a larger number of unknowns, and more strongly associated with
the word *politique*.[87] This is emblematic of the relationship of *politiques* to
print culture. The 1595 edition of the *Satyre ménippée* was published
with a 'Printer's Discourse' ('Discours de l'imprimeur') in which the
printer notes similar problems of piracy and invokes the wider public
enabled by print:

> I have also heard complaints about a bookseller who, either through avarice
> or jealousy, had this work printed in tiny lettering, most incorrect and
> unpleasant, and who had the temerity to leave out whatever he wished,
> which Justice should not endure. Nevertheless, the *argument* is public, and
> anyone can make additions [to it] that serve the subject.[88]

The public and relatively uncontrolled aspect of print publication allowed
the *politique* problem to proliferate; as such, print is the central arena of
enquiry in this book.[89]

---

of the League; more recently, Ian Maclean's account of the book trade demonstrates the vitality of
print culture and shows the rise of a 'new genre of political writing' that was facilitated by the
expansion of printing. See Elizabeth Eisenstein, *The Printing Press as an Agent of Change*
(Cambridge: Cambridge University Press, 1980). Eisenstein points out that early modern writers
also noted the transformative impact of print, citing Francis Bacon's claim that print 'changed the
appearance and state of the whole world', p. 3; Denis Pallier, *Recherches sur l'imprimerie à Paris
pendant la Ligue (1585–1594)* (Droz, Geneva: 1976); Ian Maclean, *Scholarship, Commerce, Religion:
The Learned Book in the Age of Confessions 1560–1630* (Boston, MA: Harvard University Press,
2012) p. 70; See also Racaut, *Hatred in Print*, as well as *Histoire de l'édition française tome 1. Le livre
conquérant du Moyen-Âge au milieu du XVIIe siècle*, ed. by Henri-Jean Martin, Roger Chartier, and
Jean-Pierre Vivet (Paris: Promodis, 1982), Zemon Davis, *Society and Culture*, pp. 189–226, and the
chapter 'Pamphlets and Persuasion', in Andrew Pettegree, *Reformation and the Culture of Persuasion*
(Cambridge: Cambridge University Press, 2005), pp. 156–84.
[87] La Boétie uses *politique* once, adjectivally, in the *Discours*: Etienne de la Boétie, *De la servitude
volontaire, ou Contr'un*, ed. by Malcolm Smith (Geneva: Droz, 1987) p. 34.
[88] 'Aussi l'ay-je oüy plaindre d'un Libraire, qui par avarice ou jalousie des autres, a fait imprimer cet
œuvre en petits characteres, mal corrects et mal plaisants, et a esté si temeraire, d'y oster ce qu'il a
voulu: ce que la Justice, ne devroit pas endurer. Toutefois l'argument est public, où chacun peut
faire des additions qui servent à la matière.' *Satyre Ménippée*, ed. by Martial Martin (Paris:
Champion, 2007), p. 157.
[89] On sixteenth-century French conceptions of the public, see Emily Butterworth, *The Unbridled
Tongue: Babble and Gossip in Renaissance France* (Oxford: Oxford University Press, 2016),
pp. 10–12, and Eisenstein, p. 102.

However, there are many arresting uses of *politique* in manuscript sources such as correspondence, or trial documents, or in private works such as L'Estoile's journal. Manuscript letters are quoted infrequently in what follows, but are often referenced in the texts I focus on in detail. Stuart Carroll has analysed a telling reference to 'political justice' in a letter written by the Lieutenant General of Guyenne in 1560, and suggests that this bears the influence of La Boétie.[90] A more comprehensive account of uses of *politique* in trial documents in particular might also enable a broader sense of the impact of changes in the use of *politique* across the class spectrum, and demonstrate the variation among more localised cases, giving a denser texture to the claims made here about the imbrication of the discursive with the social. Some cases show contestation of the meaning of *politique* in real-world conflict. The record of a trial in Lyon where a man accused of murder reports having been called a 'bigarré ['mixed/motley'] politicque' by his adversary evokes the political vocabulary of Lyon in the late stages of civil war, and the consequences of uses of *politique* for individual, non-elite lives.[91] I refer at various stages to the experiences of real people – mostly the writers themselves – implicated in their own or others' uses of *politique*, who are either empowered or, more often, endangered by association with the term. The real-world consequences of uses of *politique* are especially present in Chapter 5. But readers will not find case studies of individuals or communities, and only limited discussion of those who did not participate in print production. As the author of the 'Printer's Discourse' in the *Satyre ménippée* might put it, the study in this book does not present a closed case; others may offer additions that serve the subject.

Politics and *Politiques*

A particularity of this book and its methods arises from its focus on politics, and on *politiques*. What are the politics of *politiques*?[92] Keywords

---

[90] Stuart Carroll, 'Political Justice and the Outbreak of the Wars of Religion', *French History*, 33.2 (2019), 177–98 (p. 177). See BNF MS Fr 3186 fol. 127.

[91] Papin, 'Duplicité et traîtrise', p. 4; MS AN X2B 165, 1591-07-19. Thanks to Tom Hamilton for this reference.

[92] On the relation between literary techniques and tropes, and politics or public discourse, see *Metaphor and Discourse*, ed. by Andreas Musolff and Jörg Zink (New York, NY: Palgrave Macmillan, 2009), especially Christ'l De Landtsheer, 'Collecting Political Meaning from the Count of Metaphor', pp. 59–78, and Jonathan Charteris-Black, 'Metaphor and Political Communication', pp. 97–115. On the use of keywords and glossaries as political theory, see Emily Apter, *Unexceptional Politics: On Obstruction, Impasse, and the Impolitic* (London: Verso,

approaches expose the politics inherent to language use; Williams is remembered as a Marxist critic, while Edward Said's defence of philology calls on public intellectuals to pursue a kind of postmodern humanism that might be a route to liberation for marginalised and exiled groups.[93] Recent work on early modern terminology follows Said's injunction in some ways by excavating the gender politics in the use of words like 'avarice', 'curiosity', and 'discretion'.[94] In this book I also show the gendered dynamics of the characterisation of *politique* as masculine agent of power.[95] This is a crucial aspect of early modern political writing: as Anna Becker has shown, political thought in the early modern period was deeply gendered, with gender a 'primary way of signifying relationships of power'.[96] My account of politics and *politiques* is, moreover, concerned with the emergence of a particular political class, its fortunes and interests, and with their language use as a sign of their (albeit limited) agency in this process: in tandem I consider who was excluded from participating in politics according to their visions of it.

Politique as a focal point for conceptual arguments and debates about what kind of person incarnates political action, political wisdom, and political error, also has a bearing on theorisations of what politics actually *is*. Firstly, in this book at least, politics is a word, occupying several different parts of speech. I look extensively at the differences between *la politique* and *le politique* wherein the former could be translated as 'politics' and the latter either 'the political', or, more often, 'the political person'. I will suggest that early modern philological attention to the grammatical range of politics and *politiques* might be a key legacy of the sixteenth-century *politique* problem, and a fundamental aspect of politics as a phenomenon in early modern thought. Modern theorists of the

2018). Apter develops what she calls 'a vocabulary for the microphenomenology of political life', p. 4.

[93] Said, p. 83.

[94] See Kenny, *The Uses of Curiosity*, pp. 310–424; Patterson, *Avarice*, pp. 78–119; Timothy Chesters, 'Discretion', in *Renaissance Keywords*, pp. 103–17, esp. pp. 109–13.

[95] For an account of misogynistic politics as a product of patriarchal structures of thought, see Jane Flaz, 'Political Philosophy and the Patriarchal Unconscious: A Psychoanalytic Perspective on Epistemology and Metaphysics', in *Discovering Reality: Feminist Perspectives on Epistemology, Metaphysics, Methodology, and Philosophy of Science*, ed. by Sandra Harding and Merrill B. Hintikka, 2nd ed. (Dordrecht: Kluwer, 2003) pp. 245–82.

[96] Anna Becker, 'Gender in the History of Early Modern Political Thought', *The Historical Journal*, 60.4 (2017), 843–63 (p. 846). See also Anna Becker, *Gendering the Renaissance Commonwealth* (Cambridge: Cambridge University Press, 2019) and Hanna Pitkin, *Fortune Is a Woman: Gender and Politics in the Thought of Niccolò Machiavelli* (Berkeley, CA: University of California Press, 1984).

phenomenology of politics tend to think of it as relational. Elizabeth Frazer has described the concept of politics as a 'complex' operating across several relational dimensions, which are: state–society–individual; publicity–secrecy; deliberation; openness–closure.[97] This book explores early modern French politics across and beyond these dimensions, but a keywords study of the term *politique* – of how it was contested, and used to contest the nature of politics – lends itself to particular focus on deliberative understandings of the political, since *politique* is subject and object in (as it happens, often unsuccessful) deliberation, on a spectrum between strong praise and extreme blame.[98]

The seemingly endless mobility of *politique* within these deliberative acts places it at the open end of an openness–closure spectrum, wherein there can be no final settlement or definitive decision, evoking Chantal Mouffe's understanding of politics as necessarily 'agonistic', against Jürgen Habermas's proposition of a deliberative politics that aims at resolving *agon* and building consensus.[99] Habermas refers to consensus as 'communicative recognition'; my book is all about attempts to recognise *politiques* and trigger recognition and re-cognition in the reader. Within this, I show that any such recognition is at best partial and in any case always offers multiple possibilities. In this sense I understand the political in the sixteenth century in sympathy with Mouffe's theorisation of contemporary politics, showing *politique* operating as a dynamic element within a fundamentally quarrelsome discourse that necessarily constructs and deconstructs concepts and forms, through the use of that word and others.[100] Privileging 'agonistic' over 'democratically consensual' understandings of the political is a way of following the clues given in the poem *Description*

---

[97] Elizabeth Frazer, 'Political Theory and the Boundaries of Politics', in *Political Theory: Methods and Approaches*, pp. 171–95 (p. 194).

[98] This way of conceptualising politics maps imperfectly on to theorisations of deliberative and epideictic rhetoric that would have been more familiar to early modern writers; this underlines the long-standing connection between conceptualisations of politics, rhetoric, and communication. Victoria Kahn has shown how deliberative rhetoric and the possibilities it was thought to offer were central to the reception of humanist practice across Europe in which the story of the term *politique* has its place. See *Rhetoric, Prudence, and Skepticism*, p. 20.

[99] See Jürgen Habermas, *Postmetaphysical Thinking: Philosophical Essays* (Cambridge: Polity, 1992); and Chantal Mouffe, *The Democratic Paradox* (London: Verso, 2000), esp. pp. 80–107.

[100] Alain Viala has described the creative and socially constructive impact of literary quarrelling. See Alain Viala, 'Un temps de querelles', in *Le temps des querelles*, ed. by Jeanne-Marie Hostiou and Alain Viala (=*Littératures classiques*, 81 [2013]), 5–21, esp. pp. 18–19. Mouffe has a related view of the creative potential of productive tensions expressed in linguistic form, and draws on philosophy of language (especially on Richard Rorty and pragmatics) to make this point, p. 9.

du politique, which bemoans a lack of imposed consensus (figured as harmony) and describes the *politique* as the embodiment of discord.[101]

Despite the differing contexts with which Habermas and Mouffe are concerned, conceptualisations of consensus are particularly relevant to a study of the sixteenth-century *politique* because, as I discuss above, it has been taken as both representative of and the means of achieving the fragile post-war consensus encapsulated by the Edict of Nantes.[102] Moreover, although most if not all sixteenth-century writers considered democracy deeply undesirable, the liberal historians I discuss above saw in the Wars of Religion and the supposed *Politique* triumph the proto-democratic seeds of modern governmental forms. I argue rather that the term *politique* is involved in attempts at imposing, negotiating, and refusing consensus, and that tracing its uses in texts within and beyond the literary canon demonstrates some of the power dynamics at work in literature. Given the frequency of deadlock and destructive failures of dialogue, sixteenth-century French politics in fact seems to have the qualities of what Emily Apter defines as 'unexceptional politics': that is, the politics of circumstances profoundly marked by contingency and by 'baffled institutional authority'.[103] Apter's point is that 'unexceptional politics' involve phenomena for which 'classical political theory and political science have no names'.[104] 'The political' as expressed in sixteenth-century uses of the term *politique* operates outside the boundaries of the normative political models outlined by theorists from Plato to the present (tyranny, monarchy, democracy, etc.), constantly seeking and testing those theoretical and institutional forms.

We shall see below how the term *politique* is often placed on one extreme or the other in sixteenth-century writing ('friend', or 'enemy', for instance) precisely because it incarnates dubious compromise. Its mobility between such categories allows modern readers to place the word in a kind of ethical no man's land that some call pragmatic compromise: a middling term for the middle ground, occupying what Terence Cave refers

---

[101] Unlike the anonymous poet, Mouffe does not see conflict or disharmony as inherently bad; nor was disharmony always considered negative in early modern thought: Teresa Bejan has recently analysed the early American thinker Roger Williams's view that cacophony might be the best state any mixed society can hope for, with lasting implications for the nature of civil society in the modern United States. See Bejan, pp. 50–82.

[102] Some critics also take inspiration from the early moderns to make sense of modern political experience. See Victoria Kahn, *The Future of Illusion: Political Theology and Early Modern Texts* (Chicago, IL and London: University of Chicago Press, 2014), esp. pp. 2–22.

[103] Apter, p. 4.   [104] Ibid., p. 9.

to as a 'median zone' ('zone médiane').[105] Cave derives this term from Aristotle's *meson* (middle term) between opposites, used to define terms and thus reach definitive judgement. In Cave's account of Renaissance ethics, this system of oppositions offered no precise middle that could be counted on: as such the 'middle term' is mobile, occupying a 'zone' rather than a fixed location.[106] The so-called *Politiques* came to be known in history-writing as a group that followed the 'middle path' of compromise between polarised opposites during the civil wars; I argue here that the 'middlingness' of *politique* is also a function of uses of the word itself, which in turn developed out of Renaissance habits of reading, thinking, and conceptualising ethical problems at the frontiers between deliberative consensus, autocratically imposed meaning, and chaotic, murderous dis-agreement. This book explores the agonistic tensions of the *politique* 'zone médiane' that go beyond the *agon* articulated by Mouffe precisely because there was no stable governmental form, democratic or otherwise, no French state beyond the theoretical, imaginary, or incipient. Therefore, the writers I discuss are seeking not just representation but the forms that would make representation possible, in ways that depend to greater and lesser extents on dialogue: staged dialogues between characters who embody ideas and problems; real dialogues between writers and readers whose survival might depend on the consensus, or common ground, that their writing and reading has the potential to create.

The political landscape of sixteenth-century France is in many ways an alien and alienating one for readers in the twenty-first century, even if its sectarian conflicts and debates over the importance and the limitations of toleration may remind readers of contemporary politics.[107] The struggles of various writers to reimagine, understand, or rationalise their political communities, and their relationship to or identification with their leaders (both monarchs and 'politicians'), are defined by specific historical cir-cumstances: early modern French culture has as much to teach the contemporary world through its differences as through its similarities to the world of today. The book does not, then, present an origin story; nor does it draw simplistic analogies in which yesterday's assassinated *politique* is today's murdered politician. Nor do I make the argument that

---

[105] Terence Cave, *Pré-histoires: Textes troublés au seuil de la modernité* (Geneva: Droz, 1999), p. 85.
[106] Ibid., p. 99.
[107] If anything this book might offer part of a genealogy, with Foucault's emphasis on accident and displacement in genealogical accounts. See Michel Foucault, 'Nietzsche, la généalogie, l'histoire', in Michel Foucault, *Dits et écrits 1954–1988*, ed. by D. Defert and F. Ewald, 4 vols. (Paris: Gallimard, 1994), II, pp. 136–56.

contemporary French attitudes to secularism, integration, and toleration have explicit roots in the Wars of Religion. I view the resonances of sixteenth-century politics in the present more as recurrences of particular forms rather than as the outcome of identifiable processes.[108] The demonisation and lionisation of political figures, the radicalisation of political (and polemical) discourse, the currency of insults and name-calling, and the question of whether moderate paths are desirable or even possible, are common phenomena then and now. At the heart of my exploration of the problems of form and representation that gather around uses of the term *politique* is the problem of decidability (that is, of definition) raised above: the question of meaning itself, and whether it remains fundamentally open, or whether some questions really can be closed. Who decides meaning, and how, and in whose interests? Can conflicting aims – built from essentially conflicting visions of the value of life and the purpose of society – be made to speak to one another, be reconciled? If yes, how so? If not, what is lost? All these are the questions urgently asked, and tentatively, provisionally answered, in sixteenth-century uses of the term *politique*.

---

[108] This stance is influenced by Felski's sense of the 'logic of recognition' that readers may experience when reading (*The Uses of Literature*, p. 14), and Fredric Jameson's philosophy of (literary) history. He has pointed out the ideological double bind of antiquarianism versus facile claims for relevance in historical and literary studies, and suggests a philosophy of history that 'is capable of respecting the specificity and radical difference of the social and cultural past while disclosing the solidarity of its polemics and passions, its forms, structures, experiences, and struggles, with those of the present day'. Fredric Jameson, *The Political Unconscious: Narrative as a Socially Symbolic Act* (London: Methuen, 1981), p. 18.

CHAPTER 2

Pre-Histories and Word Histories

Weeds in the Garden of France

How to account for the rise of the word *politique* to prominence and controversy in sixteenth-century writing? Looking back on a century of strife, Etienne Pasquier saw new uses of *politique* as an unhappy phenomenon born of accident and malign influence. At the opening of the eighth book of his enormous work of history, *Les recherches de la France*, the writer and jurist lamented that 'the greatest misfortune that can befall a Republic is when, whether by fortune or discourse, we see a people diversifying themselves ['se bigarrer'] with partial words'.[1] This view of linguistic misadventure as a matter both of fate and of 'discourse' suggests a negotiated balance between human agency (figured as authorship) and the vagaries of fortune in the making of unwanted words. The lament opens a chapter entitled 'Du mot Huguenot', in which the author blames 'Courtizans' for the initial use of *Huguenot*, and goes on to describe the sub-categories that grew from *Huguenot* and *Catholique* as if the process were a form of spontaneous cell division that eventually produced *politique*, considered worse than *Huguenot*:

[1] 'Le plus grand Malheur qui puisse advenir en une République, c'est lors, que soit par fortune, soit par discours, l'on voit un peuple se bigarrer en mots de partialitez.' Etienne Pasquier, *Les recherches de la France*, ed. by Marie-Madeleine Fragonard and François Roudaut, 3 vols. (Paris: Champion, 1996), III, p. 1670. For the publication history of Book Eight of the *Recherches*, see Pasquier, *Recherches*, III, p. 1496 n. 1. For an account of the genesis, approach, and source material of the *Recherches*, see Fragonard and Roudaut, 'Introduction', in Pasquier, *Recherches*, I, pp. 3–41. On Pasquier, see also George Huppert, *The Idea of Perfect History: Historical Erudition and Historical Philosophy in Renaissance France* (Urbana and Chicago, IL: University of Illinois Press, 1970), pp. 28–69; 'Etienne Pasquier et ses *Recherches de la France*', = *Cahiers V. L. Saulnier*, 8 (1991), especially the contributions by Colette Demaizière (pp. 23–33) and Arlette Jouanna *Le pouvoir absolu* (pp. 105–19), on Pasquier's ideas about language and on his proposition for the 'mythical origins' of the French state respectively. See also James H. Dahlinger, *Etienne Pasquier on Ethics and History* (New York, NY and Oxford: Peter Lang, 2007) and *Saving France in the 1580s: Writings of Etienne Pasquier* (New York, NY: Peter Lang, 2014).

[*Politique* is a] word which in little time spread across France, and was formed in the middle of our two opposing parties, the *Huguenots* and the *Papists*, whom we have since called *Catholics*, from which, as if from a seedbed, were produced many offshoots of partiality, now *associated Catholics*, now *malcontent Catholics*. It was only in our most recent troubles that the *Catholic* party produced this further subdivision of *Politique*, who was considered of worse condition than the *Huguenot*, because he argued for peace.[2]

With his definition of the middling location of the *politique* person, and identification of a *Politique* party emerging only at the very end of the wars, Pasquier articulates here some of the key traits of the *politique* identified by historians, although he sees little good in the categorisation.[3] Many writers blamed poor use of language for the *politique* problem. What makes Pasquier's version stand out is his sense of the blend of contingency and agency that gives the word its meaning, and his own particular history with the weed-like word. For the Pasquier of the *Recherches*, the words that grew from a seedbed of 'partialities' give meaning to each other, and *politique* is one term amongst them. Thirty years earlier the same Pasquier had written a dialogue in which a main character was named Politic (*Le pourparler du Prince*, 1560), a figure who mediates between different kinds of knowledge to give the Prince the best possible counsel, and does so by mitigating the influence of a potentially pernicious 'Courtizan'. In this passage from his *Recherches*, Pasquier does not relate the brief rise of the anti-League *politique* to earlier uses of either *politic* or *courtizan*, his own included. Why? What had changed? What ideas and trends influenced those early uses? To address these questions, in this chapter I present the semantic field around *politique* in the sixteenth century, treating it as a kind of 'conversation politicque' ('political conversation': a phrase used in Rabelais's *Gargantua*, discussed below).[4] The chapter is at once a word-historical overview and a 'pre-history', in the sense that I treat a number of

---

[2] 'Mot qui en peu de temps s'épendit par toute la France, se formant au milieu de nous deux partis contraires, le *Huguenot* et le *Papiste*, que nous appellâmes depuis *Catholique*: desquels, comme d'une pépinière furent produits plusieurs rejettons de partialitez, tantost de *Catholiques associez*, tantost de *Catholiques malcontents*. Il n'est pas qu'en nos derniers troubles, le party *Catholique* ne fut encore subdivisé en *Politique*, que l'on estimoit de pire condition que le *Huguenot*, parce qu'il plaidoit pour la paix.' Pasquier, *Recherches*, pp. 1676–77. This passage is cited as emblematic of the period in Elie Barnavi and Robert Descimon, *La Sainte Ligue, le juge et la potence: L'assassinat du Président Brisson (15 novembre 1591)* (Paris: Hachette, 1985), p. 29.

[3] On impartiality as a virtue in seventeenth-century Europe, see *The Emergence of Impartiality*, ed. by Kathryn Murphy and Anita Traninger (Leiden and Boston, MA: Brill, 2014).

[4] *Gargantua* refers to 'conversation politicque' in a discussion with Frère Jean in *Gargantua*; see François Rabelais, *Œuvres complètes*, ed. by Mireille Huchon (Paris: Gallimard, 1994), p. 110.

texts written prior to the civil war, and therefore prior to the rise of *politique* as a keyword, that express doubt or 'trouble' (to borrow Terence Cave's terms about 'pre-history') concerning its meaning and application.[5] These 'troubles' informed the field (literally imagined by Pasquier as growing from a 'seedbed') from which later versions of *politique* emerged, through processes that were both contingent – shaped by contextual 'fortune' – and also actively shaped, through writing, or 'discourse'. The weed-like *politique* and other such words emerged from a semantic field that was also a literary one, and self-consciously so.

Pasquier's metaphor of the seedbed and its offshoots evokes the horticultural imagery used by writers such as Geoffroy Tory and Joachim Du Bellay to analyse and promote the newly prominent French language: Tory's *Champ fleury* ['Field of Flowers'], *c.* 1529, depicted French, and implicitly France, as a flowered garden that could be yet perfected.[6] Plant metaphors were a means both of praising French and of discussing variation, as well as beauty and perfectibility.[7] There are many passages in Montaigne's *Essais* in which he uses organic metaphors to explore the difficult relationship between language and thought, and between language and society. The work both begins and ends with reflections on this theme: in 1.8 ('On Idleness'), Montaigne compares his mind to a fallow field, threatening to teem with 'a hundred thousand kinds of wild and useless weeds' (p. 24) unless he commits his thought to paper: hence the *Essais*.[8] I mentioned in Chapter 1 that Montaigne described the Reformation as a quarrel over words; in the last chapter, III.13, he regrets the legal disputes that 'make the world fructify and teem with uncertainty and quarrels', annotating the Bordeaux Copy with the further comment that 'the earth is made more fertile the more it is crumbled and deeply ploughed'.[9] Metaphors of fertility, and of cultivation, convey the difficulties of language as well as means for its improvement; and they express the impossibility of full control over meaning. So when Montaigne refers to Tacitus in III.8 ('On Conversation') as a 'seedbed of political and ethical discourses', the point that complications might ensue and bad seeds be

---

[5] Cave, *Pré-histoires*, p. 85.

[6] Geoffroy Tory, *Le champ fleury, ou l'art et science de la proportion des lettres* (Paris, 1529), f. ii. See also Du Bellay's *Deffense et illustration de la langue françoise* (1549).

[7] On France as a 'Garden of Letters', see Hampton, *Literature and Nation*, pp. 1–30, and on horticultural metaphors, see Louisa Mackenzie, *The Poetry of Place: Lyric, Landscape and Ideology in Renaissance France* (Toronto: Toronto University Press), pp. 20–21.

[8] 'foisonner en cent mille sortes d'herbes sauvages et inutiles' (p. 54).

[9] 'En semant les questions et les retaillant, on faict fructifier et foisonner le monde en incertitude et en querelles', p. 1113.

produced is implicit; this is made explicit in an earlier chapter, II.17 ('On Presumption'), in which Montaigne writes (in reference to Machiavelli) that 'political matters' were, in particular, a 'fine field open for vacillation and dispute' (p. 603).[10]

Pasquier opens Book Eight of his *Recherches de la France* with a discussion of the development of the French vernacular; in his work the connections between common (or uncommon) language and community (or its splintered version) are clear.[11] Pasquier's use of the verb 'bigarrer' (to diversify, variegate, or render in multiple colours) further connects his account of linguistic change with others.[12] That language and its variability were key preoccupations for Renaissance writers is well known thanks in large part to the work of Terence Cave.[13] French writers took up such questions with alacrity, but these preoccupations were broadly European, not just French. Two treatises by Erasmus, *De copia* (1512) and *Lingua* (1525), are lodestones in critical accounts of how Renaissance writers addressed the pleasurable and painful possibilities of linguistic variety. Cave writes of the widespread 'urgent desire, in all camps, to seal the leaks and prevent the fragmentation of the logos', even in this age of linguistic *copia*, which goes some way to explaining Pasquier's regret over the unwanted linguistic weeds springing up and spoiling the garden of France in the civil war period, even as his *Recherches* celebrate elsewhere the variety and idiosyncracy of French.[14] Variety, or 'bigarrure', was all very well in certain textual contexts, but when words start to *do* things in the world, causing people to vary themselves ('se bigarrer'), linguistic change becomes a problem: the word *politique*, in particular, became a problem; indeed, later on in the wars, 'bigarré' was a negative quality explicitly associated with *politique*.[15]

---

[10] 'C'est une pepiniere de discours ethiques et politiques', p. 986; 'Notamment aux affaires politiques il y a un beau champ ouvert au bransle et à la contestation', p. 694.

[11] Pasquier, *Recherches*, III, p. 1496.

[12] Estienne Tabourot wrote two collections entitled *Les bigarrures* ('Variations'), the first in 1572 and the second in 1585.

[13] Terence Cave, *The Cornucopian Text: Problems of Writing in the French Renaissance* (Oxford: Clarendon Press, 1979), esp. pp. 157–68. See also Ian Maclean, *Interpretation and Meaning in the Renaissance: The Case of Law* (Cambridge: Cambridge University Press, 1992); Emily Butterworth, *The Unbridled Tongue: Babble and Gossip in Renaissance France*, esp. pp. 13–26; and Timothy J. Reiss, 'The Idea of Meaning and Practice of Method in Peter Ramus, Henri Estienne, and Others', in *Humanism in Crisis: The Decline of the French Renaissance*, ed. by Philippe Desan (Ann Arbor, MI: University of Michigan Press, 1991), pp. 125–32.

[14] Cave, *The Cornucopian Text*, p. 157.

[15] On anxiety over the consequences of linguistic proliferation, see also Reiss, 'The Idea of Meaning'. One later association of *politique* and *bigarré* is Anon., *Responce au cartel d'un politique bigarré qui ne s'est osé nommer* (Lyon, 1591).

The incompatibility between the universalising and transcendent impulses of humanism, and the uncontrollable multiplicity and inherent epistemological instability wrought by those who sought to fulfil those same impulses, has been described by Philippe Desan as the 'apple in the worm of humanism'; Cave describes Renaissance literature as a kind of 'fallen garden', echoed by Tzvetan Todorov's description of early modern literature as an 'imperfect garden' ('jardin imparfait').[16] Here, I locate the various *politiques* present in this earthly garden, be they roses, thorns, or weeds.

Origins

It makes little sense to speak of sixteenth-century origins for *politique* when the vernacular term had already been in use for several centuries, and yet sixteenth-century writers consistently registered their impression that it had changed and was still changing in fundamental ways. During these decades of change, *politique* seemed to be endlessly new. In the early seventeenth century, Jacques-Auguste De Thou attempted to clarify the origin of the plural substantive *politique* as it had come to be used ('Politicorum nominis origo': 'the origin of the appellation "politiques"'), but his conclusions were vague. He traced the term's origin to a moderate faction that developed in the wake of the Saint Bartholomew's Day massacres. Earlier in his history, however, he had described as 'politici' those who followed the traditional religion and lobbied for peace from 1568, a gloss that seems to reflect a post hoc historical categorisation as well as being potentially representative of a new kind of word use that developed in the 1560s.[17] Thus, in De Thou, origins blur and merge. In 1573 the *Président* of the Rouen *Parlement* described *politique* as 'newly introduced'; in 1589 a Leaguer pamphlet described the word as 'newly used'.[18] Clearly, in these instances, the same word may have very

---

[16] Philippe Desan, 'The Worm in the Apple: The Crisis of Humanism', in *Humanism in Crisis*, pp. 11–34; Cave, *Cornucopian Text*, p. 180; Tzvetan Todorov, *Le jardin imparfait: La pensée humaniste en France* (Paris: Grasset, 1998), p. 11. Gardens were not only a matter of metaphor in this period: garden design received much attention in the period of cultural flourishing presided over by François Ier. See Danièle Duport, *Le jardin et la nature: Ordre et variété dans la littérature de la Renaissance* (Geneva: Droz, 2002).

[17] Quoted in Ingrid de Smet, *Thuanus: The Making of Jacques-Auguste de Thou (1553–1617)* (Geneva: Droz, 2006), pp. 240–41.

[18] Letter quoted in Jouanna, *Le pouvoir absolu*, p. 177; *Le karesme et mœurs du Politique où il est amplement discouru de sa manière de vivre, de son Estat & Religion* (Paris: Pierre-Des-Hayes, 1589), p. 5.

different meanings; what it retains is novelty, with all its potential for disruption and dissonance. This is reproduced in Pasquier's account in the *Recherches* of the new and disruptive iteration of *politique* in the final phase of the wars.

The sixteenth-century 'conversation politicque' was, however, both continually renewed *and* influenced by longer-term intellectual developments and linguistic trends. Some of the longer-term influences correlate with the interrelated intellectual and linguistic 'streams' that Pocock and Pagden identify as the main languages of political theory in early modern Europe: 'political Aristotelianism', 'classical republicanism', 'political economy', and 'the science of politics'.[19] Interacting with and shaping these 'languages' was more than a century's worth of moral and political thought developed in, and about, the Italian city states.[20] James Hankins has recently described the political project of Italian humanism as 'virtue politics': a 'new way of thinking about politics' that focused on improving the character and behaviour of ruling elites; this could also be understood as another 'political language' influential on French thinking about politics and *politiques*.[21]

The different languages of early modern politics, and indeed of *politiques*, are also the different tongues of Latin and Ancient Greek, alongside the modern vernaculars. The story of the word *politique* in French is, after all, partly that of its emergence as a vernacular term: a translation – and indeed, adaptation – of the Latin *politicus*. *Politicus* itself is a corruption, a Latinized Greek term; Ciceronian Latin (and Cicero himself, in *De officiis*) used the *civil* word group to refer to matters now generally categorised as 'political'. But in the sixteenth century, French literary-linguistic culture was increasingly open to Greek influence (as was that of much of Renaissance Europe following the impact of the Aldine Press and others). French thinkers increasingly turned to Greek political philosophy by the middle of the century. French was frequently defined with and against Italian; these shifts ought to be understood in the context of Franco-Italian rivalry, in which French thinkers and poets painted France as a new

[19] Anthony Pagden, 'Introduction', and J. G. A. Pocock, 'The Concept of Language and the *métier d'historien:* Some Considerations on Practice', in *The Languages of Political Theory in Early Modern Europe*, ed. by Anthony Pagden (Cambridge: Cambridge University Press, 1987), pp. 1–18 and 19–38.

[20] Hans Baron, *The Crisis of the Early Italian Renaissance: Civic Humanism and Republican Liberty in an Age of Classicism and Tyranny* (Princeton, NJ: Princeton University Press, 1955).

[21] James Hankins, *Virtue Politics: Soulcraft and Statecraft in Renaissance Italy* (Cambridge, MA: Harvard University Press, 2020), p. 54.

Athens, to rival the Greco-Roman revivals occurring in Italy. Proximity between Ancient Greece and France was sought (and fostered) at a lexical level, as demonstrated by a near-contemporary of Pasquier, Henri Estienne, a Protestant scholar and member of the celebrated printing family, who wrote a treatise on the 'natural' connections between the French and Greek languages.[22] This may explain the use of *politique* instead of or in tandem with *civil*, in some of the examples discussed below.

The apparent 'Greek turn' in French political thought should not, however, be overestimated. The Classical Latin and Neo-Latin cultures were influential throughout the period, and distinctions between 'Greek' and 'Latin' were frequently bridged. The Greco-Latin hybrid, *politicus*, had long been a reference to the Aristotelian curriculum of moral philosophy taught at the Sorbonne (*ethica*, *politica*, and *oeconomica*). Nicolai Rubinstein shows how the term *politicus* was treated with lively engagement in commentaries of Aristotle from Aquinas onwards; he sees the epicentre of work on the Latin term as late Medieval and Renaissance Italy, where it was also a substantive in active use in legal discourse (some Medieval lawyers referred to themselves as 'politici').[23] Hankins suggests that duplicitous 'habits of mind' developed through the legal and diplomatic occupations of humanists who were professionally obliged to be persuasive at all costs, and to argue *pro* and *contra*; this, indeed, could be one influence on a disagreement that occurred in the 1530s between Thomas More and a counsellor named Saint German over the appellation 'polytyke', which More uses to mean duplicitous (although, tellingly, More contributes to the apparent newness of politics in his time by describing 'polytykes' as a 'kynd of thynkers ... as I never to my remembrance have herde of before').[24] More wrote this diatribe less than two years before his execution; fifteen or so years before that, his *Utopia* (1516), written in Latin, had imagined a state largely free of such failings. Latinate-Italian legal contexts were replicated and altered in French legal

---

[22] Henri Estienne, *Traicté de la conformité du langage françois avec le Grec* (Paris: Robert Estienne, 1569).

[23] See Nicolai Rubinstein, 'The History of the Word *Politicus* in Early Modern Europe', in *The Languages of Political Theory in Early Modern Europe*, pp. 41–57.

[24] James Hankins, 'Humanism and Modern Political Thought', in *The Cambridge Companion to Renaissance Humanism*, ed. by Jill Kraye (Cambridge: Cambridge University Press, 1996), pp. 118–40. More writes that he's heard his opponent refer to a group of thinkers called 'polytykes' who 'purposely saye evyll and openly speke heresye, and for all that thynke well'. Thomas More, *The Complete Works*, ed. by J. B. Trapp, 15 vols. (London and New Haven, NJ: Yale University Press, 1963–97), IX, pp. 84–85.

writing, where a more idealistic vision of the political man – 'homo politicus' – developed, representing 'in many minds ... that compound Renaissance ideal of scholarship and social utility, of private learning and public virtue'.[25] At the turn of the sixteenth century, then, in the context of increasing vernacularisation, *politicus* and *politique* were flexible terms that referred to a kind of expertise that was itself potentially characterised by flexibility, associated with a kind of ideal union of theory and practice, and, in the case of the Hellenised Latin *politicus*, already a kind of hybrid creature.

Rubinstein argues that the essential early sixteenth-century French context for both the term *politicus* and its vernacular iteration, *politique*, was the theorisation of constitutional monarchy.[26] Given that this was at least theoretically the prevailing political system, this seems hard to refute, and yet other contexts emerge even in Claude de Seyssel's *Grant monarchie de France* (1515), held to be the clearest articulation of constitutionalist principles. For instance, in a passage representing the state as a 'mystic body', Seyssel describes its progress from formation to inevitable decline and fall, in which the initial phase is 'assembly through civil and political union'.[27] This image of a primordial civil and political union characterising any human society recalls Aristotle's view of man as political animal, and shows the adjectival *politique* operating beyond any one normative structure. For Seyssel, the term *politique* is flexible and sometimes rather general; *police* (meaning administration, or rule) is an important constitutional keyword, but *politique* is not simply its adjectival offshoot.[28] Meanwhile the term *police* itself in sixteenth-century French was not only a constitutionalist sub-heading; Estienne's *Conformitez*, for instance, refers it back to Ancient Greek by emphasising the connections between *police* and *politeia*.[29]

---

[25] Kelley, *The Beginnings of Ideology*, pp. 203–11. This is reminiscent of Hankins's 'virtue politics'.

[26] Rubinstein, p. 52. This was the idea of a constitutional monarchy in which checks and balances – 'justice', 'religion', and 'police' – regulate monarchic power, differentiating this model from what classical theory described as 'tyranny' and also from the model that came to be known as 'absolutism'. See Claude de Seyssel, *La monarchie de France, et deux autres Fragments politiques*, ed. by Jacques Poujol (Paris: Librarie d'Argences, 1961).

[27] 'Tout ainsi advient aux corps mystiques de la société humaine; car, après qu'ils sont assemblées par une civile et politique union, ils vont par quelque temps en accroissant et multipliant', Seyssel, p. 108.

[28] See Rebecca Ard Boone, *War, Domination, and the Monarchy of France: Claude de Seyssel and the Language of Politics in the Renaissance* (Leiden and Boston, MA: Brill, 2007), p. 18. Boone suggests that *police* is to Seyssel what *virtù* is to Machiavelli. On the fortunes of the concept of the 'police' in the sixteenth century, see Nicholls, *Political Thought in the French Wars of Religion*.

[29] Estienne, *Traicté de la conformité du langage françois avec le Grec*, p. 165.

Pocock suggests that the ideal historian become conversant with and able to identify the different 'codes' of political thought in order to select the most important, as Rubinstein does.[30] The polysemy of the semantic field at the start of the sixteenth century indicates, however, that there is no one 'essential' French context for the term *politique*.[31] The 'languages' in which *politicus* and *politique* operated were porous and interconnected. The rise of the substantive form in the mid-sixteenth century accompanied intellectual and socio-political developments that could well be described according to a number of sub-languages but were at once more and less than the sum of such parts, and by the time François I died in 1547, the seeds were sown for the *politique* weeds that various writers complained of later in the century.

Politique was then a hybrid term and flexible by definition at the dawn of the sixteenth century. But the broader linguistic context made writers more conscious of this flexibility. Close attention to language use was encouraged by the promotion of French to official court language in 1530; also in 1530, at the instigation of Guillaume Budé, François Ier opened the *Collège royal* as a centre of humanist study. A highly ambitious king renowned for his patronage of the arts, and less renowned for his military exploits (his Italian campaigns were notably unsuccessful), François dreamed of a united France becoming increasingly powerful within an ever more interconnected world.[32] Over the course of his reign, power shifted towards his court and the *Parlements*, and towards humanist cultural and educational practices, accompanied by a renewal in the study and practice of law.[33] The development of the vernacular, then, was consciously informed by language users who formed the growing elite group of lawyers and royal associates, and it was influenced by their practices of sociability as well as by ideas about art, law, linguistic and poetic convention, and good government.[34]

---

[30] Pocock, 'The Concept of Language', p. 23.

[31] This point is similar to Ita Mac Carthy's account of 'grace' (*grazia/gratia*) as the product of a blend of influences, resulting in a word 'adaptable to a multiplicity of ends'. Mac Carthy, *The Grace of the Italian Renaissance*, p. 49.

[32] Anne-Marie Lecoq, *François Ier imaginaire. Symbolique et politique à l'aube de la Renaissance française* (Paris: Macula, 1987), p. 15.

[33] On law, see Kelley, *The Beginnings of Ideology*, pp. 172–93, and *The Foundations of Historical Scholarship*, pp. 242–56; and Ian Maclean, *Interpretation and Meaning in the Renaissance: The Case of Law* (Cambridge: Cambridge University Press, 1992), pp. 125–35.

[34] See Philip Ford, *The Judgment of Palaemon: The Contest between Neo-Latin and Vernacular Poetry in Renaissance France* (Leiden and Boston, MA: Brill, 2013).

Like Pasquier, who we recall blamed 'Courtizans' for the rise of the term 'Huguenot', many writers were also concerned with *who* was responsible for linguistic change, and it is clear that those who were held responsible for linguistic corruption were also held, by some, to be responsible for political (and even religious) error. Tory writes that there are great natural virtues to be found in plants ('herbes'), stones ('pierres'), and words ('parolles') but that different kinds of person attempt to deform and corrupt the latter (he cites frothing Latinists, jokers, and jargon-spouters).[35] He nonetheless advances the sincere hope that the already admirable style of French spoken in the *Parlements* and at court could be improved. Henri Estienne took a less fond view of courtly language: he begins his treatise on French and Greek with an assertion that his intention is not to speak that varied French ('ce langage François bigarré' – again using the term 'bigarré' negatively) which changes its colours daily according to the whims of 'monsieur le Courtisan', or 'monsieur du Palais'.[36] The language users awarded power here are courtiers and lawyers. In Italian, the modern vernacular was often referred to as *cortegiano* ('courtly' or 'of the court') – so the association here between courtiers and contemporary language use may be another Italian import; Estienne in fact explicitly criticises 'italianised' French in the same passage.[37] As for 'monsieur du Palais', lawyers in the period were well aware of their role in manipulating and altering language: Ian Maclean has pointed out that language change in legal contexts was held to be a continuous process.[38] Courts, both royal and legal, were in large part the location of transformations in language, meaning, and power.

Although himself a lawyer, and certainly in many ways a product of Renaissance humanism, Jean Calvin set up an opposition between appropriate religious attitudes and the pleasures of irreverent or experimental linguistic, literary, and philosophical endeavour so central to the humanist project. In his well-known diatribe, the *Excuse aux Nicodemites* (1544), Calvin castigated all those whose flexibility and ability to see things in more than one light made them moral hypocrites; all those, in sum, capable of using language to redescribe bad things as good ('tous ceux qui diront le mal estre bien').[39] Calvin identified 'pronothaires delicatz' as the second in a list of four kinds of Nicodemite. 'Pronothaires delicatz'

---

[35] 'Aux Lecteurs', in Tory, n.p.   [36] 'Preface', in Estienne, n.p.
[37] Mac Carthy, *The Grace of the Italian Renaissance*, p. 45.
[38] Maclean, *Interpretation and Meaning*, p. 133.
[39] Jean Calvin, 'Excuse aux Nicodemites', in Jean Calvin, *Three French Treatises*, ed. by Francis M. Higman (London: Athlone Press, 1970), pp. 131–54 (p. 138).

might be translated as 'delicate gentleman officers': here, he is targeting the men of court (he also describes them as 'mignons de court') who are happy to read and discuss the gospel with fine ladies to the extent that it doesn't interrupt their pleasures; possibly, he is criticising the evangelical circle around Marguerite de Navarre. A 'courtisant', writes Calvin brusquely, may well jest and mock ('parler en risée et moquerie') but not in matters of divine importance.[40] The third type of Nicodemite, meanwhile, are humanist syncretists who use Platonism ('idees platoniques') to convert Christianity into Philosophy; happily, not all educated people are like this – otherwise, says Calvin, he would favour the extermination of all human knowledge ('science humaine') so as not to risk the corruption of good Christians.[41] Calvin names a sequence of professional types who might turn out to be Nicodemites: lawyers, judges, doctors, philosophers, and theologians.[42] These were precisely those who, according to contemporary writers, were responsible for changes in language use.

Calvin attacked 'Nicodemites' at an early stage in his career, at a time when Protestantism was on the rise in France, and François's light was dimming. The coming of the Reformation and in particular the arrival of Calvinism in France certainly complicated existing dynamics of language and power, but the French religious landscape had been unstable for some time: already a part of the power struggle. Following the signing of the Concordat of Bologna in 1516 (a 'spectacular deal' for a Gallican Church that would be affiliated with Rome but in large part self-directing), François had wielded considerable personal power over church and state, threatening the balance of *police*, *justice*, and *religion* that had been the hallmark of late Medieval French constitutionalism, sparking protests in the Sorbonne and *Parlements* alike.[43] Bergin describes the ancient Theology faculty of the Sorbonne as the 'oracle of Christendom' between 1500 and 1550, but its authority at home was increasingly subject to challenge.[44] Negotiations and disagreement over how the newly empowered Gallican Church should be ruled made France vulnerable to confessional dispute and institutional change.[45]

---

[40] Calvin, 'Excuse aux Nicodemites', p. 138.   [41] Ibid., p. 139.   [42] Ibid., pp. 139–40.
[43] Bergin, pp. 9–10. On French understandings of the role of the monarchy in late Medieval and early modern France, see Colette Beaune, *Naissance de la nation France* (Paris: Gallimard, 1985).
[44] Bergin, p. 13.
[45] François and his advisors seem to have been attracted by what is now called humanism at least partly for what Patrick Baker has recently described as its core selling point in Italy: the offer of cultural refinement both as a means of perfecting society and as a remedy for social and political tensions. See Patrick Baker, *Italian Renaissance Humanism in the Mirror* (Cambridge: Cambridge University Press, 2015), p. 5.

Within this increasingly tricky religious context, another meaning that can be inferred from *politique* is as a general reference to 'non-religious legal and ethical norms', since the primary textual references were Classical rather than Biblical, and given the distinction between 'religion' and 'police' made by Seyssel and others. A Canon of Lyon Cathedral was already complaining in the 1560s that 'worldly *politiques*' self-interestedly put the human ahead of the divine.[46] The question of the proto-secular nature of political thought and of *politique* attitudes in the Reformation period is a vexed one. It is clear that the pressure placed on the previously vaunted unity of faith, law, and monarchy in France ('une foy, une loy, un roy') put politics into potential conflict with faith as never before, and yet religious devotion was, in different ways, likely to have been part of the everyday lives and motivations of more or less all the writers discussed in this book, including those who advocate a degree of separation between politics and religion in certain legal contexts.

Perhaps deliberately rendering unity in faith and government unnecessary, Calvin seems to imply that *politique* meant non-spiritual, and vice versa. In his chapter on 'Christian Liberty' in his *Institutes of the Christian Religion*, of which the first French edition was published in 1541, he describes the double regime under which man lives: one 'political, or civil' (again demonstrating the paired Greek and Latinate terms), and the other 'spiritual'.[47] In 'On Civil Government', Calvin more or less prescribes obedience to civil law, arguing that 'spiritual liberty' can coexist with 'civil servitude' and that in any case it would be barbarous for Christians to reject the *police*, because they can increase its resemblance to the kingdom of heaven. But he also argues that the state has a duty to protect religious dignity, and suggests a vision of an ideal earthly realm in which the spiritual and the political are aligned.[48]

Ultimately, then, in his prevarication about whether and how Protestants might live peaceably in a Catholic realm, Calvin does not quite maintain a distinction between that which is *politic* and that which is *spirituel*, eventually incorporating the political into the spiritual as a

---

[46] Gabriel de Saconay, *Discours des premiers troubles advenu à Lyon*, quoted in Jouanna, 'Politiques', p. 1211.

[47] Jean Calvin, *Institution de la Religion chrétienne (1541)*, ed. by Olivier Millet (Geneva: Droz, 2008), pp. 1505–06.

[48] Calvin, *Institution*, pp. 1582–85. Skinner points out that Calvin is a 'master of equivocation' on this point, and argues that he leaves increasing room for resistance theory across the various editions so that the definitive Latin version of 1559 is altogether more favourable to civil disobedience. See Skinner, *Foundations*, II, p. 192. Ralph C. Hancock argues that Calvin ultimately incorporates the political into the religious in *Calvin and the Foundations of Modern Politics* (Ithaca, NY, and London: Cornell University Press, 1989), p. 34.

subordinate sphere of action. Calvin's contribution to the history of the term *politique* is thus to emphasise its distinction from religious law, *and* to undermine that apparent separation, as well as to hint at an ideal or improvable version of politics that might better manage the essential duality of man. *Politique* did not, then, necessarily stand in opposition to spiritual or theological concern: the relationship between the two spheres was unstable.[49] This put pressure on the meaning of *politique* and con-tributed to the 'trouble' accompanying the word towards the middle of the sixteenth century.

In the period leading up to the death of François I, uses of *politique* in France were unstable, influenced by cultural change in Europe, and by the encroaching shadow of religious and political conflict. The next part of the chapter is a series of case studies that show how this played out in particular texts written in the early, middle, and late sixteenth century: in each, *politique* is a 'textual disturbance' that carries some, or many, of the resonances I have traced up to this point. The texts in question are connected, a kind of genealogy. I nonetheless treat each as a singular entity, with its own imagination and concerns.

The first two writers I discuss produced literary reimaginings of politics during the reign of François I. The first text in question is a practical, thoughtful handbook written to guide a prince: Guillaume Budé's *De l'institution du Prince* ('On the Education of a Prince'); the next is Rabelais's *Gargantua*, a fictional representation of a prince's education. Following that, I examine dialogues written in the run-up to civil war by Louis Le Caron and Etienne Pasquier. The chapter then concludes with analysis of two texts marked by the civil wars, and that respond in some way to earlier uses of *politique*: François de la Noue's *Essais politiques et militaires*, and Montaigne's *Essais*.

Between Philosophers and Princes before 1550: Budé and Rabelais

Guillaume Budé's great contribution to French letters was his work on antiquity, and on Greek in particular, a legacy he attempted to guarantee by founding the *Collège royal*. Most of his work and correspondence was written in Latin. Given Budé's primacy as a conduit of Greek and Latin learning, it seems likely that his classically inflected conception of politics

---

[49] As discussed above, Cave refers to the fragmentation of the *logos* in Renaissance thought; Hancock argues that Calvin is anti-theological in the sense that God has no *logos* and is permanently beyond human comprehension, p. 21.

influenced the conceptual and semantic fields that shaped later understandings of what politics was, and of what it could be. His only published vernacular text was *De l'institution du Prince*, printed posthumously in the 1540s but begun *c.* 1519.[50] He wrote it in the earliest years of François's reign, to win the favour of the King (in which endeavour he was obviously successful); beyond that, it seems he intended it only for circulation in manuscript form.[51] The writing of the manuscript was influenced by his association with the King's boyhood tutor, François Desmoulins, whose beautifully illustrated *Traité des vertus* ('Treatise on the Virtues') had been written for an earlier phase of François's education; this relationship, the demands of the genre, and the rise of French as the language of court may all have moved Budé to write in French, albeit somewhat reluctantly.[52]

The publication history of *De l'institution* is chequered to say the least. The original manuscript, thought to have been more or less identical to one now held at the Bibliothèque de l'Arsenal, was essentially a series of Plutarch-inspired apothegms that encouraged the King to support poets and historians in order to heighten his glory.[53] Budé is thought to have revised the manuscript extensively before his death, but there is no definitive printed version. Recent work, moreover, has shown that the earliest printed editions date not to 1547 as previously thought, but to 1544, in Lyon; Bénévent and Walsby argue that a renewed interest in Budé's treatise on education was therefore tied less to the death of François I in 1547 than to the uncertain contexts of the King's illness, increasing factionalism, and rumblings of confessional conflict that marred the end of his reign.[54] The year 1544 is also a landmark in printed political thought in French, as the date of one of the earliest French translations of

---

[50] On the complex printing history of *De l'institution*, see Christine Bénévent and Malcolm Walsby, 'Lost Issues and Self-Censorship: Rethinking the Publishing History of Guillaume Budé's *De l'institution du Prince*', in *Lost Books: Reconstructing the Print World of Pre-Industrial Europe*, ed. by Flavia Bruni and Andrew Pettegree (Leiden and Boston, MA: Brill, 2016), pp. 239–75.

[51] Marie-Madeleine de la Garanderie, *Guillaume Budé, philosophe de la culture*, ed. by Luigi-Alberto Sanchi (Paris: Garnier, 2010), p. 257.

[52] Sylvie Le Clech-Charton, *Guillaume Budé, l'humaniste et le prince* (Paris: Rive neuve, 2008), p. 190.

[53] The Arsenal manuscript has been transcribed by Claude Bontems et al. in Claude Bontems, Léon-Pierre Raybaud, and Jean-Pierre Brancourt, *Le Prince dans la France des XVIe et XVIIe siècles* (Paris: Presses universitaires de France, 1965), pp. 77–140.

[54] Christine Bénévent and Malcolm Walsby, 'Lost Issues and Self-Censorship: Rethinking the Publishing History of Guillaume Budé's *De l'institution du Prince*', in *Lost Books: Reconstructing the Print World of Pre-Industrial Europe*, ed. by Flavia Bruni and Andrew Pettegree (Leiden and Boston, MA: Brill, 2016), pp. 239–75 (p. 272.)

Machiavelli's work: Jacques Gohory's version of the *Discorsi* (*The Prince* was translated in the following decade).

The two Parisian editions of Budé's treatise (Larrivour, 1546 and Foucher, 1547) are fairly different; the Foucher is closer to the long manuscript revised by Budé, whereas the Larrivour has been extensively altered by others. Bénévent and Walsby consider it likely that the Lyon edition of 1544 was prepared by none other than the scholar Etienne Dolet, who was burnt at the stake for heresy in 1546, and that Dolet may also have had a hand in the Larrivour text.[55] The Foucher editor, Richard Le Blanc, announced that his edition was intended to correct the mistakes of the previous imprint and provide a better guide for students of public administration and servants of the Christian prince.[56] However, the Larrivour was by far the more influential in early modern Europe, owned by Edward VI of England (whose reign began in 1547) and later by Marie de Medici and/or Louis XIII (possibly used for his education) as well as Cardinal Mazarin.[57] The differing editions and their fortunes show that Budé's text was not a stable entity between 1519 and 1547, and that it was associated with contemporary controversy through its likely contact with Dolet; Budé, whose wife was a prominent Protestant, was himself suspected of having converted to Calvinism before his death.

Uses of *politique* vary across the different editions of *De l'institution*, with the printed text containing more uses, and more developed ones, than the Arsenal manuscript. In that manuscript, Budé's focus is more on the importance of eloquence and the necessity of patronage; he refers to 'a circle of liberal arts and political sciences [*sciences politiques*]', emphasising the ultimate coherence of all types of learning (a point that is retained in other editions).[58] By contrasting liberal arts and political sciences, and putting emphasis on the political among the sciences, the Budé of 1519 was already developing a different vocabulary of princely education to Desmoulins, in whose treatise the word *politique* does not appear (by contrast, there are many references to prudence).[59] In the printed editions, this 'circle' is referred to as an 'Encyclopedia'; Rabelais is credited with the first printed use of this term in vernacular French, but Huchon suggests Budé's *Pandecta* (1508) as his source, and argues, moreover, that in his

---

[55] Bénévent and Walsby, pp. 272–73.
[56] Guillaume Budé, *Le livre de l'institution du Prince, au Roy de France treschrestien Francoys premier de ce nom* (Paris: Foucher, 1547), pp. aiiir–v.
[57] Bénévent and Walsby, pp. 252–53.
[58] Budé, 'De l'institution du Prince', ed. Bontems et al., p. 95.
[59] François Desmoulins, *Traité des vertus cardinales*, BNF MS Fr12247.

revisions of *De l'institution* Budé placed greater emphasis on the differences between forms of knowledge in order to more fully elaborate a manifesto for the necessity and utility of the *Collège royal*.[60] This goes some way to explaining how *politique* became more prominent in the printed texts.

There are three particularly developed uses common to both the Foucher and the Larrivour editions. Firstly, *politique* is used as an adjective early in both texts to qualify a form of prudence.[61] Secondly, in a discussion of Alexander the Great's education by Aristotle, 'political science' is held as a crucial part of the education of a ruler, passed from philosopher to prince, and indeed to anyone involved in government.[62] Thirdly, at the very end of the text, Budé comments that many learned ancients were extremely wise but often lacked knowledge of 'political philosophy'; this develops into praise of Solon, who was by contrast most excellent in this area.[63] In the latter example, the two editions are almost identical; by criticising the ancients (Solon excepted), perhaps Budé (and his editor) imply that the moderns might need to develop political philosophy further. In the first two examples, *politique* appears alongside references to law, indicating the proximity of these disciplines and forms of authority. In the Alexander example, the main difference between the two editions is that in the Larrivour, the section is introduced as a reflection on the issue of how to balance the nobility's right to a level of self-determination with the Prince's overall control of civil law: this was a controversial question in the context of the rising factionalism of the 1540s, and is not posed in the Foucher.[64] The Larrivour variant seems to offer knowledge of 'science politique' as a solution to this potential threat to civic harmony.

Despite the positive, constructive assertions of the importance of political science, the description of civil prudence in an early section of the text shows that *politique* is already a troublesome term in Budé because of a distinction drawn between moral and political actions. In the later passage on Alexander the Great, the author refers to 'moral and political doctrine', and emphasises that these are strongly connected and unproblematically complementary: this 'doctrine' mostly likely refers to Aristotle's *Ethics* and

---

[60] Mireille Huchon, 'Rabelais, les universités et la mobilité: les phantasmes du Pantagruel à des fins de propagande', in *Les échanges entre les universités européennes à la Renaissance. Colloque international organisé par la Société française d'Étude du Seizième Siècle*, ed. by Michel Bideaux and Marie-Madeleine Fragonard (Geneva: Droz, 2003), pp. 143–58 (pp. 148–49).

[61] Budé (Foucher) pp. 9v–10v; Guillaume Budé, *De l'institution du prince* (Paris: Larrivour, 1547) [facsimile edition Farnborough: Gregg Press, 1966], p. 19.

[62] Budé (Foucher), p. 97; Budé (Larrivour), p. 118.

[63] Budé (Foucher), p. 191; Budé (Larrivour), p. 203.   [64] Budé (Larrivour), p. 118.

Politics, and makes a less stark distinction between what is moral and what is *politique*, but a distinction nonetheless. However, in the early passage in question, on prudence, knowledge is presented as potentially destructive. Both editions stress the dangers of misapplied intellectual endeavour: vanity, error, ambition, and 'hallucinations' (a rare early modern instance of this now common term used only in the Foucher).[65] All these things assail human reason and cause people to make bad choices. In this passage, in the midst of an extremely long sentence that is slightly different in each edition, there is a reference to 'civil prudence', which is qualified as 'more political [*politique*] than moral', and connected to 'rigorous' and 'magistral' law: 'magistral' here, according to Cotgrave's dictionary, can mean both 'relating to the work of a magistrate' and 'artificial, skilful, cunning'.[66] *Politique* civil prudence is ethically confusing in Budé's text, all the more so given the tricky syntax. A rough (and slightly trimmed) translation of the Larrivour would be: 'Reason, the privilege and gift of the intellectual mortal creature, may well accommodate all kinds of dissimulation and follow the senses called common by the Orators, believing things that shouldn't be believed. Thus ['par ce moyen'], our reason favours civil prudence...'[67] In the Foucher, it goes as follows: 'Reason ... accommodates and lends obedience to dissimulation or to common sense, and to civil prudence ...'[68] It is not clear in either text whether *politique* prudence is man's error, or the solution to man's error. Surely neither Budé nor his editors would likely have intended to cast rigorous law-making as mistaken or vain; nor would they necessarily intend to cast the value of the adjective *politique* into doubt, considering that they recommend 'science politique' elsewhere. And yet the ethical value of that which is *politique*, here, is ambiguous, and there are associations with accommodation and flexibility in the same passage.

There are several instances in the Larrivour where *politique* is added, when it is not present in the apparently more authentic Foucher text; one such instance is a retelling of Plutarch's story of Fabius Maximus, who says

[65] Budé (Foucher), p. 9v.
[66] 'plus politicque & introduicte sur les façons de la police, que sur l'ordre des mœurs, qu'on appelle, morale', Budé (Larrivour), p. 19; 'plus est politicque, que moralle, et conjoincte par affinité trop plus a droict rigoureux magistral', Budé (Foucher), p. 10.
[67] 'la raison, à qui toute congnoissance appartient par le singulier privilege, & bienfaict ottroyé de toute ancienneté à la Creature mortelle intellective, veult bien s'accommoder et porter toute patience, & dissimulation aux sens que les Orateurs appellent communs, et les croire de ce, qu'il ne debueroient. Par ce moyen, celle nostre raison favorise la prudence civile, qui est plus politique & introducte sur les façons de la police, que sur l'ordre des mœurs, qu'on appelle, morale', Budé (Larrivour), p. 19.
[68] 'la raison ... accomode, et prete patience, ou dissimulation, ou commence au sens, qui s'appelle commun par les orateurs, et à prudence civile, qui plus est politicque, que moralle', Budé (Foucher), pp. 10–10v.

to his son: 'you are Rome'. The author adds that this is insofar as political authority can be universally represented by a single person, and as long as this person's honour is undiminished either by word or deed. This virtuous figure incarnating political authority could be a monarch, or any representative of 'the people', or they could be a person like Fabius's son, who is particularly politically skilled in word and deed.[69] Examples such as this from the Larrivour edition make it tempting to imagine that the more politically controversial, and influential, edition does more with the term *politique*. But there is one striking use in the Foucher that does not appear in the Larrivour, in a chapter on the high esteem in which rulers of antiquity held learned men. Budé notes that natural law and political law can be corrupted, 'unless they are corrected, and tempered, by mixed, ambidextrous men ('hommes meslés') who help with both hands'.[70] This evocation of a mixed person who might be able to stave off corruption is worth emphasising in light of later coruscating critiques of the hybrid *politique* later in the century. In the same chapter, Budé gives a long description of an ideal ruler and his 'learning, practice, and exercise of political faculties' ('facultés politiques').[71] Since he emphasises this person's nobility (no 'middling genealogy' could produce such a person), it seems that this character might most likely be a prince, but it could include his highest advisors and nobles; after all, the Foucher text is dedicated not to Henri II but to Claude de Lorraine. Here, then, we see Budé (or his 1547 editor) imagining a type of person suited to government, advised by a 'mixed man'.

Overall, in Budé, *politique* is a relatively prominent term. The form of expertise it denotes relates to Aristotle most obviously, but also to a broader range of Classical authorities (including Plutarch and Solon). As well as its complex interweaving with the virtue of prudence and the practice of law, the adjective is also attached to the following nouns: *philosophie* (philosophy), *gouvernement* (government), *doctrine* (learning), *droict* (law), and *prudence*. More loosely associated terms are *publique* and *police*. This semantic field indicates the meeting of different 'languages' of political thought in Budé's text, the increasing prominence of *politique* learning, and its use across different spheres of learning and action. All this, given the word history outlined earlier, is perhaps to be expected. Budé was instrumental in the transfer of Greek and Latin vocabulary and ideas to early modern France, and indeed to early modern French, as we have

---

[69] Budé (Larrivour), p. 154.
[70] 'sinon qu'ilz soyent corrigées, et attemperees par hommes meslées, et ambidextres. qui s'aydent de deux mains', Budé (Foucher), pp. 76–77.
[71] Budé (Foucher), p. 82.

seen with other terms like 'encyclopedie' and 'hallucination'; the humanist project of which he was a leader involved the unsettling of both the intellectual landscape and the lexicon at large.[72] *Politique*, in his *De l'institution*, is one more unsettled, troublesome term: this is not especially surprising either. But what is more compelling in a text written so early in the century is the ambiguity introduced in the opening section on prudence, the moral doubt attached to *politique*, and the fact that both editions emphasise character or persona in discussions of political action, such as the intriguing 'mixed' figure who appears in the Foucher edition.

In Budé's *De l'institution*, *politique* is a kind of object that passes between the prince and his teachers; it qualifies forms of expertise and *is* a form of expertise in its own right. Rabelais, a contemporary of Budé's who was active in courtly circles, and who wrote him at least one letter, was also concerned with humanist education and scholarship.[73] Gargantua's letter to his son in *Pantagruel*, an epistle to a Prince about the importance of humanist culture, is reminiscent of the earliest version of *De l'institution*. For Rabelais *politique* is less strictly something between a prince and his teacher than between a prince and his advisor or associate – as well as between the text and its reader – leading to a testing or reimagining of what government and politics could be.

Published around the midpoint between the first and last versions of Budé's *De l'institution*, *Gargantua* contains a smaller number of uses of *politique*: here I consider two of only four occurrences in the whole of his *œuvre*.[74] The first, in the prologue, invites the reader to interpret the text that follows as revelatory in some way of the nature of 'l'estat politicq':

> By careful reading and frequent meditation, break the bone and suck out the substantific marrow – that is to say what I mean by those Pythagorean symbols, in the certain hope of being made more astute and brave by the said reading; for in this you will find quite a different taste and more abstruse doctrine, which will reveal to you some very lofty sacraments and horrific mysteries, concerning both our political state (*estat politique*) and our domestic life (*vie oeconomique*).[75]

---

[72] Humanists like Budé may have rather intended to settle, colonise, or otherwise reshape their intellectual landscape in a more fixed form, but their enterprises had more unsettling effects. See Desan, 'The Worm in the Apple', p. 12.

[73] For a translation of Rabelais's 'Letter in Latin, with much Greek', addressed to Budé, see Donald Frame, *The Complete Works of François Rabelais* (Berkeley, Los Angeles, CA and Oxford: California University Press, 1992), pp. 735–37.

[74] The others that I have found are in the *Tiers livre*, associated with 'juste' and 'justice', see Rabelais, pp. 356 and 499.

[75] 'Puis par curieuse leçon, et meditation frequente rompre l'os, et sugcer la sustantificque mouelle. C'est à dire: ce que j'entends par ces symboles Pythagoricques avecques espoir certain d'estre faictz escors et preux à ladicte lecture. Car en icelle bien aultre goust trouverez, et doctrine plus absconce,

This comes as part of Rabelais's figuration of his reader as a diligent dog able to find the marrow ('sustantificque mouelle') of his text – it turns out that part of that 'marrow' might be 'politicq'. Whether Rabelais meant this seriously or not, this use of 'politicq' paired with 'estat' could be read as an early example of what Skinner described as the new vocabulary of the state, and the concomitant rise of the term 'state' in European vernaculars.[76] Moreover, its appearance alongside 'œconomique' evokes the Aristotelian curriculum. Rabelais's use here is therefore consistent with the story of a shift taking place in how politics was understood, reflected in word use. Rabelais's texts are an exuberant blend of many different types of writing and vocabularies; this blend is self-consciously, satirically constructed, as if the reader is invited to be conversant with multiple idioms in the style of Pocock's ideal historian, and at the same time the invitation is laced with mockery and challenge, testing the limits of interpretation and meaning.[77] If, in his prologue, Alcofribas/Rabelais offers his reader a role in an interpretive challenge, where would the *politique* 'marrow' be found? A straight reading of Rabelais's four (or five) books reveals many of the political genres and 'sub-languages' outlined by Pagden, Pocock, and Skinner, and more, with their focus on the education of a prince, military practices, and engagement with Classical authorities on what Budé defined as 'science politique'. The title of Budé's *De l'institution du Prince* itself seems to fit squarely in the 'advice manuals for princes' 'sub-language' of politics, but it has been observed that this title is somewhat misleading; indeed, both Rabelais and Budé enact the meeting of diverse associations and 'languages' in their prose.[78]

Rabelais's characters are constantly travelling, and searching: what they seek, and what they often find, is text, or simply words themselves (for example, the 'frozen words' near the end of the *Quart livre*), the reader's own quest helped and hampered by Rabelais's neologisms and wordplay.

---

laquelle vous revelera de tres haultz sacremens et mysteres horrificques, tant en ce que concerne nostre religion, que aussi l'estat politicq et vie oeconomique', Rabelais, p. 7; Frame, p. 4.

[76] Quentin Skinner, *Foundations*, II, p. 352.

[77] On multiplicity of meaning and the limits of interpretation in Rabelais, centred on the 'substantificq mouelle', see Gérard Defaux, 'D'un problème l'autre: herméneutique de l' "altior sensus" et "captatio lectoris" dans le Prologue de *Gargantua*', *Revue d'histoire littéraire de la France*, 85 (1985), 195–216; E. M. Duval, 'Interpretation and the "Doctrine Absconce" of Rabelais's Prologue to *Gargantua*', *Etudes rabelaisiennes*, 18 (1985), 1–17; François Rigolot, 'Interpréter Rabelais aujourd'hui', *Poétique* (1995), 269–85; more generally, see also François Cornilliat, 'Interpretation in Rabelais, Interpretation of Rabelais', in *The Cambridge Companion to Rabelais*, ed. by John O'Brien (Cambridge: Cambridge University Press, 2011), pp. 43–56.

[78] Bénévent and Walsby, p. 240.

Supposing that one version of Rabelais's 'marrow' were a word, and the word *politique* itself, then the 'lofty sacraments' and 'horrific mysteries' pertaining to the 'political state' might be found towards the end of *Gargantua*. In Chapter Forty, Gargantua and Frère Jean discuss monastic withdrawal from the world. Their discussion of the monastic rule points the reader towards the alternative abbey of Thélème (Chapter Fifty-Two), with its alternative (absence of) rules. These passages locate the term *politique* in a series of conversations about space, community, and belonging. In Chapter Forty, the term *politicque* appears in opposition to *retraict* (withdrawal, or 'privy'). The discussion opens with Eudemon turning the view of monks as having withdrawn from the world on its head; instead he asks why monks are excluded from 'all good companies'.[79] Gargantua agrees that monks attract extreme opprobrium, and can explain why:

> The determining reason is that they eat the shit of the world, that is to say the sins, and as shit-eaters, they are cast back into the privies (*retraictz*)*: such are their convents and abbeys, separate from political conversation (*conversation politicque*) as are the privies from a house.[80]

Here, 'conversation politicque' designates what might be roughly described as 'the social world' (toilets and monasteries being, by contrast, places of isolation). This anticipates later characterisations of the *politique* (such as Le Caron's, discussed below) as occupied with the management of public affairs. The elastic realm of 'conversation politicque' could be a positive space, where 'all good companies' can be found, though this is undercut by the image of the world at large as a producer of shit/sin (for all that shit has some positive associations in Rabelais). In sixteenth-century French, 'conversation' is more or less synonymous with 'commerce', as well as intercourse or interaction; the word also refers, quite loosely in this period, to dialogue, so that perhaps Frère Jean and Gargantua are, by talking in this way, engaging in a 'conversation politicque' that distinguishes Frère Jean, the exceptional monk, from all the rest. This moment can therefore also be read as a conversation about rules, and customs, especially considering that the word 'conversation' is also defined in Nicot's *Thresor de la langue française* as 'consuetudo, conversatio, usus',

---

[79] Rabelais, p. 110.
[80] The asterisk indicates the beginning of a section present in Huchon's *Pléiade* that is missing from Frame's translation. 'La raison peremptoire est: par ce qu'ilz mangent la merde du monde, c'est-à-dire les pechez, et comme mache-merdes l'on les rejecte en leurs retraictz: ce sont leurs conventz et abbayes, separez de conversation politicque comme sont les retraictz d'une maison', ibid., p. 110. Frame, p. 93.

which connotes a set of meanings corresponding broadly to habit, regular use, and association – communal links and practices. *Conversatio morum* also meant the uptake of the rules of a monastic order, so 'conversation politique' could be a play on that phrase, suggesting adherence to a different kind of rule, and the construction of an alternative community.

The opening of Chapter Fifty-Two ('How Gargantua Built for the Monk the Abbey of Thélème') describes the construction of that alternative community, and may therefore be at once the embodiment of a 'conversation politique' (the communal practice of Thélème) and the product of the 'conversation politique' (the dialogue in Chapter Forty). Chapter Fifty-Two invites comparison to Chapter Forty on a structural level, and not simply because a new kind of (anti-) monastery is being imagined.[81] A problem is raised (in this case, Frère Jean being fussy about his post-war reward), and answered in a manner qualified as 'determining' (*peremptoire*). 'Peremptoire' is a legal term used to introduce a definitive or quashing argument; Frère Jean thus effectively closes the case by stating that he cannot belong to or run a 'real-life' monastery:

> But the monk gave him the determining answer that he wanted no charge or government: 'For how,' said he, 'Could I govern others, who cannot possibly govern myself? If it seems to you that I have done, or might do in the future, service pleasing to you, grant me this, to found an abbey of my own devising.'[82]

Is this exchange also a 'conversation politicque'? If so, it is a discussion that initially seems to reject the semantic field around *politique* operating in Budé's text(s): government and law are banished. Frère Jean rejects the monasteries (and the *gouvernement* they offer), indicating a lack of desire, and a lack of ability resulting from a lack of knowledge, although ironically, questioning one's own self-governance was, as we will see below in Le Caron, a common topos of political discourse, considered a precursor to good rule by Plato. Frame translates the final word quoted above as 'devising', but the French is 'devis', which also means motto, or phrase, placing emphasis on the power of sets of words to conjure worlds into

---

[81] For critical comparisons of Rabelais's two abbeys, see, for example, Guy Demerson, *Rabelais* (Paris: Balland, 1986), pp. 54–55, and Miernowski, '"Politique" comme injure', pp. 353–56.

[82] 'Mais le moyne luy fist responce peremptoire, que de moyne il ne vouloit charge ny gouvernement, "Car comment (disoit il) pourroy je gouverner aultruy, qui moy-mesmes gouverner ne sçaurois? Si vous semble que je vous aye faict, et que puisse à l'advenir faire service agreable, oultroyer moy de fonder une abbaye à mon devis"', Rabelais (Huchon), p. 137; Rabelais (Frame), p. 116. Frame translates 'peremptoire' as 'decisive', which certainly sounds better in English but loses the legal connotations and the connection to the phrasing of Chapter Forty.

being. The ungoverned state he then establishes famously follows a single motto, 'Fay ce que vouldras', or 'do as you will': this is a distillation of the opening lines of Chapter Fifty-Seven: 'All their life was laid out not by laws, statutes, or rules but according to their will and free choice.'[83] Thélème thus stands as separate from the standard 'conversation politique' as did the useless 'shit-eaters'; an idealised vision of communal liberty and pleasure emerges, with all undesirables excluded – notably, only 'well-born' people are allowed since they are the only ones likely to use their free will appropriately. And the genesis of this exclusive free state was a conversation between Gargantua and Frère Jean that suggested that the whole enterprise depended on past and future service from the monk to the prince; in other words, a measure of autonomy depends on the will of the prince, enabled – implicitly – by 'conversation politicque'. Much is made in Chapter Forty of the ideal qualities of Frère Jean himself: 'he's no bigot; he's no ragamuffin; he's honourable, cheerful, determined, good company ...' (precisely the qualities required in Thélème).[84] This excellent interlocutor is then able to use his standing with his prince to create an elite community.

Politiques in Dialogue(s) *c.* 1550–68: Le Caron, Pasquier, L'Hospital

Between Budé and his prince, as between Gargantua and Frère Jean, conversation is crucial in establishing good politics; dialogue, implicit or explicit, may be the making of good *politiques*. Indeed, dialogue is a key context for the term *politique* in the sixteenth century both literally, in formal terms, and metaphorically, in the meetings of figures, ideas, and languages – this is a further aspect of the influence on French political writing both of classical models of political dialogue and of Italian humanist dialogues.[85] Next, I examine dialogues published on the threshold of

---

[83] 'Toute leur vie estoit employée non par loix, statuz, ou reigles, mais selon leur vouloir et franc arbitre', Rabelais, p. 148.

[84] 'il n'est pas bigot, il n'est point dessiré, il est honeste, joyeux, deliberé, bon compaignon ...', ibid., p. 111; Frame, p. 93.

[85] On dialogue in early modern Europe, see Jon R. Snyder, *Writing the Scene of Speaking: Theories of Dialogue in the Late Italian Renaissance* (Stanford, CA: Stanford University Press, 1989); Colette K. Winn, *The Dialogue in Early Modern France 1547–1630: Art and Argument* (Washington, DC: Catholic University of America Press, 1993); Anne Godard, *Le dialogue à la Renaissance* (Paris: Presses universitaires de France, 2001); Jean Vignes, 'Dialogue', in the *Dictionnaire du littéraire*, ed. by Alain Viala and Paul Aron (Paris: Presses universitaires de France, 2002), pp. 147–49; Eva Kushner, *Le dialogue à la Renaissance: Histoire et poétique* (Geneva: Droz, 2004); *Printed Voices: The Renaissance Culture of Dialogue*, ed. by Dorothea Heitsch and Jean-François Vallée (Toronto, Buffalo, and London: University of Toronto Press, 2004). Most of these works treat 'high'

civil war and during the period in which the word *politique* came to be a keyword, *c.* 1550–68.

The 1550s were an exceptional moment for the dialogue form in France. They were in fact an exceptional literary moment more broadly: Pelletier du Mans published his translation of Horace's *Ars poetica* in 1545, with a preface in defence of the vernacular, and Du Bellay's defence of the French language was published in 1549; Ronsard's *Odes* and *Amours* appeared in the first half of the 1550s. This was also a time of high political tension, marked by the arrival of Calvin's pastors from 1555, and of a certain muscular optimism about what France might become.[86] Expressing both optimism and latent anxiety about the future of France, Louis Le Caron (also known as Charondas, another long-lived lawyer, b. 1534, d. 1613) and Etienne Pasquier wrote dialogues that can be considered threshold texts in the narrative presented in this book. They were written as France was on the brink of civil war, and their works make compelling use of a substantive form of *politique* (spelt *politic*) to refer to a particular kind of person who embodies and manages the best kind of political action.

Le Caron's two *Courtisan* dialogues were published in 1556, and Pasquier's *Pourparler du Prince* in 1560. The works appeared at a time of high tension, after the death of Henri II in 1559. Although the Wars of Religion are considered to have begun with the Massacre at Vassy in March 1562, religio-political conflict had been escalating in the preceding years.[87] The three dialogues have many similarities. They centre on the role of the prince, and so certainly belong to the 'advice manuals for princes' (or 'mirror for princes') genre; they are both influenced by Plato as well as other key figures of Classical political thought; they have also been read as staging either a transition from constitutionalism to 'absolutism' (Le Caron) or a defence of constitutional monarchy (Pasquier).[88]

---

culture; Tatiana Debaggi Baranova has also looked at the dialogue form in polemical pamphlets during the Wars of Religion, in *A coups de libelles: Une culture politique au temps des guerres de religion (1562–1598)* (Geneva: Droz, 2012), pp. 416–35. Transnational dialogue has received particular attention in recent years; see Helen Hackett, *Early Modern Exchanges: Dialogues between Nations and Cultures, 1550–1750* (Farnham: Ashgate, 2015).

[86] See Robert M. Kingdon, *Geneva and the Coming of the Wars of Religion in France 1555–1563* (Geneva: Droz, 1956, repr. 2007), esp. pp. 54–64. Mackenzie writes that 'in the 1550s, France seemed poised to put itself on the map culturally, politically, cartographically, and linguistically' – but that everything went wrong with the outbreak of war in 1562 (p. 5).

[87] For example, confessional difference heightened family feuds and civic unrest in the Agenais: see Stuart Carroll, 'Political Justice and the Outbreak of the Wars of Religion'.

[88] Jouanna, *Le pouvoir absolu*, pp. 23–70, esp. pp. 24–34 and 60–70. Jouanna gives an overview of these interpretations but doubts the implied dichotomy between the two models.

In their attempt to instil the imaginary ruler with a particular political kind of virtue, they surely also exhibit traces of what Hankins sees as the 'virtue politics' that characterised Italian political writing in the previous century.[89] Their dialogues explore the relation between the prince and philosopher, and explicitly introduce an idealised figure, a skilled actor in the circles of power, who will mediate this relationship by speaking wisdom, if not truth, to power: the *politic*.

Le Caron and Pasquier knew each other. They were jurists who frequented the court and gained reputations as men of letters; this model of the writer-jurist was a prominent one in an age of literary-legal confluence.[90] Pasquier wrote poetry and four dialogues before the *Recherches*. Le Caron also wrote poetry, and his *Courtisan* dialogues were published with a number of others that present a kind of early modern vernacular canon: one on knowledge, featuring Rabelais as a discussant; another the Platonic-inspired *Claire, ou la beauté*, on aesthetics; and also *Ronsard, ou de la Poësie*, in which a character called 'Etienne Pasquier' appears representing oratory to the poet. The full titles of Le Caron's *Courtisan* dialogues are *The Courtier: That the Prince Must Philosophise, Or, On True Wisdom and Royal Philosophy*, and *The Courtier II: Or, On True Wisdom, and in Praise of Philosophy*.[91] The influence of Castiglione's *Book of the Courtier* (first printed in Italy in 1528) is clear.[92] Pasquier's *Pourparler du Prince* (1560) also features a character called Le Courtesan; both authors, technically courtiers themselves, seek to distinguish between good and bad *courtesans*, and seem to decide that a morally upstanding *courtesan* is actually a *politic* (we recall once again how the later Pasquier blamed 'courtizans' for the spread of partial words).

---

[89] Hankins writes that Humanist virtue politics was uniquely possible in the context of the Italian city states, *Virtue Politics*, p. 501. Part of the point of 'virtue politics' is that these rulers ruled thanks to their virtue, not because of hereditary position. Any transfer to the French context is, like all translations, imperfect.

[90] See *L'écriture des juristes. XVIe–XVIII e siècle*, ed. by Laurence Giavarini (Paris: Champion, 2010), and Stéphan Géonget, 'La parole vertueuse du juriste. Les exemples de Jean Papon, Louis Le Caron et Claude Le Brun de la Rochette', in *Valeur des lettres à la Renaissance. Débats et réflexions sur la vertu de la littérature*, ed. by Pascale Chiron and Lidia Radi (Paris: Champion, 2016), pp. 95–108. George Hoffmann also emphasises the important connection between literature and law in *Montaigne's Career* (Oxford: Clarendon, 1998), pp. 132–34.

[91] 'Le Courtisan, que le Prince doit philosopher, Ou, de la vraie sagesse et Royale philosophie'; 'Le Courtisan II, Ou de la vraie sagesse, Et des louanges de la Philosophie', in Louis Le Caron, *Dialogues*, ed. by Joan A. Buhlmann and Donald Gilman (Geneva: Droz, 1996), pp. 59–124 and 125–80.

[92] See Peter Burke, *The Fortunes of the Courtier: The European Reception of Castiglione's Corteggiano* (Cambridge: Polity, 1995). Neither Le Caron's text nor Pasquier's is, however, treated by Burke.

Le Caron's first *Courtisan* dialogue is between a character called Le Caron and another called Philarete (lover of virtue); in the second, the Le Caron character is in dialogue with Le Courtisan. The texts are also in implicit dialogue with their ancient sources, since much of the content is a translation or paraphrase of works of Classical moral philosophy. In both, the ultimate goal of the discussion is to establish how to maintain ordered rule ('ordre et police'), and peace ('repos'); the term *police* here then corresponds to a set of rules with the implication that these are in place for the purpose of balance and harmony. Order and harmony also depend on good behaviour by individuals: *police* is further figured as self-government, the prince needing to 'police' himself before all others, with philosophy as aid.[93] In the second dialogue, Le Caron and Le Courtesan discuss tyranny, and whether the prince is synonymous with the law. Le Caron solves the problem of all power resting in the hands of one individual by imagining a prince who has absorbed the crucial lessons of philosophy and is both more and less than a single person, anticipating Jean Bodin's portrayal of the monarch as a placeholder, the embodiment of abstract centralised power, in his theory of sovereignty.[94] The healing power of an enlightened prince depends, for Le Caron, on an acceptance of Plato's notion that an ideal state is born from symbiosis between a prince and a philosopher (mediated here by the Le Caron character).[95] The *police*, then, appears as something that emerges and is defended through managed symbiosis.

Le Caron uses the word *politique* infrequently. The main use as a noun occurs principally at the end of the first dialogue. Other notable instances are adjectival, attached to 'laws' (as in 'political laws') in a list of things that promote civic peace. 'Political laws' figure in Le Caron's account of how human society developed from the state of nature (the 'long sleep' of ignorance), when men began to act for the common good, and finally enclosed the city with walls, 'yielding to the political laws and constitutions of their Kings, Princes, and Magistrates, or whatever other name they had for those who governed them'.[96] Here, the names of those involved in

---

[93] 'Comment pourroit-il contenir une multitude, qui n'useroit de la police de soi-mesme?', Louis Le Caron, 'Le Courtisan', p. 72. This is the topos of the correlation between self-discipline and aptitude for government discussed in Plato's *Republic*.

[94] On the monarch as the embodiment of power in the pre-modern period, see Ernst Kantorowicz, *The King's Two Bodies: Studies in Medieval Political Theology*, 7th ed. (Princeton, NJ: Princeton University Press, 1997).

[95] Plato, *Republic*, 8, 471c–502c.

[96] 'se flechir aux lois politiques et constitutions de leurs Rois, Princes, Magistratz, ou si d'autre nom leurs gouverneurs estoient appellez'. Le Caron, 'Le Courtisan', p. 68.

government are uncertain, as if there may be other names and types. This anticipates the close of the dialogue: Le Caron concludes by describing a person, distinct from both philosopher and courtier, who will facilitate the symbiosis between 'The Prince' and 'The Philosopher' (gender is not emphasised, but masculine pronouns are used). This person is referred to as 'our politic'.[97] Le Caron presents the coming of the Politic person as a kind of evolutionary process that has already occurred. In a sense, the process came to fruition in antiquity; indeed, the passage in which 'our politic' appears is an almost exact reproduction of the section of Plutarch's *Moralia* that treats precepts of statecraft.[98] But the portrait of a *Politic* begins in the future tense: rather than changing laws suddenly, 'he *will* do better to adapt to popular custom at first, until he has gained the good opinion of the people: and when he sees that custom is in some way contrary to reason, he *will* then be able to suggest how, under the Prince's authority, it may be corrected' [my italics]: 'our Politic', then, could be a tacit innovator.[99]

The Le Caron character comments further on the adaptable qualities of the Politic; rewriting a passage in which Plutarch criticises 'court flatterers', Le Caron attacks *courtesans* who, like fowlers imitating the calls of birds, try to imitate the gestures of *seigneurs* to curry favour: Le Caron states that it is abject to always conform to the mistakes either of princes or of the multitude.[100] The use of key naming vocabulary like *courtesan* and *seigneur* updates the Greek for contemporary France: the 'other names' referenced early in the dialogue. The other change to the Plutarch in this section is the point that a courtier might conform to the views either of the Prince or of the people, where Plutarch only suggests conformity with the Prince, and control of the people.[101] Le Caron's Politic, then, exists more in a middle ground between royalty and populace. The critique of *courtesans* imitating birdsong also echoes contemporary debates on imitation that were central in Renaissance poetics: over what was the bad kind (uncreative, 'servile')

---

[97] It seems that in Le Caron, the –c ending differentiates the substantive from the adjective, denoted by a –que ending.

[98] Plutarch, *Moralia*, tr. by Harold North Fowler, 15 vols. (Cambridge, MA: Harvard University Press, 1936), x, pp. 167–73. On Plutarch, see Sophia Xenophontos, *Ethical Education in Plutarch: Moralising Agents and Contexts* (Berlin: De Gruyter, 2016), especially chapter 5, 'Politics as a Site of Moral Education', pp. 126–50.

[99] 'Il fera donc mieux s'accommoder dès le commencement aux mœurs du vulgaire, jusqu'à ce qu'il ait gaigné envers lui quelque bonne opinion de vertu: et lors s'il veoit la coustume estre en aucune chose contraire à la raison, il advisera comment par l'autorité du prince elle pourra estre corrigée.' Le Caron, 'Le Courtisan', p. 120.

[100] Plutarch, x, p. 167.   [101] Ibid., p. 167.

and the good (innovative, renewing).[102] Our Politic must be a discerning and timely imitator, knowing when to introduce alteration, and so engaging with politics poetically, in a manner of speaking; indeed, Le Caron (the author) is performing this task in his translation.[103]

Later in the same passage, more aesthetically inflected advice is given: just as 'one must touch the strings of [an] instrument not forcefully but with softness and measure, so the discourse of the one whom we are instructing must be full of honourable gentleness and naivety, not painted in the overly exquisite and overwrought colours of the Schools or Theatres'.[104] What seems particularly important in this piece of advice for the Politic, aside from the suggestion that he should be neither stereotypical Sorbonne sophist (such as had already been critiqued by Geoffroy Tory) nor overwrought actor, is the point that he must have expert command of language to avoid the many threats with which he is faced.[105] The Politic must also render himself so accomplished that he never shows himself to be blameworthy ('qu'il ne monstre rien en lui, qui puisse estre blâmé'), for after all, every word, action, and gesture of one elevated to such dignity of position will be observed by others.[106] It is striking here that the Politic must only *seem* blameless, because he is forever being watched: to be political is a performance, even if political language ought not to sound too theatrical.

Although Le Caron suggests that the best political actors behave equally well at home and in public, the implication remains that the surface matters, to an extent, more than the interior, for all the work Le Caron the author does to imbue his ideal political actor with profound philosophical virtue. This marks a contrast with other exemplary figures, most obviously in *Claire* (Claire meaning 'fair' and 'clear'), in which the eponymous speaker is 'Claire by name, nobility, and virtue'.[107] The Politic character of *Le Courtisan* is similarly expected to unite aesthetic and moral properties, for the effective management of the common good, but lacks

---

[102] Thomas M. Greene, *The Light in Troy: Imitation and Discovery in Renaissance Poetry* (New Haven, NJ: Yale University Press, 1982), pp. 189–96.

[103] This recalls Sophie Smith's emphasis on poetic 'making' or poesis in politics, discussed in Chapter 1.

[104] 'Mais comme (selon les Musiciens) il faut toucher les cordes de l'instrument non par force, ains par douceur et moien: ainsi l'oraison de celui, lequel nous instituons, doit estre pleine d'honorable gentilesse et naiveté, non fardée de couleurs trop exquises et recerchées des escholles ou Theatres.' Le Caron, 'Le Courtisan', p. 122.

[105] On Le Caron's concern with eloquence, see Géonget pp. 99–102.

[106] Ibid., pp. 120–21. This discussion of internal and external morality further reprises themes of Plato's *Republic*, especially chapter 6.

[107] Le Caron, 'Claire, ou de la beauté', in Le Caron, *Dialogues*, pp. 302–42 (p. 304).

the ethical transparency conferred on Claire by her name. This calls to mind later critiques of *politique* people saying one thing and secretly thinking or doing another, as well as Calvin on Nicodemites. Here, Le Caron presents the accommodating, altering, performative nature of political action as a strength, perhaps unintentionally showing that this strength could also become a drawback.

The tension between outward moral virtue and inner imperfection is not then exactly alluded to by Le Caron either as character or as author, so concerned is he with perfectibility; *Claire* is presented as the pinnacle and summary of the dialogues. But in fact, these final pages of the first *Courtisan* dialogue present a Politic negotiating a delicate path between all kinds of bad behaviours and threats to his position. Moreover, the closing phrases concerning how the Politic will hold social classes in their proper place by the exercise of virtue, rather than by violent force, cannot but convey proleptic irony given the chaos that would shortly engulf France, even if those later referred to as *politiques* did their best to find non-violent ways of ending that chaos. And if Le Caron's *politic* fixes the social order in place, his own position within it is unclear. The text had already asserted the elevated 'dignity' of the Politic, and the last words of Le Caron's final speech define *noblesse* (nobility) not as fortune or especially ancient lineage, but by the more flexible conditions of good birth (which seems marginally less exclusive than 'ancient lineage') and, most significantly, learned virtue.[108] The Politic, then, seems to earn part of his *noblesse* by his learning and good actions (whereas Claire simply *is* noble).[109] Though idealised as skilled negotiator, highly educated leader, and effectively the incarnation of civic virtue who will bring peace to the polity, he carries with him the tensions and socio-political shifts of the moment.

There is some suggestion that Pasquier wrote his *Pourparler du Prince* in response to Le Caron's *Courtisans*; we might then see the Politic character in the *Pourparler* as an extended vision of how 'our politic' might conduct himself.[110] The real-life context is also reinforced in the preface, in which the narrator might reasonably be loosely identified with the author, since he refers to the illness that forced the real Pasquier to take time away from the law in 1559. The *Pourparler* is a discussion between characters named

---

[108] Le Caron, 'Le Courtisan', p. 123.
[109] Again, this seems reminiscent of Hankins's concept of 'virtue politics' in which legitimacy may be earned through behaviour rather than by birthright, see above, n. 89.
[110] Béatrice Sayhi-Périgot, 'Commentaire des *Pourparlers*', in Etienne Pasquier, *Pourparlers*, ed. by Béatrice Sayhi-Périgot (Paris: Champion, 1995), pp. 270–533 (pp. 298–302).

L'Escolier [The Scholar], Le Philosophe [The Philosopher], Le Courtesan [The Courtier], and Le Politic. The first three make lengthy responses to an opening statement by the Politic reformulating Plato's philosopher-prince problem: 'You all believe', says the Politic, 'that a prince must be a philosopher, but you each establish different principles.'[111] The term *politique* (with spelling variants) appears rarely in the body of the text; its primary use is as the name of the character. This character hears, and then responds to, the propositions of the others. Each offers, in the Politic's view, an imperfect model of the philosopher-prince: he summarises the problems with their proposed models of education before they start ('if your speeches ['discours'] take place ['tiennent lieu'], you will make of your prince either a scholar, or a hermit, or perhaps a tyrant') and extensively criticises them after they have spoken.[112] The link between language and action is a confident one here: their 'discours' could strongly impact on reality (this is an ambiguous but generally more positive account of what 'discours' can achieve than is expressed in the section of Pasquier's *Recherches*, cited at the opening of this chapter).

The Escolier proposes a scholarly prince whose power and glory will come from extensive reading and mastery of eloquence; the Politic casts doubt on this, instead recommending a restricted reading list made up of Plato's *Republic*, Cicero's *De officiis*, and Horace's *Sententiae*, supplemented by as much good history as possible.[113] The Philosophe emphasises the vanity and vice of man, and advises that the King reject the world and learn not to fear death; the Politic tentatively approves of this suggestion but warns that a prince unafraid of death could behave recklessly, and says moreover that the prince is likely to be disheartened by such an education; this reads as a critique of Stoic indifference and of Plato's austere vision, for all that the *Republic* and later Neo-Platonisms represent crucial influences on this text.[114] The Courtesan is third to speak, advancing a theory of tyranny that has been described as 'Machiavellian'; the Politic gives this shortest shrift.[115] He concludes *Le pourparler* with a critique of tyranny, advocating the importance of the *Parlement* moderating between the king

---

[111] 'En effet, vous estes tous de cest avis, qu'il faut un prince philosophe: mais vous establissez divers fondements de ceste philosophie.' Pasquier, 'Pourparler du Prince', in *Pourparlers*, pp. 51–106 (p. 53).

[112] 'si vostre discours tiennent lieu, rendrez-vous vostre prince ou escolier, ou hermite, ou paravanture tyran'. Ibid., p. 53.

[113] Pasquier, 'Pourparler du Prince', pp. 56–57 (the Escolier's praise of eloquence) and 82–83 (the Politic's refutation of the Escolier).

[114] Ibid., pp. 61–66 (The Philosophe) and 88–89 (the Politic's refutation of the philosopher).

[115] Sayhi-Périgot, 'Commentaire', p. 282.

and the people, with due emphasis on the role of the *Magistrat*: in every well-policed Republic, the people are subject to Magistrates, and the Magistrates to the law.[116] This certainly seems an advancement of a model of constitutional monarchy, but the characterisation of the Politic as moderator both incorporates and goes beyond that particular political language.

The 1560 *Au lecteur*, not reproduced with subsequent editions, introduces the *Pourparler* as drawn from the common run of things ('tirez du commun cours de ce temps'), and opens with a description of Pasquier's process: he reflected at length ('Je pourpensay longuement'), and has constantly been rethinking his text ('toutefois repensen en moy').[117] Together, the terms 'pourparler', 'pourpenser', and 'repenser' suggest a certain kind of careful thinking and discussion.[118] *Pourparler* is hard to translate; Béatrice Sayhi-Périgot comments that it is unusual in sixteenth-century French, particularly as a substantive, and suggests that it refers to a general kind of discussion focused on the future.[119] In Pasquier's *Pourparler*, this kind of thought and discussion involves juxtaposition and eventual synthesis of varied positions and opinions. There are references throughout the text to the dialogic form: before the characters start talking, 'Pasquier', the narrator who introduces the discussion, says that he has been inspired by the differences of humour and judgement; he compares the meeting of minds that takes place in the dialogue to the violent encounter of stone and steel, bringing forth sparks that, finding the right target, then light a great fire.[120]

This fire, indeed, has been lit in the heart of 'Pasquier', who has appreciated these 'honest altercations'. The Courtesan agrees to participate in the debate precisely because of this tradition of productive altercation in

[116] Pasquier, 'Pourparler du Prince', pp. 70–80 (The Courtesan), and 90–100 (the Politic against tyranny).

[117] Etienne Pasquier, *Un Pourparler du Prince* (Paris, 1560), p. ii.

[118] Perhaps this is the kind of 'slow' thinking that Cave and others consider to be a literary-critical kind of inferential cognition. See Terence Cave, *Thinking with Literature: Towards a Cognitive Criticism* (Oxford: Oxford University Press, 2016), pp. 21–24.

[119] Béatrice Sayhi-Périgot, 'Introduction', in Pasquier, *Pourparlers*, pp. 9–50 (p. 18). One other instance of 'pourparler' is found in Henri Estienne's *Traité preparatif à l'apologie pour Heredote* (1566), in which two characters, Eudoxe and Brute, discuss false miracles, 'parlant pour mutuel pourparler', which seems to suggest that they are speaking for mutual adancement of thought. See Henri Estienne, *Traité preparatif à l'apologie pour Heredote*, ed. by Bénédicte Boudou, 2 vols. (Geneva: Droz, 2007), II, p. 1104.

[120] Pasquier refers to the 'diversité d'humeurs' which are 'assez divers de jugement': 'de laquelle diversité se tiroy je pourtant profit ainsi que, par le heurt & attouchement violent du caillou avec l'acier, on voit ordinairement sortir quelques estincelles, lesquelles receuillies en bonne amorse allument puis apres un grand feu'. 'Pourparler du Prince', p. 51.

which a plurality of voices is heard.[121] The Politic is then at the heart of a complex processing of terms and ideas, and – in this somewhat idealised account – manages to synthesise them to close the dialogue with the image of a successful, happy, and harmonious Republic. Small wonder, then, that the 'Pasquier' character at the beginning suggests that the Politic is the authoritative voice: without wishing to undermine the authority of 'wise courtiers', he suggests that they are more likely to favour the part of the Politic than of the Courtesan, who would seem to have a similar name to them ('qui semblera avoir quelque conformité de nom avec eux').[122] Here, 'Pasquier' effectively suggests that 'sages Courtizans' ('wise courtiers': we note here that, like later iterations of *politique*, a courtier can be qualified as the good, wise kind) have more in common with the Politic than those with whom they have 'conformité de nom'. In a way, Pasquier is suggesting that names can and should change, and is problematising the category of the courtier through this staged encounter with 'mon Politic'.

Although he did not make any reference to his own Politic in his discussion of partisan language in the *Recherches*, Pasquier did reflect again on his dialogue in the 1596 edition with the benefit of such hindsight as was available to him. What is striking is that in this edition of the *Pourparler*, the real Pasquier still held the same, or a similar view as in 1560, even if the term *politique* had in the intervening period undergone the series of mutations that made being at least one kind of *politique* potentially very undesirable. It seems as though, despite his awareness of the *politique* produced by the toxic seedbed of the 1580s–90s, Pasquier wanted to defend a positive meaning of the appellation; he also played a role in generating the post hoc history of the so-called *politique* party in the 1590s, as Warren Boutcher has shown.[123] The note to the opening of the *Pourparler* added in 1596 reads:

> It was thirty-two years ago that this *Pourparler* was printed for the first time, with the first book of the *Recherches*. After three characters [in the dialogue] had discussed three differing opinions of what care the sovereign Magistrate should have in the management of his Republic, ultimately the author came to share the view of the Politic, which is to say, that the Prince should serve the public good in all things and should not seek his own particular advantage, to the detriment of his subjects.[124]

---

[121] 'comme en vos brigues et congregations solonelles l'on a coustume de passer par la pluralité des voix, je te donne encores, avec le Politic, le mien'. 'Pourparler du Prince', p. 54.

[122] Ibid., p. 53.

[123] Boutcher refers to Pasquier's 'quasi-public role as a *politique* historian of France', *The School of Montaigne*, II, p. 80.

[124] 'Il y a trente-deux ans, qu'avecq le premier livre des Recerches, ce Pour-Parler fut imprimé la premiere fois, dans lequel après avoir sous trois personnages discouru trois diverses opinions sur le soing que le Magistrat souverain doit avoir au maniement de sa République, en fin l'autheur se

In the dialogues of Le Caron and Pasquier, a person or character who is called Politic emerges as an authoritative negotiator of the terms, roles, ideas, and attitudes that the adjectival *politique* can comprehend; the word appears as a synonym for managed plurality in these accounts of what political discussion could and should be between truth and power, or between the philosopher and the prince. The Politic incarnates intellectual virtues and also, crucially, exhibits particular power of thought and expression, made clear through Pasquier's conception of the productive *pourparler* and Le Caron's parallel between the Politic and the musician. We have also seen associated names – *Magistrat, Courtesan* – that will have varying importance in connection with *politique* in the following decades. In these texts, the meaning of *politique* is formed in dialogue, and the function of the person who may then be named as *politique* is to manage and facilitate the kind of dialogue that enables the creation and maintenance of the best kind of *police*: a literary-political skillset.

Pasquier's *Pourparler*, between 1560 and 1596, negotiates a delicate path between the abstract *police* and the real world that the author inhabited. The *Pourparler* and *Le Courtisan I* and *II* demonstrate porosity between fiction and reality, particularly given that Pasquier identifies with his narrator and his Politic character, and both authors appear as a character of one kind or another in their own dialogues. The boundaries between fiction and reality wear particularly thin when Pasquier intervenes thirty-six years after its initial publication to align himself with the Politic of his dialogue.[125] In the context of the civil war that broke out two years after the first appearance of the *Pourparler du prince*, the connection between the ideal (or fictional), and the real, and the impact of words and texts, became increasingly troubled, just as the difficulties of acting in politics were magnified.

The real figure who came to incarnate the difficulties of acting in politics was Michel de L'Hospital. As Emily Butterworth describes, he opened the 1560 meeting of the Estates General calling for an end to the language of factionalism, in terms similar to Pasquier's condemnation of 'offshoots of partiality'.[126] He attempted to mediate between competing factions and different confessional groups, but his efforts did not succeed: he resigned,

---

ferme en celle du Politic, qui est l'utilité publique à laquelle le Prince doit se rapporter toutes ses pensées & non se s'advantager en particulier, à la foule & oppression de ses subjects.' 'Pourparler du Prince', p. 51 n. 1.

[125] Pasquier, *Pourparler*, p. 53.   [126] Butterworth, *Poisoned Words*, p. 12.

or was discharged, from his office as Chancellor in 1567 and thereafter lived a secluded life until his death in 1573, although his work was still being printed.[127] At the end of the wars, L'Hospital was condemned in polemic as 'author and patron of the *politique* mistake' (although *erreur politique* here could simply be translated as 'the political mistake').[128] The nineteenth century would rehabilitate him as a liberal hero, and in 1960 he even appeared on a French postage stamp; L'Hospital's literary and historical afterlife is one of failed (or frustrated) strategy and then of posthumous vindication.[129] It is within this narrative that he appears in histories both of sixteenth-century politics and in histories of the term *politique*, in which he is frequently presented as the paradigmatic *politique* figure of the early part of the wars.[130]

In 1558, between the publications of *Le Courtisan i* and *ii*, and Pasquier's *Pourparler*, at the height of L'Hospital's success as a statesman, Joachim Du Bellay published his sonnet sequence, *Les regrets*. Sonnet 167 is in praise of L'Hospital, presenting him as a model for how to avoid vice, and who, as Du Bellay writes in the second verse, is so perfect as to practically elude all description. The verse ends, indeed, with a comparison to Plato.[131] In short, in this verse L'Hospital appears as an idealised statesman of the kind that Le Caron and Pasquier imagined. The three men were all connected to one another within a wider literary-political circle centred on the Morel salon in Paris (associated with the *Pléiade* poets; the circle facilitated the entry of poets such as Ronsard into courtly

[127] On Michel de L'Hospital, see Denis Crouzet, *La sagesse et le malheur: Michel de L'Hospital, chancelier de France* (Seyssel: Champ Vallon, 2002), and especially *De Michel de L'Hospital à l'Edit de Nantes*, ed. by Wanegffelen.

[128] *Description de l'homme politique de ce temps*, p. 4. See Daniel Ménager, 'L'image de Michel de L'Hospital de la Pléiade à la Ligue', in *De Michel de L'Hospital à l'édit de Nantes*, pp. 151–64.

[129] This is the account affectingly retold by Denis Crouzet in *La sagesse et le malheur*. L'Hospital's own view of government did not always involve the kind of pragmatic vision he was later associated with. Denis Crouzet and Marie Seong-Hak Kim write that L'Hospital was deeply wedded to Christian principles with a Ciceronian gloss (*caritas* as *amicitia*, according to Crouzet), and that he was a stubborn, inflexible political leader who became known for pragmatism despite himself. See Denis Crouzet, 'Grâce et liberté dans les *Carmina* de Michel de L'Hospital', and Marie Seong-Hak Kim, '"Nager entre deux eaux". L'idéalisme juridique et la politique religieuse de Michel de L'Hospital' in *De Michel de L'Hospital à L'Edit de Nantes*, pp. 223–42 and 243–54. On his nineteenth- and twentieth-century afterlives, see Jacqueline Lalouette, 'Vie et déclin du souvenir de Michel de l'Hospital en France (XIXe et XXe siècles)' in the same volume, pp. 175–220. There is an image of the stamp on p. 220.

[130] Pagden, 'Introduction', p. 2. Loris Petris writes that the idea of L'Hospital as 'father of the *politiques*' is an anachronistic myth, in *La plume et la tribune: Michel de L'Hospital et ses discours (1559–1562)* (Geneva: Droz, 2002), p. 275.

[131] Joachim Du Bellay, *Les regrets* (Paris: Gallimard, 1967), p. 198.

circles) in the decades preceding the civil wars.[132] The circle was also a meeting point of various 'languages'; not just Latin, French, and Greek, but also poetics, and streams of religious thought categorised variously as Erasmian and Ciceronian, which were clearly also influenced by Plato and Platonism.[133] Philip Ford described this group as being at the 'centre of the *politique* tendency'; I'd suggest that this group is at the centre of an early phase of one kind of political thinking, in which different discourses met with a common aim of maintaining royal power and advancing culture as they understood it, rather than being representative of a singular *politique* movement.[134]

Indeed, the diversity of uses of the term *politique* in and around this circle at the outbreak of the civil wars is exemplified by a reference to 'political justice' ('justice politique') in a letter written by the Lieutenant General of Guyenne to Catherine de' Medici in 1561 about the demands of rebels in the area.[135] Stuart Carroll reads this as a reference to Aristotelian conceptions of justice and suggests that this vocabulary was influenced by Etienne de la Boétie, who was assisting the Lieutenant General in his attempts to quell unrest in this area; La Boétie, translator of Plutarch and Xenephon, and author of poetry as well as of the *Discours de la servitude volontaire*, certainly had the kind of learning increasingly referred to as *politique*, and had connections with the *Pléiade* group and other members of the Morel circle.[136] La Boétie's varied sources of political thinking (practical experience, Plutarch, the Morel salon, Aristotle) and the influence he may have had on his colleague in Guyenne shows the practical and theoretical complexity of thinking about politics and *politiques* around the outbreak of war beyond the ideas of any strictly defined cohort or political language.

Within this complex picture, Michel de L'Hospital is a tricky figure to situate between endogenous and exogenous uses of the term *politique*. In his history of France, printed from 1581, La Popelinière writes that L'Hospital decided to 'take the straight path of the *homme politique*, not favouring anyone in particular but serving the King and the country, having to use incredible stratagems to keep each side in their place'.[137] Still, *politique* is not a keyword of L'Hospital's speeches of the 1560s; he

---

[132] Ford, *The Judgment of Palaemon*, esp. chapter seven: 'The Morel Salon: A Microcosm of the *Res Publica Litterarum*', pp. 205–25.

[133] Ford, p. 223.   [134] Ibid., p. 223.   [135] Carroll, 'Political Justice', p. 177.

[136] Ibid., p. 177.

[137] 'Mais s'estant proposé si tost qu'il eut esté estably en sa charge de cheminer droit en homme politique, et de ne favoriser ni aux uns ni aux autres, ains de servir au roy et à sa patrie, il luy falloit

uses the term relatively rarely. In one of these instances, in 1561, he advocates changing 'human and political [*politique*] laws', according to the nature of the people: stasis is impossible, owing to the inconstancy of man.[138] This echoes Le Caron's discussion of *politique* laws and is reminiscent of his representation of 'our *politic*' as accommodating, and Budé's sense of the need for flexibility; the association between *politique* and 'human' also evokes the kind of contrast between the human and divine spheres that Calvin and others grappled with. In 1567, in a valedictory address given to the Paris *Parlement*, *politique* appears again in adjectival form in an appraisal of French monarchs in the late Medieval period, and their relation with the *Parlement*: Medieval kings, he says, were more inclined to consult the *Parlement*, and so were 'more *politique* and popular than they are now that they hold [power] on a knife-edge' ('plus politiques et populaires qu'ilz ne sont maintenant qu'ilz tiennent du tranchant').[139] What L'Hospital does with *politique* here is mix a 'constitutionalist' use of *politique* with an implicitly irenicist stance, while implying that the former belongs to the past, but that the latter is nonetheless predicated on negotiation and on smooth dialogue between the *Parlement* and the king.[140] It would be an exaggeration to suggest that these uses from 1561 and 1567 are in any way representative of a stance that L'Hospital intended to be understood as *politique*, but it is clear that he associates *politique* with flexibility, and with debate and discussion.

The risks inherent to being a Politic are implicit in *Le Courtisan I* and II, and in *Le pourparler du prince* (what would happen should the sparks provoked by 'honest altercation' land somewhere dangerous?). Le Caron and Pasquier presented their *politic* characters as ideal negotiators – and as Sylvie Daubresse notes, seeking harmony through dialogue and negotiation was key to the idealised vision, held by L'Hospital and others, of what

---

user de merveilleux strategemes pour contenir uns et autres en leurs bornes.' Popelinière, *Histoire*, p. 331.

[138] 'Aussi les lois humaines et politiques ne peuvent tousjours demourer en ung estat mais les fault changer quelquefois selon que le peuple est.' Michel de L'Hospital, in *La plume et la tribune I*, p. 411. On this speech, see Oliver, p. 105.

[139] Michel de L'Hospital, *Discours et correspondance: La plume et la tribune II*, ed. by Loris Petris (Geneva: Droz, 2013), pp. 94–95.

[140] On attempts at peace-making during the religious wars, see Mark Greengrass, *Governing Passions: Peace and Reform in the French Kingdom, 1576–1585* (Oxford: Oxford University Press, 2007); Penny Roberts, *Peace and Authority during the French Religious Wars c. 1560–1600* (Basingstoke: Palgrave Macmillan, 2013), and Jérémie Foa, *Le tombeau de la paix. Une histoire des édits de pacification (1560–1572)* (Limoges: Pulim, 2015).

a *Parlement* was for.[141] In light of their connections with L'Hospital's circle, and his place in histories of *politiques* and politics, Le Caron's and Pasquier's dialogues bring L'Hospital's failures of discourse and dialogue into relief. It seems that the ideological impulses present in Pasquier's evocation of meetings of differing minds, and in Le Caron's faith in language (and in poetry) to help create a better *police*, had limited power. In a speech given at Moulins criticising the ambitions of rogue judges in 1566, published as a *Remonstrance*, L'Hospital opened referencing the dialogues of antiquity (by Plato and Cicero) and suggested that his own 'propos' gained authority if understood as the product of his implicit dialogue with the monarch, who was present in his audience at Moulins.[142] However, no amount of *discours*, *remonstrance*, or *dialogue* could resolve the conflict that would last another thirty years after L'Hospital's fall. Le Caron, Pasquier, and in a sense L'Hospital, offered models of politics and *politic[-que]s* in the 1550s and 1560s that in some ways seemed destined to fail, and yet can, with hindsight, be considered coordinates that mark the field from which the keyword *politique*, with its emphasis on the persona or particular person who practised politics with flexibility and linguistic dexterity, would emerge.[143]

La Noue and Montaigne: Surviving Fragments

An excavation of uses of *politique* between *c.* 1519 and *c.* 1562 shows it as a means of mediation, particularly between the monarch and the philosopher, but also between established law and princely judgement, and between the monarchy, the nobility, and the *Parlements*. Leading up to the outbreak of civil war, what it evoked above all was risky but potentially productive dialogue; the figure of a person who might conduct that dialogue, and facilitate the wider conversation between different interests and groups, was named by Le Caron and Pasquier as *Politic*, and tacitly by Budé as a 'mixed man'; Rabelais's conduit might be Frère Jean. Such characters are instrumental in the creation of better, even of perfected, political states. All these writings show preoccupation with class and status; the shadowy *politique* figure both works within the existing elite and is a kind of parvenu. In another context – 1530s England – Thomas More had criticised the duplicity of 'polytykes': an early instance of a meaning

---

[141] Daubresse, *Le Parlement de Paris*, pp. 164–65.
[142] L'Hospital, *Discours et correspondance*, pp. 80–81.   [143] Cave, *Pré-histoires* I, pp. 15–18.

of *politique* that became very common later in the century in French. These contexts provide a basis on which the principles (and mythology) of the semi-fictional *Politique* party were founded; that Pasquier was actively imagining what a *politic* might do *c*. 1560 informed his later role in shaping the history of the war period.

The final part of this chapter considers texts produced later in the wars (1570s–*c*. 1590). This period is the focus of the rest of this book; in the chapters that follow, we consider Bodin's *République*, Le Roy's translation of Aristotle's *Politics*, Monarchomach dialogues, polemical pamphlets, and more. Before moving onto these texts and contexts, I discuss two more writers who contribute to the *politique* seedbed: François de la Noue and Michel de Montaigne. After decades of civil war, what, if anything, remained in their writings of the kind of *politique* that was more able to balance alternatives, or for whom *politique* as a conceptual framework could present the possibility of peaceful, or even happy resolutions? How are surviving fragments of the pre-1562 *politique* mitigated by the new, more openly violent and dangerous context of war?

By 1589, and the publication of François de La Noue's *Discours politiques et militaires*, the term *politique* has reached a level of prominence such that it appears in the title of a contemporary work rather than simply as a reference to a work by Aristotle; like Frère Jean, the warrior monk, La Noue also links the political and the military, in the title of his book, and in his life. La Noue, also known as 'bras-de-fer' ('Iron Arm') for the prosthesis he wore, was a Protestant nobleman who distinguished himself in battle. By the late 1580s, he and most of his compatriots were, however, tired of war. In his work, *politique* appears in a discussion of how to maintain harmony between fundamentally different confessional groups who must share territory. In La Noue, the 'peace', 'harmony', and 'order' that good politics and *politiques* facilitate in earlier texts come to the fore, and he argues extensively for political peace ('concorde politique').[144] He is at pains to establish the difference (as well as the connection) between 'la souveraine concorde' (overall peace) and that maintained between men (i.e. 'concorde politique': political concord), and also to excuse himself from discussing the religious aspect further because he is an *homme politique*, not a theologian:

> There, one will find that sovereign concord is that which we must have with God, for he who does not worry about contradicting God will hardly be

---

[144] François de La Noue, *Discours politiques et militaires* (Geneva: Droz, 1967), e.g. p. 100.

able to get along with other men ... But since discourse on this point belongs more to theologians than to the *homme politique*, I will not discuss it further.[145]

This statement comes at the end of the *deuxieme discours*, or second chapter. The third, however, is all about how religious disagreement is no grounds for civil dispute, and is the chapter that concludes with the call for 'concorde politique', in which La Noue openly occupies theological territory. At forty pages in length, this third chapter amounts to much more than 'a word or two', despite what La Noue says:

> A theologian would have written a book on such a topic, but I content myself with having said only a word or two about it, as much to try and moderate somehow our harshness, which divides us too much, as to rekindle, too, our charity, so that at the very least, it may serve to reunite us in a good political [*politique*] peace.[146]

In some ways, the point about prioritising *politique* peace over religious unity is exactly what historians have associated with *politique* attitudes: a prioritisation of the political over the religious. But if political peace is represented as distinct from religious unity here, it is not entirely distinct from religion itself, since charity, or *caritas*, was a crucial Christian ideal. As a Protestant, it is clear what La Noue would stand to gain in personal and spiritual terms from such concord, but also as a Protestant, he does not fit the typical story of the term *politique* as a tool used by radical Catholics against moderates.[147] La Noue, effectively referring to himself as 'l'homme politique', and putting *politique* in the title of his treatise, as Justus Lipsius had (in Latin) three years earlier, was also drawing on a tradition of erudition that was increasingly being labelled as political, rather than making direct reference to the controversy around *politique* at the time of publication, lamented by Pasquier in the *Recherches*.

La Noue has, though, a more modest sense than earlier writers as to what 'a good peace' might be: 'some kind of' moderation of disagreements.

---

[145] 'Là trouvera-on que la souveraine concorde est celle que nous devons avoir avecques Dieu; car celuy qui ne se soucie de luy contrarier, mal-aisément se pourra-il bien accorder avec les hommes ... Mais pource que le discours de ce point appartient plustost aux théologiens qu'à l'homme politique, je m'en tairay', p. 61.

[146] 'Un theologien eust fait un livre sur ceste matiere, mais je me contente d'en avoir seulement dit un mot, tant pour essayer de moderer en quelque façon nos aigreurs, qui nous separent trop, que pour reschauffer aussi nostre charité, afin que cela nous serve au moins à nous reünir en une bonne concorde politique', p. 100.

[147] The peace did not come soon enough for La Noue, who died following a wound sustained at the siege of Lamballe in 1591.

That he seeks moderation 'somehow' ('en quelque façon': the means are also uncertain) could be read as a doubling of the idea of moderation, with 'façon' moderating the verb 'moderer'. Throughout, La Noue underplays the potential impact of his ideas, while emphasising that they will be of service and be useful (*servir* [to serve], and *utilité* [utility], are key words in his text). Much of the work is about the terrible present state of France and its risk of irreversible decline. Towards the end of the third chapter, building towards the call for 'political peace' quoted above, La Noue complains about the ease with which insults are thrown (as L'Hospital had twenty years previously). La Noue emphasises that the word 'heretic' in particular has been misused: he wishes to moderate, and thus minimise, such failures of language.[148] In other words, he seeks to make a modest intervention in public life by using language that might act directly to soothe the present grave problems that are in part problems of language.

The author of the preface is his co-religionist Philippe Canaye (the sieur du Fresne), another Protestant writer and jurist who served under both Henri III and Henri IV; in his preface to La Noue's *Discours* he writes that he has been thrown together with La Noue by the 'misery of the time' (both were in exile in Geneva), and that he discovered in his friend's papers a series of very useful observations on the present state of France and persuaded him to share them with the public. He further adds:

> The author did not amuse himself by forging some Idea of Utopian perfection, like some Philosophers ancient and modern; rather he learnt to accommodate himself so much to our taste and disposition, and offers his advice with such evident facility and usefulness, that if we do not benefit from it, either for public purposes or for our particular selves, we would have only our own hardened minds and lack of care to blame.[149]

This account of the *Discours* seems to enact a separation between philosophers in general, and writing categorised as *politique et militaire*, which has more to do with 'our taste and disposition'. La Noue, says Canaye, has been accommodating to the conditions of the time, just as Le Caron indicated that 'our politic' ought to be. Canaye's description tells the reader that what is to come does not imagine a better or alternate society as a kind of amusing exercise (perhaps this describes the author's view of

---

[148] La Noue, pp. 87–91.

[149] 'L'autheur ne s'est point amusé à forger une Idee de perfection Utopienne, comme quelques Philosophes anciens et modernes, mais il s'est estudié à s'accommoder tellement à nostre gout et disposition, et propose ses conseils avec une facilité et utilité si evidente, que si nous n'y profitons, soit pour le public, ou pour nostre particulier, nous n'en devons accuser que nostre endurcissement et nonchalance', pp. 1–3.

More's *Utopia*), but considers how to manage the systems that are already in place. His advice, potentially useful for both private and public purposes, is so self-evident that only lost souls and the lazy could fail to benefit. This confidence about the 'real' application of the text seems to be built on the fact that it makes no attempt to 'forge some Idea of Utopian Perfection'. This marks a move away from a Platonic or nascent utopian tradition of political writing alongside which the earlier uses of *politique* I have outlined sit more easily (Rabelais engages with this tradition, and Thélème has been read as a kind of utopia).[150] Canaye suggests, instead, that La Noue follows the example of Tacitus, thereby bringing a new author into the frame of the *politique* reading list either prescribed or implied in all of the texts that make significant use of the term.[151] In La Noue, *politique* may qualify 'concord', and is loosely born of a friendship with Canaye, who imagines a wider social function for the text, but the model is not one of vibrant dialogue or conversation.

His contemporary, Montaigne, manages a discussion that retains a more dialogic form, addressing writers ancient and modern throughout his work. His annotation to II.17 on the Bordeaux Copy, refers to La Noue as among the greatest of his time, for the 'constant goodness, the gentle conduct, and the conscious affability' that he has shown 'amid such injustice' (p. 610).[152] On Tacitus, Montaigne is again in sympathy with La Noue and Canaye, writing that 'his service is more suited to a disturbed and sick state, as ours is at present; you would often say that it is us he is describing and decrying' (p. 874).[153] As I mentioned at the opening of this chapter, Montaigne places Tacitus at the top of a *politique* reading list in III.8, calling his histories a seedbed of political and ethical reflections, 'for the provision and adornment of those who hold a place in the

---

[150] On the idea of utopia, see Cave, *Utopia in Early Modern Europe*, pp. 67–86. Cave calls Rabelais's fictions some of the most inventive imitations of More's *Utopia*, and describes Thélème as a 'Utopian chateau', p. 67.

[151] Some consider that a move from Ciceronian to Tacitean rhetoric as the model for political writing occurred across the sixteenth century. See Salmon, 'Cicero and Tacitus', who sees Pasquier and Montaigne as architects of this shift, and considers it a result of 'the triumph of *politique* thinking', pp. 330–31. This move is staged – perhaps even parodied – in the *Satyre ménippée*. See Chapter 6 of this book.

[152] 'La constante bonté, douceur de mœurs, et facilité consciencieuse de Monsieur de la Noue, en une telle injustice de parts armées', p. 701. La Noue's reputation as a soldier and man of letters may have earned him more esteem than Montaigne's *Essais* originally inspired in the first years after the appearance of the 1588 edition; Boutcher, *The School of Montaigne*, p. 20.

[153] 'Son service est plus propre à un estat trouble et malade, comme est le nostre present: vous diriez souvent qu'il nous peinct et qu'il nous pinse', p. 987.

management of the world'.[154] Like Canaye, Montaigne introduces some kinds of writing as a service, and as having the potential to not only describe the present (unhappy) world but also to have an impact on its management. Some of his first and closest readers in France and outside it viewed his *Essais* as offering precisely this kind of service: the clichéd but nonetheless partly persuasive memory of Montaigne as pragmatic sage is also part of the story of Montaigne *politique*.

Montaigne certainly champions moderation repeatedly in the *Essais*, not least in 1.30, 'Of Moderation', where he writes that extreme positions (in this case, philosophical extremes) make man 'incapable of any political administration' (p. 178).[155] But representations of Montaigne as belonging to a *Politique* group really only developed after the author's death. Like Michel de L'Hospital, Montaigne was retrospectively drawn into a canon of lawyerly *Politique* writers and public figures after his death and after the end of the wars by writers including De Thou and Pasquier who were seeking to 'fashion a pre-history and a moral philosophy for the fragile Henrician concord'.[156] The *Essais* were further drawn into the lexical and generic *politique* 'field' in translation, where they gained titles that evoke the good version of the *politique* seedbed, as well as La Noue's *Discours* and Montaigne's own description of Tacitus; in English, Florio calls them *The Essayes or, Morall, Politike, and Militarie Discourses*, and in Italian they are *Discorsi morali, politici et militari*. The presence of the word moral and *morali* in these titles also demonstrates continued proximity (and yet separation) of the moral and the political.[157]

The exact nature of Montaigne's politics remains, however, a matter of much discussion. The *Essais* are themselves a seedbed of political and ethical reflections; many critics associate him with some kind of *politique* position but differ as to their definitions of that position.[158] And although

[154] 'une pepiniere de discours ethiques et politiques, pour la provision et ornement de ceux qui tiennent rang au maniement du monde', Montaigne, p. 986 [Frame p. 872; Frame translates *pépinère* as 'nursery']. On this chapter of the *Essais*, see Quint, *The Quality of Mercy*, pp. 102–44.

[155] 'incapable de toute administration politique', p. 204.

[156] Boutcher, *The School of Montaigne*, p. 24. On the late sixteenth-/early seventeenth-century reception of Montaigne, see pp. 10–80.

[157] See *The Essayes or Morall, Politike and Militarie Discourses of Lo: Michaell de Montaigne, Done into English by J. Florio* (London, 1603), and Montaigne, *Discorsi morali, politici, et militari, tr. dal sig. G. Naselli* (Ferrara, 1590). These titles are testament to the fact that political writing was becoming increasingly prominent and that advertising Montaigne as a political expert would be a way to attract readers. On Naselli's translation see Boutcher, *The School of Montaigne*, II, pp. 134–40; and on Florio, pp. 189–271, esp. pp. 189–203.

[158] See, for instance, Fontana, pp. 8 and 82, and Philippe Desan, *Montaigne: A Life*, tr. by Steven Rendall and Lisa Neal (Newark, NJ: Princeton University Press, 2017) [this is a translation of

in recent decades Montaigne's activity in politics and diplomacy have received much critical attention, the *Essais* are also explicitly framed as a retreat from public life in 1.8 ('Of Idleness').[159] John O'Brien has discussed the extent to which 'retreat' is an important motif in the *Essais*; that the connections between Montaigne's life, his writing, and the world in which he lived and wrote, are hard to grasp, and are the object of ceaseless critical revision, perhaps demonstrates the success of the strategies mapped out by O'Brien.[160]

Montaigne is somewhat evasive even in the chapters of the *Essais* that most engage with contemporary politics – in which he refers more to 'party' than to *politiques*. In II.19, 'Of Freedom of Conscience', written in the aftermath of the Edict of Beaulieu (1576), which accorded Protestants the greatest toleration of any edict before the Edict of Nantes, Montaigne writes that 'the best and soundest side [*party*] is undoubtedly that which maintains both the old religion and the old government [*police*] of the country' (p. 615), but he then criticises those who show excessive zeal.[161] This is surely aimed at the less tolerant of the staunch Catholic factions, who were dismayed by compromises made at Beaulieu. Still, the chapter is relatively ambivalent about the freedom of conscience that some Catholics despised, rather than being a robust defence or celebration (one reason modern readers may, according to Biancamaria Fontana, find this chapter 'confusing, or even disappointing', even if she reads it as an ardent plea for toleration).[162] Montaigne's somewhat minimalist approach to toleration here evokes what Skinner described as the 'merely *politique* defence of

---

Montaigne. Une biographie politique, published in 2014], p. 184. Desan writes that Montaigne 'became a *politique* after having long thought that the initial religious disorders had been resolved with firmness'.

[159] On Montaigne's version of prudent political engagement, see also Ulrich Langer, *Vertu du discours, discours de la vertu: Littérature et philosophie morale au XVIᵉ siècle en France* (Geneva: Droz, 1999), pp. 161–79, and 'Montaigne's Political and Religious Context', in *The Cambridge Companion to Montaigne*, ed. by Ulrich Langer (Cambridge: Cambridge University Press, 2005). See also Richard Scholar, 'Reasons for Holding Back in Two Essays by Montaigne', in *The Emergence of Impartiality*, pp. 65–86, and *Montaigne and the Art of Free-Thinking* (Oxford: Peter Lang, 2017), pp. 115–16. Many writers have attempted to plot the intricacies of Montaigne's political stance, and his career; recent works beyond O'Brien and Langer include Géralde Nakam, *Montaigne et son temps. Les événements et les essais. L'histoire, la vie, le livre* (Paris: Gallimard, 1993); Hoffmann, *Montaigne's Career*; Fontana, *Montaigne's Politics*; Desan, *Montaigne: A Life*; and Boutcher, *The School of Montaigne in Europe Volume 1: The Patron-Author* (Oxford: Oxford University Press, 2017).

[160] John O'Brien, 'Retrait', in *Montaigne politique*, pp. 203–22.

[161] 'le meilleur et le plus sain party est sans doute celuy qui maintient et la religion et la police ancienne du pays', p. 706.

[162] Fontana, p. 82.

religious liberty'; in making this defence, however, Montaigne makes no mention of *politique*.[163]

In III.10, 'Of Husbanding One's Will', concerning his tenure as mayor of Bordeaux, he repeats his criticism of excessive zeal: 'I adhere firmly to the healthiest of parties, but I do not seek to be noted as especially hostile to the others and beyond the bounds of the general reason' (p. 942).[164] He leaves it to his readers to infer that 'the healthiest of parties' is a loose assemblage of moderate Catholic royalists; the lack of specificity leaves ambiguity and places emphasis more on the critique of zeal and on his willingness to praise qualities in his opponents other than their politics ('Should we not dare say of a thief that he has a fine leg?', p. 942).[165] Once again, there is no connection made between 'party' and *politique*. In the three examples thus far discussed where he does use the word *politique*, firstly it qualifies a kind of thought and of writing in III.8, then a 'field open to dispute' in II.17, and in I.30 a form of administration hampered by extreme positions. These uses (praising Tacitus, acknowledging Machiavelli, and critiquing excess) indirectly engage with the civil war setting, but they are also relatively generic adjectival uses that recall the semantic field around *politique* in pre-war philosophical writing. As this chapter draws to a close, I discuss two further instances of Montaigne's *politiques*, from I.31 and III.9. Rather than using the word in a way that engages with the immediate context of the 1570s–80s, these examples show Montaigne striking up a conversation with Plato that challenges political idealism.

In terms of *politiques* more ideal than real, Montaigne has an equivocal relation to those whom Canaye and other sixteenth-century readers would recognise as philosophers dealing in 'Ideas'. His treatment of Plato recalls in some ways the texts by Le Caron and Pasquier which speculate about the possibilities of how, and under whose influence, a better or even ideal community might be established and maintained.[166] In I.31 ('On Cannibals'), Montaigne writes that he wishes Plato could have seen the New World and how it exceeded the state that he imagined; one reading of

---

163 Skinner, *The Foundations of Modern Political Thought*, II, p. 244. The reference to 'mere' or 'minimal' toleration recalls Teresa Bejan's account of 'mere civility' in the Anglo-American context, Bejan, *Mere Civility*.

164 'Je me prens fermemant au plus sain des partis, mais je n'affecte pas qu'on me remarque specialement ennemy des autres, et outre la raison generalle', p. 1058.

165 'N'oserions nous dire d'un voleur qu'il a belle greve?', p. 1058.

166 See Richard Scholar, 'Montaigne et la "vanité" des utopies', *Revue de synthèse*, 137.3–4 (2016), 321–43, on Montaigne's engagement with utopia in the context of Plato.

'On Cannibals' is that a distorted vision of a real place (the New World) is offered as a foil to a completely imaginary republic in order that Montaigne can condemn from a distance practices in his own society.[167] The chapter explores historical and textual precedents for the Discoveries, and problematises the word 'barbare'/'barbarous': 'each man calls barbarism whatever is not his own practice' (p. 185).[168] This observation leads to the following, on government:

> For indeed it seems we have no other test of truth and reason than the example and patterns of the opinions and customs of the country we live in. *There* is always the perfect religion, the perfect government [*police*], the perfect and accomplished manner in all things. (p. 185)[169]

Thus Montaigne takes up the question that we have seen posed variously so far from Rabelais to Pasquier, of what might constitute 'the perfect religion' (especially if *religion* is understood as 'rule' as well as 'religious belief') and 'the perfect *police*', suggesting that perception of perfection is governed by habit, and by the workings of human reason that Montaigne has just demonstrated can often be faulty. This also potentially undermines Montaigne's statement in 11.19 that maintaining the established religion and government is *undoubtedly* 'the best and soundest side'.

It is at this point in 'On Cannibals' that Montaigne engages Plato in a conversation marked out by discourse verbs. Plato speaks first: 'All things, says Plato, are produced by nature, by fortune, or by art' (p. 185; recalling Pasquier's pairing of 'fortune' and 'discourse').[170] Plato's philosophical imagination, Montaigne then says, could not stretch to a vision of the world such as the early moderns experienced it. Initially he is saying this more or less to himself: 'il me prend' ['it strikes me'], 'il me desplait' ['it displeases me'], 'il me semble' ['it seems to me']).[171] But then Montaigne speaks back to Plato (speaking back to the philosopher, a kind of truth to a kind of power):

---

[167] On 'On Cannibals' as a critique of contemporary French mores, see, for example, Hoffmann, 'Anatomy of the Mass: Montaigne's Cannibals', *PMLA*, 117.2 (2002), 207–21, and John O'Brien, '"Le propre de l'homme": Reading Montaigne's Cannibals in Context', *Forum for Modern Language Studies*, 53.2 (2016), 220–34.

[168] 'chacun appelle barbarie, ce qui n'est pas de son usage', p. 211.

[169] 'Comme de vray nous n'avons autre mire de la verité, et de la raison, que l'exemple et idée des opinions et usances du pays où nous sommes. Là est tousjours la parfaicte religion, la parfaicte police, parfaicte et accomply usage de toutes choses', p. 211.

[170] 'Toutes choses, dit Platon, sont produites ou par la nature, ou par la fortune, ou par l'art', p. 212.

[171] pp. 212–13. These are my translations, since Frame does not reproduce the reflexivity.

> This is a nation, I should say to Plato, in which there is no sort of traffic, no
> knowledge of letters, no science of numbers, no name for a magistrate or for
> political superiority, no custom of servitude, no riches or poverty, no
> contracts, no successions, no partitions, no occupations but leisure ones,
> no care for any but common kinship, no clothes, no agriculture, no metal,
> no use of wine or wheat. The very words that signify lying, treachery,
> dissimulation, avarice, envy, belittling, pardon – unheard of. How far from
> this perfection would he find the republic that he imagined: *Men fresh
> sprung from the gods* [Seneca]. (p. 186)[172]

In the list of negatives that makes up the perfection of this 'nation', we are
told that there is 'no name for a magistrate or for political superiority
[*supériorité politique*]'. This appearance of *politique* attached to 'supériorité'
places it in a list of things not present in a seemingly better place.

Are we then to understand that *politique* is implicitly Greek and
explicitly corrupt, and that a happy *police* would not be governed by this
difficult term, as the New World apparently is not? But the dialogue with
Plato in 'On Cannibals' is counterbalanced by the reporting of actual life
in Brazil, where ancient and modern are contrasted and overlapping
(Montaigne suggests towards the end that the language of the New
World resembles Greek).[173] This mitigates the sense that knowledge of
the New World can be a corrective to the old, and the idea of perfection
fades, until the chapter concludes almost dismissively, bringing in another
unnamed voice that cannot look past superficial cultural differences: 'All
this is not too bad – but what's the use? They don't wear breeches'
(p. 193).[174] What, in the end, can be learnt from difference if such surface
matters are a stumbling block? Still, this final dismissal contains a lesson of
sorts, at the start of the sentence. The example set by the New World has
moved from 'perfection' to 'not too bad': the dialogues of 'On Cannibals'
offer a perfect *police* as an idea or a thought experiment, removed from real
experience which can only really be 'not too bad'.

Montaigne's address to Plato about the quasi-miraculous bareness of life
in the New World (swiftly undermined by the wealth of detail that

---

[172] 'C'est une nation, diroy je à Platon, en laquelle il n'y a aucune espece de trafique; nulle
cognoissance de lettres; nulle science de nombres; nul nom de magistrat, ny de superiorité
politique; nul usage de service, de richesse ou de pauvreté; nuls contrats; nulles successions; nuls
partages; nulles occupations qu'oysives; nul respect de parenté que commun; nuls vestemens; nulle
agriculture; nul metal; nul usage de vin ou de bled. Les paroles mesmes qui signifient le mensonge,
la trahison, la dissimulation, l'avarice, l'envie, la detraction, le pardon, inouies. Combien trouveroit
il la republique qu'il a imaginée, esloignée de cette perfection: *viri a diis recentes*', pp. 212–23.

[173] Ibid., p. 220.

[174] 'Tout cela ne va pas trop mal: mais quoy? Ils ne portent point de haut de chausses', ibid., p. 221;
Frame p. 193.

follows), echoes the list of negatives in Chapter Fifty-Seven of *Gargantua*: in Thélème there are also no 'laws, statutes, or rules' (this is similarly swiftly undermined by a wealth of material detail and a description of strictly policed behavioural codes in the abbey, as in Thomas More's *Utopia* itself: problematisation of the desirability of utopia, and the lack of freedom there, is integral to the tradition from its earliest phases). Montaigne's list of negatives also echoes another earlier text: Calvin's chapter 'On Christian Liberty'.[175] In the *Institutes*, Calvin criticises the Anabaptists and anyone else who might be precipitous in their attempts to overthrow the state: no one inspired by the gospel should claim their Christian liberty to the extent of recognising no earthly master.[176] This would only work, says Calvin, in a kind of negative paradise: those who recognise no master but Christ 'think that things can only go well if the whole world is converted to a new form, in which there are no judgements, laws, or Magistrates'.[177] Calvin's blend of beatific transcendence via both faith and pessimism about the world and its salvation is not discernibly attractive to Montaigne. Still, what the two have in common is that neither is convinced by the possibility of an earthly paradise, or the realisation of the ultimate negative situation, the 'no-place' of u-topia. Politics, laws, and magistrates inhabit the alternative semantic field of the real, the often less-than-desirable, the sometimes 'not too bad'.[178]

In Montaigne, the term *politique* might best be read as a problem or 'trouble' that he is annexing in discursive space. It is more problem than solution, in contrast to what Budé, Le Caron, and Pasquier (at least in 1562), and, in his own way, La Noue all imply in their uses of the term.

---

[175] Montaigne does not directly engage with Calvin in the *Essais*; not a shocking omission for a Catholic writer in the civil war context, although he was not shy about praising more conciliatory Protestant authors like La Noue. Montaigne also drew heavily on the Calvinist Jean de Léry's travel narrative for the exaggerated negations in the account of what the Tupinamba did not have; cannibalism in the chapter has been read as a metaphorical exploration of the Reformation drama of transubstantiation, so the confessional context is certainly multilayered. Andrea Frisch, *The Invention of the Eyewitness: Witness and Testimony in Early Modern France* (Chapel Hill, NC: University of North Carolina Press, 2004), pp. 18 and 157; Hoffmann 'Anatomy of the Mass'; O Brien, 'Reading Montaigne's Cannibals'.

[176] Calvin, *Institution*, pp. 1581–82. The editor, Millet, suggests the critique of the Anabaptists, whom Calvin does not directly name, p. 1581 n. 2.

[177] 'ilz ne pensent pas que la chose puisse bien aller, si tout le monde n'est converty en une nouvelle forme en laquelle il n'y ayt ne jugemens, ne Loix, ne Magistratz'. Calvin, *Institution*, p. 1581.

[178] This attitude seems present in Montaigne's comments in II.19 on the policy of toleration pursued by the monarchy: 'having been unable to do what they would, they have pretended to will what they could', p. 619 ('n'ayans peu ce qu'ils vouloient, ils ont fait semblant de vouloir ce qu'ils pouvoient', p. 710). Here, again at the close of a chapter, Montaigne emphasises the incompatibility of the possible and the desirable.

Montaigne occupies a middle ground between Pasquier's *Pourparler* and his *Recherches*. In the *Essais*, political alternatives, counter-narratives, and productive conversations survive, but *politique* carries with it shades of discord and dissatisfaction. Certainly, in 1.30 and 1.31, which offer visions of politics and contain uses of *politique*, politics is both vulnerable to error and to the passions (1.30) and seems in itself somewhat undesirable (1.31).

In another later chapter, 'On Vanity' (III.9), addressing his own reluctant participation in public service, Montaigne returns to Plato, in a manner that both reprises and adjusts his negative framing of politics. Montaigne refers to Plato as the 'master workman in all political government', who nevertheless abstained from practising it:

> Political philosophy may condemn, for all I care, the meanness and sterility of my occupation, if I can once acquire a taste for it, as he [Montaigne's father] did. I am of the opinion that the most honourable occupation is to serve the public and be useful to many. *The fruits of genius, virtue, and all excellence are most rewarding when they benefit some neighbour* [Cicero]. For my part, I stay out of it; partly out of conscience (for in the same way I see the weight attached to such employments, I see also what little qualification I have for them; and Plato, a master workman in all political government, nevertheless abstained from it); partly out of laziness [*poltronerie*: can also mean cowardice]. (p. 883)[179]

The reader should note the humour in Montaigne's claim that political work and Ciceronian neighbourliness are the greater parts of excellence, but that he himself demurs from engaging out of conscience (and laziness). Still, by implication Montaigne is portraying himself as a kind of minor 'workman in political government', who, like Plato, has removed himself from pursuing such work ('telles vacations') out of modesty and cowardice (this lack of heroism contrasts with Budé's account of how Alexander was advised to diligently apply himself ['vaquer'] to moral and political philosophy). The term *politique* is associated with public service in this passage, but the work of writing about it is dislocated from actually *doing* it, unlike in the passage praising Tacitus in III.8. And yet Montaigne was, in the real world, 'doing politics', mostly without an official political position (except

---

[179] 'La philosophie politique aura bel accuser la bassesse et sterilité de mon occupation, si j'en puis une fois prendre le goust, comme luy. Je suis de cet avis, que la plus honnorable vacation est de servir au publiq et estre utile à beaucoup. *Fructus enim ingenii et virtutis omnisque praestantiae tum maximus accipitur, cum in proximum quemque confertur.* Pour mon regard je m'en despars: partie par conscience (car par où je vois le poix qui touche telles vacations, je vois aussi le peu de moyen que j'ay d'y fournir; et Platon, maistre ouvrier en tout gouvernement politique, ne laissa de s'en abstenir), partie par poltronerie', pp. 996–97.

when he was mayor of Bordeaux), and as this passage clearly states, Plato was both a 'master workman of politics' and *not* a political actor. The possibility remains here then that writing and theorising about politics is a way of performing the service that Montaigne claims to be avoiding out of weakness and humility.

In Montaigne, boundaries and potential points of overlap between real and ideal practice – between the written and the lived – are thus tested and twisted in some of the few passages where the adjective *politique* appears. Much has been made of the *Essais* as a kind of extended dialogue between various selves, between texts, authors, ideas, and so on.[180] In this sense they thus represent a survival of the principles of discussion and of a convivial humanist ideal of conversation, enabled by his so-called retirement from certain kinds of politics even as he continued his political career in the 1580s in various roles from mayor of Bordeaux to general go-between between warring princes.[181] Montaigne and his *Essais* are implicated in, and yet distinct from, the uses of *politique* that made it so 'key' in writing during the Wars of Religion. Perhaps Montaigne's 'retreat' from politics was not so much that as a strategic retreat from *politiques*. In this spirit, Montaigne is not a central figure in any chapter of this book on politics and *politiques*, but his work is a crucial context, and in a way incarnates the field (or the seedbed) in which the main primary texts are situated. The texts I have analysed in this chapter are, in different ways, all 'seedbeds' from which versions of politics and *politiques* may have sprung by means of chance or of intention.

---

[180] See Terence Cave, *How to Read Montaigne* (London: Granta, 2007), pp. 96–105.

[181] Montaigne's supposed retirement, his reluctance, and his abstentions could be in tacit dialogue with Rabelais's discussion of different kinds of 'retraictz' in *Gargantua*; whether 'retrait' means 'privy' for Montaigne at any point would be interesting to consider.

PART II

c. *1568–78*

CHAPTER 3

Wise Politiques? *Jean Bodin and Loys Le Roy*

Interest in who exactly embodies good political action is a feature of the whole canon of Western political philosophy; in its earliest iterations we find Aristotle's figure of the statesman (*politikos*), or Plato's dialogue of the same name. The possibilities open to such a person were powerfully reworked in early modern France. We saw in the previous chapter that some writers were imagining the important role of a person named *politic* as France descended into civil war. In the preface to his translation of Aristotle's *Politics*, written a few years after Pasquier's *Pourparlers*, Louis Le Roy rewrites the commonplace 'man is a political animal' (*Politics*, 1253a2), concluding that despite man's natural disposition to live in groups, his negative qualities (his passions) frequently threaten to destroy community. Enter the special person with the capacity to manage this threat:

> It has been necessary to impose some laws so as to tame such afflictions, and to return [society] to the straight path of justice. Certain excellent persons [or characters, 'personnages'] who grasp political ability have attempted such remedies.[1]

Le Roy names these persons 'legislators' rather than *politiques* (in the title of the preface, it is legislators who practise politics). But what this passage demonstrates is his view that certain people – *excellent* people – who have true political ability are crucial for stable communities. In this chapter I turn to two canonical texts of political thought that argue for the central importance of politics as a discipline, and theorise the role of the political person extensively: Bodin's *Six livres de la République* (1576) and Loys Le Roy's translation and commentary on *Les Politiques d'Aristote* (1568; reprinted 1576).

---

[1] 'Il a esté necessaire proposer quelque commandemens, à fin de domter telles affections, & les remettre en droicte voye de justice. Aquoy aucuns excellens personnages entendans la faculté politique, se sont efforcez remedier', *Les Politiques d'Aristote, tr. en fr., avec expositions, par L. le Roy* (Paris: Vascovan, 1576), p. aiiij^v. All further references to Le Roy's translation and commentary will be to this edition. I am using the 1576 edition in order to look at the text as it was printed in the year of the publication of Bodin's *République*.

Despite differences of form, these texts have much in common. Both synthesise and compare ideas and anecdotes to offer various kinds of *politiques* to their reader, as a form of textual diplomacy in troubled times. Both respond at length to the classical canon of political thought, not least to Aristotle; both aim to update the discipline of politics for their war-torn age from a more-or-less Catholic position.[2] The need for communal harmony – and for skilled *politiques* – was especially urgent during the period in which these texts were written and printed. Le Roy wrote the preface cited above, first published as a pamphlet in 1567, during the second phase of fighting in the civil wars, after the uneasy peace that had held between 1563 and 1567. In the late 1560s and early 1570s, a period marked by the fall of Michel de L'Hospital, the consolidation of rival Protestant and Catholic factions, and the brutal massacres of Saint Bartholomew's Day in August 1572, the Wars of Religion became more deeply entrenched and uses of *politique* more ambiguous, conflicted, and urgent.

Bodin (1529/30–96) and Le Roy (1510–77) exploit the power and flexibility of politics to construct their own versions of it, and to explore the powers of the political practitioner. Although both were responding to the crisis of the civil wars and massacres, and in Bodin's case in particular to Huguenot resistance theory (which I discuss further in the next chapter), their work emerged from a broader context. They inherited the intellectual mantle of Budé, and were similar in profile to Louis Le Caron and Etienne Pasquier in that they were legally trained, historically minded, and held various public offices. They had strong ideas about how *politiques* ought to behave, and a more enigmatic sense of how *politique* they were themselves. John O'Brien writes that 'a number of authors in the late Renaissance [were] faced with the troubling difficulty of attempting to assert a proper sphere of action for the prudent man and his special cognitive powers'.[3] In the work of Bodin and Le Roy the term *politique* names both a version of this 'prudent man' and his 'special powers'. In Le Roy's commentary, and in Bodin's *République*, among the roles and personas identified as useful or deleterious for statecraft, the *politique*

---

[2] Their uses support Demonet's view that uses of *politique* in this period arise at the intersection of the reception of classical texts with current events. Demonet, 'Quelques avatars du mot "politique"', p. 33.

[3] John O'Brien, 'Aristotle's Prudence, and Pyrrho's', in *Au-delà de la Poétique: Aristote et la littérature de la Renaissance/Beyond the Poetics: Aristotle and Early Modern Literature*, ed. by Ullrich Langer (Geneva: Droz, 2002), pp. 35–45 (p. 36).

emerges as a powerful, even visionary, figure, invested with all the various kinds of understanding that meet in *la politique*.

The narrative of special (or terrible) men emerging from a fertile (or corrupting) landscape of texts and ideas is common in historical writing.[4] In their real careers, both Bodin and Le Roy had mixed success as 'special men' emerging from what Jehasse called the golden generation of French humanists, trying to rise to the challenges of their age; in their writings they hint at this process of emergence, with touches of long-suffering patience, aspiration, and bombast in their portrayal of the *politiques* who might steer the nation to a better course.[5] This was a process of self-conscious construction involving no small amount of self-fashioning, where the roles of *politiques* (written and lived) are problematised and reformulated, to the exclusion of other things that *politique* could have meant, and of other people who by definition could not then qualify as *politique*.[6] The aptitude of certain kinds of men, born of a particular intellectual landscape, for prudent political action, is not accidental or inevitable, but – much like meaning itself – at least partly engineered in writing, and a kind of politics in itself.

The *République* and the *Politiques d'Aristote*

Le Roy and Bodin (especially Bodin) are often evoked (and often together) in discussions of sixteenth-century political thought, and often referred to as *politiques*.[7] They were also read together; Gabriel Harvey wrote in the 1580s that you could not step into a Cambridge student's study without finding its occupant reading either Bodin's *De republica* (his self-translation of the *République* into Latin) or Le Roy's translation of Aristotle (in fact, Harvey wrote that people were reading Le Roy's 'expositions' of Aristotle, placing Le Roy in a kind of 'first author' position).[8]

---

[4] Richard Tuck's book on philosophy and government in the early modern period portrays Grotius, Selden, and Hobbes (all born in the 1580s) as the products (and fulfilment) of a European intellectual tradition that includes in its margins the works I discuss in this chapter. See Tuck, *Philosophy and Government*.

[5] Jehasse: 'grande génération humaniste'. See Jean Jehasse, 'Loys Le Roy, maître et émule de Jean Bodin', in *Etudes sur Etienne Dolet: Le théâtre au XVIe siècle: Le Forez, Le Lyonnais et L'histoire du livre, publiées à la mémoire de Claude Longeon*, ed. by Gabriel-André Pérouse (Geneva: Droz, 1993), pp. 251–64 (p. 251).

[6] Stephen Greenblatt, *Renaissance Self-Fashioning from More to Shakespeare* (Chicago, IL: University of Chicago Press, 1980).

[7] Marie-Luce Demonet also refers to Bodin and Le Roy, alongside Pasquier, as the '"vrais" politiques' ('"real" *politiques*') of the period, in 'Le politique "nécessaire" de Montaigne', p. 35.

[8] Quoted in Howell A. Lloyd, 'Introduction', in *The Reception of Bodin*, ed. by Howell A. Lloyd (Leiden and Boston, MA: Brill, 2013), pp. 1–20 (p. 2).

Their works played a part in the rising status of the keyword *politique* in erudite discourse, evident in the proliferation of political works in the years surrounding the publication of Bodin's treatise and Le Roy's translation: Guillaume de la Perrière's *Miroir politique* (written well before the author's death in 1565 but printed in 1567); François de la Rosière's *Six livres de la politique* (a much briefer treatise than Bodin's *République* published together with a reprint of Le Roy's pamphlet on the political arts in 1574); and François Grimaudet's *Opuscules politiques* (1580).[9] Later on, La Noue's *Discours politiques et militaries* (1587) and especially Justus Lipsius's *Politicorum sive Civilis doctrinae libri sex* (1589) confirmed the inauguration of politics – now explicitly named as such – as a central intellectual pursuit in early modern Europe. The emphasis on *politique* in these texts (and in some cases on its Latin equivalent) was part of wider changes in education and thought, influenced by developments in legal studies and the rise of history.[10] Ian Maclean has identified a 'new genre of political writing' in sixteenth-century Europe, facilitated by the increasing profitability and widespread dissemination of printed scholarly books.[11] Maclean notes that this new genre arose, in part, from the commentary tradition; by considering both Bodin's original and methodologically novel treatise and Le Roy's extensive commentary, this chapter thus treats two key interrelated forms of high-cultural political writing in the period.[12]

Both authors discussed here are well known, Bodin more so, but the details of their biography are worth noting to give a sense of their intellectual and social contexts. Loys Le Roy, disciple of Guillaume Budé and inheritor of Denis Lambin's chair in Greek at the *Collège royal*,

---

[9] See *Unmasking the Realities of Power*, ed. by De Bom, and Howell A. Lloyd, *Jean Bodin, 'This Preeminent Man of France': An Intellectual Biography* (Oxford: Oxford University Press, 2017), pp. 116–17.

[10] Werner L. Gundersheimer, *The Life and Works of Louis Le Roy* (Geneva: Droz, 1966), p. 47. See also Grafton and Jardine, *From Humanism to the Humanities*. On history, see Huppert, and Anthony Grafton, *What Was History?* (Cambridge: Cambridge University Press, 2007, repr. 2012). On law, see Ian Maclean, *Interpretation and Meaning in the Renaissance: The Case of Law* (Cambridge: Cambridge University Press, 1992). On the connections between developments in legal and historical approaches, see Julian H. Franklin, *Jean Bodin and the Sixteenth-Century Revolution in the Methodology of Law and History* (New York, NY and London: Columbia University Press, 1963), and Kelley, *The Beginnings of Ideology*, and *The Foundations of Modern Historical Scholarship: Language, Law, and History in the French Renaissance* (New York, NY and London: Columbia University Press, 1970).

[11] Ian Maclean, *Scholarship, Commerce, Religion*, p. 70. See also Annabel Brett, *Changes of State: Nature and the Limits of the City in Early Modern Natural Law* (Princeton, NJ and Oxford: Princeton University Press, 2011), p. 10.

[12] See also Charles Schmitt, 'The Rise of the Philosophical Textbook', in *The Cambridge History of Renaissance Philosophy*, ed. by Charles Schmitt, Quentin Skinner, Eckhard Kessler, and Jill Kraye (Cambridge: Cambridge University Press, 1988), pp. 792–805.

published his major original work, *De la vicissitude ou de la variété des choses en l'univers* ('On Vicissitude, or the Variety of All Things in the Universe') in 1575, two years before his death.[13] Le Roy was Budé's pupil and protégé – his first published work, the *Vita Budaei*, was Budé's funeral oration. He rose to prominence from relatively low beginnings, having studied theology in Paris, and law in Toulouse.[14] He was secretary to the Bishop of Rieux, and was sent on various diplomatic missions, before being given an office in the Paris *Parlement* in 1559. In the 1550s he devoted his attentions to the project of translating a series of ancient Greek texts, such as Plato's *Symposium* (1558), and in the 1560s, alongside translations of Xenophon, and Aristotle's *Politics*, he wrote a number of political pamphlets. One of these was the praise of politics: *De l'origine, antiquité, progres, excellence, & utilité de l'art politique* ('On the Origin, Antiquity, Progress, Excellence, and Use of the Art of Politics', 1567). This text was republished numerous times, and used as the preface, with a new title, to his translation of Aristotle's *Politics* in the 1568 and 1576 editions. The new title for the pamphlet-preface reads:

> On Politics ['De la Politique'], on the most renowned legislators who practised it, and on illustrious authors who wrote about it, especially Plato and Aristotle, with a summary and comparison ('conference') of their *Politics*, translated from Greek into French by Loys Le Roy (p. aiij).[15]

This summarises Le Roy's concerns in the translation and paratexts: to define politics and describe those who practise it, to give an updated account of political theory in the French language, and to offer a synthesised reading of ancient authorities on the subject. The practical means of the 'conference' (meeting) between ancient and modern is the translation from ancient Greek into the vernacular, updating two millennia of political thought for 'our time and homeland' ('nostre aage et patrie') (p. 2).

---

[13] On Le Roy, see *Loys Le Roy: Renaissance & vicissitude du monde*, ed. by Daniel Duport (Caen: Presses universitaires de Caen, 2011). Le Roy has been the object of three single-authored monographs in the last 150 years: Abraham Becker, *Un humaniste au XVIe siècle: Loys le Roy (Ludovicus regius) de Coutances* (Paris: Lecène, Oudin et Ci, 1896), Gundersheimer, *The Life and Works of Louis Le Roy*, and Enzo Sciacca, *Umanesimo e scienza politica nella Francia del XVI secolo: Loys Le Roy* (Florence: Olschki, 2007). On Le Roy and Budé, see Katherine Macdonald, *Biography in Early Modern France: Forms and Functions* (London: Legenda, 2007), pp. 27–44.

[14] Gundersheimer, p. 10.

[15] 'De la Politique et des legislateurs plus renommez qui l'ont pratiquee, et des autheurs illustres qui en ont escrit, specialemet de Platon & Aristote, avec le sommaire & conference de leurs Politiques, traduittes de Grec en François par Loys le Roy'.

Jean Bodin also came from relatively humble stock, although his family was 'comfortable' and not without 'means and connections'.[16] He received his early education from Carmelite monks in Angers, before moving to the Sorbonne under the protection of the Bishop of Angers in 1540. Like Le Roy, he studied and practised law in Toulouse, before returning to Paris in 1560 and embarking upon a career in the *Parlement*. In the 1570s he was attached to the household of the Duc d'Anjou (the king's youngest brother – in this context he was associated with the group known as 'malcontents', and with what became known as a *politique* conspiracy), and he represented the third estate at the *Estats de Blois* in 1576.[17] Bodin was a controversial figure throughout his career, and likely a heterodox thinker, whose interests spanned an enormous range of topics.[18] His written output consisted of a number of lengthy treatises, mostly in Latin; his first published work was an oration on the importance of humanist education, *Oratio de instituenda in republica juventute ad senatum populumque Tolosatem* (*Address to the Senate and People of Toulouse on the Education of Youth in the Commonwealth*, 1559), followed by his famous method of history, the bestselling *Methodus ad facilem historiarum cognitionem* (1566).[19] He is also remembered for his intervention in economic theory, for instance his *Response to Malestroit* of 1568 about price inflation. In 1578 he published a textbook of legal methodology, *Juris universi distributio*. His two vernacular works are a treatise on sorcery (*De la démonomanie des sorciers*, 'On the Demon-Mania of Witches', 1580), and the *République*.

The *Six livres de la République* are an enormous work that somewhat defy generic categorisation, since they encompass economic and constitutional theory, critiques of ancient and modern philosophy, historical reflections, and biblical commentary. The originality and influence of Bodin's theories of citizenship and sovereignty are well documented, though the question of his overall contribution to political thought is not closed; Howell A. Lloyd has pointed out that Bodin also rejected

---

[16] On Bodin's beginnings and the difficulty of identifying him in the historical record, see Lloyd, *'This Pre-eminent Man of France'*, pp. 2–5 and 14.

[17] The Duke of Anjou's circle have been described variously as *malcontents* and *politiques*. See Holt, *The Duke of Anjou and the Politique Struggle*. The origin of association between this group and the term *politique* is in Simon Goulart's *Mémoires*, discussed in the following chapter.

[18] Lloyd writes that Bodin's faith is ultimately mysterious despite his evident preoccupation with religion and his belief that he was a prophet of sorts. Lloyd, *'This Pre-eminent Man of France'*, pp. 259–61.

[19] Lloyd thinks a print run of 1,000 books is not unlikely, Lloyd, *'This Pre-eminent Man of France'*, p. 91. Lloyd's biography also analyses minor Latin works that are little known today.

mixed constitutions and emphasised the role of the magistrate, and Sara Miglietti has argued that a holistic reading of the *République* shows that it also offers a new, non-juridical understanding of territory as a 'political technology'.[20] It is clear that Bodin, like Le Roy, intended to offer an updated, and urgently needed, vision of what politics could do. In the preface to the *République*, he writes that his purpose is to 'enlighten' or 'clarify' ('esclaircir') a field (*la science politique*) currently steeped in ignorance, and that he is writing in the vernacular because the civil wars have pushed France to a state of barbarism that the Latin tongue could not articulate.[21] The famous theory of sovereignty is articulated in 1, 8. The lengthy text around this chapter is a blueprint for the good exercise of sovereign power. Each of the six books has a different focus. Briefly: Book I establishes theoretical principles; Book II looks at the different kinds of rule (popular, aristocratic, monarchy, tyranny); Book III the role of officials (especially magistrates) and institutions; Book IV the rise and fall of various kinds of Republics; Book V examines laws and penalties; and Book VI discusses censorship, state finances, monarchy as the best form of government, and the underlying divine harmony that, according to Bodin, governs the universe.[22] The work is dense, repetitive, and long, and it is therefore tempting to focus on isolated chapters that concern a particular

---

[20] Lloyd, *'This Pre-eminent Man of France'*, p. 137; Sara Miglietti, 'Sovereignty, Territory, and Population in Jean Bodin's *République*', *French Studies*, 72.1 (2018), 17–34. There is much scholarship devoted to Bodin's political theory. See in particular Simone Goyard-Fabre, *Jean Bodin et le droit de la République* (Paris: Presses universitaire de France, 1990); *Politique, droit et théologie chez Bodin, Grotius et Hobbes*, ed. by Luc Foisneau (Paris: Kimé, 1997); *Bodin a 400 anni dalla morte: Bilancio storiografico e prospettive di ricerca*, ed. by A. E. Baldini, *Il Pensiero politico*, 30.2 (Florence: Olschki, 1997); Jean-Fabien Spitz, *Bodin et la souveraineté* (Paris: Presses universitaire de France, 1998); and Cesare Vasoli, *Armonia e giustizia: Studi sulle idee filosofiche di Jean Bodin* (Florence: Olschki, 2008). Julian Franklin writes: 'The account of sovereignty in the work of Jean Bodin was a major event in the development of European political thought', in 'Sovereignty and the Mixed Constitution: Bodin and His Critics', in *The Cambridge History of Political Thought*, ed. by J. H. Burns (Cambridge: Cambridge University Press, 1992), pp. 298–328 (p. 298). See also Goyard-Fabre, esp. p. 9. More general recent works on Bodin include: Marie-Dominique Couzinet, *Jean Bodin* (Paris: Menini, 2001); Julian Franklin, *Jean Bodin* (Aldershot: Ashgate, 2006); *The Reception of Bodin*, ed. by Lloyd; and Lloyd's new intellectual biography, *'This Pre-eminent Man of France'*. See also Turchetti's extensive introduction and notes in Jean Bodin, *Les six livres de la République: De republica libri sex / livre premier liber 1*, ed. by Mario Turchetti and Nicolas de Araujo (Paris: Classiques Garnier, 2013).

[21] Jean Bodin, *Les six livres de la République*, ed. by Christiane Frémont, Marie-Dominique Couzinet, and Henri Rochais, 6 vols. (Paris: Fayard, 1986), *Préface*, pp. 14 and 10. All further references to the *République* will be to this facsimile edition, since only the first volume of Turchetti's bilingual edition is currently available.

[22] On Bodin's theology, see Marie-Dominique Couzinet, 'La logique divine dans les *Six livres de la République* de Jean Bodin', in *Politique, droit, et théologie chez Bodin, Grotius et Hobbes*, pp. 47–70. See also Ann Blair, *The Theater of Nature: Bodin and Renaissance Science* (Princeton, NJ: Princeton University Press, 1997).

relevant topic (for instance, sovereignty), but scholars concur that the work is best understood as a whole.[23]

In the writing of Le Roy and Bodin, *politique* is multifaceted: a means of referring to other texts, a means of defining a discipline and categorising knowledge, and embodied in a figure whose expertise in the former made him (and it had to be a him) uniquely suited to the challenges of government in the context of civil war and political uncertainty. My purpose here is to examine in detail how they defined politics and *politiques*, rather than giving an account of their political thought, although I could hardly write about their conceptions of politics without taking their substantive positions into account. The connection between theory and practice was central for both authors: a connection evident in their uses of *politique*, which referred to both abstract knowledge and the knowledgeable person who would put it into practice. The authors assert the novelty of their *politiques* by means of detailed comparison of (and with) various sources ancient and modern. Aristotle figures as both exemplary and inadequate *politique*: it is with and against him that Bodin and Le Roy fashion their own skilled *politique* negotiator and rule-maker, as well as reshaping and in a sense creating the canon of political thought for their readers. The last part of the chapter is concerned with the masculine substantive, which absorbs the power of the abstract and adjectival uses. What do *politiques* do in Le Roy and Bodin's view, how do they do it, and who, indeed, might they be?

Introducing *La Science Politique*

In the French academy by the mid-sixteenth century, developments in teaching practice and in thought had resulted in 'a constant agitation of a group of interrelated terms: teaching (*doctrina*); learning (*disciplina*); method (*methodus*); art (*ars*); and science (*scientia*)'.[24] All of these became associated with the abstract substantive *politique* or were used in conjunction with the adjectival form. Le Roy calls politics an art; Bodin more commonly refers to it as science or philosophy. Both assert that it is in ascendancy. Of the hundreds of instances of substantive and adjectival uses of *politique* in Le Roy's translation of Aristotle, and the approximately fifty

[23] Marie-Dominique Couzinet, 'On Bodin's Method', in *The Reception of Bodin*, pp. 39–65 (p. 62); Miglietti, p. 32.
[24] Walter J. Ong, *Ramus, Method, and the Decay of Dialogue: From the Art of Discourse to the Art of Reason* (Cambridge, MA: Harvard University Press, 1958), p. 156.

uses in Bodin's *République*, the term is particularly common in paratextual material, especially the prefaces.[25] In Bodin, *politique* is also used more frequently in the opening to various chapters than in the body of the arguments, in the kind of integrated preface that Gérard Genette describes as characteristic of pre-modern writing.[26] These prefatory uses define the texts as *politique*, and make the authors' claims about the meaning of *politique* prominent in each work. Bodin writes that his text focuses on 'several Political questions [questions Politiques] that to me seem in need of being well understood' (p. 11). The five uses of the term in the preface are clustered around this statement, on this page, and are all adjectival (political questions – 'questions politiques'; political discourse – 'discours politiques'; political science – 'science politique'; political philosophy – 'philosophie politique'), using *politique* to qualify types of knowledge and forms of expression. By referring to politics as a question in need of resolution, Bodin in particular is acknowledging what I have called the *politique* problem.

For Le Roy, *politique* defines an area of study that itself defines and delineates the related landscapes of knowledge and power, so that the word performs the action that it describes. We see this particularly at the close of the preface, in which *la politique*, quasi-personified, appears at the head of a long sentence describing how 'she' governs all constituent members of a community:

> She nourishes children, lifts the heart of young men, softens the troubles of the aged, sustains the poor, conserves the rich, pleases the good, satisfies the wise, guides magistrates, directs Kings and Emperors, rules the *estats**, balances out the superior and the inferior, ornaments prosperity, and consoles adversity. (p. biv)[27]

---

[25] Mario Turchetti says there are more than fifty in 'Bodin as Self-Translator of His *République*: Why the Omission of "Politicus" and Allied Terms from the Latin Version?', in *Why Concepts Matter: Translating Social and Political Thought*, ed. by Martin J. Burke and Melvin Richter (Leiden and Boston, MA: Brill, 2012), pp. 109–18 (p. 112). I have counted forty-seven: six in the *Préface* (pp. 11–12); twelve in Book I (pp. 31, 36, 52, 107, 109, 179); two in Book II (pp. 40, 80); one in Book III (p. 45); eight in Book IV (pp. 98, 101, 109, 149, 152, 153, 212); thirteen in book V (pp. 11, 19, 41, 42, 43, 67, 80, 98, 125, 141, 156, 165); and eight in Book VI (pp. 35, 82, 102, 163, 196, 234, 257, 261).

[26] Gérard Genette, *Seuils* (Paris: Seuil, 1987), pp. 7–8.

[27] 'Elle nourrit les enfans, eleve le cœur des jeunes hommes, adoucit les molestes des plus aagez, soustient les pauvres, conserve les riches, plaist au bons, contente les sages, guide les magistrats, conduict les Roys et Empereurs, regit les estats, balance les superieurs et les inferieurs, orne la prosperité et console l'adversité.' **Estats* in the sense of 'estates': the main social groups (and hierarchy) under the *Ancien Régime*.

Le Roy tends to use the noun more in his preface, Bodin the adjective. This is likely because Le Roy is explicitly trying to inaugurate the 'restitution' of politics as the 'mother of disciplines, [and] mistress of manners' ('mere des disciplines, maistresse des mœurs', p. aiij'). This paraphrases Aristotle's point at the opening of his *Nicomachean Ethics* that politics is the 'master art' (*NE*, 1094a–b). Bodin's *République*, meanwhile, attempts to adjust the ways in which various spheres of expertise are *politique*. However, it is not always absolutely clear whether a use of *politique* is adjectival or nominal, or whether it refers to a text (as in 'Aristotle's *Politiques*') or a person. Indeed, texts and thinkers are to some degree coextensive in lexical and syntactic terms.

A central claim made by both authors is for the novelty of their works and their relevance for the contemporary moment. Bodin justifies his enterprise by suggesting that the body of existing 'Political discourses' needs updating and extending, 'since Plato and Aristotle cut their *discours Politiques* so short that they rather left an appetite for more' (*Préface*, p. 11).[28] In his preface to the *Politiques d'Aristote*, Le Roy similarly suggests that *la politique* is a discipline in need of greater attention; he opens by praising the successes of his age (the Discoveries; the 'restoration of learning'), but then laments the lack of attention that politics has received, despite its central, governing importance. As such, both emphasise their attempts to do something new with something very old: Le Roy is helping to restore *la politique* to its rightful place in the intellectual canon by elucidating Aristotle's thorny text; Bodin is picking up where Aristotle and Plato left off. They were also, in a sense, picking up where Budé left off. For Budé, the lessons of the ancients were for the moderns to absorb and implement, without direct acknowledgement of the enormous historical gulf between, say, Alexander the Great and François I; Bodin and Le Roy, by contrast, are more painfully aware of peculiarly contemporary demands on political thought and action.

Budé had emphasised the role of the teacher, and of teaching. Late in his own life, Le Roy – Budé's pupil – also became a teacher, holding the Chair in Greek at Budé's *Collège royal*. In his inaugural lecture he announced his intention to profess not Greek but 'politica', by which he means his interpretation of Greek political thought, which he describes as matters ('res') most serious or pressing ('graves'), important ('praeclaras'), and that have been neglected ('omissas negligentur'); he expresses this view again,

---

[28] 'car Platon et Aristote ont tranché si court leurs discours Politiques, qu'ils ont plustost laissé un appetit'.

and more fully, in his translation of Aristotle.[29] Did all this amount to a new politics, or a restoration of politics?

Their philological and methodological approaches were, if not entirely new, consistent with their moment. Bodin and Le Roy were using and responding to new methods of reading, and of organising information and argument, influenced both by Ramist practical methodology and by commonplacing techniques.[30] Their uses of *politique* were also born of an early modern version of interdisciplinarity made possible by humanist methods, through which the domains of law and history became increasingly important for considerations of politics. Greengrass comments that 'one of the striking features of the *République* is Bodin's determination to ground the rook in the interstitial space between politics, history and law, between the way things are, and the way they should be'.[31]

Bodin and Le Roy were trained jurists; Bodin also published a legal textbook in 1578.[32] The reinforced connection between politics and law had many precedents. The figures of jurisconsult and *politique* were already associated in Latin legal discourse; in his *Commentarius de jurisprudentia Muciana* (1559), Baudouin writes 'Jurisconsultus hoc est Homo Politicus' ['the Jurisconsult is the Political Man'].[33] In Chapter 2 I discussed the late medieval legal-political ideal of the *homo politicus* identified by Donald Kelley, and also showed that legal habits were associated with politically inflected linguistic innovation (and malpractice), and that lawyers like Pasquier and Le Caron devoted attention to how politics ought to be conducted. We know that Budé associated *droit* and *politique*, and

---

[29] Loys Le Roy, *Prolegomena Politica. Oratio ab eo habita Parisiis inito professionis Regiae, in ennaratione Politicorum Aristoteles* (Paris: Morel, 1575), p. 10.

[30] Marie-Dominique Couzinet, *Histoire et méthode à la Renaissance: Une lecture de la Methodus de Jean Bodin* (Paris: Vrin, 1996), p. 21; Ann Moss, *Printed Commonplace Books and the Structuring of Renaissance Thought* (Oxford: Clarendon, 1996), p. 154 n. 25; Francis Goyet, *Le sublime du 'lieu commun': L'invention rhétorique dans l'Antiquité et à la Renaissance* (Paris: Champion, 1996), p. 667. See also Ann Blair, *Too Much to Know: Managing Scholarly Information before the Modern Age* (New Haven, CT: Yale University Press, 2010). Although commonplacing provided a base structural form for experiences as diffuse as 'thought', 'memory', and 'reading', Moss shows there was a great diversity of methods and practices in this period. Indicating Bodin's particularity within the broader structure, Maclean refers to him as a 'systematiser', in *Interpretation and Meaning*, pp. 26 and 122. On Bodin and Ramus, see Couzinet, 'On Bodin's Method', in *The Reception of Bodin*, pp. 39–65, and Vasoli, pp. 45–46 and 90.

[31] Mark Greengrass, 'The Experiential World of Jean Bodin', in *The Reception of Bodin*, pp. 67–96 (p. 87).

[32] Bodin aspired to a professorship of law in Toulouse; see Franklin, *Jean Bodin and the Sixteenth-Century Revolution in the Methodology of Law and History*, p. 63. On Bodin's view of the law, see Maclean, *Interpretation and Meaning*, pp. 26–27.

[33] Quoted in Kelley, *The Beginnings of Ideology*, p. 203.

I mentioned at the opening of this chapter that Le Roy indicated in his preface that legislators were the key practitioners of politics.

In Bodin's *République*, the substantive *politique* emerges alongside and against the figures of jurisconsult and legislator. Bodin's second preface to the *République*, written (in Latin) for the third edition (1578) is, indeed, more focused on the figure of *jurisconsultus* than on the *politicus*.[34] This second preface describes how the lawyer must make a special effort to work out how to situate himself according to social mores, citing a legal commonplace that could be roughly translated as 'who makes laws for the lawyers?': 'Aut illut juriscosultorum carmen, HOC JURE UTITUR, qui quo jure utitur nesciat?'[35] Since Bodin announces in the first chapter that his intention is to follow 'political rules' (I, 1, p. 30), perhaps *politiques* make laws for the lawyers. The legal context is especially privileged in the semantic field that defines and is defined by the adjective *politique* in Bodin's work. In this way, he uses the term *politique* to do work that Le Roy explicitly describes in his preface: to regulate and direct other disciplines relating to the construction and maintenance of republics, particularly law: 'it is in accordance with her [la politique] that all other particular, local, or temporal laws must be ordered, ruled, moderated, and explained' (Le Roy, p. aiiij) – this recalls Budé's description of the role of a 'mixed man' moderating between various types of law (discussed in Chapter 2).[36] In linking *politique* so specifically with legal expertise and practice, Le Roy and Bodin were both replicating long-standing obvious connections between law and government, and reinforcing the link between those who ruled and the members of the growing and increasingly prominent legal profession.

Given the varied precedents for their work, the most obvious 'newness' in both cases is linguistic, the product of Bodin's apparently desperate decision to write in the vernacular, and Le Roy's undertaking the first vernacular translation of the *Politics* from Greek.[37] Although I do not have

---

[34] See the translation by Mario Turchetti and Sara Miglietti in Bodin, *République* (2013), pp. 126–41.

[35] Bodin, *République* (2013), p. 135.

[36] 'C'est elle [la politique] sur laquelle toutes autres loix particulieres, locales ou temporelles, doivent estre dressees, reiglees, moderees, exposees.'

[37] This was a new enterprise, as Le Roy claimed, although it was not the first vernacular translation of Aristotle's *Politics*: Nicolas d'Oresme translated William Moerboke's Latin version into French *c.* 1268. Between Oresme and Le Roy, the majority of translations of Aristotle were from Greek into Latin, including Jacques Lefèvre d'Etaples's translation and commentary that applied humanist philological practice to the original Greek for the first time (1506). See Charles B. Schmitt, *Aristotle and the Renaissance* (Cambridge, MA and London: Harvard University Press, 1983), pp. 36 and 44, and David Lines, 'Lefèvre and French Aristotelianism on the Eve of the Sixteenth Century', in *Der*

the linguistic expertise to give a detailed account of the quality of Le Roy's translation and his manipulation of the Greek, a general point to make is that, as Melissa Lane has recently pointed out in her account of the figure of the Archon (office-holder), there is slippage in Classical Greek between verb and noun forms: this flexibility may have influenced the slippage between substantive and other forms in Le Roy's uses of *politique*.[38] In a broader sense, both Le Roy's work and Bodin's can be seen as acts of translation, given that Bodin announces that he has had to render in French what would otherwise have been in Latin (owing to the drought of learning brought on by the civil wars, p. 10), and that both are concerned with a transfer of knowledge from classical and contemporary (principally Italian) theory to France, and French practice, in an act of *translatio studii*.[39]

This linguistic novelty, however, is connected to another important way in which Bodin's and Le Roy's *politiques* were, necessarily, new: their presentism. This is born of their attention to historical context and particularly to their contemporary moment and its historicity. Bodin and Le Roy were instrumental in the emergence of history as a distinct discipline; Bodin with his method of history published in 1566, and Le Roy with his pamphlet on history of the same year, and his major work, *De la vicissitude*, which articulates a broad-ranging historical vision.[40] For Bodin, the *République* is the fulfilment of his proposed historical method. In the *Methodus*, he writes that history explains the present and enables us to deduce what the future will be.[41] The printing history of Le Roy's *œuvre*

Aristotelismus in der Frühen Neuzeit – Kontinuität oder Wiederaneignung? ed. by Günter Frank and Andreas Speer (Harrassowitz: Wiesbaden, 2007), pp. 273–89.

[38] Melissa Lane, 'Office and Anarchy', in *Constitutions before Constitutionalism: Classical Greek Ideas of Office and Rule* (Oxford: The Carlyle Lectures, 16 January 2018). On Classical Greek political vocabulary, see also Melissa Lane, *Greek and Roman Political Ideas* (London: Pelican, 2014), pp. 12–14.

[39] Karlheinz Stierle, '*Translatio studii* and Renaissance: From Vertical to Horizontal Translation', in *The Translatability of Cultures: Figurations of the Space Between*, ed. by Sanford Budick and Wolfgang Iser (Stanford, CA: Stanford University Press, 1996), pp. 55–67. The transfer of knowledge from Italy to France was a major dynamic of French Renaissance culture, and was acted out in the legal sphere in the debate over the *mos gallicus* and the *mos italicus*. See Maclean, *Interpretation and Meaning*, pp. 73 and 122, and Kelley, *The Beginnings of Ideology*, pp. 178–79. On Bodin's use of translation in his conception of sovereignty, see also Oisin Keohane, 'Bodin on Sovereignty: Taking Exception to Translation?', *Paragraph*, 38.2 (2015), 245–60.

[40] See Philippe Desan, *Naissance de la méthode: Machiavel, La Ramée, Bodin, Montaigne, Descartes* (Paris: Nizet, 1987), and Couzinet, *Histoire et méthode à la Renaissance*.

[41] 'ex quibus non solum praesentia commodè explicantur, sed etiam futura colliguntur': 'this not only explains the present situation, but also elucidates the future'. Jean Bodin, 'Methodus ad facilem historiarum cognitionem', in *Œuvres philosophiques de Jean Bodin*, ed. by Pierre Mesnard (Paris: Presses universitaries de France, 1951), pp. 105–277 (p. 112).

suggests a particular elision of *politique* and *histoire*; *Consideration sur l'histoire* ('Consideration of History') was subsequently printed with *L'excellence de l'art politique*, a joint edition that was reissued in 1570, 1571, 1576, and 1599. Le Roy similarly states that history will 'instruct the present and the future'.[42] He refers to his commentary as a political history ('une histoire politique') in the *Argument* to Book II of the *Politiques d'Aristote*:

> Thus I have laid out a political history, a collection of all kinds of things ancient and modern that I have come to know, through reading or other research, all to adjust ('adjouster') the *Politics* of Plato and Aristotle, a very necessary thing both for an understanding of their works and for a knowledge of the political faculty. (pp. 65–66)[43]

Le Roy is advancing a method ('histoire politique') that will enact a transfer from one kind of knowledge to another more practical kind: from political history to political faculty, a move mimetically reinforced by the structure of his sentence. He makes his motivation for this explicit in the *Argument* to Book I, where he writes that he intends to bring together the ancient and modern sources for the benefit of an overall 'political work' ('l'œuvre politique') that transcends any single text (p. 2).

In their different ways Bodin and Le Roy also turn away from the habits of many other writers now considered to have been working on 'politics': instead of taking the education and action of the prince as their central focus, they announce their intention to look at overarching systems of appropriate knowledge and action, and situate figures, such as the sovereign, the jurisconsult, the magistrate, and the *politique*, within these systems. These systems are defined by the abstract term *politique*: Bodin announces his intention to follow political rules ('suyvre les reigles Politiques') in his treatise (I, I p. 30); Le Roy refers to 'la politique' as the principal rule, or law ('la principale reigle') (p. biv). These systems will be adjusted according to pressing contemporary needs, leading to a marriage between their theorisations of normative systems and a contingent pragmatism. The apparent paradox between synthesis and historicism in their approaches to their source material is the product of this marriage. The effect of Le Roy's commentary on Aristotle, even more so than Bodin's

---

[42] Loys Le Roy, *Consideration sur l'histoire françoise, et l'universelle de ce Temps, dont les merveilles sont succinctement recitées* (Paris: Morel, 1567), p. Diiij.

[43] 'A ceste cause j'ay dressé une histoire politique, un receuil de toutes sortes, anciens & modernes, dont j'ay peu avoir la cognoissance, par lecture ou par autre recherche, le tout pour adjouster aux Politiques de Platon & Aristote, comme chose tresnecessaire à l'intelligence de leurs livres, et à la cognoissance de la faculté politique.'

approach in the *République*, is to suggest that there is no such thing as purely theoretical, context-free politics; no politics without history.

Aristotle's *Politiques*?

An significant element of Le Roy's and Bodin's new or updated *politiques* is their treatment of texts and authors classified as *politique*. They define their own work in relation to what has come before (in Bodin's case), and comment on and in some cases adjust earlier work (Le Roy's commentary does this most obviously and extensively, but Bodin consistently quotes, comments, and adjusts in the *République*). In this way they participate in the early modern contestation of the figure of the (political) philosopher, with particular attention to [his] socio-political role, and begin to make an argument about what their own contributions are.[44]

Exploration of the role and status of the philosopher in these works occurs most explicitly in analysis of one in particular: Aristotle. The most visually evident use of *politique* in Le Roy's translation is a plural: 'les Politiques d'Aristote', which appears on the title page and at the head of every other page in the body of the text. But Le Roy's *politiques* are not exclusively Aristotle's – they respond to a broad range of sources, of which the most important intertext is Plato's *Republic*, although Le Roy's translation of the *Republic* was published only posthumously (in 1599). In assembling and critiquing such a range of sources, Le Roy's *politiques* become something like his own. By translating into the vernacular and emphasising the needs of contemporary readers, his project place him within the *Pléiade* mission of illustrating and advancing the French language, as well as representing an early articulation of what would become the Quarrel of Ancients and Moderns (latent in his many juxtapositions of ancient and modern) – his gesture of using a chair in Greek to profess politics can also be understood as a 'modern' intervention within the nascent quarrel.[45] Being tentatively 'modern' in 1576 does not entail

---

[44] See *The Philosopher in Early Modern Europe: The Nature of a Contested Identity*, ed. by Conal Condren, Stephen Gaukroger, and Ian Hunter (Cambridge: Cambridge University Press, 2006), especially 'Introduction', pp. 1–16. The editors argue that the early modern philosopher was a 'persona' adopted to solve particular philosophical problems, fashioned through the classical political vocabulary of office holding, as were other categories associated with office such as that of judge or counsellor. See pp. 7–10. The fashioning of the *politique* persona should be considered part of this process.

[45] Duport, 'Introduction', p. 7; Anthony Grafton suggests that Bodin and Le Roy's attitudes to history identify them as early examples of *Modernes*, see Grafton, p. 174. I discuss a potential sixteenth-century articulation of the *Querelle*, and the place of Le Roy's *De la vicissitude* therein, in 'A

rejection of the ancient; the critical relation to Aristotle, Plato, and others is one of productive tension.

Le Roy is 'modern' in the sense that Aristotle and Plato are only a beginning. On the page, Le Roy often outwrites Aristotle, with lengthy italicised commentary on a single sentence, using Aristotle's precepts as a starting point. The outcome of the 'conference' of ancient and modern sometimes undermines Aristotle: for example, when Aristotle suggests in Book 1 that the Greeks are suited above all others to the practice of empire, Le Roy observes that Aristotle is moved to this view by patriotism but that since his death Greece has been colonised multiple times.[46] The transition from Roman to Byzantine Empire is described as a 'translation' (p. 10) – an insight into Le Roy's view of his own activity of translation, of changing words or names, of bringing objects under the control of different regimes of language and thought.[47]

The practice of translation and commentary had been a key feature of Aristotelianism since the early Middle Ages.[48] Aristotle commentary did not escape humanist influence. This genre was important in the development of scholarly manuals and in Renaissance reassessments of classical thought; the commentaries of John Case in England (1588) and Johannes Magirus in Germany (1597) demonstrate that Loys Le Roy was not the sole innovative commenter in the period.[49] Through his method of contextualising and synthesising, his approach contrasts not so much with 'Aristotle', but with pre-Renaissance 'Aristotelians' working in the

---

Sixteenth-Century Modern? Loys Le Roy's *De la vicissitude*', *Early Modern French Studies*, 37.2 (2015), 76–92.

[46] This reflects contemporary accounts of Greece as exceptionally subjugated; Vives asked in 1529 whether 'any people, or indeed any person at all, ever suffered such an extreme condition of slavery as that which is now suffered by Greece?', quoted in Malcolm, *Useful Enemies*, p. 207.

[47] Sciacca gives a list of Le Roy's named sources, p. 136. Le Roy's practice of 'translation', in this example in particular, reflects the connection between *translatio studii* (knowledge transfer) and *translatio imperii* (power transfer) in pre-modern conceptions of language and translation. See Ernest Curtius, *European Literature and the Latin Middle Ages*, tr. by Willard Trask (London: Routledge, 1953), pp. 27–30.

[48] Copenhaver and Schmitt agree that Renaissance philosophy was conducted within a fundamentally Aristotelian framework but that Aristotle's reputation was in decline in the period. Between 1500 and 1650 there were more than 6,000 commentaries on various parts of the *Corpus Aristotelicum* written in Europe (though relatively few in the vernacular): see Brian P. Copenhaver, 'Aristotelianisms', in *The Columbia History of Western Philosophy*, ed. by Richard Popkin (New York, NY: Columbia University Press, 1999); Schmitt, *Aristotle and the Renaissance*; Heinrich Kuhn, 'Aristotelianism in the Renaissance', in *Stanford Encyclopedia of Philosophy* (2005) https://plato.stanford.edu/entries/aristotelianism-renaissance [accessed 3 August 2020]. On Paris as the centre of efforts to 'reinterpret and reform Aristotelianism', see Lines, 'Lefèvre and French Aristotelianism on the Eve of the Sixteenth Century'.

[49] Schmitt, 'The Rise of the Philosophical Textbook', p. 801.

scholastic tradition in which philosophical validity was logically intuited rather than derived from context or experience.[50] Relevant experience and awareness of the contemporary moment are crucial for political excellence in Le Roy's view. Repeatedly he emphasises the real-world implications of his project and the practical aspects of *politique* knowledge; in the dedicatory epistle to Henri III he reiterates what he had written ten years earlier in the preface to his translation of Xenophon: that 'politics consists of usage' ('la politique consiste en l'usage', p. aii). Echoing contemporary concerns about the need for practice and for practical education, he consistently emphasises the need for both experience and book learning, referring to *la politique* as 'that science which is imperfect without learning and experience combined' ('cette science qui est imparfaicte sans le sçavoir et l'experience ensemble', p. aiij').[51]

In the *République* Bodin manages a balance between announcing his originality and acknowledging his many influences.[52] Within this, Plato holds a special place for Bodin as for Le Roy: the geometrical harmony to which Bodin aspires in Book VI, and which he presents as the ultimate aim of good government (v, 6, pp. 303–12) bears testament to this. He makes clear, however, that the Romans have come closest to achieving the kind of Republic he is interested in building (I, I, p. 37).[53] Whether Bodin's *Politiques* are Aristotle's to any extent is a matter for debate; Bodin is remembered as outspokenly anti-Aristotelian, but some critics emphasise his debts to the Stagirite.[54] Although Bodin makes clear and definitive breaks with Aristotle, like his later reader, Hobbes, he nonetheless

---

[50] Schmitt, *Aristotle and the Renaissance*, p. 5.

[51] Tuck, p. 25. On the general trend for emphasis on 'use' and 'practice', see Grafton and Jardine, p. 168.

[52] Lloyd describes Bodin as a 'prismatic agent' in the transmission of ideas. See Lloyd, 'Introduction', in *The Reception of Bodin*, p. 2. Bodin examines and recalibrates ideas from Plato to Cicero to Aquinas to Machiavelli. He was, as Skinner points out, also conversant with Stoic humanism; see *Foundations*, II, pp. 284 and 279. See also Goyet, *Le sublime du lieu commun*, p. 670, and Tuck, p. 52.

[53] Bodin's preference for Rome evokes another aspect of the *Querelle des Anciens et des Modernes*; writing about the debates of the following century, Larry Norman shows that being 'Modern' was often a matter of asserting the supremacy of Rome over Greece, in *The Shock of the Ancient: Literature & History in Early Modern France* (Chicago, IL and London: University of Chicago Press, 2011), pp. 21–22.

[54] Tuck puts Bodin at the forefront of what he terms the 'new, anti-Aristotelian science', pp. 26–27 and 62. Others emphasise continuity with Aristotelian frameworks. Marie-Dominique Couzinet emphasises his Aristotelian vocabulary, Vasoli argues that Bodin's approach follows 'una direttiva aristotelica', and Jehasse notes that, on a formal level, Bodin imitates the structure of Aristotle's *Politics* even if he rearranges the order of contents. See Marie-Dominique Couzinet, 'On Bodin's Method', in *The Reception of Bodin*, pp. 36–65 (pp. 60–61); Vasoli, pp. 90–91; Jehasse, p. 263.

manages and retains Aristotelian influences as he constructs his own vision of politics.[55]

Bodin disagrees with Aristotle on several key points, notably on the relation between economics and politics (I, I), on slavery (I, 5), and on citizenship (I, 6). He typically begins his chapters asserting that no writer (or, as we shall see below, no *politique*) has tackled the subject before, or that Aristotle has done so mistakenly; *Polit. d'Aristote* appears frequently in the margins of the early editions of the *République*, and most of these notes signal a correction of Aristotle's principles. Thus Bodin highlights the distinctiveness of his own contribution to a long conversation about politics. But in the introductory gestures his references to Aristotle are more ambiguous than those who emphasise his strident anti-Aristotelianism might allow; much later in the *République*, in VI, 5, on the highly controversial question of whether it is advisable to elect a monarch (Bodin says not), he writes that the topic has led even the best writers astray: 'not only those who are simple and little acquainted with political science, but even those who are considered the most sufficient'; he goes onto comment that 'Aristotle himself considered that monarchs could be elected' (VI, 5, p. 197).[56] If Aristotle is among 'the most sufficient', this reminds us that Aristotle is useful to Bodin, to work both with and against. Elsewhere, Bodin introduces Aristotle as 'an ancient *politique*' (V, 2, p. 80), and earlier in the same chapter, as part of his argument against usury, writes that 'this law has always been held in esteem by legislators, and by the greatest *politiques*: that is, Solon, Lycurgus, Plato, and Aristotle' (V, 2, p. 67).[57] Here, then, Aristotle has his place among the greatest *politiques* of history.

Ultimately, for Bodin the ends justify the theoretical means, and in this sense his *politiques* are a composite of thousands of sources that belong to none but him. He ends on a note of neo-platonic idealism, but in the opening chapter of the first book (on the ultimate end ['fin principale'] of a

---

[55] Ryan writes that while Hobbes 'despised' Aristotle's *Politics* and *Ethics*, he 'silently appropriates [Aristotle's] views on many occasions'. See Ryan, pp. 425–26. Bodin may also have been influenced, like Hobbes, by Aristotle commentary. Sophie Smith has argued that Hobbes's view of democracy was influenced by early modern commentaries on Aristotle in 'Democracy and the Body Politic from Aristotle to Hobbes', *Political Theory*, 46 (2018), 167–96.
[56] 'non seulement les simples et peu entendus en la science politique, ains encores ceux là qui sont estimez les plus suffisans'; 'mesmes Aristote est d'avis qu'on eslise les monarchques'. Anna Becker argues that, even if Bodin criticises Aristotle, he 'held Aristotle to have provided the fundamental categories for thinking about the political'. Becker, *Gendering the Renaissance Commonwealth*, p. 109. See also Ann Blair, *The Theater of Nature*, p. 218.
[57] 'Ceste loy a tousjours esté fort estimee de tous legislateurs, et des plus grands politiques: c'est à sçavoir Solon, Lycurgue, Platon, Aristote.'

good republic) Bodin emphasises that his project is contained by the limitations of what he views as possible:

> Yet we do not wish to figure a Republic of Ideas without effects, such as Plato and Thomas More Chancellor of England have imagined. Rather we will content ourselves with following the Political rules as closely as possible. In so doing, we cannot rightly be blamed, even if we have not achieved the goal we aimed for, any more than the master navigator swept aside by a storm, or the doctor conquered by disease, will be esteemed the less, as long as the latter has governed his patient well, and the former his vessel. (I, I, p. 31)[58]

The phrase, 'Republic of Ideas' evokes both the general idea of a republic of letters and its effects on government, and the specific problem of how Plato's ideal realm might influence the construction of a republic. Bodin places himself – as will François de la Noue fifteen years later – in an anti-utopian stream of political thought in which 'Political rules' (be they Plato's or anyone else's) can only be approximately followed in pursuit of curative and conservative political goals. The negative framing is amplified by Bodin's anticipation of failure to meet the given goal and his statement that, if we have at least tried, we cannot be blamed for that failure. The relation between theory and practice, then, is a tense one: ideas alone will not suffice, and their effects are in doubt.

Le Roy is more positive about Plato's 'example of political perfection' ('exemplaire de perfection politique') but says it is more divine than earthly: those who wish to will conform to this model 'by as close an imitation as they can manage' ('par imitation le plus près qu'ils pourront', p. aiiij[v].). These pragmatic approaches evoke none other than Aristotle, for whom the political goal was not 'the best state' but the 'best possible (or practicable) state'.[59] And yet, although the language of practically applied political knowledge (*phronesis*) originates with Aristotle, such pragmatism almost inevitably leads both writers away from Aristotle, since it is contextually determined. Bodin notes that 4,000 years of known world history have shown slavery to be a constant source of problems (specifically

---

[58] 'Toutefois nous ne voulons pas aussi figurer une Republique en Idee sans effect, telle que Platon, et Thomas le More chancelier d'Angleterre ont imaginé, mais nous contenterons de suyvre les reigles Politiques au plus pres qu'il sera possible. En quoy faisant, on ne peut justement estre blasmé, encores qu'on n'ait pas attaint le but où l'on visoit, non plus que le maistre pilote transporté de la tempeste, ou le medecin vaincu de la maladie, ne sont pas moins estimés, pourveu que l'un ait bien gouverné son malade, et l'autre son navire.'

[59] Aristotle, *Politics*, 1288b37. See Ryan, p. 105. In the Renaissance, Aristotle's work was not standardly held up as an example of practical philosophy: Ramus criticised Aristotelians for their emphasis on intellectual as opposed to practical virtues. See Tuck, p. 25.

uprisings and discord): writing from his late perspective (as he understands it), in a very different world to Aristotle's, he thus criticises slavery on pragmatic rather than ethical grounds, as it has proved too imprudent (1, 5 p. 106).[60] As in Le Roy's commentary, the relation of attraction and repulsion to Aristotle and others is part of a process of fashioning the substantive *politique*, and of constructing the nascent canon of the newly inaugurated discipline of politics, in which Classical texts are there to test and adjust, and Aristotle and Plato are prominent, but not singular, *politiques* themselves.

Prudent *Politiques*

Budé wrote that an education in 'science politique' was necessary for those in government; such an education would confer prudence, a surety against the errors that inevitably befall leaders otherwise.[61] In earlier writings, such as Desmoulins's political handbook, the *Traité des vertus*, prudence was the principal keyword of political virtue, without any mention of the word for politics itself. Half a century later, in Bodin and Le Roy, the terms *prudence* and *prudentia* are strongly associated with *politique*.[62] The association is also made in Le Roy's wider *œuvre*. He defines his printed collection of Latin opuscules, the *Prolegomena politica*, as the sum of accumulated prudence ('summa prudentia cumulata').[63] At the opening of *De la vicissitude*, we find *politique*, *usage*, and *prudence*, in a summary of intellectual virtues: 'The body politic encompasses justice, strength, prudence, temperance, religion, military expertise, counsel, magistrates, and private citizens' ('Au politique justice, fortitude, prudence, temperance,

---

[60] Despite Bodin's critique of slavery, Malcolm shows that his views on servility, servitude, slavery, and feudal ties were complex. See *Useful Enemies*, pp. 211–16. Still, in the century that saw the establishment of the Atlantic slave trade, Bodin's effective rejection of slavery reflects the comparatively limited participation of France in the early years of that trade, for all that the later French colonial record was no less brutal than that of its rivals. See Michael Harrigan, *Frontiers of Servitude: Slavery in Narratives of the Early French Atlantic* (Manchester: Manchester University Press, 2018). In general, Bodin and Le Roy were more interested in the 'old world' of the Ottoman Empire than in the Atlantic world. See Noel Malcolm, 'Positive Views of Islam and Ottoman Rule in the Sixteenth Century: The Case of Jean Bodin', in *The Renaissance and the Ottoman World*, ed. by Anna Contadini and Claire Norton (Aldershot: Ashgate, 2013), pp. 197–220.

[61] Budé (Larrivour), p. 118. Victoria Kahn writes that 'prudence' was understood in the sixteenth century (with references to Classical texts) as 'the intellectual virtue of right judgement about our actions'. See *Rhetoric, Prudence, and Skepticism*, p. 21. See also Francis Goyet, *Les audaces de la prudence: Littérature et politique aux XVIe et XVIIe siècles* (Paris: Classiques Garnier, 2009).

[62] On prudence as a key concept in early modern political thought, and the transition from politics as prudence to politics as political science, see Maclean, 'From Prudence to Policy'.

[63] Le Roy, *Prolegomena*, p. 3.

religion, militie, judicature, finance, conseil, magistrats et privez' ['politique' is adjectival here, and agrees with 'corps']).[64] It is noticeable here that within this body we find both concepts and human agents demonstrating the connection between abstract and (human) concrete in Le Roy's thought.

For Bodin, the link with prudence is also strong in Latin, as a translation of *politique*; the word *politica* is, indeed, markedly absent from *De Republica*, although in the 1584 preface there is a use of *politica* – 'politica decreta' – indicating the way that the term retains strength as a disciplinary marker in paratextual discussion.[65] Turchetti attributes the absence of *politica* from Bodin's Latin to linguistic purism: the influence of Leonardo Bruni's argument that Cicero and Seneca didn't use this term, but translated the Greek as *civilis*.[66] It is testament, however, to the strength of the vernacular term *politique* that Bodin does not always simply translate it as *civilis* or *civitatis*; each translation is effectively a gloss, often with *prudentia* at its heart, for instance 'an act of a *politique* master so wise that nobody revolted against it' becomes 'prudence governs without provoking sedition' ('prudentia sine seditione gestum est').[67] Quelling sedition is a primary function of the *politique*, brought into being partly – as Bodin explains in his preface – to end civil discord.

Bodin is more polemical than Le Roy with respect to contemporary political writing, stating in the preface that, since Plato and Aristotle, writing qualified as political philosophy has been dangerously mistaken: this 'has given occasion to the disturbance and overturning of great polities' ('chose qui a donné occasion de troubler et renverser de beaux Estats') (*Préface*, p. 11). Bodin promises a different kind of political writing to guide the troubled French kingdom to safety, marked as different, and more urgent, by being in French rather than Latin. His emphasis on political 'questions' evokes both an earlier Latinate culture of Scholastic disputation and *quaestiones*, but also contemporary works, not least the *Question politique* (*c.* 1570; attributed to Jean de Coras), a Huguenot work advocating resistance against the monarchy.[68] Clearly,

---

[64] Loys Le Roy, *De la vicissitude* (Paris: Morel, 1575), p. 5.
[65] Turchetti, 'Bodin as Self-Translator', p. 109; Bodin, *République* (2013), p. 150. Turchetti translates 'politica decreta' as 'les principes politiques', p. 151.
[66] Ibid., pp. 116–17. Pierre Mesnard translates 'civilis' and its cognates in the *Methodus* as *politique*, e.g. *Méthode*, p. 19; 'Methodus', p. 121.
[67] Turchetti, 'Bodin as Self-Translator', p. 113: 'un traict de maître politique si sagement qu'il n'y eut personne qui s'en remua'.
[68] [Jean de Coras], *Question politique: S'il est licite aux subjects de capituler avec leur prince*, ed. by Robert M. Kingdon (Geneva: Droz, 1989). Although the use of *politique* in the title signals the increasing prominence of the term in general, the text itself doesn't problematise *politique*; it focuses

questions politiques could threaten the ship of state: as such, they ought to be properly handled. Bodin opens his preface with the image of the ship threatened by imminent wreck; he prays for its safe arrival at the 'Port of Safety' for which the text to follow will be a guide to safe passage through the resolution of various 'questions *politiques*' (p. 10).[69]

This part of Bodin's preface echoes Le Roy's dedicatory letter to Henri III, suggesting that the tempest of war ('l'horrible orage de guerre civile') could make way for peace and order if God is willing and if the prince agrees to govern prudently (p. ajii). Le Roy goes on to demonstrate that knowledge to which *la politique* refers is a spur to action, the pivot between thought ('we know') and potential deed ('duty, 'offices' etc.), finally launching a list of verbs at the end of the sentence:

> We know through this science the duty of Princes towards their subjects; that of magistrates between themselves and concerning private citizens; which offices are the most necessary or most honest; what obedience, honour and reverence inferiors owe their superiors; in what manner they buy, sell, alter, rent, give, receive, promise, contact, plead. (p. iiij)[70]

In Bodin and Le Roy, *politique* indicates correct action, and so is an enabler of *praxis*, often figured as prudence.[71] Both offer the term *politique* as a key to the management of change. The passing of time, then, is a crucial context to the connection between the word and its referents. This, too, is a function of the prudent politics they seek to articulate; prudence is a quality associated since Cicero with an ability to predict or anticipate

on the meaning and potential of the word 'capituler', italicising this keyword and its cognates throughout. The strong stance of Bodin's preface as a whole has been interpreted as countering Huguenot resistance theory (see Skinner, *Foundations*, p. 285).

[69] On this metaphor in Bodin's preface, and political shipwreck metaphors in sixteenth-century France, see Oliver, pp. 101–39.

[70] 'Nous cognoissons par ceste science le devoir des Princes envers ses subjects: celuy des magistrats entre eux et avec les privez: quelles offices sont plus necessaires ou plus honnestes: quelle obeissance, honneur et reverence les inferieurs portent à leurs superieurs: quelle maniere ils gardent à achepter, vendre, permuter, louer, donner, recevoir, promettre, contacter, plaider.'

[71] The different ways in which *la politique* manages *vicissitude* (Le Roy) and transcends fateful circumstance (Bodin) is reminiscent of Machiavelli's concept of *virtù*, wherein *virtù* triumphs over the caprices of *fortuna*. On Machiavelli's *virtù* see for example Quentin Skinner, *Visions of Politics II: Renaissance Virtues* (Cambridge: Cambridge University Press, 2002), pp. 160–85, and for a broader assessment of fortune and prudence in the Italian Renaissance, see Mario Santoro, *Fortuna, ragione e prudenza nella civiltà letteraria del Cinquecento* (Naples: Liguori, 1966). Althusser added his part to the long-standing debate about the scandal and originality of Machiavelli by saying that it was rooted in his emphasis on practice: 'Il nous interpelle à partir d'un lieu qu'il nous appelle à occuper comme "sujets" (agents) possibles d'une pratique politique possible'/ 'He interpellates us from a place that he calls us to occupy as potential subjects (agents) of a possible political practice.' Louis Althusser, *Machiavel et nous* (Paris: Tallandier, 2009), p. 72.

future events, on the basis of historical knowledge.[72] At different moments Bodin and Le Roy describe this knowledge as a kind of clairvoyance; this is part of the privileged vision that *politique* knowledge confers. Both Bodin's treatise and Le Roy's translation and commentary are, in part, surveys: of existing knowledge; of global history; of types of state; of the various roles assigned to people in society. These surveys offer pragmatic readings of Aristotle and others, in order to construct composite *politiques* that represent the pinnacle of all-seeing political knowledge.

We have already seen how Le Roy personified abstract politics as a soothing, fair-minded female figure, *la politique*. But for the incarnation of *politique* knowledge, the person who puts this knowledge into action, both texts evoke a masculine substantive, *le politique*. The special knowledge, and associated cognitive power, of a *politique* person is indicated in the association between *sage* ('wise') and *politique*, and linked to evocations of prudence.[73] In Bodin and Le Roy, as in their wider intellectual context, the figure of the *prudens*, the prudent man, is strongly associated with that of the wise man, the *sapiens*.[74] There are instances of Bodin translating *le politique* into Latin as *prudens legislator* ('prudent legislator', once again highlighting the importance of the legal context and the closeness of *legislateur* and *politique* for Bodin as for Le Roy).[75] Both authors are concerned with instructing and improving these 'prudent and wise persons' as well as demonstrating and – as we shall see – embodying, the qualities of these men. The person who unites wisdom and experience to practical effect, and who therefore has the authority to command is often described as *politique*. The adjective is generally attached variously to 'man', 'philosopher', and most commonly in Bodin, 'the sage', or 'wise man'; other associated nouns are, variously, 'the prince', 'magistrates', and

---

[72] Andrea Brady and Emily Butterworth, 'Introduction', in *The Uses of the Future in Early Modern Europe*, ed. by Andrea Brady and Emily Butterworth (London: Routledge, 2009), pp. 1–19 (p. 3).

[73] For an exploration of the resurrection of the classical ideal of *sapientia*, see Cesare Vasoli, 'The Renaissance Concept of Philosophy', in *The Cambridge History of Renaissance Philosophy*, ed. by Eckhard Kessler, Jill Kraye, Charles B. Schmitt, and Quentin Skinner (Cambridge: Cambridge University Press, 1998), pp. 55–74, esp. p. 61. The pre-eminent example of an early modern French discussion of *sagesse* is Charron's *De la sagesse*, which borrowed heavily from Montaigne and Bodin and was published just after the end of the civil wars in 1601.

[74] Kahn has pointed out that this was common in the period, the result of Cicero's conflation of *prudentia* and *sapientia* in *De officiis*. Kahn, *Rhetoric, Prudence, and Skepticism*, p. 201 n. 19. An example of this proximity is Le Roy's dedication to Henri III, in which the opening line describes the king as already surrounded by 'a good number of prudent and wise persons ('bon nombre de prudens & sçavans personnages', p. aij). Guillaume Budé glossed the connection (and difference) between prudence (*prudentia*) and wisdom (*sapientia*) in *De philologia*. Guillaume Budé, *Philologie/ De philologia*, ed. and tr. by Marie-Madeleine de la Garanderie (Paris: Belles lettres, 2001), p. 18.

[75] Turchetti, 'Bodin as Self-Translator', p. 113.

'jurisconsults'. These are all broadly civil categories, belonging in Henri
III's Palace Academy, the humanist study, or the *Parlement*; despite
Bodin's syncretist gestures religion is consistently presented as a separate
field of action and enquiry from that defined by *la politique*.[76]

Le Roy and Bodin were Catholic, but neither refers to the contemporary
Church very often; faith is always the more abstract *religion*, and references
to the civil wars are not framed in confessional terms. In this respect the
authors seem to be staking out a space in which civil actors (*politiques*) can
resolve questions that they are determined to understand in civil (*politique*)
terms. Le Roy, in his commentary of Aristotle v, 2, highlights the
separation of 'la religion' and 'la police', arguing that they are served
by different kinds of magistrates (p. 395) – Bodin draws a similar admin-
istrative distinction between the two in the *République* (III, 7, p. 383).[77] In
I, 3, Bodin specifically disassociates 'moral discourse' from 'that
which is *politique*', leaving the former to 'Philosophers and Theologians'
(p. 52). A further distinction between ethics (*la morale*) and politics is also
made in I, I:

> The principle end of [the well-ordered Republic] lies in contemplative
> virtues, although political actions precede them, and the least illustrious
> come first: such as those taken to make necessary provision for the main-
> tenance and defence of the lives of subjects. And yet such actions relate to
> moral actions, and these to intellectual life, the end of which is contempla-
> tion of the greatest subject that exists and is imaginable. (I, I, pp. 36–37)[78]

Here, 'political actions' are necessary to facilitate 'contemplative virtues',
belonging to a separate but related sphere to the moral and intellectual; at
the most basic level they are carried out to preserve life, but ultimately
serve the greater 'end', which is contemplation of the divine. *Politique*
pragmatism, condemned so vituperatively later in the period, appears here

---

[76] On Henri III's Palace Academy, see Greengrass, *Governing Passions*, pp. 42–54. Still, we should not
underestimate Bodin's zeal for using legal and political means to pursue nominally spiritual or
religious projects, such as his persecution of witches. Lloyd points to Bodin's obsession with sorcery
as one way in which the religious and the spiritual were at the heart of his preoccupations, and his
politics. Lloyd, *'This Pre-eminent Man of France'*, p. 170.

[77] Sophie Nicholls shows the important role of his conception of *police* in Bodin's political thought
and gives an account of attempts made in the 1570s to reunite 'religion' and 'police', for example by
René Choppin in *De sacra politia* ('On the Sacred Polity', 1577). See Chapters 5–6 of *Political
Thought in the French Wars of Religion*.

[78] 'Nous ferons mesme jugement de la Republique bien ordonnee, la fin principale de laquelle gist aux
vertus contemplatives, jaçoit que les actions politiques soyent preallables, et les moins illustres
soyent les premieres: comme faire provisions necessaires, pour entretenir et defendre la vie des
subjects: et neantmoins telles actions se rapportent aux morales, et celles cy aux intellectuelles, la fin
desqelles est la contemplation du plus beau subject qui soit, et qu'on puisse imaginer.'

as a necessary stepping-stone to moral good. It is indicative of shifting political vocabulary that political action here is described as 'necessary' rather than prudent; like Machiavelli, Bodin will characterise politics as the art of the necessary, but to a different end, since Bodin seeks neither civic virtue nor the glory of the city unless as stepping-stones to the static harmony he imagines will result from the proper distribution of sovereign power in a nascent nation state.[79]

Bodin's *Sages Politiques*

When used to describe a kind of person, *politique* appears most often in Bodin in conjunction with *sage* ('wise'), rather than any cognate of 'prudent', especially in Books IV to VI, which are, broadly speaking, concerned with administration in practice rather than with establishing principles and structures as in Books I–III.[80] Between *sage* and *politique* it is sometimes unclear which is the noun and which the adjective, whether together they indicate 'a wise person whose wisdom concerns politics' or 'a *politique* who is wise'. Where *politique* reads more as the noun, it might have been necessary to qualify [him] as 'wise' in order to indicate that he is *not* one of the bad *politiques* with whom later writers become obsessed. Machiavelli figures in Bodin's preface as an unwise *politique*.[81] In that discussion of Machiavelli, Bodin writes that diligent readers (who have 'wisely weighed, subtly resolved, and discussed political issues in a learned manner') will agree that Machiavelli has never truly sounded the depths of political science (*Préface*, p. 12).[82] Bodin then concludes the preface by inviting his reader to 'censure at their discretion' the text that follows ('censurer à vostre discretion') (*Préface*, p. 14).[83] The *sage politique*, as well as an idealised administrator, will also be – like him – a proficient reader of ancient, legal and biblical texts, and also, of course, of Bodin's own text.

---

[79] On the French reception of the Machiavellian concept of necessity, see Demonet, 'Le politique "nécessaire" de Montaigne', pp. 17–18.

[80] Uses of *sage Politique* or *sages politiques* in Book IV: pp. 98, 101, 109, 149, 212; in Book V: pp. 11, 125; in Book VI, pp. 82, 163, 257. These account for *c.* 20 per cent of all uses of the term in the *République*.

[81] On the reception of Machiavelli in the sixteenth century, see Sidney Anglo, *Machiavelli: The First Century* (Oxford: Oxford University Press, 2005), especially the section on France, pp. 183–324.

[82] 'ceux qui ont accoustumée de discourir doctement, peser sagement, et resoudre subtilement les hauts affaires d'estat, s'accorderont qu'il n'a jamais sondé le gué de la science Politique'.

[83] Chesters writes that 'discrétion' has four particular associations in the French Renaissance: separation, judgement, prudence and secrecy; in Bodin the dimensions of judgement and prudence seem to be at work. Chesters notes that the doublet 'sage et discret' is very common. See Chesters, 'Discretion', pp. 105–06.

A strong thrust of Bodin's argument in 1, 1 is that the number of people who could ever be described as wise is inevitably very small, though they are desperately needed to help a society manage its unfortunate variety of customs and laws (1, 1, p. 32).[84] Primarily, the role outlined by Bodin for these *sages politiques* is to maintain the stability of the state. For example, in 1, 5, the *politique* figure is the subject in a maxim-like phrase: 'the wise *politic* is not he who expels thieves from the Republic but he who prevents them from entering' (1, 5, p. 109); their means of doing so is the establishment of poorhouses, following the example of Paris, Lyon, and Venice.[85] The wise *politique* of the *République* is, moreover, imbued with an exceptional level of agency, able to counter the tempests and twists of fate that Bodin describes as the scourge of republics. Book IV is concerned with political change (and its apparent synonym, 'ruin'). In the final subsection of the IV, 3, under the title 'The wise *politique* must follow the work of God in the government of this world' ('Il faut que le sage politique suyve les œuvres de Dieu au gouvernement de ce monde'), Bodin makes it clear that the role of the *Politique* is to resist sudden change (IV, 3, p. 109). He emphasises that change should be 'gentle and natural, if possible, and not violent or bloody' ('doux et naturel, si faire se peut, et non pas violent ny sanglant', p. 10). In the same chapter Bodin argues that 'the wise' escape astrological influence thanks to their learning. The 'sage Politique' in particular can use his wisdom to alter the future and effectively cheat fate:

> If then we have discovered that astral power, which we believed unavoidable, can weaken, and wise Doctors have found ways of changing illness and diverting fevers from their natural course in order to cure the sick more easily, why can the wise *Politique*, who foresees the changes that naturally arise in Republics, not prevent their ruin with advice and appropriate remedies? (IV, 3, p. 98)[86]

---

[84] Goyet's analysis of the restricted circle of the truly prudent leads him to a similar conclusion: he loosely translates this exclusive group as 'the happy few', Goyet, *Les audaces de la prudence*, p. 29. Scholar describes Montaigne's imagined group of freethinkers in the same terms, *Montaigne and the Art of Free-Thinking*, p. 107.

[85] 'Or le sage politic n'est pas celuy qui chasse de la Republique les voleurs, mais celuy qui les empesche d'y entrer.' On the 'contestation of the boundaries of political space in the early modern period', see Brett, *Changes of State*, pp. 3–7.

[86] 'Si donc on a descouvert que la force des astres, qu'on pensoit inevitable, se peut affoiblir, et que les sages Medecins ont trouvé des moyens pour changer les maladies, et alterer les fievres contre leur cours naturel, à fin de les guarir plus aisement: pourquoy le sage Politique prevoyant les changemens qui adviennent naturellement aux Republiques, ne previendra par conseil et remedes convenables la ruïne d'icelles?'

The *sage Politique* uses his agency to provide 'advice et remedies' and so to conserve the state via a kind of vision ('foresees') of corruptions that threaten the body politic. The fading power of astrology and rise of human agency here may originate in a reading of Machiavelli, and also evokes changing scientific perceptions of the solar system.[87] What this amounts to is counter-revolution in the most literal sense of the term: a wise *politique* can act against the movements of the stars, against fortune's wheel.

In the preceding chapter we saw that for writers like Budé and Le Caron, political action was fundamentally flexible and accommodating of change. Bodin's reimagining of politics is a blueprint for the management of gradual change, ultimately intended to eliminate all deviation. His preference for gradual change echoes some of what Montaigne suggests in his chapter on custom (I, 23, 'Of custom, and not easily changing an accepted law'). Their respective positions must be understood as responses to the chaos wrought by civil war but these anti-change agendas may now read as conservative, again in literal terms.[88] Certainly there is more to such attitudes than a simple desire to preserve life and property. The role assigned by Bodin, albeit loosely, to those he qualifies as *politique* is not to reform, or to preserve liberty: that is not how they use their exceptional agency. Bodin's wise *politique* is reactionary, a discerning cog within a rigid overall structure that ideally would change as little as possible. Unlike Montaigne, who criticised Bodin for his failure to see that things could have 'different faces', Bodin believes in a singular (though complex) shape to truth and justice, and his *politiques* are its administrators.[89] He even makes it clear that thought crimes of a certain order (wishing to kill, or even *thinking* about killing the sovereign) should be prosecuted (II, 5, pp. 75–76). He makes it the task of politics to consolidate power and minimise alteration and threat to the centre of power embodied by the

---

[87] John M. Najemy, 'Machiavelli and History', *Renaissance Quarterly*, 67.4 (2014), 1131–64.

[88] The conservatism of these writers is debatable. Montaigne was writing a new, experimental genre (the 'essay'), and Bodin attempting a new account of the political – both are prepared to do away with norms if they deem it necessary. Still, Montaigne is frequently described as conservative (see Jean Starobinski, *Montaigne en mouvement* [Paris: Gallimard, 1982, repr. 1993], pp. 459–542, esp. 500–25), and on such terms, Bodin is arguably more conservative than Montaigne; both of their approaches to change seem in some ways to foreshadow, for instance, Burke's reaction to the French Revolution. It should hardly need stating, however, that pre-modern conservative views are not the same as modern Western conservatism, with which Bodin's extensive government and powerful multitude of lawyers and magistrates would sit uneasily. See Corey Robin's definition (and critique) of conservatism in *The Reactionary Mind: Conservatism from Edmund Burke to Sarah Palin* (Oxford: Oxford University Press, 2011), pp. 13–16.

[89] Montaigne, II, 32, p. 667: 'But it is folly to judge by one feature things with so many aspects' ('Mais c'est folie de juger d'un traict, les choses à tant de visages', p. 763).

sovereign. This, theoretically, would eventually make politics superfluous: ultimately, harmonious administration should transcend political management of necessity and contingence (this kind of management could be understood as the 'least illustrious' primary political actions described in Book 1).[90]

This was not how Le Roy defined political action. In contrast with Bodin's goal of fixity, Le Roy places greater faith in politics as innovation within inevitable vicissitudes.[91] This is a core part of the difference between the two writers and a consequence of Le Roy's sense of the inextricable link between politics and history: for him, this is not something to transcend. In his conception of how people will be able to work with *la politique*, Le Roy emphasises its creative function, facilitated by the right kind of teaching:

> Whoever tries to found a new administration ['police'], restore a ruined one, conserve an ancient one, reform a corrupted one, or run the administration of one which is well established, if he is born to politics, well instructed and experienced in it, with the good judgement to consider at length the nature of each kind of state, its beginnings, its growth, strength, decadence, changes, and how one begins as another ends: he will do it much better if he is thus educated, and well-prepared. (p. biv)[92]

Here, the person acting politically in a number of ways might be starting, rebalancing, and reforming, as well as conserving and administering established states.

Politique Self-Fashioning

Le Roy and Bodin subtly identify themselves with the powerful *politiques* who govern the limits and applications of *la politique*: within the use of the term to denote a particular kind of man, there occurs a version of self-fashioning and self-promotion. Greengrass has made this point with respect to Bodin, and emphasised the impact of his experience as a

---

[90] For all that Bodin disavows More's *Utopia*, this is a kind of utopian negativity: links could be drawn with the discussion in Chapter 2 of a link between the 'no-place' of utopia and the desirability of a world with no politics and *politiques*.

[91] Their views of change and reaction may be where they differ, too, in their reception of Aristotle, especially of *Politics*, v, on factions and constitutional change.

[92] 'Quiconque entreprendra fonder nouvelle police, redresser la ruinee, conserver l'ancienne, reformer la corrompue, administrer l'establie, s'il est né à la politique, bien instruit et experimentee en icelle, ayant jugement de considerer murement la nature de chacune, leurs commencemens, acroissemens, forces, decadences, mutations, & comment l'une prent fin en l'autre: le fera beaucoup mieux ainsi endoctriné & preparé.'

député on his writings.[93] This self-fashioning is associated with the emergence of the new *élite savante* in French society to which Bodin and Le Roy belonged: the *noblesse de robe*, that group whose positions as lawyers, magistrates, and so on gave them increasing social capital. These positions were not evenly or fairly distributed; Lloyd comments that Bodin's career was a struggle in a context in which offices were increasingly purchased rather than awarded on merit.[94] Perhaps in order to improve their chances, despite their lack of inherited wealth, these authors worked to reinforce their own position within an implicitly constructed genealogy of *politique* experts. In so doing, they reinforce a hierarchy in which most people are excluded from participating in government.

At the conclusion of his preface to *Les Politiques d'Aristote*, after the list of verbs attached to *la politique*, Le Roy connects the abstracted feminine *politique* to the masculine plural, via a gerund in the same passage that I discussed above:

> She nourishes children, lifts the hearts of young men [. . . etc.], promising perpetual praise to true *politiques* ('vrais politiques') in recompense for their extreme labours, and the indignities they often receive in the form of attacks and troubles. (p. biv)

If these attacks and troubles seem prophetic of the avalanche of abuse later directed at so-called *Politiques*, Le Roy may have also been thinking of his career up to that point, characterised by large output and little patronage (Gundersheimer writes that 'penury was the paramount fact of Le Roy's material existence').[95] It could also be a reference to the struggles of philosophers defined by Bodin and Le Roy as *politiques*; Aristotle and Plato were exiled, and the death of Plato's teacher, Socrates, was the pre-eminent example of the danger of speaking truth to power in the ancient world. Le Roy opens his next sentence with the phrase 'concerning myself' ('au regard de moy'), saying that he has long frequented the courts of princes and is therefore in a position to reap the fruits to be found in joining together a reading of Aristotle and Plato with real experience of modern court life (p. aiij^v). Le Roy thus invites his reader to associate him with political expertise, and with the long-suffering true *politique*.

Bodin is also engaged in advertising himself as an innovator and new authority on political science; numerous references to Bodin as 'the Aristotle of the sixteenth century' are the measures of his success in

---

[93] Greengrass, 'The Experiential World of Jean Bodin', pp. 76–80.
[94] Lloyd, *'This Pre-eminent Man of France'*, p. 93.   [95] Gundersheimer, p. 71.

establishing himself as an authority on politics for the modern age.[96] Bodin
directly refers to a number of ancient figures, both rulers and writers, as
politiques, beginning with Polybius ('considered the wisest *politique* of his
time') in the preface (p. 12). As I mentioned above, Bodin frequently
names Aristotle as *politique*, for instance in v, 2 (p. 80), at the head of a list
that is a kind of genealogy of *politiques* whose works Bodin is updating and
bringing together rather than replacing. Bodin also raises the question of
who can, or ever could, live up to the great *politiques* of history: 'Who
could ever be like the great Augustus in political prudence?' he asks in iv, 6
(p. 152).[97] But the ancients set a standard to live up to, and one that can
even be surpassed – even if the moderns, not least Machiavelli, have too
often got it wrong. Bodin's treatment of Machiavelli is fraught, but that
does not mean that Machiavelli is excluded from being *politique*, or even
from being wise: I have already indicated Bodin's use of Machiavelli's ideas
at various points. In the preface, Machiavelli is the only modern source
named, and thus implicitly credited with reviving political science, albeit
with evil consequences. Bodin's unacknowledged debts to Machiavelli in
the *République* may be most obvious in in v, 5 ('If it is good to arm
subjects and give them military training, to fortify towns, and to wage war'
/ 'S'il est bon d'armer et aguerrir les sujets, fortifier les villes, et entretenir la
guerre') in which he deals with 'the military and political [= *politique*] arts'
(v, 5, p. 156).[98] In the introduction to the chapter, in which Bodin
introduces his primary question (essentially: is a militarised society a good
idea?), he writes that the question is a difficult one: he will do his best,
but leave a conclusion to the wiser *politiques* ('[aux] plus sages *politiques*')
(v, p. 125).[99] Here, with the comparative 'plus sages politiques', Bodin
comes close to naming himself among the *politiques* of his text; while
conceding to greater authorities, Bodin subtly places himself among them.
And more: he associates himself with Machiavelli here, if indirectly, since
Machiavelli is a *politique* who has written extensively about the art of war.
Machiavelli could then be allowed as one of the 'sages politiques' to whom

---

[96] See Lloyd, 'Introduction', in *The Reception of Bodin*, pp. 1–20 (p. 2).

[97] 'Qui fut onques semblable à ce grand Auguste en prudence politique?'

[98] Sidney Anglo has pointed out Bodin's possible use of Machiavelli in this chapter; see Anglo,
p. 542. Anglo writes that Machiavelli's *Arte della guerra* used many commonplace *topoi* and so it is
hard to infer direct influence on writers dealing with this subject. Lloyd also points out that iv, 1
(on change in governmental forms) is also considered Bodin's Machiavellian chapter par
excellence, Lloyd, '*This Pre-eminent Man of France*', p. 127.

[99] 'Je mettray le plus sommairement que faire se pourra, et ce qu'il me semble pour le mieux, laissant
toutefois la resolution aux plus sages politiques.'

Bodin refers as greater authorities on the subject. At a stretch, this could even be a suggestion of further reading.

There is one instance in Bodin's *République*, at the opening of v, 6 (on alliances and treaties between princes), where the *politique* appears as a noun in its own right: 'This chapter depends on the previous, and should not be neglected, since neither Jurisconsult nor *Politique* has treated it' (v, 6, p. 165).[100] The phrase in v, 6 is an almost exact *reprise* of the introduction to 1, 8 where Bodin asserts the need to define sovereignty 'since no Jurisconsult or political philosopher' has ever done so. v, 6 stands out as the only use of 'politique' on its own. Since 'sage politique' is used fairly frequently in Book vi, it could hardly be argued that this moment marks any kind of fundamental shift, but it may still represent a minor threshold moment at which all the philosophy, wisdom, and learning with which *politique* is associated across the *République* have been sufficiently absorbed that the word *politique* can stand alone, as a kind of abbreviation for relevant knowledge and the wise application thereof. Since Bodin, who was, although trained as a jurisconsult, more of a go-between between different offices of power and influence, embarks upon attempts to define and treat subjects thus far neglected, he cannot be ruled out from being *politique* by his own definition in this context.

Neither Bodin nor Le Roy would have considered that they could be criticised on the grounds of elitism or exclusivity. Plato's 'gold, silver, and bronze' castes and descriptions of a 'guardian' class were even more overtly exclusionary. In Aristotelian terms, hierarchies of power were considered natural and biologically determined. Cicero, too, is clear that the many should be governed by the few, who had to be both well-born and wealthy.[101] As such, Bodin is quite unusual in his lack of stipulations about a *politique*'s family background: the number of people with appropriate wisdom and discretion is small enough that his *politiques* are by definition an exclusive group. Le Roy, on the other hand, despite rising to prominence from a relatively lowly background, frequently describes the true *politique* as both born and made, 'being born reasonable and *politique*', and 'born to politics' (*Préface*, p. biv). There is a slippage in the potential identity of this *politique* person in Le Roy; since in the 'born to politics' example he is referring to the prince or King, rather than the adviser, lawyer, or teacher, but elsewhere he Le Roy indicates that

---

[100] 'Ce traicté depend du precedent, qui ne doit pas estre laissé, attendu qu'il n'y a ni Jurisconsulte, ni Politique, qui l'ait touché.'
[101] Ryan, p. 142.

education and experience can make the right kind of man *politique*. The 'true *politiques*' evoked at the end of the preface seem a much broader category, and one that includes the author. Still, while Le Roy and Bodin, with their non-noble backgrounds, experienced a form of social mobility produced by their humanist training and facilitated by church education, neither is especially interested in facilitating such a path for others.

In terms of the wider principles of social hierarchy, in keeping with Aristotle's view that some are naturally born to servitude and some to politics, Le Roy, unlike Bodin, does not challenge the institution of slavery/servitude. Although Bodin is knowledgeable about non-European cultures and is exceptionally admiring of the Ottoman Empire, both authors broadly locate *politique* knowledge in Europe.[102] What this amounts to is a tacit policing of the boundaries of the select *politique* community: the abstract term *politique* is a tool of definition; *politique* people in the text delineate the borders of the wider community; and texts defined in some way as *politique* do the same for the shifting group of people identified as *politiques*, to the exclusion of the majority of the world population, and of all women. The exclusions of women, effeminate men, and non-Western Europeans from political authority are, moreover, connected. Le Roy writes in his commentary on v, 5 that the prince is mistrusted by his subjects when he shows himself to be 'variable, light, effeminate, and cowardly' (p. 357). He then discusses the Assyrian King, Sardanapalus, who reportedly would have preferred to be female, and who brought his kingdom to ruin. Geographically oriented gender anxiety is present in v, 1 of the *République*, in which the effeminacy of 'southern' peoples is a crucial reason for their lack of political supremacy, and is given as a cause of the failure of the Moorish peoples to ever conquer hypermasculine France (v, 1, p. 19). For Bodin, the Ottomans Turks were fundamentally a 'Northern' people who had moved southwards, hence the admirable qualities of their empire.[103]

Le Roy strengthens the exclusivity of *politique* in his translation. We have already seen how 'good' Latinate translations of the Greek *politikos* were established by Bruni, via Cicero, as located in the *civilis* word group. Le Roy follows this rule in some instances, notably in his translations of the phrase 'man is a political animal'. At the beginning of this chapter I cited his rewriting of the phrase. The full excerpt is as follows:

---

[102] See in particular Bodin's cosmographical survey in v, 1, and Malcolm, 'Positive Views of Islam and Ottoman Rule', and *Useful Enemies*, especially p. 74 (on the *Methodus*) and pp. 153–58 (on the *République*).

[103] Malcolm, *Useful Enemies*, p. 220.

> For although man is naturally civil, and more sociable than any other animal, and therefore has the gift of reason and speech in order to communicate, nonetheless he is subject to passions that often trouble him, and to unpleasant desires that incessantly drawn him away from the good, and so it has been necessary to propose some laws ... (p. iij)[104]

In his translation of the phrase 'political animal'/ 'zoon politikon' in the main text of the *Politics* itself, Le Roy has 'civil animal', and in his commentary notes that the city is made up of 'men who are naturally civil and *politique*' ('hommes naturellement civils & politiques') (pp. 14–15). But are all men in the city always both *civil* and *politique*?

Directly following the discussion of man as a civil/political animal, Le Roy arrives at the section on 'obedience and empire', in which civil society is organised according to two kinds of governmental relationships: 'seigneurial' and 'politique'; translating 'mastery' as 'seigneurial' incorporates French vocabulary of social hierarchy. Aristotle writes that models for these two kinds of government can be found in man himself, since his soul has mastery over the movements of his body, while 'the political and royal intellect' ('l'intellect politique et royal') controls his desires and thoughts (p. 30; Aristotle *Politics*, 1254b2). A further separation between 'politique' and 'seigneurial' is made in Le Roy's commentary on slavery/servitude, where Le Roy writes that 'le politique' is 'concerned with those who are free and equal by nature, between whom there are vicissitudes of commanding and obeying: the seigneurial concerns those who are serfs by nature' (p. 40). In Le Roy's interpretation of Aristotle, all society is *civil*, and within that there are *politique* and *seigneurial* relationships. His earlier statements about the pertinence and use of his translation and commentary rather suggest that this concerns his own moment rather than being a purely historical account of power and hierarchy in Aristotle's Athens.

For Le Roy, then, *politique* defines social hierarchies as well as forms of government and of political agency; it reinforces the superiority of a small group of men over the majority of their fellow men, and certainly over women.[105] The exclusion of women, in theory at least, from some political roles does not, however, mean that women are not important in thinking

---

[104] 'Car jaçoit que l'homme soit naturellement civil, & plus sociable que nul autre animal, & soit à cest effect doué de raison & de parole pour la communication: toutefois estant subject aux passions qui le troublent souvent, & aux convoitises mauvaises qui le retirent incessamment du bien, il a esté necessaire proposer quelques commandemens ...'

[105] On gender and female authority in early modern France, see Julie Hardwick, *The Practice of Patriarchy: Gender and the Politics of Household Authority in Early Modern France* (Pennsylvania, PA: Pennsylvania State University Press, 1998); Thierry Wanegffelen, *Le pouvoir contesté: Souveraines d'Europe à la Renaissance* (Paris: Payot, 2008); Domna Stanton, *The Dynamics of*

on politics or the political in the period. Indeed, attention to gender and the policing of gender roles – with gender understood not as a shorthand for 'women' but as a nexus of relations implicating masculine, feminine, and all the overlaps between them – was a structuring device of early modern political thought, as Anna Becker has shown.[106] We see this literalised in the personification of the abstract noun, *la politique*, as a calming, balancing female figure who distributes justice evenly and consoles the (implicitly male) 'true *politiques*' who act in her name.

This kind of incarnation of an abstract ideal in a venerated female figure is fairly typical for this period; we saw it in Chapter 2 in Le Caron's *Claire*. Such veneration does little for real women. Le Roy's translation stays very close to Aristotle on this issue. Translating the now notorious section on women's reduced intellectual capacity (*Politics*, 1260a4), Le Roy renders the opening as a statement that husbands control wives 'politiquement' ('politically') (p. 64).[107] Political relationships between men denote equality of birth, but a high-born woman is not awarded equal status:

> The husband commands his wife politically, not because there is equality between them, or vicissitudes of command that do not and should not exist; this authority is defined as political by the vigour, strength, authority, gravity, and prudence of words and deeds that nature commonly gives in greater quantity to the male than to the female. (p. 64)[108]

This passage places all the qualities associated with *politique* across the text explicitly in a masculine agent: vigour, authority, prudence and so on. Le Roy's only comment on this is to note that one Durant, a *politique* Magistrate, exemplified all the qualities denied women by Aristotle (p. 64); his commentary reinforces Aristotle's misogyny. In sum, among men, some are governed by the rules of *la politique* and could be *politique* themselves (there is a vicissitudinous movement within this group as to

---

Gender in Early Modern France: Women Writ, Women Writing (Farnham: Ashgate, 2014). The fashioning of a masculine *politique* subject is not just about controlling, excluding, and subjugating the feminine: it is part of an interrogation and policing of masculine identity. See Long, *Masculinity in Crisis*. See also Becker, 'Gender in the History of Early Modern Political Thought', and *Gendering the Renaissance Commonwealth*.

[106] Becker writers that 'gender structured the politicial', in *Gendering the Renaissance Commonwealth*, p. 227.

[107] Aristotle, *Politics*, 1259a37. On this section see Becker, 'Gender in the History of Early Modern Political Thought', pp. 16–17: she shows how the figure of the wife becomes *political* and by analogy the citizen becomes a kind of wife to the state in early modern political thought.

[108] 'Le mary commande la femme politiquement, non pour le regard de la parité de l'homme et de la femme, et vicissitude de commander qui ne sont ny doivent estre en eux: mais à la vigueur, force, auctorité, gravité, prudence en faicts et dicts, que nature donne communément plus grand au masle que à la femme.'

who actually wields power at different moments), and some are 'serfs by nature'; women are entirely relegated to servility through their apparently innate relative lack of *politique* qualities.

Politics and marriage were especially 'strongly intertwined' in this period.[109] In *République* 1, 3, Bodin establishes an analogous relation between the state and the family, and within this draws an analogy between marriage and statecraft.[110] He refers to the Aristotelian trope discussed above about the soul controlling the body and the intellect controlling the mind; this is his opening gesture, before saying that he will leave the moral aspect of the question to 'philosophers and theologians', and instead focus on what is 'politique':

> Thus we leave moral discourse to the philosophers and theologians and will take up that which is political [*politique*] concerning the power of the husband over the wife, which is the source and origin of all human society. (p. 52)[111]

When he translated this passage into Latin, for 'that which is political' he gave 'quod hujus quaestionis proprium est' – what is proper, or appropriate, to the topic at hand. This at once defines the 'quaestiones' of the book, or at least of this chapter, as 'politique' (if you work backwards to the French), associates 'politique' with 'proprium', and makes the question of man's control of women as one of politics, propriety, and of property.[112] Men control (and possess) wives as they possess property; but women also define the men who are said to control them:

> How much those who take such pleasure in commanding effeminate husbands resemble those who prefer to lead the blind than to follow the wise and the clear-sighted ('clairvoyans'). For God's law and the holy tongue, which named all things according to their true nature and property, called the husband *Bahal*, that is to say lord and master, to show that it is his role to command. (p. 60)[113]

---

[109] Becker, *Gendering the Renaissance Commonwealth*, p. 223.

[110] On Bodin and the family, see Becker, *Gendering the Renaissance Commonwealth*, pp. 106–44. Becker shows how Bodin's treatment of the Aristotelian marriage is grounded in Bodin's sense of the family as a privileged structuring unit in the commonwealth. She also points out Bodin's subtle account of the 'conjugal bond' in the *République*, p. 125.

[111] 'Or nous laissons aux philosophes et theologiens le discours moral et prendrons ce qui est politique pour le regard de la puissance du mari sur la femme, qui et la source et origine de toute societé humaine.'

[112] Kathy Eden shows that *proprium* indicated both something fitting and something owned. See Kathy Eden, *The Renaissance Rediscovery of Intimacy* (Chicago, IL: Chicago University Press, 2012), pp. 26–27.

[113] 'Combien que celles qui prennent si grand plaisir à commander aux maris effeminés ressemblent à ceux qui aiment mieux guider les aveugles que de suivre les sages et clairvoyans. Or la loy de Dieu

Powerful women are figured here as preferring 'effeminate' men, and so preferring to lead the blind than be led by the wise. To be 'wise and clear-sighted' is to be squarely placed in the *politique* semantic field established in the *République*; women are thus excluded from being *politique* but also used to define *politique* men and their behaviour. The relationship is similar to that between the abstract *la politique* and the active concrete 'real *politiques*' in Le Roy. Bodin, of course, documented his hatred and fear of women in his treatise on witchcraft.[114] Nor is he shy about directly criticising female rule in the *République*, unlike Le Roy, who may have refrained owing to the patronage he sought and received from Catherine de' Medici in the 1560s. In VI, 5, invoking Salic law, Bodin argues against female rule, suggesting that female power in public government might subvert what he had established as a fundamental law of humanity in 1, 3 (male dominion over women in the private sphere) and thus contravene a key 'political rule' ('reigle politique', VI, 5, p. 234). Bodin establishes women as being under the command of men in 1, 3 near the very beginning of the six-book structure and excludes them from politics via 'a political rule' near the very end.

We thus see that for Bodin, as for Le Roy, women and the feminine are used to define what is *politique*, and *politique* is used to define their exclusion. These acts of definition and exclusion are gendered not only in their treatment of women, but as visions of controlled – and control-ling – masculinity, with male political actors stalked by the threatening potential charge of effeminacy. In real life, women had more power and agency than either author could allow; not only the queens who wielded enormous power in European courts, but – in restricted but significant ways – in networks and communities across social classes.[115] For all their pragmatism, then, Le Roy and Bodin offer a masculinised vision of politics

---

et la langue saincte, qui a nommé toutes choses selon la vraye nature et proprieté, appelle le mari *Bahal*, c'est à dire le seigneur et maistre, pour monstrer qu'à luy appartient de commander.'

[114] Stuart Clark clarifies that Bodin and his fellow demonologists were not 'only' motivated by misogyny, and demonological treatises were in fact not the most virulently misogynistic texts of their era. See Stuart Clark, 'The 'Gendering' of Witchcraft in Early Modern French Demonology: Misogyny or Polarity', *French History*, 5.4 (1990), 426–37 (pp. 429 and 431). Clark has argued that the *République* and the *Démonomanie* ought to be read as intrinsically connected in *Thinking with Demons: Witchcraft in Early Modern Europe* (Oxford: Oxford University Press, 1999), pp. 670–71. See also Lloyd, '*This Pre-eminent Man of France*', p. 170.

[115] See, for example, *The Politics of Female Households: Ladies-in-Waiting across Early Modern Europe*, ed. by Nadine Akkerman and Birgit Houben (Leiden and Boston, MA: Brill, 2014); Una McIlvenna, *Scandal and Reputation at the Court of Catherine de Medici* (London: Routledge, 2016); Suzannah Lipscomb, *The Voices of Nîmes: Women, Sex and Marriage in Reformation Languedoc* (Oxford: Oxford University Press, 2019).

that didn't precisely reflect the worlds they wrote about. We have seen that neither author left Aristotelian precepts unchallenged if they did not fit with their vision of the present and future state of France; neither wished simply to reproduce classical political philosophy without adjustment. If politics was a newly prominent and central intellectual endeavour in France in this period, its self-appointed spokesmen created within it a gender dynamic that, if unsurprising, was, in light of their own methods, by no means inevitable.

***

The *Président* of the *Parlement de Rouen* wrote in 1573 that:

> We do not intend to speak of how this word *politique* has been newly introduced and interpreted as indicating being of no religion; we use it according to the interpretation and definition given by wise men and philosophers, that is to say, knowing how to rule and govern a multitude of men.[116]

In 1573, then, five years after the first edition of Le Roy's translation of Aristotle and three years before the publication of Bodin's *République*, the term *politique* was circulating in elite discourse as a way of describing a person with a particular kind of knowledge resulting from the interpretations and definitions offered by 'wise men and philosophers'. The *président's* description of other *politiques* as potentially meaning 'being of no religion' – ominous in the context of confessional conflict, though not indicating atheism so much as a refusal to engage in partisan struggles in religious terms – anticipates the increased controversy *politique* attracted from 1576 onwards. The shadow cast by Machiavelli, the subtle divorce between ethics, religious devotion, and political action, and the pre-eminence of pragmatic prudence in their writing, all anticipate, too, the trouble to come, and the long history of *politiques* and politics as morally ambiguous or even amoral.

The *Président's* account of the term *politique* conforms to the uses of the term in Bodin and Le Roy, who use it with reference to ancient authorities (who are 'wise' and 'philosophers') in order to confer this authority on to themselves and some of their potential readers. Their uses of *politique* tell the story of a theoretical and practical response to civil war, and are the

---

[116] 'Nous n'entendons pas parler comme on a nouvellement introduit et interpreté ce mot *politicque* quasi: n'estant d'aucune religion, mais selon l'interprétation et définition des saiges et philosophes, c'est-à-dire sçavoir régir et gouverner une multitude d'hommes.' Quoted in Jouanna, *Le pouvoir absolu*, p. 177.

result of a humanist legacy, working together to shape a conceptual keyword (the feminine substantive) and its agent (the masculine substantive). The abstract term *politique*, consistently translated into English as 'politics', is often considered the neutral term in a pairing with its more mobile, polemical counterpart, *le Politique*, that refers to a person rather than to a concept (although the person, as we have seen, may be the incarnation of a concept).[117] However, I have suggested that they work in concert and that *la politique* is not neutrally framed: it can indicate reactive and/or creative politics, it is used to shape a political canon, and it operates within a fraught gender dynamic.

Le Roy and Bodin used the word *politique* to indicate the path to a solution to all manner of civil, juridical, or governmental problems, as well as to name a male person who is, in association with the abstract noun, the ultimate 'fixer'. Their writings were part of a revitalising of the field of politics as a distinct area of intellectual inquiry, and by the nature of their enterprise carry a certain optimism about the influence of thought on action, of rhetoric on reality, and the ideal on the real. Their engineering of meaning had the 'real-world' consequences of an altered curriculum at the *Collège royal* during Le Roy's tenure, as well as potentially empowering readers of various kinds of politics and *politiques* to act in legal and governmental contexts relating to the immediate crisis and beyond. Francis Goyet sees the rhetorical training that students in humanist colleges received as the training of a political elite; while acknowledging the anachronism in the analogy, he implies a similar system in place to that of the Ecole Nationale d'Administration (ENA) which supplied the Elysée with its *politiques* in contemporary France.[118] The history of the term *politique* plays its part in the early modern socio-political process of educating a new elite, with echoes in the present.

Despite their ultimately constructive sense of what *politiques* (as texts and as people) could achieve, both Le Roy and Bodin nonetheless have an ambiguous sense of man's power to change the world through sheer will. A paradoxical relationship with inevitability and contingency marks Bodin's understanding of politics in particular. While Le Roy accepted and even welcomed a degree of vicissitude, Bodin imagined the best possible world as one in which the wise actions of wise *politiques* would have predictable consequences because they would have prepared the

---

[117] See, for example, Demonet, who defines *la politique* as 'abstrait' and 'neutre', in 'Quelques avatars du mot "politique"', p. 54.

[118] Goyet, *Le sublime du lieu commun*, p. 33. President Emmanuel Macron announced the closure of the ENA in 2021, and its replacement, the 'Institute for Public Service'.

ground appropriately. Still, nothing was so predetermined about the way these authors conceptualised politics, or its real-world agents. Le Roy and Bodin style themselves as visionaries, and political action as dependent on a kind of vision or special insight, but they were by no means dominant voices in their lifetimes, and the differences between them demonstrate already the limitations of any attempt to definitively outline the proper nature and function of politics. In the next chapter, we turn to Huguenot polemicists who had their own visions of what would best serve the political community, and what kind of *politique* person should perform that service.

CHAPTER 4

A Wake-Up Call and A Call to Arms
Le reveille-matin des François *and Simon Goulart's* Mémoires de l'estat de France

The dynamism of political discussion in 1570s France, and the dangerous uncertainty it wrought, was in some ways what Jean Bodin was trying to write out of politics, notably in arguing that rebellion against a monarch is never legitimate.[1] We now turn to texts that do advocate such rebellion, often categorised as 'Huguenot resistance theory'.[2] Following the slaughter of a huge number of the country's Protestants, the exile or abjuration of many more, and the siege of the Protestant stronghold at La Rochelle, Protestant writers began to publish arguments that doubted or under-mined royal authority, suggesting that the French monarchy had become degraded, and the king a tyrant. Some of the most significant were in Latin: François Hotman's *Francogallia* (1573), Théodore de Bèze's *De jure magistratum* (1574), and the anonymous *Vindiciae contra tyrannos* (1579), but the works I discuss here are the best-known vernacular contributions to the discussion. In this chapter I turn from treatise and translation to dialogue and diatribe, with particular attention to two anonymous works. These are the *Reveille-matin des François* (a pair of dialogues first published in full in 1574) and a dialogue called 'Le Politique', which appears in Simon Goulart's *Mémoires des estats de France sous Charles IX* (1576–78). I also more briefly treat a work called 'Discours politiques', also in Goulart's *Mémoires*. The word *politique* appears most obviously in the title of the texts from Goulart's *Mémoires*, and in the *Reveille-matin* as the name

---

[1] Bodin, II, 5, p. 75. Becker and others show, however, that repudiating his direct contemporaries was not Bodin's main aim in the *République*. Becker, *Gendering the Renaissance Commonwealth*, p. 108.
[2] The phrase refers to works by French Huguenots theorising resistance to the authority of the monarch if the monarch's actions compromise their faith, thus acting in a manner incompatible with his role as purveyor of justice. They are not arguing against monarchy per se. Authors grouped under this heading are referred to in French criticism as 'monarchomaques'. For a detailed analysis of Huguenot resistance, see Quentin Skinner, *The Foundations of Modern Political Thought*, II, esp. Part III, pp. 189–349. See also Knecht, pp. 190–97, and Paul-Alexis Mellet, *Les traités monarchomaques: Confusion des temps, résistance armée et monarchie parfaite* (Geneva: Droz, 2007).

of one of the principal characters in both dialogues: 'le Politique', 'a French *Politic Seigneur*'.

These works do not break with the erudite traditions discussed in previous chapters but combine erudition and polemic. Their concern with preventing tyranny and their use of the dialogue form reflect the influence of earlier ideas (constitutionalism) and earlier texts (like the works of Le Caron and Pasquier discussed in Chapter 2). Paul-Alexis Mellet has argued, moreover, that – just as Bodin did not write the *République* exclusively for his immediate political moment – the Saint Bartholomew's Day massacres should not be considered the primary intellectual context of 'Huguenot resistance theory' even if this was surely a critical factor in the number of texts, the timing of their publication, and their frantic reception.[3] As always, longer-term intellectual processes and shorter-term contingencies intermingle in the representations of politics in these texts.

While the contexts and influences are varied, the form is perhaps even more so. All the texts are composite constructions, explicitly polyphonic in the dialogue form, and implicitly so in their organisation and construction. The mixing of 'original' narrative, criticism, and citation is as tangled as any postmodern 'bricolage' and problematises author–text relations in ways that anticipate J. Hillis Miller's deconstructionist characterisations of text and citation as alternately playing the roles of 'host' and 'parasite'.[4] Goulart's *Mémoires* and the *Reveille-matin* mix the works of several different authors, often without attribution; the most famous, or notorious, of such textual borrowing (or 'hosting') is a lengthy extract from La Boétie's *Discours de la servitude volontaire* in the *Reveille-matin*, delivered by the Politique without naming the author. The extract is mobilised in order to inspire readers to fight for freedom of worship.

Quentin Skinner has shown that the question of what exactly might constitute liberty was a consuming one in early modern political thought, and that there were arguments for religious freedom in this period that went at least as far back as Pico della Mirandola's search for universal truths in every religious tradition.[5] In Chapter 2, I mentioned how Skinner contrasts principled arguments for freedom with the 'merely *politique*

---

[3] Mellet, *Les traités monarchomaques*. The range of references in the texts to classical and contemporary authors and various political questions supports Mellet's view.
[4] J. Hillis Miller, 'The Critic as Host', *Critical Inquiry*, 3 (1977), 439–77.
[5] Skinner, *Foundations*, p. 244.

defence of religious liberty'.[6] However, as we shall see in this chapter, Huguenot writers attempted to harness the contemporary force of politics and *politiques*, to make their principled defences of liberty political, and *politique*, in their own terms. This led at least some of them to personify the *politique* in ways that defy the traditional narrative of *politique* moderation, and to further trouble the relation between politics, *politiques*, and Machiavelli. As we shall see, the relation between 'Machiavel' and *politique* is not one of straightforward negative association.

The Borrowers: The *Reveille-matin* and the *Mémoires*

The *Reveille-matin*, according to Robert Kingdon the 'most popular and widely circulated piece of Protestant propaganda' of the period, appeared under a pseudonym with a false printing location on the frontispiece.[7] Scholarly disagreements concerning the circumstances of its composition and publication demonstrate the complexity and enduring evasiveness of clandestine print culture. Kingdon considers that, despite its own claim to have been printed in Edinburgh, the *Reveille-matin* was printed in Strasbourg by the same press that issued a German version of Rabelais's *Pantagruel* and *Gargantua* so as to put Rabelais's anti-clericalism to work for the anti-Catholic cause; the most recent editors of the text, Jean-Raymond Fanlo, Marino Lambiase, and Paul-Alexis Mellet, suggest based on typographical analysis that it may rather have been printed somewhere in the German Palatinate, possibly Heidelberg.[8] The author question is also vexed.[9] It may be that there were several authors and editors, given the variation of 'voices' across the texts, some of whom were there without permission. Baranova suggests, based on her study of Pierre de L'Estoile's collection which contains pamphlets bearing strong resemblances to sections

---

[6] Prior to Saint Bartholomew's Day the author of *Question politique*, attributed to jurist Jean de Coras, was already making the question of Huguenot liberty a *politique* question. See above, pp. 111–12.

[7] Robert M. Kingdon, *Myths about the St Bartholomew's Day Massacres 1572–1576* (Cambridge, MA: Harvard University Press, 1988), p. 70.

[8] See 'Introduction', in *Le reveille-matin des François*, ed. by Jean-Raymond Fanlo, Marino Lambiase, and Paul-Alexis Mellet (Paris: Garnier, 2016), pp. 7–138 (pp. 112–16).

[9] Donald Kelley sees similarities between the *Reveille-matin* and another work attributed to Nicolas Barnaud, *Le miroir des françois* (Paris, 1582), which is also a series of dialogues; the fifth dialogue is between a character called 'Politique' and 'Themis' (a figure for law). He considers that Barnaud held an idealistic, humanist-inspired view of the role of the *homo politicus*. See Kelley, *The Beginnings of Ideology*, p. 204. Kingdon doubts this potential attribution, p. 70. For a summary of current views on the authorship of the *Reveille-matin*, see Fanlo, Lambiase, and Mellet, pp. 87–107. They acknowledge continuities between the *Miroir des françois* and the *Reveille-matin* but doubt that Barnaud was the author of either.

of the *Reveille-matin*, that there must have been at least eight different authors.[10] Kingdon posits an English author for the first part of the second dialogue, which amounts to a lengthy critique of Elizabethan religious policy, and suggests that the final section of the first dialogue must have had a different author to the rest of it because, essentially, the prose is less lively (he calls it 'dry').[11] By contrast, Fanlo, Lambiase, and Mellet stand against the multiple-author position; they are sufficiently persuaded by continuities of style and content across the two dialogues that they argue for one supremely erudite author, and draw an admiring character sketch of this individual, probably residing in Geneva, who united humanist learning with reformist zeal, their identity mysterious to this day.[12]

The most direct engagement with the idea of an author in the text itself is the pseudonym on the frontispiece, 'Eusèbe Philadelphe Cosmopolite'. This name encourages the reader to imagine either a group of authors, or a member of the Reformed faith representing a group position; 'Eusèbe' refers to the Church historian Eusebius, 'Philadelphe' is a transliteration of the Greek for 'brotherly love', and 'Cosmopolite' emphasises both the internationalism of the dialogues and multiplicity potentially of both place and of people. The name 'Eusèbe Philadelphe' was used by Nicolas Barnaud as well as by Théodore de Bèze and Hugues Doneau; Iagolnitzer thinks that the pseudonym implies a network of authors – she suggests that a group that included Barnaud, Doneau, Goulart, and François Hotman compiled much of the *Reveille-matin*. Hotman has been posited as a main editor, but Iagolnitzer casts doubt on this, suggesting that although he may have brought together many of the materials, he left it to Doneau to write it up.[13] Overall it seems persuasive that there may have been a 'lead' author with a network of contributors. The hypothesis of a network of prominent Protestant men of letters being responsible for the *Reveille-matin*, directly and indirectly, perhaps goes some way to explaining how the *Discours de la servitude volontaire* ended up in print

---

[10] Baranova, *A coup de libelles*, p. 189.

[11] Kingdon, pp. 79 and 75. Kingdon suggests the prominent Elizabethan puritan, Thomas Cartwright. It is worth noting, however, that this serves Kingdon's overall argument about the international and internationalising focus of Protestant writings in the post-Saint-Bartholomew period. This has been questioned by Huchard, who emphasises the specificity of the French context for which, in her view, the authors were primarily writing. See Kingdon, p. 72, and Cécile Huchard, *D'encre et de sang. Simon Goulart et la Saint-Barthélemy* (Paris: Champion, 2007), p. 10.

[12] Fanlo, Lambiase, Mellet, 'Introduction', pp. 87–91.

[13] Mitchiko Iagolnitzer, 'La publication du "Discours de la servitude volontaire" dans les "Dialogi" ou le "Reveille-matin des Français"', *Bulletin de la société des amis de Montaigne*, 18–19 (1976), 99–108 (pp. 107–08).

in its pages, having up to this point only circulated among a limited audience in manuscript form.[14] Moreover, this would also point to the form in some way reflecting the process of composition: dialogue and discussion within this network of readers and writers led to the printed dialogues of the *Reveille-matin*, whether compiled by one hand or several.

The *Reveille-matin* dialogues were quickly translated into several languages, and widely circulated across Europe, though owing to the criticism of Elizabeth I, and the radical propositions made by the prophet Daniel, who appears at the end of the first dialogue, they was not universally well received even by committed Protestants.[15] The activities of a well-organised and highly motivated network of Calvinists operating from their central hub in Geneva to spread the Reform across France, in a targeted and initially very successful campaign, have been well documented.[16] But by the 1570s, as the reception of the *Reveille-matin* shows, the leading pastors in Geneva were not entirely in control of their flock; some of their most talented and prolific propagandists, horrified by events in their homeland, threatened to go rogue.

One such rogue-in-the-making was Simon Goulart, whose output in various fields was so prolific and diverse – as an editor, translator, adaptor, commentator, historian, historiographer, mediator between Calvinists and Lutherans, and author of *nouvelles*, essays, poems, and of one very unsuccessful play – that he has been called a 'seismograph' of cultural trends and contemporary thought.[17] Born in 1543, he converted to Calvinism in Paris while studying law in the 1560s, and was ordained as a pastor in 1566. His reputation was sufficiently established in Geneva by the 1570s that he was commissioned by the authorities to write corrections to Bodin's *République* (largely concerning the depiction of Geneva), which were incorporated into the clandestine edition of the *République* that was printed in 1577; Lloyd notes that Bodin incorporated many of these changes into his own second edition.[18] Goulart was one of the most prolific and widely read literary pastors, though he eventually fell foul of the Genevan authorities. He is perhaps best remembered for his *Mémoires*

---

[14] On Protestant letter networks, see Mark Greengrass, 'Informal Networks in Sixteenth-Century French Protestantism', in *Society and Culture in the Huguenot World 1559–1685*, ed. by Raymond A. Mentzer and Andrew Spicer (Cambridge: Cambridge University Press, 2002), pp. 78–97; especially concerning the use of manuscript letters and their use in the rising martyrology genre, pp. 61–71.

[15] Kingdon, p. 76.   [16] See, for example, Salmon, *Society in Crisis*, pp. 117–46.

[17] Olivier Pot, 'Quand la Polygraphie devient une poétique', in *Simon Goulart: Un pasteur aux intérêts vastes comme le monde*, ed. by Olivier Pot (Geneva: Droz, 2013), pp. 7–53 (p. 7).

[18] Lloyd, '*This Pre-eminent Man of France*', p. 118.

de l'estat de France sous Charles IX, a three-volume set of *recueils* of which the first appeared in 1576, although, somewhat perversely, the third volume was intended as the introductory one. It is this third volume – a mixture of treatises, letters, and documents – with which I am concerned here, and indeed particularly with the second edition, published in 1578.[19]

In the mid-1570s, Huguenot leaders were working towards an alliance with the moderate Catholic nobility who felt pushed out by the Guises and perhaps, too, doubted Charles IX and Catherine de' Medici after the recent bloodshed. This faction rallied around Charles IX's youngest brother, the Duc d'Alençon (they are sometimes referred to as the 'Malcontents'). With this alliance in mind, the first edition of the *Mémoires* was intended to persuade, or at least not to alienate, moderate Catholics. However, the alliance broke down, and thus Goulart felt free to include more radical resistance texts in his second edition, notably the 'Discours politiques', which calls for the assassination of a tyrannical ruler.[20] The *Mémoires*, although one of the most widely referenced sources for histories of that phase of the civil wars, were not reprinted again in the sixteenth century, despite the fact that Goulart's other writings were sought after (or perhaps, as Gilmont suggests, even informally commissioned) by a variety of printers throughout his career.[21] It is likely that this work was not reissued due to the controversy attached to parts of its content – the second edition of volume three was publicly burned in Bordeaux in 1579.[22]

Like the *Reveille-matin*, Goulart's *Mémoires* bring together many different 'voices'. Goulart's own narrative, with occasional use of first-person pronouns, is interspersed with works by other authors, usually anonymous, of various political and confessional persuasions.[23] Uses of the term *politique* reflect this diversity. The most frequently cited is a fragmentary narrative labelled in the margin as the 'Commencement des Politiques qu'on appelle et des divers changements advenus depuis' ('The beginning

---

[19] There are actually two second editions. The one I have used is the slightly later one, known as the 'petits caractères' version. See Jean-François Gilmont with Amy Graves-Monroe, 'Les *Mémoires de l'estat de France sous Charles IX* (1576–1579) de Simon Goulart: bilan bibiliographique', *Etudes d'histoire du livre*, 11 (2015) https://revues.droz.org/index.php/HCL/article/ view/2326/3890 [accessed 15 January 2021].

[20] This is Amy Graves-Monroe's understanding of the expansion of the 1578 editions, see Amy Graves-Monroe, *Post tenebras lex: Preuves et propagande dans l'historiographie engagée de Simon Goulart (1543–1628)* (Geneva: Droz, 2012), p. 117.

[21] Jean-François Gilmont, 'Simon Goulart et ses imprimeurs', in *Simon Goulart*, ed. by Pot, pp. 257–70 (p. 270).

[22] Graves-Monroe, p. 124.   [23] See Graves-Monroe, p. 109.

of the so-called *Politiques*, and the changes that have occurred since'),
which Goulart wrote himself and which describes what is also known as
the 'Malcontent' conspiracy around d'Alençon in 1574, with which Bodin
has sometimes been associated.[24] In the title of this fragment, Goulart
draws attention to the appellation and fuels the suggestion that a party
sometimes known as the *Politiques* were working at various times towards a
political alternative during the wars, although the integrity of any
'Malcontent' group has been cast into doubt in the same way as that of
any so-called *Politique* party.[25] In fact, instances of *politique* in Goulart's
Mémoires point to a more complex set of uses and associations. A key
example the 'Discours politiques' referenced above: as well as opposing
tyranny, this work is a lengthy exposition of appropriate forms of government, appearing under the full title, 'Political discourses on the diverse
powers of God in the world, on the legitimate government of the same,
and the duties of subjects' ('Discours politiques des diverses puissances
estampilles de Dieu au monde, du gouvernement légitime d'icelles, & du
devoir de ceux qui y sont assujettis'). Towards the beginning of volume
three in both the first and second editions, the dialogue *Le Politique*
appears, with the full title given as:

> *Le Politique*. Dialogue treating the power, authority, and duty of Princes;
> the different types of government; how far tyranny should be borne; if in
> extreme oppression it is legitimate for subjects to take arms to defend their
> lives and liberty, and when, how, by whom and by what means this must
> and can be done.[26]

The dialogue is introduced by the anonymous author in a prefatory epistle
to his nephew, a lawyer in 'one of the French *Parlements*'; he says he is
writing to console himself and to offer his nephew both pleasure in reading
and relief from suffering (p. 44), and that the dialogue that follows is
roughly an account of conversations that they have had (p. 47). But the
dialogue is between abstracted figures: Politie (who represents liberty, 'la
liberté des peuples') and Archon (sovereign authority, 'l'authorité des

---

[24] See Franklin, *Jean Bodin*, p. 79.
[25] Kelley, *The Beginnings of Ideology*, pp. 47–48; Beame, p. 356.
[26] 'Le Politique. Dialogue Traitant de la puissance, authorité, & du devoir des Princes: des divers
gouvernemens: jusques ou lon doit supporter la tyrannie: Si en une oppression extreme il est loisible
aux sujets de prendre les armes pour defendre leur vie & liberté: quand, comment, par qui, & par
quel moyen cela doit & peut faire'. 'Le Politique' in Simon Goulart, *Mémoires de l'Estat de France,
sous Charles Neufiesme. Troisième volume. Seconde Edition, reveue, corrigee & augmentee* ([?], 1579),
pp. 44–83 (p. 44). All further references to Goulart's *Mémoires* will be to this edition unless
stated otherwise.

Princes').[27] Whether or not this uncle and nephew ever existed or had these conversations, this introduction describes a process of inspiration and composition similar to that which may have brought forth the *Reveille-matin*: conversations, and letters, between dismayed Protestants trying to enact a kind of restoration of common purpose, hope, and justice in writing, as it was not yet possible in person. These writers likely had similar educations and frames of reference to those previously analysed in this book, but different politics and *politiques*.

The anonymous author of *Le Politique* doesn't use *politique* again in the preface; one wonders whether Goulart may have added this word to the title. *Le Politique* is followed in the *Mémoires* by the full text of La Boétie's *Discours de la servitude volontaire*, which seems to be the product of a thematic organisation by the editor. Goulart's narrative then reprises without any obvious break on the printed page, only the author's brief introduction: 'It is time to return to the subject that has been deferred a little for the sake of the treatises inserted above' (p. 99^v).[28] Jan Miernowski contends that Goulart strategically mixed the texts in the *Mémoires* so as to make it difficult for the reader to tell who had written what, and to know when one thing finished and the overarching narrative thread was being picked up again – the transition between the *Discours de la servitude volontaire* and the return to the overall *propos* is an example of this technique, which Miernowski refers to as Goulart's ventriloquism.[29] Ventriloquism is a key technique in all the works I discuss in this chapter, since authors animate their concept of politics and make it speak, most obviously in the *Reveille-matin*'s Politique character.

---

[27] Archon of Athens was a citizen-sovereign elected by his people; a 'magistrat souverain', as Bodin put it, deciding in his famous chapter on sovereignty that Archon did not hold true sovereignty. Perhaps he had read 'Le Politique'. Bodin, I, 8, pp. 183–85. The connection between the words 'Politie' and 'Politique' is not entirely clear; the first dictionary definition of 'Politie' is in the *Littré*, which gives the same Greek etymology as 'politique' and notes a medieval use of the word 'Politie' by Christine de Pizan associated with 'droit' ('law') and 'droictement' ('correctly', or 'legally'). See 'Politie', in Emile Littré, *Dictionnaire de la langue française* (Paris: Hachette, 1872–77) http://artflsrv02.uchicago.edu/cgi-bin/dicos/pubdico1look.pl?strippedhw=politie [accessed 3 August 2020]. Ian Maclean shows that the concept of 'policy' in the modern sense of the term was not yet current in this period, in 'From Prudence to Policy'. Politie, like Alithie in the *Reveille-matin*, is female; although the evocation of a feminine figure who embodies an abstract ideal is hardly unusual (and Le Roy comes close to something similar with *la politique*), these dialogues certainly give more space to nominally female voices than most of the other texts analysed in this book.

[28] 'Il est temps de reprendre le propos qui a esté differé quelque peu pour les traitez sus inserez.'

[29] Jan Miernowski, 'La mémoire des massacres chez Simon Goulart et les origines de la fable Protestante', in *Simon Goulart*, ed. by Pot, pp. 143–58 (p. 157).

The *Politique*'s Wake-Up Call

The title of the *Reveille-matin des françois*, which Kelley translates as 'Alarm Bell', but could also be something like 'Wake-Up Call for the French People', announces the text as one meant to inspire action.[30] It consists of two dialogues. The first edition, printed in 1573, contained only the first, which takes place at the house of Alithie (a figure for truth; her name derives from the Greek *aletheia*, meaning truth or disclosure) in Hungary, under Ottoman Turkish rule.[31] It may initially seem that the implication is that truth has been forced to travel beyond Christian realms and settle in the land of its avowed enemy. However, contemporary attitudes to Islam and to the Ottoman Empire were more nuanced than this, as Noel Malcolm has shown. The location of the first dialogue may rather reflect the fact that a few contemporary writers praised Ottoman policies of religious toleration in this period, especially in newly conquered Hungary.[32] Perhaps the writer(s) of the *Reveille-matin* were genuinely impressed by the Ottoman approach to diverse populations and saw it setting an imitable example, just as Bodin admired aspects of Ottoman rule – certainly, Alithie says that she is safer and freer in Ottoman territory than in other lands ruled by 'so-called Christians' ('ceux qui se disent Chrestiens', p. 166). Besides, although both Catholics and Protestants regularly attempted to smear one another by associating them with non-Christian religions and Islam in particular, some Protestant leaders and theologians were interested in cooperation with the Ottomans – and at least one writer believed that Ottoman rule in Hungary created an opportunity for all its Christian inhabitants to freely convert to the reformed faith.[33] As such, Athilie's decision to settle in Hungary reflects contemporary accounts of that region as one of possibility.

Alithie is attended by a French refugee, Philalithie, whose name simply means lover of truth, and who thus plays the role of right-thinking listener, or reader. Philalithie introduces two other French exiles, the

---

[30] Kelley, *The Beginnings of Ideology*, e.g. p. 204.
[31] The name 'Alithie' in contemporary dialogues is relatively rare, but this is not an isolated incidence. Likely inspired by the *Reveille-matin*, Simon Goulart wrote a character called *Alithie* in his 1585 play, *Pastorale*. See Christian Grosse et Ruth Stawarz-Luginbühl, '"La Pastorale" (1585) de Simon Goulart: Théâtre et tradition bucolique au service d'une célébration politique', in *Simon Goulart*, ed. by Pot, pp. 431–52. Parts of what is now Hungary were annexed by the Ottomans in 1541.
[32] Malcolm, *Useful Enemies*, p. 93; the *Reveille-matin* may thus be part of what Malcolm calls a 'new paradigm' for the place of the Ottoman Empire in political thought, characterised by a sense that Western powers might benefit from imitation of Ottoman practice, pp. 137–38.
[33] Ibid., pp. 94–103.

Historiographe (Historiographer or Historian), and the Politique. In the discussion that follows, the Historiographe gives an account of the rise of Calvinism in France, and the ensuing persecution of Protestants, in particular the days leading up to the Saint Bartholomew's Day massacre, with a long description of the massacre itself. The Politique is presented as companion and helper of the Historiographe, analyses his story, and suggests conclusions (such as that Catherine de' Medici should never have been made regent). At the end of the dialogue, a character named Eglise ('Church') arrives, and introduces the prophet Daniel to the company. Daniel issues a kind of manifesto (introduced as 'loix et ordonnances politiques', 'political laws') for a new society centred on liberty of conscience for French Huguenots.[34]

Daniel essentially suggests extreme localisation of powers, or, as Kingdon puts it, the 'dismemberment of France' into hundreds of small city states on the Genevan model.[35] This vision of a federalised France centred on the fortified towns currently at war with one another was in some ways a more realistic proposal than Bodin's vision of centralisation, as though the state were analogous to a single family and a single town. The Historiographe and the Politique, Catholic at the start of the *Reveille-matin*, are persuaded by what they hear, and convert to the Reformed faith (they swear loyalty to the Eglise character); this conversion is signalled from the opening in the *Argument* (summary) of the first dialogue, which also states that after the conversation has finished, the Historiographe will travel to tell 'neighbouring princes and nations' about 'the French tragedies, and their duties towards the good' ('les Tragedies Françoises & leur devoir envers les bons', p. 164).[36] The Politique is sent to inform the oppressed French people of Daniel's orders.

The second dialogue begins with the joyous reunion of the Politique and the Historiographe after their travels. In case his conversion was ever in doubt, the scene opens on the Politique in a tavern in Friburg in Brisgau singing Psalm 74; the Historiographe overhears him and is delighted to find his friend.[37] The dialogue is each telling the other what they have

---

[34] *Le reveille-matin des Francois*, pp. 141–308 (p. 279). All further references will be to this edition.
[35] Kingdon, p. 76.
[36] Conversion was an integral part of the Calvinist mission, see Pettegree, *Reformation and the Culture of Persuasion*, pp. 1–9.
[37] Singing the Psalms in French was one of the most recognisable parts of Calvinist worship. Calvin and Clément Marot began translating the Psalms in the 1530s; the work was finished by Théodore de Bèze, who completed the Calvinist metrical Psalter in 1562. Pettegree, *Reformation and the Culture of Persuasion*, pp. 55–62.

learnt during their travels – followed by the Politique issuing 'a short treatise on resistance theory'.[38] The text concludes with their call for rebellion against tyranny. Daniel had appeared at the end of the first dialogue with a manifesto for a new society. At the end of the second, the Politique urges the French to rise up against their 'voluntary servitude' to tyrannical leaders: this is the excerpt from the *Discours de la servitude volontaire* mentioned above, which makes La Boétie the unwitting Daniel of the second dialogue.

Although the Politique in the *Reveille-matin* becomes an ally of truth and emissary of the Reformed church, when he is first introduced to Alithie alongside the historian, her response is mistrustful:

> I am easier seeing one of them accompanying you than the other, for I know that one is necessary and useful to aid memory and serve posterity – and the other is most often pernicious and damaging, especially if he cut his teeth at the court of certain Kings and Princes well known to you. Still, I can assure myself that such people as the *Politiques* of today would not easily turn you away from our friendship, if you still remember well what I have taught you. (p. 1)[39]

Alithie's comments about her new guests are addressed to her friend, Philalithie. For her, the Historiographe can only be helpful but the Politique is likely to be 'pernicious and damaging' and to have been corrupted by his peers; she allows him entry only because she trusts that Philalithie has not forgotten the lessons he has learnt from her. The sense that the Politique's contribution would be invalidated if he has been too close to certain kings and princes stands in contrast to Le Roy's boast in the preface to his translation of Aristotle that he is particularly qualified to comment on politics precisely because he has frequented royal courts (Le Roy, p. 2); it also undermines Aristotle's point in the *Nicomachean Ethics* that political experts require political experience (*NE*, 1095a), if that experience can be so corrupting. But overall, the 'pernicious and damaging' status is not fixed, only 'most likely': there can be such thing as a *politique* who is welcome in the house of truth. The initial reception of the Politique by Alithie leaves room to manoeuvre, and the mobility of the Politique in both spiritual and actual space across the discussions that follow (in which

---

[38] Kingdon, p. 83.

[39] 'Je suis plus aise de te voir accompagné de l'un que de l'autre, sachant combien l'un est nécessaire et profitable pour aider à la mémoire, et servir à la posterité: et l'autre, le plus souvent pernicieux et dommageable, principalement s'il est nourry à la cour d'aucuns Rois et Princes que tu cognois bien: toutesfois, si tu as tousjours bonne souvenance de ce que je t'ay enseigné, je m'asseureray que telles gens que les Politiques d'aujourd'huy, ne te destourneront facilement de l'amitié que tu me portes.'

the Politique both travels through Europe and converts from Catholicism to Protestantism) then serves to show that *politique* as a substantive noun incarnates, in this text, a considerable degree of mobility between various axes, not least that between perceived good and evil.[40]

The authors ultimately establish their Politique character as trustworthy, and more than that, as a figure with powers of discernment and authoritative judgement, but the potential moral/ethical stance taken by somebody called *politique* is more obviously dubious here than in the other texts I have so far discussed. In Le Caron's *Courtesan* dialogue the negative alter ego of 'our Politic' exists only to the extent that a reader could imagine that 'someone else's Politic' might not be so exemplary. For their part, Bodin and Le Roy were concerned about bad politics, and about those who lacked the wisdom, discretion, and prudence to read, think, and do politics well, but did not directly criticise people named *politiques*. Here, we see the bad *politique* character who dominated the discourse later in the period beginning to emerge.

The bad *politique* is not yet let loose, however. Alithie will not allow it. She is introduced as the embodiment of truth in the *Argument* (p. 164).[41] 'Dis-closure' is a more literal translation of 'A-letheia', the meaning of which may be more legible to modern readers through the image of Lethe, the river of oblivion in the underworld of Greek mythology: *Aletheia* then means the opposite of closure, oblivion, and concealment, and could also be translated as 'unconcealed'. Her role in the text, in keeping with this name is, then, to clarify meaning through disclosure. Viewed in this way, in her role as 'host' of the conversation and of the various textual fragments cited and analysed in the course of the discussions, she is there to eliminate the shadows with which multiple and conflicting meanings obscure truth and unity of sense; she is there to resolve the encounters and contestations present in words like *politique*. In this sense she also presents a vision of true and appropriate politics as ultimately discoverable; as something that can be faithfully represented.[42] The title of the text itself, the 'wake-up call'

---

[40] The setting connects the *Reveille-matin* to the tendency of Protestant writers to represent themselves as foreigners to France, as observed by George Hoffmann in *Reforming French Culture: Satire, Spiritual Alienation, and Connection to Strangers* (Oxford: Oxford University Press, 2017), esp. pp. 47–72. On migration in the period, see Heinz Schilling, *Early Modern European Civilisation and its Political and Cultural Dynamism* (Hanover, NH and London: Brandeis University Press, 2008), pp. 33–64.

[41] 'Alithie, c'est-à-dire la vérité'.

[42] By naming the host character Alithie the authors can be understood as mobilising the mimetic function of literature in order to represent truth as they would like it to be. Victoria Kahn points out the significance of *aletheia* in the Platonic tradition as received in the early modern period; Plato

can be connected to this suggestion of discoverable truth; the text, and the host character, facilitate this process of discovery and awakening.

The differentiation between the Politique in the dialogue and the dangerous 'Politiques of today' occurs across the first dialogue. The Politique character is not a thinly veiled portrait of any contemporary individual active in these events, and so may carry more of the positive connotations of *politique* present in contemporary writing. The authors of the *Reveille-matin* make his apparent position as detached from the contemporary conflict work for their purposes. In contrast, for example, with the later *Dialogue d'entre le Maheustre et le Manant* (1593; discussed in Chapter 6), in which both characters introduce themselves according to their allegiance in the contemporary conflict, the Politique of the *Reveille-matin* enters the dialogue with mention of his history and no stated allegiance other than to truth, and only halfway through the first dialogue does he mention that he is a Catholic who has fled France in horror at the atrocities committed there (although both his original faith and conversion are signalled in the *Argument*).

Throughout the first dialogue, the Politique acquires ideological content. When we meet him, he is something of an empty vessel, if associated by his name with 'pernicious *Politiques*' and arguably imbued with the power conveyed by the abstract noun. He is then 'filled' with ideas relating to specific events recounted by the Historiographe, and these ideas are ratified by the approval of Alithie. The Politique's status as an embodiment of intellectual abstraction is potentially compromised by the detailed recounting of recent history, but in fact the writers manipulate this to create a Politique with a clear stance on contemporary events who is nothing like the duplicitous courtly *politiques* feared by Alithie. Thus, the Politique is 'historicised' in a way that recalls Le Roy's and Bodin's emphasis on history in politics. The writer(s) mobilise tropes of Renaissance dialogue to animate a Politique that corresponds with the powerful, elevated *politique* found in Bodin's *République*, in order to lend authority to their agenda (which is, in no small part, an excoriation of monarchs across Europe, from Charles IX to Elizabeth I and so on, as well

---

contrasts it with 'doxa' (opinion) as part of his problematisation of rhetoric and poetics. Victoria Kahn, *The Trouble with Literature* (Oxford: Oxford University Press, 2020), p. 12. The Greek notion of *aletheia* has its place in the longer history of representation in Western art, as Christopher Prendergast shows in *The Order of Mimesis: Balzac, Stendhal, Flaubert, Nerval* (Cambridge: Cambridge University Press, 1986), p. 11. 'Aletheia' was also a keyword of twentieth-century thought after Heidegger drew on the etymological sense of the term in *Being and Time*, and as part of his aesthetic thought. See Martin Heidegger, *Being and Time*, tr. by Joan Stambaugh (Albany, NY: SUNY Press, 2010), p. 204; 'The Origin of the Work of Art', in *Poetry, Language, Thought*, tr. by Albert Hofstadter (New York, NY: Harper and Row, 1967), pp. 15–89 (e.g. p. 56).

as promotion of the Calvinist cause). Alithie orchestrates a transition to political engagement. In distinguishing the Politique from 'les Politiques d'aujourd'hui', then, the authors of the *Reveille-matin* draw on elite discourse to create a different kind of *politique*, but one who is ultimately no less engaged in the contemporary moment. In so doing, their use of the term represents an unusual one in the sense that their Politique is – or becomes – a committed Protestant, rather than acting as the moderate Catholic go-between characterised as *politique* by historians.[43]

The positive Protestant framing of Le Politique in *Le Reveille-matin* is made possible with the shadowy 'Politiques of today' as his foil. What might the phrase 'Politiques of today' have meant to readers? A survey of contemporary uses suggests that Alithie's negative associations at the outset of the *Reveille-matin* are not typical. The 'moderate Catholic' substantive meaning was current; the authors of the *Reveille-matin* drew on it to create a Catholic *politique* so persuadable that he became Protestant. The pamphlet *L'allegresse chrestienne de l'heureux succès des guerres de ce royaume* ('Christian Gladness at the Happy Success in the Wars in this Kingdom') provides another example of the *politique* as moderate Catholic. This poem celebrating the Saint Bartholomew's Day massacres denounces Gaspard de Coligny and extrapolates from that a denunciation of all those who shared his faith; such posthumous attacks explain the Historiographe's wish to exonerate Coligny in the *Reveille-matin*. Perhaps the most high-powered attack on Coligny was Pibrac's notorious letter to Stanislas Elvidias, justifying the massacres; the Politique of the *Reveille-matin* pities Pibrac for having had to speak such untruths ('se desdire', p. 116).[44] The author of *L'allegresse chrestienne* both praises the desecration of Coligny's body in death (which actually occurred) and continues a metaphorical dragging through the mud in verse; Coligny is the foil to the hero of the pamphlet, Charles IX, who has saved the kingdom by ordering the massacres. The poem as a whole is not so much an argument as an expression of jubilation at recent acts of mass murder; the existence of a dissenting view is briefly raised and dismissed:

> In any case I know well that each time some *politique*
> Will say it's not for a King to punish a heretic.
> It is then not for the King to maintain his own authority,
> Since without an established church, his throne cannot be.[45]

[43] One of the first of these historians seems to have been Simon Goulart, in the fragment 'Commencement des politiques qu'on appelle', p. 99ᵛ.
[44] Pibrac, apologist of *La Saint-Barthélemy*, was, we recall, the dedicatee of Bodin's *République*.
[45] 'Je sçay bien toutes fois que quelque politique/ Dira, ce n'est au Roy, de punir l'hérétique./ Ce n'est donc pas au Roy de maintenir son sceptre, / Son trosne, sans l'eglise estably ne peut estre' [Jean

These four lines suggest that a *politique* view could be a kind of proto-*laïcité* in which secular power has no jurisdiction over the spiritual realm (Bodin and Le Roy seemingly favour separate, if not necessarily equal, jurisdictions; the author disagrees, presenting the church as the foundation of royal authority). This view is not unique: in the letter of 1573 cited in the conclusion of the previous chapter, the president of the *Parlement* in Rouen defined the word 'politicque' as designating one who did not take sides in the confessional conflict but knew how to govern a multitude of men.[46] We also have Goulart's fragment (discussed above) associating *politiques* with the group around the François d'Alençon, later Duc d'Anjou. François Hotman wrote in a letter of 1574 that a group of 'nobles, *robins*, and merchants' who had been imprisoned in Paris were calling themselves *politiques* and arguing for a return to the ancient constitution of France and a meeting of the Estates General.[47] Hotman was not in Paris at the time, and this supposedly *politique* point of view is suspiciously close to his own argument in the *Francogallia*; but this comment does show a Protestant writer in the mid-1570s suggesting proximity between Protestants and *politiques* either real or fictional, akin to the alliance staged in the *Reveille-matin* (of which Hotman may also have been an editor).

Other pro-Charles Catholic pamphlets do not use the word *politique* at all, and nor do most Catholic sources critical of Charles; for example, the Duc d'Alençon's *Declaration*, made at Dreux in 1575, could very loosely be described as a 'malcontent' manifesto, and makes no use of the term.[48] Greengrass has written that the most notorious *politique* of the age was Catherine de' Medici, but she is not described thus in the *Discours merveilleux de la vie, actions et déportements de Cathérine de Médicis, royne mere* (translated into English in 1575 as *A Mervaylous Discourse upon the Lyfe, Deedes, and Behaviours of Katherine de Medicis, Queene Mother*) which likely had a Protestant author and/or editor, and is credited with establishing her reputation as manipulative and malevolent.[49]

Touchard], *Allegresse chrestienne de l'heureux succès des guerres de ce royaume, et de la justice de Dieu contre les rebelles au Roy, & comme de droit divin, est licite à Sa Majesté punir ses sujets, pour la religion violée* (Paris: J. de Roigny, 1572), n.p.

[46] Quoted in Jouanna, *Le pouvoir absolu*, p. 177.   [47] Quoted in Jouanna, 'Politiques', p. 1212.

[48] See *Declaration de Monseigneur Francois fils & frere de Roy. Duc d'Alençon, &c. Contenant les raisons de sa sortie de la Court* (Paris, 1575).

[49] Greengrass, *France in the Age of Henri IV*, p. 15; Nicole Cazauran, 'Introduction', in *Le discours merveilleux de la vie, actions, et déportements de Cathérine de Médicis, royne mere*, ed. by Nicole Cazauran (Geneva: Droz, 1995), pp. 11–54 (pp. 11–12); see also pp. 360–64.

Beyond the 'moderate Catholic' meaning, adjectival uses in the Protestant works I discuss here are fairly similar to those in previous chapters, perhaps unsurprisingly given that they were writing at almost the same time as Bodin and Le Roy. The adjective qualifies a form of expertise, a kind of writing, and a kind of rule. In *Le Politique* and 'Discours politiques' in Goulart's *Mémoires*, other than the uses in the title the most frequent form is adjectival, as part of 'loix politiques' ('loix politiques' is also one of the only adjectival uses in the *Reveille-matin*, and introduces Daniel's edicts). In *Le Politique*, there is one occasion when, as the characters are discussing examples of rebellion against unjust monarchs, Politie qualifies the checking of Solomon's excessive spending by a prophet as 'a purely *politique* (political) example' – which Archon then counters with 'one which is only about religion' ('un qui est purement pour la religion': a rebellion against Joram, son of Jehoshaphat, who tried to introduce false gods [p. 68]). This moment of contrast between *religion* and the adjectival form of *politique* in *Le Politique* indicates potential opposition between religion and politics, even as the title of the dialogue indicates an attempt at resolution, and Politie attempts in her speeches to make politics work for religion.

All this points to a dynamic situation in which uses of the term relate to a fracturing of the traditional view of France as 'le royaume trèschrétien', a nation unified by a single faith. The *Reveille-matin* and *Le Politique* invent characters called Politie and Le Politique to mend these fractures, in moves both similar and – in ideological terms, often strongly opposed – to those of Bodin and Le Roy. Unlike League-affiliated polemicists, who – as we shall see in the next chapter – turn against the *politique*, the Huguenot writers here take advantage of the term's mobility and attempt to work it to their own advantage by fixing it in a particular form, so that *politique* opposes not religion itself, but his alter ego, the bad *politique*. And the bad *politique* par excellence is, of course, Niccolò Machiavelli – or rather, the sensationalised version of him who appeared in Huguenot polemic as the ideological inspiration of the massacres.

Le Politique contre Machiavel

As Sidney Anglo has shown, the French reception of Machiavelli was instrumental in the development of the Florentine's sulphurous reputation, and the development of 'Machiavellian' as an adjective indicating unprincipled, self-serving, and power-hungry behaviour.[50] This negative

---

[50] See Anglo, pp. 271–324.

reception was forged in Protestant writing in the wake of Saint Bartholomew's Day. The first French translations of his work were popular enough that *Il Principe* and the *Discorsi* were read widely in France from *c.* 1550; his influence on contemporary writers such as Le Roy and Montaigne has been much discussed and debated, and although Bodin disavowed Machiavelli he borrowed extensively from him.[51] In the preface to the first translation of the *Prince* (1553), the translator Guillaume Cappel had praised Machiavelli as an expert in all things 'Politique': '[he] has so well treated all parts of Politics that he has already attracted as much praise as all others put together have been praised for their work on any one part of it'.[52] As Cappel's hard sell indicates, 'Machiavelli' and 'politics/*politique*' could be connected in an approbatory way.

In 1571, a new translation was printed, this time by Jacques Gohory, who had already translated the *Discorsi*; he also translated the dedication to Lorenzo de' Medici, affirming a connection between the names of Machiavel and Medici. After the massacres of 1572, in the context of the vilification of the Florentine Queen Mother, Machiavelli's reputation as an expert in 'all parts of Politics' suffered in tandem. Knecht writes that it was rumoured that Catherine de' Medici 'had brought up her children on Machiavelli's *Prince*, and that Anjou always carried a copy in his pocket'.[53] The *Discours merveilleux* refers to Machiavelli as a highly influential *politique* at the Valois court:

> The Florentines, for the most part (as those who know them will say) are little concerned with their conscience. They want to seem religious but not to be so, and make a great case (as did Machiavelli, one of their foremost *politiques*, in his advice to his prince) of what the ambitious Ixion would so often say in former times:
>
> *Try to have the reputation of a righteous man,*
> *Without the actions or good works.*
> *Only do the things that you can see*
> *Will be a means of furthering your own profit.*[54]

[51] On Le Roy and Machiavelli, see, for example, Maria Elena Severini, 'Premessa', in Loys Le Roy, *De la vicissitude ou variété des choses en l'univers, La traduzione italiana di Ercole Cato*, ed. by Maria Elena Severini (Paris: Classiques Garnier, 2014), pp. 7–13 (pp. 12–13). On Montaigne and Machiavelli, see n. 66.

[52] [Il]a si bien traité toutes les parties de Politique qu'il est acquis desja autant de louenge en toutes, que tous les autres ensemble sur chacune.' *Le Prince de Nicolas Machiavelle secrétaire et citoien de Florence*, trans. by Guillaume Cappel (Paris: Estienne, 1553), p. aiiii.

[53] R. J. Knecht, *Catherine De' Medici* (London: Longman, 1998), p. 164.

[54] 'Les Florentins, pour la pluspart (comme disent ceux qui ont mangé quelque peu de sel avec eux) se soucient peu de leur conscience: veulent sembler religieux et non pas l'estre, faisans grand cas

Here, Machiavelli appears as a courtly *politique* like Aristotle or Scipio in Bodin's *République*: as an author, or an authority, using theory to improve practice – except that he's doing the opposite. It is important to note that at this stage, though, where Machiavelli reception intersects with the keyword *politique*, the description of Machiavelli as 'one of their foremost *politiques*' only partially passes the negative associations with 'Machiavel' onto *politique*, and *politiques* in general are not directly blamed for the massacres. In the *Reveille-matin*, the '*politiques* of today' are indirectly held responsible for the atrocities but counterbalanced by the example of the Politique character, who is capable, in more ways than one, of reforming. Anti-Machiavellian writing makes *politique* an object of greater contestation, rather than one of pure vilification.

We have already seen this at work, albeit briefly, in the previous chapter, in Bodin's preface to the *République*, written in the anti-Machiavellian context of the time of publication – Bodin writes a paragraph on 'a Macciavel' (the use of the indefinite article suggests that 'a Macciavel' is already a type, or stock character). He concludes that any reasonable reader would reach the opposite conclusion to Cappel: Machiavelli has actually misunderstood everything about politics.[55] Bodin thus joined the voices calling to shut Machiavelli out of political discourse, of which the loudest was Innocent Gentillet, whose *Discours sur les moyens de bien gouverner et maintenir en bonne paix un royaume ou autre principauté, contre Nicolas Machiavel* ('Treatise on the means of good government and maintaining peace in a kingdom or other principality, against Nicolas Machiavel', 1576) so came to typify anti-Machiavellian writing that it is more commonly known simply as the *Anti-Machiavel*. In his preface, Gentillet cautiously praises 'the art of Politics', with the caveat that it is not as reliable as mathematics (in contrast to Bodin's aspiration for synchronicity between the two arts) and thus requires extremely delicate judgement, properly applied.[56] He describes his aim in the work that follows in terms that echo Bodin's critique of 'un Macciavel':

(comme aussi Machiavel l'un de leurs premiers politiques le conseille à son prince) de ce qu'avait jadis fort souvent en la bouche l'ambitieux Ixion: Cherche d'avoir d'homme droit le renom / Mais les effects et justes œuvres non. / Fay seulement cela dont tu verras / Que recevoir du profit tu pourras', *Discours merveilleux*, p. 133. In Greek mythology, Ixion murdered his father-in-law. Cazauran attributes this citation of Ixion to Amyot's translation of Plutarch (p. 299 n. 18).

[55] Bodin, *République*, Préface, p. 12.
[56] Innocent Gentillet, *Anti-Machiavel, Edition de 1576*, ed. by C. Edward Rathé (Geneva: Droz, 1968), p. 30.

> My goal is only to show that Nicolas Machiavel, Florentine, formerly
> secretary of the Republic (now Duchy) of Florence, has understood little
> or nothing of this political science of which we speak, that he has developed
> entirely bad maxims, and that he has built from these not a science of
> politics, but of tyranny.[57]

Anglo points out that Gentillet's reading reduced Machiavelli's writings to
(sometimes poorly translated) maxims and aphorisms that distorted the
content of his work, commenting that he was in this respect a 'typical
Renaissance reader'.[58] Gentillet was neither the first nor the last to take
this approach to Machiavelli; the excerpt from *Discours merveilleux* quoted
above makes a marginal reference to Chapter 15 of *The Prince* (on
reputation, and how the Prince should not try to be wholly good) and
reduces this chapter (in which Machiavelli says that it would be preferable
if princes were entirely virtuous, but 'because of conditions in this world,
princes cannot have those qualities, or observe them completely') to four
lines of verse that instruct the Machiavellian prince to try to appear good
without actually being good in any way.[59]

   The characters of the *Reveille-matin*, are both 'typical Renaissance
readers' and typical 1570s readers of Machiavelli. Daniel explicitly refers
to 'the maxims of Machiavelli' (p. 278), warning that these have no value
when it comes to God's judgement. Machiavelli is mentioned twice in an
anonymous letter quoted by the Historiographe supposedly sent to the
Admiral de Coligny before his murder warning him of dangers at court: a
key part of the warning is that the King has been persuaded by 'the
doctrine of Machiavelli' not to tolerate religious diversity; Chapter 18 of
The Prince (on whether and when Princes should keep their word) is
mentioned as especially influential (pp. 197–98). The Politique also refers
to the Florentine twice, to say that his views are 'pernicious heresy in
statecraft' despite the King seeming to follow them (pp. 182–83). In the
second reference, Machiavelli is presented as the teacher of Catherine de'
Medici (pp. 251–52), who in turn persuaded the King that he need not
keep his promises (this is a somewhat unfair digestion of Chapter 18 of
The Prince). In the *Reveille-matin*, then, the Politique character is thus
partly an Anti-Machiavel himself. Where the Historiographe reports the

---

[57] 'Mais mon but est seulement de montrer que Nicolas Machiavel Florentin, jadis secrétaire de la
   republique (maintenant duché) de Florence; n'a rien entendu, ou peu, en ceste science politique
   dont nous parlons, et qu'il a prins des maximes toutes meschantes, et basta sur celles non une
   science politique mais tyrannique', ibid., p. 31.
[58] Anglo, p. 299.
[59] Niccolò Machiavelli, *The Prince*, tr. by George Bull (London: Penguin, 2004), p. 66.

influence of Machiavelli and Daniel confirms that God disapproves, it is for the Politique to say that Machiavelli fails in statecraft as well as in spirituality. As such, the authors create in him a character who can rescue politics from Machiavelli.

In *Le Politique*, Politie is also critical of 'Machiavel and the other modern *Politiques*', again sounding rather like Bodin in his preface to the *République*.[60] She makes this criticism in a discussion with Archon over whether pagan political thought is compatible with Christianity. Like Gentillet, Politie emphasises the need for good judgement:

ARCHON: It well seems that there is great compatibility between what God ordained for the civil *police* in his laws, and what the Pagans said about this matter.

POLITIE: This must be judged with discretion. For God has considered this matter so carefully, that he wants the *police* to be maintained through charity and fear of his name, and for the conservation of states ['estats'] to be recognised as the work of his hand. Philosophers, legists, and other *politiques*, who are illuminated in prudence and experience only by the light of nature, often do not care to conserve the greatness and dignity of states ['estats'], and their rulers, and to make them perpetual. In the third book of the *Republic* Cicero wishes, through the power of the world's eternity (just as Platonists also believed the world to be eternal), to make the city eternal. Machiavelli and other modern *politiques* have studied hard in order to teach the means of this kind of maintenance but they forget the principal part of it. (p. 49)[61]

The semantic field here is very similar to the one explored in earlier chapters, with the links made between philosophers, lawyers, and 'other *politiques*'; the references to Cicero and Plato; the emphasis on 'prudence and experience'. The critique of Machiavelli is somewhat subtler than in Gentillet and in the *Reveille-matin*. Machiavelli is positioned at the heart of a potential conflict between pagan morality (whose goal is an eternal city on earth) and Christian morality in which the state is maintained in God's

---

[60] Here Politie makes polemical use of the term 'modern', as Le Roy did with different effect.

[61] 'ARCHON: Il semble bien qu'il y a grande convenance entre ce que Dieu a ordonné de la police civile en ses loix, et ce que les Payens en ont dit. POLITIE: Il en faut juger avec discretion. Car Dieu y a esgard tellement, qu'il veut qu'elle se maintienne par charité & crainte de son nom, & que la conservation des estats soit reconnue de sa main, & les Philosophes, legistes, & autres politiques, qui ne sont esclairez en leur prudence & experience, que de la lumiere naturelle, n'ont bien souvent esgard à conserver la grandeur & dignité des estats, & des conducteurs d'iceux, & de les rendre perpetuels. Ciceron au troisiesme livre de la Republique veut sus le patron de l'éternité du monde (comme les Platoniques le cuident estre eternel) rendre aussi la cité eternelle. Machiavel et les autres politiques modernes s'estudient fort à enseigner les moyens de ceste manutention, mais ils omettent le principal.'

name 'through charity and fear', and the only access to anything eternal is through religion: hence Machiavelli and his fellow *politiques* seem to emphasise the means of preserving a city but omit to consider the principal part (which is God).[62]

The conflict Politie evokes, in which she is on one side and 'Machiavel and other modern *politiques*' are on the other, comes close to evoking what Isaiah Berlin described as the true scandal of Machiavelli's politics: not the divorce of ethics from politics, but the portrayal of Western politics as caught between two incompatible ethical models, one pagan, and one Christian. The former, Berlin writes, is associated with qualities such as public order, greatness, and discipline, and the other with charity, submission to the will of God, and a prioritisation of the salvation of the individual soul over any social or civil goal.[63] Thus Berlin paints Machiavelli as the man who lifted the veil on the fundamental impossibility of syncretism between the Classical and Judeo-Christian traditions in the political sphere; without wishing to pronounce on the veracity, or not, of this binary, I might add that it could be a particular problem arising between the Classical tradition and Protestant interpretations of the Judeo-Christian tradition, with their emphasis on individual salvation as an interior process, or even as predetermined (Luther's justification by faith alone; Calvin's theory of predestination) rather than as the result of good works and civic action. This could suggest a confessional explanation as to why *Le Politique* in particular seems to make Berlin's thesis for him about the problem with Machiavelli, though not necessarily about the fundamental paradox of syncretism. What this does to the meaning of the word for 'politics' in *Le Politique* is certainly, moreover, to make it an object of suspicion and contestation: something to be manipulated, and if possible, recuperated.

Overall, the text called *Le Politique* and the character named Le Politique are anti-Machiavels as a means of opposing Charles IX and Catherine de' Medici, as a way of identifying what makes a *politique* good, and also as another way of opposing the way in which faith and

---

[62] Although for Bodin, 'the means' were anything that would facilitate the principal divine force governing the universe, and so there is less conflict for him between ends and means, the view expressed by Politie here is not entirely at odds with what he says about the principality of the divine at the end of *République* I, 1.

[63] Isaiah Berlin, 'The Originality of Machiavelli', in Isaiah Berlin, *Selected Writings: Against the Current, Essays in the History of Ideas*, ed. by Henry Hardy (Oxford: Clarendon Press, 1991), pp. 25–79 (pp. 44–45). For a subtler account of early modern thinkers grappling with ideas about virtue according to both Christian and pre-Christian frameworks, see Michael Moriarty, *Disguised Vices: Theories of Virtue in Early Modern French Thought* (Oxford: Oxford University Press, 2011).

politics are drifting apart in the discourse (a process facilitated, even encouraged in some sense, by the likes of Bodin). Within this, the *Machiavel* word group interacts in a complex way with *politique* – Machiavelli stands, effectively, as an example of a bad *politique* in opposition to the one imagined by these writers, who is able to argue for diversity in religion within one state, and who is still able to prioritise religion in politics. Through stabilising this character's ethical and political project these authors seek to control the meaning of the word and its dangerous mutability; discretion, good judgement, and faith are all required. Machiavelli's own ideas, mostly from *The Prince*, are extracted and distorted as part of this project. This interaction between *politique* and Machiavel can be understood as the French experience of Pocock's 'Machiavellian moment', which he defined as the problem of attempting to build and maintain stable and lasting communities in the face of great conflict, and apparently inevitable instability.[64] For Pocock, the 'Machiavellian moment' occurs when the fundamental instability of politics itself emerged as a kind of truth, in which 'to act in politics is to expose oneself to the insecurities of human power systems, to enter a world of mutability and *peripeteia* whose history is the dimension of political insecurity'.[65] This problem is dramatised in *Le Politique* and *Le reveille-matin* in their uses of the word 'politique' even as the writers seek to solve it.

One of Montaigne's rare uses of the term *politique*, and even rarer references to Machiavelli by name, seems to evoke the same problem: 'Notably in political matters, there is a fine field open for vacillation and dispute ... Machiavelli's arguments, for example were solid enough for the subject, yet it was very easy to combat them.'[66] This moment in II, 17 ('Of Presumption'), contains the more stable adjectival use of *politique*, attached to 'matters', and yet the presence of Machiavelli a few lines later, associated with the term ('for the subject'), with both cautious praise of the Florentine and allusion to the anti-Machiavellian context, shows Montaigne absorbing changes in use of the word at the same time as commenting on what he sees as the fundamentally contested and changeable nature of politics as a field of enquiry. The reference to the 'open field' ('champ ouvert') recalls his description of Tacitus's writing as an ethical and political seedbed (p. 872/p. 986), as well as Pasquier's condemnation

---

[64] Pocock, *The Machiavellian Moment*, pp. vii–ix.   [65] Ibid., p. 36.
[66] 'Notamment aux affaires politiques il y a un beau champ ouvert au bransle et à la contestation ... Les discours de Machiavel, pour exemple, estoient assez solides pour le subject; si, y a-il eu grand aisance à les combattre', p. 694.

of the seedbed that spawned all the insults of the League period, *politique* included. Here, in II, 17, Montaigne is once again on the outside looking in, commenting on the uncontrollably productive and destructive potential of texts defined as *politique*.

If this is a 'Machiavellian moment' in Montaigne, it is connected to a '*politique* moment' in which uses, and understanding, of the term *politique*, as of politics as an arena for thought and action, are highly unstable. Many critics have drawn links between Montaigne and Machiavelli, with III, 2 ('De l'Utile et de l'Honneste') treated as the paradigmatic example.[67] Here in II, 17, Montaigne is acknowledging the 'vacillation' and 'dispute' provoked by Machiavelli and attributing them to the kind of writing that it is, rather than to Machiavelli's particularly nefarious, brilliant, or shocking intervention. Montaigne's use of Machiavelli in II, 17 can therefore be read as a comment on the 'fine field' of politics: a point about politics itself, rather than about Machiavelli on his (or indeed, on Montaigne's) own terms. These few lines in the middle of the *Essais* may seem emblematic of Machiavelli's reception in 1570s France, but Montaigne is taking Machiavelli as an example of a particular moment in politics. The history of the term *politique*, here again, offers a reversal of narratives that place Machiavelli at the centre of a web of instability and intrigue: instead, Machiavelli as he was read and understood in 1570s France is emblematic of the conflict reflected, and fought out, in uses of the term *politique*.

The *Politique* Reader, between Liberty and Servitude

Machiavelli is not the only author to be manipulated in the name of a certain kind of politics, or to be named as *politique*, for better or for worse. In this final section, I explore how the term is mobilised in a debate about what liberty is and what it should be, and how this involved appropriation of the work of La Boétie.

In *Le Politique*, Politie and Archon's discussion of Machiavelli comes as part of a discussion about how to read. Directly after Politie's speech on Machiavelli, Archon suggests that he should simply be read selectively:

---

[67] David Schaefer, for example, views Montaigne as distinctly Machiavellian, particularly in III, 3. See David Schaefer, *The Political Philosophy of Montaigne* (Ithaca, NY: Cornell University Press, 1990), pp. 247–94. This view is criticised by David Quint, in *Montaigne and the Quality of Mercy*, p. 39. See also Valérie Dionne, *Montaigne, écrivain de la conciliation* (Paris: Garnier, 2014), pp. 67–92.

ARCHON: One must take the good and leave the bad.
POLITIE: On the contrary, men always turn the scraps and rubbish in authors'
                writings into pearls and ornaments. (p. 49)[68]

As well as making a seemingly sardonic comment about the widespread
practice of collecting *sententiae* and maxims, Politie is arguing that a text
can only be judged in its entirety: an argument for textual integrity that
takes on an ironic aspect in light of Goulart's borrowings. Depending on
how we read her opening 'au contraire' ('on the contrary'), she either
agrees with Archon, and regrets that readers generally take the worst
elements of a text and treat them as precious insights, or she disagrees:
one must not attempt to read selectively because readers always confuse
swine for pearls. It seems at least that the author is demanding of Politie's
reader what the character advocates in her critique of Machiavelli: reading
with discretion.[69] Throughout *Le Politique*, Politie's main function is as a
reader and critic, providing glosses mostly on Biblical texts but also several
times on Cicero (whom she criticises in conjunction with Machiavelli, but
quotes approvingly later on [p. 74]). The Politique in the *Reveille-matin*
has a similar role; he offers commentary and analysis of the
Historiographe's story. His purpose in the text is explicitly linked to
critical judgement in the *Argument*: 'The Politique helps the
Historiographe to tell the story and points out the mistakes made on both
sides as they go' (p. 164).[70] In the first dialogue in particular, the Politique
character offers readings not only of Machiavelli but also of a number of
other texts, ancient and modern. Here, then, he plays a similar role to the
narrative voice of Bodin's *République* or Le Roy's *Politiques d'Aristote*:
gathering sources and differentiating between them. The most frequently
discussed Ancient is Cicero, again, while the most striking reading of a
Modern is the gloss on Ronsard's *Franciade*, his unfinished (and highly
political) history of France.[71]

The Politique cites the episode in the *Franciade* in which Bodille, in
ancient France, rebelled against a tyrannical king and killed him and his
pregnant queen.[72] The Politique speculates that 'true French Catholics'

---

[68] 'ARCHON: Il en faut prendre le bon & laisser le mauvais. POLITIE: Au contraire, les hommes font
toujours des perles & ornemens de la racleure & ordure des escrits des autheurs.'
[69] We saw in Chapter 3 how Bodin also required his reader to use their discretion.
[70] 'Le politique aide l'historiographe au récit de l'histoire & marque incidemment les fautes faites de
tous les deux costez.'
[71] Pierre Ronsard, *La Franciade*, ed. by Paul Laumonier, Raymond Lebègue, and Guy Demerson
(Paris: Nizet, 1983).
[72] On this citation, see Fanlo et al., 'Introduction', p. 18.

('les vrais catholiques françois') might bring forth a 'new Bodille', and expresses a kind of mock surprise that Ronsard was so daring as to tacitly encourage this: 'How is it possible that Ronsard published this?' ('Comment est-il possible que Ronsard ait publié cela?', p. 255). He repeats this surprise a couple of pages later: 'God, what is this? Who has ever seen things so well described under other, covert names?' ('Dieu, qu'est-ce là? Qui vit jamais descrire mieux les choses dessous noms couverts?', p. 257). He continues to discuss the Bodille example, and concludes, 'Be assured, Alithie, that Ronsard is marvellously subtle: he really knows how to cut to the quick' ('Asseure-toy Alithie, que Ronsard est merveilleusement subtil, il sçait bien pinser sans rire', p. 258). Alithie agrees, and says she is glad of it, because Ronsard's writing will move readers to do their duty, while his subtlety will save him from being put to death by the tyrant king, or being forced, as Pibrac was, to speak against his own judgement ('se desdire', p. 259).

Thus, in the discussion of Ronsard, the Politique reads the Bodille episode as subtly conforming to Huguenot resistance theory, and in doing so, effectively rewrites that part of the *Franciade* into a nascent resistance canon, at the same time as problematising the term *catholique* (implying that 'true French Catholics' will side with the Huguenots against tyranny). This is also a dig at Ronsard, who wrote polemical poetry supporting the Catholic cause (collected as the *Discours des misères de ce temps*), was a target of Protestant polemicists, and engaged in heated disputes with Théodore de Bèze. The Politique, then, in a similar fashion to Politie, embarks on a process of reading and borrowing from other texts in a manner so active that it amounts to rewriting. It would seem that the Politique character, like Politie in *Le Politique*, is something like Anglo's 'typical Renaissance reader', and as such he may also be (like Gentillet too, in his rewriting of Machiavelli into maxims that he rebuts) an increasingly typical Renaissance writer.

Terence Cave sees the sixteenth-century symbiosis between active reading, writing, and rewriting as one of the fundamental changes in approaches to text that occurred in the early modern period, rendering it distinct, in this way at least, from Medieval and earlier periods. He credits Erasmus with theorising this shift, which he qualifies as, broadly speaking, anti-Ciceronian.[73] The effect was to reverse the balance of power between author as authority and reader as interpreter: it is the reader who gives the

---

[73] Terence Cave, *Retrospectives: Essays in Literature, Poetics and Cultural History*, ed. by Neil Kenny and Wes Williams (London: Legenda, 2009), p. 13.

text meaning, which can therefore only be a contingent one. For Cave, subjectivity of interpretation is thus intimately connected to a growing consciousness of readerly subjectivity, in which 'the reader as an independent subject is beginning to impose himself and his own discourse as primary: the quotation is integrated into a new context authorised by the re-writer'.[74] This leads to what Cave refers to as a 'topos of textual appropriation': a phrase that certainly seems to sum up both the writing practice of the various authors of the Protestant texts I discuss here, and the interpretive process enacted by Le Politique and Politie.[75]

In this way, the fragmentation of conceptions of politics, and the concomitant introduction of plurality to what had been the traditional view of a political community as a singular, universal phenomenon (in Maclean's account), meets the change in reading practices that Cave has outlined.[76] Cave describes this as a 'generative' reading process with a new emphasis on both the writer's and the reader's subjectivity: '[forcing] readers to constitute themselves in their turn as subjects'.[77] His discussion is centred on the reconfiguration of relations between text and individual reader; Montaigne is his key example, but he also cites the *Heptameron*, and Erasmus's *Convivium religiosum* – all his examples either contain dialogue or, like the *Essais*, operate on the principle of bringing different texts into dialogue with each other. This idea of 'generative reading' is differs from the relationship that Bodin sets up in his *République*, where he himself is an extraordinarily active interpreter – a kind of ur-reader who has done most of the hard work for you –while his own reader is more a recipient of predigested content, even if they must still practise discretion. For the readers of these Huguenot texts, as for Cave's 'active readers', more work remains.

But where the dialogues in the *Reveille-matin* and *Le Politique* differ from the texts discussed by Cave is not only in their less-than-canonical literary status, but in the goal of the heuristic exercise that these borrowed, appropriative texts and characters offer their readers: these texts attempt to reinforce readers' efforts to constitute themselves in their turn as *Huguenot* subjects or sympathisers, as well as to compel others to join them, in an attempt to support and expand a community in the wake of the crises that had led to its extreme dispersal. They appeal to the reader's agency, but not so that they may do as they see fit: the 'wake-up call' is intended to marshal the reader, rather than to make them free to choose their own view of the

---

[74] Cave, *Retrospectives*, p. 14. [75] Ibid., p. 15. [76] Maclean, 'From Prudence to Policy', p. 9.
[77] Cave, *Retrospectives*, p. 16.

purpose of politics and of what would constitute the good of the community. The reader is theoretically spurred, like the Politique in the *Reveille-matin*, to reorganise society into a set of Protestant communities where Catholic Christendom used to be. The borrowed text that makes the most direct (and perhaps most compelling) appeal to the reader is La Boétie's *Discours de la servitude volontaire*, in both the *Reveille-matin* and the *Mémoires*, the latter of which incorporated the *Discours* in full (neither mentions the author).[78] And in these authors' borrowings from La Boétie, there are key connections with the term *politique*.

In the *Mémoires*, the anonymised *Discours* is printed immediately after the dialogue *Le Politique*, and the marginal gloss that appears beside the reprised narrative following it is the 'Commencement des Politiques qu'on appelles, & des divers changemens, advenus depuis' (p. 99*v*). Here, then, the *Discours de la servitude volontaire* appears between two texts labelled *politique*; in the *Reveille-matin*, the excerpt from the *Discours* is spoken by someone called Le Politique. The effect of the citation of this controversial, flexible text is to associate this *Discours* with a certain kind of *politique*, and in so doing to harness the *Discours* to serve an aggrieved, and radicalised, Protestant agenda.[79] The politics of La Boétie's text, and the timing of its composition, are the subject of debate. Kingdon, accepting Montaigne's account of the genesis of La Boétie's text two decades earlier, describes it as a rhetorical exercise by a 'Catholic schoolboy', but Demerson suggests that references in the text to the *Pléiade* poets imply further revision in the 1550s, when religious conflict was brewing and *politique* was an emerging keyword in literary and political writing.[80] Ultimately, the abstract setting of the *Discours* as well as its incendiary attack on enablers of tyrants made it an ideal vehicle for writers of the 1570s concerned that the monarchy was descending into tyranny.

In the *Reveille-matin*, the Politique speaks La Boétie's words, presented as those of a Catholic author; in particular, he cites opening of the *Discours*.[81] This is quoted at length as the conclusion of the second dialogue, including this impassioned diatribe against servitude:

---

[78] See Jean-Raymond Fanlo, 'La première édition partielle du *Discours de la servitude volontaire* dans le *Reveille-matin des François et de leurs voisins*', and Cécile Huchard, '"Mise en lumière, et à mauvaise fin": Le *Discours de la servitude volontaire* de La Boétie dans les *Mémoires de l'estat de France* de Simon Goulart', in *La première circulation de la* Servitude volontaire, pp. 219–30 and 253–77.

[79] Huchard points out that this was the main available printed version of the *Discours* until the eighteenth century, 'Mise en lumière, et à mauvaise fin', p. 255.

[80] Kingdon, p. 172.

[81] Jean-Raymond Fanlo argues that selectiveness of the citation shows a certain reserve on the part of the author about the *Discours*; this is borne out in the commentary within the text. Fanlo, 'La première édition partielle', p. 226.

But, oh good God! What can this be? What will we call this? What ill fortune is it? What vice, or rather, what unhappy vice? To see an infinite number of people not obedient, but enslaved; not governed, but tyrannised ... (p. 450)[82]

When the Politique has finished this lengthy quotation, the Historiographe expresses his approval in the strongest of terms:

There is nothing truer in the human world than what you have just told us: so please God, were these fine words to be spread to the very centre of a great assembly of our French Catholics, I am sure that there would be some amongst them who would benefit from them, and none among them who would not find a new spirit in their stomachs, so to speak. (p. 455)[83]

It is interesting that it is Catholics the Historiographe mentions here, rather than Protestants. This recalls the reference to 'true French Catholics' in connection with Ronsard's Bodille; both instances evoke a desire for an alliance against the tyrannical Charles IX between Protestants and moderate Catholics, and/or potentially the kind of conversion experience that the Politique has in the first dialogue. That these 'fine words' ('beaux mots') should be distributed among the populace and breathe new life into them ('un nouvel esprit dans le ventre') gives a new thrust to La Boétie's description of what he hopes for from the average enslaved citizen, that is, the will to be free, which is the first means of actually being free.[84] Since this is now a message for French Catholics, this rewriting of La Boétie's *Discours* as a Politique's call to arms (in a text whose title explicitly announces such a call) reframes this group as one of enslaved citizens who desire freedom. The fairly aggressive rereading (and rewriting) of La Boétie seems slightly paradoxical in its attempt to compel readers to breaking free from what they perhaps do not perceive as tyranny. This is what Montaigne complains about in 1, 28, 'De l'amitié', where he writes about his friendship with La Boétie, and his reason for not

---

[82] 'Mais, ô bon Dieu! que peut estre cela? comment dirons-nous que cela s'appelle? quel malheur est celui là? Quel vice, ou plustost quel malheureux vice, voir un nombre infini de personnes non pas obeir, mais servir; non pas estre gouvernés, mais tirannisés', Etienne de la Boétie, *Discours de la servitude volontaire, ou contr'un*, ed. by Malcolm Smith (Geneva: Droz, 1987), p. 35.

[83] 'Il n'y a rien de plus veritable entre les choses humaines, que ce tu viens d'enseigner: que pleut à Dieu, que ces beaux mots eussent pieça esté semez au beau milieu d'une grande assemblee de nos Catholiques François, je m'asseure, qu'ils y auroyent esté fort bien recueillis, et qu'il n'y auroit celuy d'entre eux, qui n'en fist bien son profit: nul auquel ils ne creassent par maniere de dire, un nouvel esprit dans le ventre.'

[84] La Boétie, p. 137.

reproducing *Discours de la servitude* in the *Essais*. Others have got there first, and in the wrong spirit:

> Because I have found that this work has since been brought to light, and with evil intent, by those who seek to disturb and change the state of our government without worrying whether they will improve it, and because they have mixed his work up with some of their own concoctions, I have changed my mind ('je me suis dédit') about putting it in here (p. 175).[85]

Just as the authors of the *Reveille-matin* described Pibrac having to speak against his true mind as 'unsaying himself' ('se desdire'), here, Montaigne is forced to go against what he had said. The authorial techniques of mixing ('meslé') run parallel to the disruption of government (the 'police'), in a way that has made it impossible, so Montaigne says, for him to make free with the work his beloved friend produced in his youth, and which was originally the means of a great friendship, rather than of civil conflict.

Indeed, the way in which the authors 'make free' with their source texts, and the Politique determines his own meaning for the texts that he cites, risk closing down the infinitely productive series of meanings and contexts implied in the relationship Cave posits between the individual reader and the text. In their attempt to free their readers, and win freedom of conscience for their co-religionists, the authors seem to be minimising the possibility of free thought, or free reading, just as they attempt to minimise the mobility of the term *politique* by anchoring it in a character who comes to represent a particular position.[86] These texts work with the diversity of thought, language use, and interpretation of various other texts, and in some ways embody plurality, but often with a view to reducing it to a form that serves their agenda. A word frequently associated with *politique* in the texts I have discussed here is *liberté* – whether in the words of La Boétie spoken by the Politique, in the description of Politie as representative of 'the liberty of the people', or in an extended passage of the 'Discours politiques' in which 'liberté' is made a crucial element in political communion:

---

[85] 'Parce que j'ay trouvé que cet ouvrage a esté depuis mis en lumiere, et à mauvaise fin, par ceux qui cherchent à troubler et changer l'estat de nostre police, sans se soucier s'ils l'amenderont, qu'ils ont meslé à d'autres escris de leur farine, je me suis dédit de le loger icy', Montaigne, p. 201. On Montaigne as La Boétie's editor, see, for example, Desan, *Montaigne: Une biographie politique*, pp. 210–16.

[86] On freethinking in this period, and Montaigne's attempt to 'think with freedom about freedom of conscience', see Scholar, *Montaigne and the Art of Free-Thinking*, esp. pp. 114–26 on 'De la liberté de conscience' (ii, 19).

If the multitude is therefore made servile, it cannot be active in political communion, since this activity is only possible in liberty. Therefore, the names 'people' and 'city' will be lost, following the etymology of these words which could only apply to free ('franc') people and not to serfs or animals. Similarly, the prince [of such a people] would be a despot, not royal and *politique*. (p. 187)[87]

In this passage, the adjective *politique* is opposed to *servil* and *despotique* – and the suggestion is that for a people and their king to be qualified as 'politique(s)', the people must be 'franc et non serfs' (which evokes Le Roy's rendering of Aristotelian vocabulary and suggestion that *politique* relationships exist among higher, or more free, beings) – here, again, *politique* is used to signal a desirable state of affairs, and of being. The Politique of the *Reveille-matin* seems the embodiment of the impulse to fulfil this desire. But if the author(s) present only one way to understand the texts that they mobilise in the name of freedom, they demonstrate some difficulties of liberty as a political end.

Memory and Projection: The *Politique* Agent

It is crucial to emphasise the textual practices at work in the construction of the Politique character, and in other uses of the term *politique* found in these texts, because this gives a sense of how these Renaissance readers, working here as writer-compilers, used citation in an active way for their own purposes rather than passively receiving influence. The works discussed here demonstrate a great degree of cross-pollination between different strands of discourse, across and beyond the 'languages of politics' explored in Chapters 2 and 3; this is clear in the names of the characters Historiographe and Politique, which recall the higher-register works of Le Roy and Bodin discussed previously, and whose roles in the text seem to carry the influences of those authors, but with different purpose and effect which cannot be seen as accidental. For these Huguenot authors, the potential of rhetorical interventions in the real pertain not simply to potential future socio-political configurations, but to present memories of the past which, after all, are only as 'real' as the means of constructing and keeping them; for Miernowski this is part of a 'poetics of memorialisation'

---

[87] 'Si donc la multitude est rendue servile elle ne peut user de communion politique, car l'usage en subsiste par liberté: par consequent le nom de peuple & de cité se perdra suivant l'etymologie de ces noms qui s'entendent estre dits de gens francs et non serfs ne bestiaux. Pareillement tel prince seroit despotique & non royal & politique.'

at work in Goulart's *Mémoires*.[88] This poetics of memory and of nostalgia is political. Alithie's project in the first dialogue of the *Reveille-matin*, of unveiling or disclosing the truth, can also be understood as a kind of wishful world-building in hindsight.

Running against the grain of contemporary Catholic narratives, the texts I discuss here offer accounts of the past, the righting of wrongs in text if not in fact, and a series of suggestions, appearing either under the title *politique*, or attached to the adjective (from Daniel's 'loix politiques' to the *Discours politiques* in the *Mémoires*) for how to create a better world to come. Critics and historians have argued that this is part of their deliberate creation of 'myths' (Kingdon) and 'fables' (Miernowski) that serve both past and future.[89] In his discussion of Goulart's process of rewriting – and of (re)writing history – Pot suggests that his is more the dream of a poet than of a religious zealot, such is his faith in the power of language, and of written texts, to change the world.[90] In one sense his faith was rewarded in the long term. Diefendorf has shown that the shared 'myths' or 'fables' invented by the authors of the *Reveille-matin* and the *Mémoires* had considerable longevity in French collective memory; they recurred in fictional, historical, and political output, even as Protestants were largely politically disenfranchised, and even after the effective expulsion of the Huguenots in 1685.[91] Their descriptions of the Saint Bartholomew's Day massacres had a rich afterlife that continued into the nineteenth-century vogue for the history of the Wars of Religion.[92]

In her discussion of Thomas More's *Dialogue of Comfort against Tribulation*, which he wrote in the Tower of London while awaiting execution, Eva Kushner suggests that the dialogue form – as well as being an 'idealised form of conversation' (in Synder's terms) connected with ideal forms of Renaissance sociability – became, in the context of confessional conflict and the persecutions that accompanied it, a form born of 'necessity and powerlessness'.[93] This certainly applies to the fragmented

---

[88] Miernowski, 'La mémoire des massacres', pp. 156–57.

[89] Kingdon, p. 5; Miernowski, 'La mémoire des massacres', p. 145.   [90] Pot, p. 39.

[91] Diefendorf discusses how the *Reveille-matin* the first instance of an account of Charles IX firing upon Protestants from a window in the Louvre, an act which would, she says, have been physically impossible. And yet the image was picked up by Bossuet and by Voltaire, and is said to have been referenced by Mirabeau in his discussions of freedom of conscience in the National Assembly. See Diefendorf, *Blood Wedding: The Saint Bartholomew's Day Massacre in History and Memory* (Boston, MA: Boston University Press, 2006), pp. 20 and 139.

[92] This reached its height, perhaps, in Alexandre Dumas's *La Reine Margot*, published in 1845; it was made into a highly successful film in 1994.

[93] Eva Kushner, 'Renaissance Dialogue and Subjectivity', in *The Renaissance Culture of Dialogue*, ed. by Dorothea Heitsch and Jean-François Vallée, pp. 229–42; Snyder, p. 6.

communities of France in the wake of the bloodiest (but not the first, or last) massacres of the civil wars, wherein families and networks were separated either for good or for the foreseeable future by bereavements, exile, abjurations, blockades, imprisonment, and so on. And there is reason to understand the dialogues in Goulart's *Mémoires*, and in the *Réveille-matin*, as being formed in such a way, not only because of what we know about the historical context, but also because of how the dialogues and speakers are introduced, such as in the letter to the nephew from the author of 'Le Politique' citing his consolatory goals and the act of writing as a necessity in the circumstances (p. 45*v*). These dialogues of the French civil wars should therefore be understood as part of a long tradition in political dialogues, running from Boethius's *De consolatione* (a dialogue between the author and Philosophy), through Thomas More, to the mostly anonymous writers and editors of the texts I discuss here.[94] In the *Reveille-matin* and Goulart's *Mémoires*, this tradition coexists with the use of various sub-genres of dialogue (didactic, humanist, conflictual, and consensual dialogues, to follow Baranova's typology: all of these elements seem present in the texts I discuss here) and intersects with other generic traditions, old and new (tragedy, *mémoire*, martyrology, history-writing, politics in the sense that Bodin understood it).[95]

Pocock describes Boethius's *De consolatione* as 'not a work of political philosophy, but the work of a political man', a political man aggrieved by misuse of power.[96] The dialogues I discuss here, also motivated by disappointment and a desire to counteract oppression, constitute (or 're-construct') a 'political man' – a man then recognisable as a good version of *le politique*. How the Politique is characterised, and how the term works within the highly complex polyphonic framework described above, has been made clear in two respects. Firstly, the word is a signpost for one of the many different generic and discursive templates borrowed and reshaped by the various authors. Secondly, in the *Reveille-matin*, the term

---

[94] Pocock sees Boethius as a paradigmatic figure in Renaissance political thought. See Pocock, *The Machiavellian Moment*, p. 36.

[95] Baranova, p. 416. Critics have noted that a keyword of these highly successful Huguenot poetics of the 1570s and beyond is *tragédie*, or *tragique* – the most famous example being Agrippa d'Aubigné's *Les tragiques*. See Jean-Raymond Fanlo, *Tracés, ruptures: La composition instable des Tragiques* (Paris: Champion, 1990). On Huguenot descriptions of the Saint Bartholomew's Day massacres as 'la tragédie des tragédies', see Huchard, p. 315. For such descriptions in the texts discussed in this chapter, see *Le Politique*, p. 44*v*, and the 'Argument' of the *Reveille-matin* (n.p.). On tragic theatre in this period, see Ruth Stawarz-Luginbühl, R., *Un théâtre de l'épreuve: Tragédies huguenotes en marge des guerres de religion* (Geneva: Droz, 2012).

[96] Pocock, *The Machiavellian Moment*, p. 36.

is paired with 'Historiographe' (the two characters are introduced as a pair in the first dialogue and are the only speakers in the second) to act as an indicator and agent of future change, while the Historiographe describes the past. These uses represent a confessionalised co-opting of the functions of historical and political writing as Le Roy and Bodin would have understood them. By investing their Politique character with exceptional agency – far more, certainly, than the authors themselves were able to exert in reality – the Huguenot 'borrowers' had much in common with Le Roy and Bodin. This demonstrates that in the mid-1570s the word experienced a moment of particularly strong construction and investment of different meanings, which no single author – or text – could contain. These varied constructions are influenced by contemporary practices of 'active' reading and rewriting, and reflect both commonplacing techniques and the practice of digesting of long-form arguments into maxims or sententiae. In other words, they show the close relationship between approaches to text (and intertexts) and approaches to politics.

In the *Reveille-matin des François* and the texts collected in Simon Goulart's *Mémoires*, the term *politique* operates as an organisational force directing the political thrust of the variously composed narratives. The choice of this particular term reflects its increasing currency in contemporary discourse, and also a desire to enact change in the 'real world' by manipulating a term imbued with agency and associated with powers of discrimination and judgement. Uses of *politique* in these texts seem to have absorbed uses and re-definitions in others, as well as making their own interventions. Within this framework, the impact of Machiavelli, and of anti-Machiavellian impulses is not, as one might have expected, one in which *politique* becomes negatively charged through increasing proximity to the figure of the 'Machiavel' (it was later that the figure of the 'politique machiavelique' was constructed by League pamphleteers). Instead, the impact of anti-Machiavellianism in the texts under discussion here is to increase the dynamism of the word *politique* and its referents; as Gentillet shows in his preface to the *Contre Machiavel*, the term, and politics itself, can still be rescued from Machiavelli. In this chapter, then, I have tried to excavate a moment in the history of the term *politique* in which a *politique* character becomes the embodiment of the various authors' positions in the increasingly contested semantic and ideological fields in which the word *politique* operated. As such, it seems that in the texts of this period the term comes to signal, and indeed embody, a 'problem of meaning' (to use Raymond Williams's phrase), whether you call that problem a 'Machiavellian moment' or the problem of liberty, or something in between.[97]

The uncertainty of French politics in the mid-1570s (including the Edict of Beaulieu in 1576 that was relatively favourable to Huguenots) may have made it seem to these authors, despite the devastating losses to their side, that structural political change might be possible. At the same time they were motivated by grief and fear of further violence. The wishful, nostalgic, memorialising poetics of these texts alert us to the varied grammars of political writing: its tenses, and subjunctive tendencies, demonstrating the engagement of the political with what is, what was, what could be, and what should be or should have been. These authors' attempts to turn *politique* into something, and indeed someone, that they can rely on to speak for their cause and provide argumentative support were not especially successful. For one thing, responses to their texts do not seem threatened by their *politiques* – the Catholic riposte to the *Reveille-matin*, written by Arnaud Sorbin, *prédicateur* to Charles IX, does not even make use of the adjectival form of the word other than in reference to Daniel's 'political laws', instead focusing on *liberté*, writing that 'We are no more lovers of Tyranny than you are, and love liberty no less than you pretend to' – it is just that he thinks they go too far, and push for 'excessive freedoms' ('dezbordees libertez').[98] Beyond this, the associations between *politique* and *liberté* (and, more loosely, *machiavel*) hold to the extent that they become part of the spectrum of negative associations around the term *politique* in League polemic, in which the *politique* becomes *libertin* (as well as *machiavelique*), as we shall see in the next chapter. These uses will represent part of the continuing process of reappropriation in which the term *politique* appears in all its different guises: having been put to use by Protestants in the mid-1570s, in the following decade the *politique* will be excoriated by their long-term opponents.

---

[97] Williams, *Keywords*, p. 22.
[98] 'Nous ne sommes non plus amateurs de la Tyrannie, que vous, & n'aimons pas moins la liberté, que vous en faites semblant', Arnault Sorbin, *Le vray resveille-matin des calvinistes, et publicains françois: Où est amplement discouru de l'auctorité des princes, & du devoir des sujets envers iceux* (Paris: G. Chaudière, 1576), pp. 7 and 71[v].

PART III

c. 1588–94

CHAPTER 5

'What Is This Monster?' The 'Bad' Politique

In March 1589, Jean Bodin rose to speak at the general assembly of the town of Laon, where he then resided. At this meeting, the town declared for the Catholic League and against Henri de Navarre. Bodin tried to speak out in favour of townspeople who had been carried off to prison overnight, but those gathered shouted him down, threatening to erect a gibbet and saying that Bodin would be first upon it. Antoine Richart (d. 1602), who recorded all this in his *Mémoires*, says that the crowd was calmed and other speakers replaced Bodin. Richart reflects on the failed *harangue* a few pages later:

> As for Bodin, he kept to himself and saw no one, however much in his speech he had tried to show his allegiance to the League, while trampling underfoot before true Frenchmen the rights and authorities of the French estates. It was in vain, for he was well known in the town as a *politicque* and dangerous catholic, showing how true a thing it is that wise men do not always show perfect discretion or judgement. It must therefore be that often they show signs of weakness in human understanding, which is what happened to Bodin in his speech at the Cathedral where he used ill-sounding words that I do not wish to repeat. This act was a significant mark against him among men of honour; his words seemed to him to be fit to make him more agreeable to Leaguers (against his conscience), by going so far in his speech as to show disdain for his King . . . but for all that, Bodin was thereafter no more employed in public affairs; the Leaguers used him only like a stick to beat imbeciles.[1]

---

[1] 'De Bodin il demeura seul sans fréquentation de personne, combien qu'en sa harangue il se fust efforcé de montrer son affection a la ligue en foullant aux piedz devant tous vraiz françois les droictz et auctoritez des estatz de France, mais en vain, car il estoit bien cogneu en la ville pour ung politicque et dangereux catholicque, dont cest une chose tres vraie que les hommes saiges nont pas tousjours une discretion ou jugement parfait. De quoy il est neccessaire que souvent se demonstrent des signes de la foiblesse de l'entendement humain tel qu'il arrivera a Bodin en sa harangue qu'il feit a ceste eglise cathedralle ou il uza des paroles assez mal sonnantes que je ne veulx réciter. Cest acte lui donna une grande tache entre les gens d'honneur, il luy sembla ces parolles estre propres pour se rendre (contre sa conscience) plus agreable aux ligueurs a s'estendre ainsy par trop en sa harangue au

Bodin had also been trying to declare his new allegiance to the Catholic League. He did the same in print in his *Lettre de Monsieur Bodin* (1590), possibly a printed version of the failed *harangue*.[2] Richart suggests that the listeners in Laon felt this declaration was not made in good faith, but rather to save his skin.[3] What the anecdote makes clear, in any case, is that Bodin's *harangue* failed because he was well known as 'a *politicque* and dangerous Catholic' (here, as in earlier instances, this could be read as adjective or noun, and is an example of the term *catholique* being problematised in conjunction with *politique*). Bodin's experience signals that, by 1589, the term *politique* had a new context, with an altered 'hum of connotations' that made the term a threat to people's lives, and was loud enough to drown out other speech (Bodin's own 'ill-sounding' words) as well as alternative uses of *politique*.[4] In the *Lettre de Monsieur Bodin*, Bodin uses the term just once, to condemn 'all the Huguenots, *politiques*, heretics, and atheists' who make up 'the party of the King of Navarre'.[5] He makes no mention of the *sage politique* of his *République*, but echoes the condemnatory uses of contemporary polemic.

By the late 1580s, the political situation in France was one of protracted crisis in the wake of Henri III's failure to broker lasting peace, the death of the heir apparent François d'Alençon and consequent prospect of a Huguenot heir, Henri de Navarre, and the refounding of the Catholic League in 1584 in reaction to this and to Henri III's failures. At this critical juncture, the figure of the *politique* – along with the word itself – takes centre stage in textual attempts to understand chaotic political circumstances and to define boundaries of belonging within this turbulence. Bodin's failed speech in Laon is evidence on the one hand of a failure of language, but on the other of the power of language: the power of a word (*politique*) to designate a person as either belonging to, or excluded from, the political community. It is a turning point in the narrative of this book, demonstrating a different way in which sixteenth-century language

mespris de son Roy, et comme depuis il feit encores a une responce quil sera dict cy apres, mais pour tout cela Bodin n'en fut davantage emploié aux affaires publicques, les ligueurs se servant de lui seulement comme d'un baston a ruer aux noix.' Antoine Richart, *Mémoires sur la ligue dans le laonnais* (Laon: Libraires de la Société; Paris: Didron-Neveu, 1869), p. 68. On Richart's *Mémoires*, and Bodin's life in Laon, see Lloyd, *Jean Bodin*, pp. 196–204. 'Like a stick to beat imbeciles' is Lloyd's translation of the phrase 'comme d'un baston a ruer aux noix', p. 201.

[2] Jean Bodin, *Lettre de Monsieur Bodin* ([?],1590). See Lloyd, *Jean Bodin*, pp. 202–04.
[3] Turchetti argues that the letter showed clear and perceptive political judgement, and that Bodin genuinely did back the League at this stage of his life. See Mario Turchetti, 'Jean Bodin', in *Stanford Encyclopedia of Philosophy* (2005) http://plato.stanford.edu/entries/bodin/ [accessed 2 August 2016].
[4] Kenny, *Word Histories*, p. 18.   [5] Bodin, *Lettre*, p. 7.

users 'did things' with *politique*. Bodin is alienated from his audience because he is *known* ('cogneu') as a *politique*. In earlier chapters, the abstract noun *politique* was an object of knowledge, a way of knowing, a person who knows: here, instead, the *politique* person is the object to be known, recognised, and rejected. The meaning of the term has, in this context, quite literally been re-cognised, re-thought; or at least, that is the kind of shift in perception that some writers attempt to provoke in their audience. These processes of (re)-cognition are integral to the *politique* problem.

In the long drama of the civil wars, with its tragedies and its absurdities, we can point to the late 1580s as the moment in which *politique* undergoes a kind of 'recognition', or *anagnorisis*, in which the term and its referents are revealed as the villains, or indeed, the monsters, of the plot.[6] Except that in the multitude of texts this moment is repeated, restaged, and always somehow incomplete, so that the shift from ignorance to knowledge managed by *anagnorisis* is never fully realised. Indeed, the mobility, and unknowability, of the term and its referents becomes perhaps *the* primary feature of the *politique* in these texts. Bodin may have been well known as a *politique*, but across the pamphlet literature I explore here, the *politique* can be tricky, hidden, nigh on unknowable, even as knowing who is *politique* is presented as vitally important. The drama of these moments of re-cognition, recognition, and failed communication then becomes that of an essential ambiguity of meaning. This reflects what is perhaps the key difficulty – and interest – of the term *politique* in this period: that it refers to *something* or *someone*, but also to nothing. Half the work of historians working on this topic has been to prove that there was no such thing as a self-identifying *politique*, or *Politique* party. In this chapter I confront the extent to which *politique* was a discursive construct, and the extent to which, at this moment of its being particularly prominent in discourse, rhetoric surrounding politics and *politiques* was a part of socio-political reality.

Mixed Merchandise: A Proliferation of *Politiques*

The word *politique* – and attempts to establish, or re-establish the way that it was understood – became a crucial tool in the dramatic confrontation

---

[6] Terence Cave, *Recognitions: A Study in Poetics* (Oxford: Clarendon, 1988), pp. 1–5. Bodin was known ('cogneu') as *politique*; Cave shows that the 'cognitio/connaître' word group was often used in Latinate renderings of *anagnorisis*, p. 5.

between the Catholic League and the fractured monarchy. This was a battle to win over the hearts and minds of townspeople across France.[7] The conflict came to a head in 1588–89. Henri III was forced to flee Paris in May 1588 on the Day of Barricades ('la journée des barricades'). In December, Henri struck back, ordering the assassination of the Guise brothers. The following year, Henri was assassinated in turn, by a monk then hailed as an avenging angel by Leaguers. In the wake of this, the already weakened French state devolved even more than it had already into various city states (including Laon), which sided with either the Protestant heir to the throne, Henri de Navarre, or with the League; the assassination of the Guise brothers transformed the urban fortunes of the League, as towns across France from Dijon to Toulouse declared their allegiance.[8] Paris was the League's heartland. For the next ten years or so, Henri de Navarre waged a series of successful military campaigns and conquered the country town by town (he besieged Laon with devastating effect in 1594), but – famously – he could not enter Paris until he had converted to Catholicism. The battles were accompanied by a huge amount of printed production from presses sympathetic to the League: they churned out news, propaganda, and anti-Navarre polemic.

There is a striking proliferation of bad *politiques* in this pamphlet material that came from France's two centres of printing, Paris and Lyon. The pamphlets are mostly anonymous, but it is likely that many of the authors were Catholic preachers who supported the League.[9] These sources are especially significant in this study for the fact that the *politique* person or persona is the primary object of these texts, rather than working as a supporting device, or being one character amongst several in a dialogue. They are mostly polemical pamphlets or *libelles*, as well as L'Estoile's broadsheet collection, *Les drolleries de la League*

---

[7] On the history of the Catholic League, see Constant, *La Ligue*, Baumgartner, *Radical Reactionaries*, and *La Ligue et ses frontières: Engagements catholiques à distance du radicalisme à la fin des guerres de religion*, ed. by Sylvie Daubresse and Bertrand Haan (Rennes: Presses universitaires de Rennes, 2015). On the League in Paris in particular, see Elie Barnavi, *Le Parti de Dieu: Etude sociale et politique des chefs de la Ligue parisienne, 1585–1594* (Brussels: Nauwelaerts, 1980).

[8] Mack P. Holt, *The French Wars of Religion 1562–1629* (Cambridge: Cambridge University Press, 2005), pp. 137–38.

[9] Cécile Huchard, 'Echoes des prédicateurs parisiens dans le *Journal du règne d'Henri IV de Pierre de L'Estoile*', in *La parole publique en ville des Réformes à la Révolution*, ed. by Stefano Simiz (Villeneuve-d'Ascq: Presses universitaires du Septentrion, 2012), pp. 181–95. On Parisian preachers, see Vladimir Angelo, *Les curés de Paris au XVIe siècle* (Paris: Cerf, 2005); on their relation with the League, see pp. 485–96.

(*c.* 1589–98).[10] Although they are brief bursts of text in comparison to enormous tomes like Bodin's *République*, they represent a significant proportion of all the primary texts discussed in this book, and almost all of them were produced in 1589–90, while Paris was under the jurisdiction of the radical Catholic *Seize*.[11] Much of the printed output of this period has been lost; there must originally have been many more texts in general, including more condemning *politiques*.[12] The texts are short; they were printed cheaply; many respond to or report key events (particularly the assassinations of the Guise brothers and Henri III). They overlap in generic terms with the short, cheap, printed works that represent an early form of 'news' and informed city populations of the outcomes of battles, councils, and the like.[13] It is therefore likely that they had a far wider

[10] Baranova argues that it is anachronistic to refer to the short, cheaply printed polemical texts I discuss here as *pamphlets* in French, and that they should rather be referred to as *libelles*, or more precisely as *libelles diffamatoires* (defamatory writings; *libelle* means 'libel' and also, more simply, 'short text'). See *A coup de libelles*, pp. 33 and 35. In English, it seems that this problem of labelling does not exist. For 'Pamphlet', the *Oxford English Dictionary* gives as its definition a handwritten or printed short text, bound without a hard cover, adding that this may indicate a 'work of a polemical or political nature issued in this form'. The first example of this particular use is, in fact, from 1588 in a work called *Briefe Discoverie of Doctor Allens Seditious Drifts*, which complains that 'Certeine ouersights in policie escaped this great politicien in this Pamphlet, which is mere politike.' Here, interestingly, we see an English use of 'politike' as a negative adjective, alongside the nouns 'policie' and 'politicien' – and a description of a 'Pamphlet' as 'mere politike', suggesting that 'pamphlet' is the term that would have been used in sixteenth-century English to describe the texts I discuss in this chapter, and that an English reader would not have been surprised to find *politiques* in these pamphlets. Source: 'Pamphlet', *n.* in *The Oxford English Dictionary* www.oed.com/search?searchType=dictionary&q=pamphlet&_searchBtn=Search [accessed 2 August 2018]. On the dating of the *Drolleries*, and for analysis of their compilation and significance, see Hamilton, *Pierre de L'Estoile and his World*, pp. 140–65.

[11] Pallier estimates that the *Ligueur* presses produced over a thousand titles over a ten-year period and that almost a third were produced in 1589 alone. See Pallier, *Recherches sur l'imprimerie à Paris*, pp. 55, 57, and 215–17.

[12] Pierre de L'Estoile describes how Senault, a leader of the *Seize*, worked with a particular printer, Nivelle, to produce a list of *politiques* to be arrested, hanged, or stabbed in Paris, the famous *Papier Rouge*, described by L'Estoile as a list of 'tous ces Politiques (qu'ils appeloient) qui estoient les plus honnetes hommes et gens de bien de Paris' – which points to the existence and circulation of more ephemeral documents targeting *politiques* that have not survived. L'Estoile's name was on the list next to 'D' ('dagué'). See L'Estoile, *Mémoires-Journaux*, v, pp. 131–32. Modern historians rely on L'Estoile's collections and journal to estimate the output of *Ligueur* printers; Pallier suggests that more than a thousand Leaguer pieces must have been printed during the years 1585–94, pp. 56–57. Baumgartner describes with regret the loss of many League documents on Henri IV's orders after his accession. See Baumgartner, pp. 18–19. Anxiety about the deleterious effects of unfettered pamphlet printing in the wake of the Wars of Religion led to sustained state censorship from the reign of Henri IV onwards. See Butterworth, *Poisoned Words*, pp. 12–13.

[13] On early modern news and information networks, see *News in Early Modern Europe: Currents and Connections*, ed. by Simon F. Davies and Puck Fletcher (Leiden: Brill, 2014). For a case study of news pamphlets, with a focus on England, which includes some analysis of the transmission of news between France and England, see Paul J. Voss, *Elizabethan News Pamphlets: Shakespeare, Spenser, Marlowe and the Birth of Journalism* (Pittsburgh, PA: Duquesne University Press, 2001). Histories of print at this time point to the strong appetite for news of all kinds in Paris during the League

audience than any of the other works I analyse in this book.[14] At this time, numerous people were named as *politique*, and pamphlets conjured up the image of hundreds or thousands more *politiques* in towns and cities across France, not just in Paris, Lyon, or Laon.[15] In the crucible of these final years of the religious wars, the term *politique* permeated everyday language to a far greater extent than it ever had before.

Perhaps because they are popular, cheap, and brief, the extent to which these texts can be considered 'literary' has been debated by critics; it has lately been the trend to argue in favour of the literary status of pamphlets and point out their varied use of literary techniques and references with the aim of pleasing, persuading, or sometimes offending the reader.[16] But if these are literary texts, what kind of literature are they? Some of the anonymous or pseudonymous authors of these pamphlets make reference to the contingent nature of their form, suggesting the perishable immediacy of their rapid-fire content. Greengrass describes the pamphlets produced in this context as 'panic literature', meant to spur the reading or listening audiences to hateful words and deeds, and to stay firm against Henri de Navarre.[17] It is my aim to analyse the hatred and violence incited by these pamphlets in their immediate context; to show the word *politique* instrumentalised as weapon. But writers of these pamphlets also situate their works in a wider literary field, and I attempt to show where their pamphlets participate in the wider political conversation that occurred in sixteenth-century France.

The late 1580s were a time of crisis and of striking literary-political production. Montaigne experienced the crisis and was a part of the productivity; he was in the capital in 1588 overseeing the final edition of the *Essais* to be printed in his lifetime, and in July of that year he was briefly incarcerated in the Bastille as retaliation for a Leaguer taken prisoner in Rouen.[18] The year 1589 also saw a landmark publication in

---

years in particular; see Pallier, p. 57. The titles of several anti-*politique* pamphlets, including some printed outside Paris, indicate that their function is very much to report on provincial affairs.

[14] Racaut estimates that printed pamphlets in the period up to 1615 reached roughly 1 per cent of the overall population, even if their content was disseminated more broadly in public preaching; Racaut, pp. 40–41.

[15] On the existential quality of the confrontation between the League and 'Politiques', see Crouzet, *Guerriers de Dieu*, pp. 249–54.

[16] Antonia Szabari discusses this trend in *Less Rightly Said: Scandals and Readers in Sixteenth-Century France* (Stanford, CA: Stanford University Press, 2010), pp. 5–8. She argues for literary readings of texts that a nineteenth-century critic referred to as 'mitraille' (p. 5).

[17] Greengrass, *France in the Age of Henri IV*, p. 8.

[18] Philippe Desan, *Montaigne: A Life*, p. 528. Earlier that year Montaigne had also been held by Protestants. Warren Boutcher comments that the lukewarm initial reception of the third volume of

European political writing, Giovanni Botero's *Della ragion' di stato* ('The Reason of State'), which was influenced by the writer's time in France in 1583–84 at the start of the troubles of the League.[19] Also in 1589, an Italian collection of political writings known as the *Tesoro politico* – short treatises, diplomatic texts, reportage – was published in Paris; this work became well known throughout Europe in the seventeenth century following its first Italian printing in Milan in 1601.[20] Jean Balsamo shows that this first printing of the *Tesoro* likely happened in France because some of its contents were circulating among the French legal elite in the 1580s, and that it was published by a group of Leaguer printers (possibly including Binet, who appears on the list in Figure 1).[21] It is intriguing, as Balsamo notes, that League-affiliated printers would have printed material that did not always show the League in a good light, but what the printing of the *Tesoro politico* in Paris in 1589 shows, at least, is the variation of political writing at this time and that political printing, even by propagandists, was not homogenous.[22]

Many of the pamphlets discussed below are written in literary style and filled with humanist allusions. The anonymous writers lived in the same cultural world, and probably had similar educations and reference points, as the other writers discussed in this book, even if they differ in style and intent. An analysis of the term *politique* in these texts requires both 'fast' and 'slow' models of inferential communication, to understand both its immediate resonance and its looser ripples of association. The 'recognition moment' of the new *politique* of the 1580s depends on both kinds of associative understanding. Literature has recently been described as 'an instrument of human cognition, continuous with spoken language yet with a longer life-span and more sustainedly reflective'.[23] The texts discussed here are more continuous with spoken language than any others analysed in this book, and in some cases offer a paucity of sustained reflection. And yet, their uses of language and argumentative constructions

---

the *Essais* was in part the result of the rebellion of the League and its consequences for the book trade between 1588 and 1594, *The School of Montaigne*, II, p. 15.

[19] Robert Bireley, 'Introduction', in Giovanni Botero, *The Reason of State*, ed. and tr. by Robert Bireley (Cambridge: Cambridge University Press, 2017), pp. xiv–xxxvi (p. xvii).

[20] Jean Balsamo, 'Les origines parisiennes du *Tesoro politico* (1589)', *Bibliothèque d'Humanisme et Renaissance*, LVII.1 (1995), 7–23.

[21] Ibid., p. 13. On League-affiliated printers see Zwierlein, *The Political Thought of the Catholic League*, pp. 31–68.

[22] Ibid., pp. 18–19.		[23] Cave, *Thinking with Literature*, p. 7.

sustain extended reflection, revealing the attempts of these authors to influence or interrupt a longer conversation, as well as to impose new meanings of the term *politique* on Parisians attempting to make sense of their surroundings in a moment of chaos and deprivation.

The titles of the pamphlets I discuss here demonstrate the new semantic field in which *politique* was operating *c.* 1589. Many of them are primarily concerned with describing *politiques* and advising the reader on how to identify them. The titles listed in Figure 1 give a sense of *politiques* operating beyond the accepted norms of the political community, through associations with *perfidie* (perfidy), *trahison* (treason), *heresie, atheisme* and so on; there is also a strong emphasis on disruptive speech: *impostures* (lies), *calomnies* (calumny), *caquet* (babble), *cartel* (challenge). The word 'bigarré', used by Pasquier in his *Recherches* and Henri Estienne in his complaints about courtly language half a century earlier, returns, showing that the 'mixed' quality of *politiques* is important. These *politiques* are both insulted and insulting. The generally quarrelsome context of the period is evoked by the encounters staged in some pamphlets between *politiques* and 'true' Catholics, and the evocation of disputes and responses: here, *politiques* are engaged in destructive, rather than constructive, dialogue. A sense that the *politiques* are hidden, disruptive elements is also clear from the revelatory intentions announced by various texts ('trahison descouverte', 'treason uncovered'; 'discours veritables', 'true discourse/speech'). The emphasis on discovery and unveiling recalls the Huguenot project of 'disclosure' discussed in the previous chapter, but revelation is endlessly deferred in these pamphlets. The title of one that appeared in Lyon in 1591 betrays a certain frustration with a *politique* 'who does not dare name himself' ('qui ne s'est osé nommer'). The *politique* not naming (him)self gives the writer an opportunity: to wield the term *politique* like a weapon, harnessing the power of naming, and name-calling, against certain ways of being, and of arguing.

Many pamphlets acknowledge the difficulty of defining and describing the *politique* even as they set out to do precisely that. The author of *Le karesme et mœurs du Politique où il est amplement discouru de sa maniere de vivre, de son Estat & Religion* ('The Lent and Manners of the *Politique* in which his way of life, State, and Religion are widely discussed', 1589) makes the following statement at the beginning of the text, with a marginal note that says 'que c'est que politique' ('what *politique* is'):

Title	Place of Publication and Printer (if known)	Date of Publication (if known)
Description de l'homme politique de ce temps avec sa foy et religion qui est un Catalogue de plusieurs heresies et athéismes, où tombent ceux qui préfèrent l'estat humain à la Religion Catholique	Paris (G. Bichon)	1588
La Foy et Religion des Politiques de ce temps. Contenant la refutation de leurs heresies	Paris (G. Bichon)	1588
Mémoires semez par quelques politics aux Estats, qui se tiennent, en la ville de Bloys. Avec la response Catholique à iceux		1588
Deux devis, d'un Catholique et d'un Politique, sur l'exhortation faicte au peuple de Nantes {...} le huitième jour de Juin, mil cinq cens quatre vingts et neuf	Nantes (N. Desmarestz and F. Faverye)	1589
Coppie de la responce faite par un polytique de ceste ville de Paris, aux precedens Memoires secrets, qu'un sien Amy lu avoit envoyés de Bloys, en forme de Missive	[Lyon (J. Pillehotte)]	1589
La Contrepoison contre les artifices et inventions des politiques et autres ennemis de la religion Catholique	Paris (A. Le Riche)	1589
Le Karesme et moeurs du Politique où il est amplement discouru de sa manière de vivre, de son Estat & Religion	Paris (Pierre-Des-Hayes)	1589
Les impostures et calomnies des Huguenots, Politiques & Atheistes pour colorer le massacre és personnes de Messeigneurs les Cardinal & Duc de Guyse par Henry de Valois		1589
L'arpocratie, ou Rabais du caquet des politiques et jebusiens de nostre aage	Lyon (J. Pattrason)	1589
Discours des trahisons, perfidies et desloyautez des politiques de Paris	Lyon (L. Tantillon)	1589
Discours veritable de la deffaite obtenue sur les trouppes des politiques et hérétiques, du pays et duché de Berry	Paris (D. Millot)	1589
La TRAHISON descouverte des politiques de la ville de Rouen		1589
La TRAHISON descouverte des politiques de la ville de Troyes	Paris	1589
Description du politique de nostre temps avec sa foy et religion qui est un Catalogue de plusieurs heresies et athéismes, où tombent ceux qui préfèrent l'estat humain à la Religion Catholique	Lyon	1591
Coppie d'une lettre escripte par un Catholique à un Politique, sur l'arrest prononcé en la Synagogue de Tours le cinquiesme d'aoust dernier	Lyon	1591
Responce au cartel d'un politique bigarré qui ne s'est osé nommer	Lyon (L. Tantillon)	1591
La Dispute d'un catholique de Paris, contre un Politique de la ville de Tours	Paris (R. Nivelle and R. Thierry)	1591
L'aveuglement et grande inconsideration des Politiques, dicts Maheustres, lesquels veulent introduire Henry de Bourbon, jadis Roy de Navarre, à la Couronne de France, à cause de sa pretenduë succession, par Fr. I. P. D. en Theologie	Paris	1592
La Trahison Descouverte des Politiques de la ville de Troyes en Champaigne, Avec les noms des capitaines & Politiques qui avoient conspire contre la Saincte Union des Catholiques	Paris (D. Binet and A. Du Brueil)	

Figure 1.   Pamphlets discussed in this chapter with the word *politique* in the title, *c.* 1588–92.
Sources: Bibliothèque nationale de France; The British Library

> But before I go any further, it would not be impertinent to give a definition of this word, *Politique*, newly used in French workshops: for people speak of *Politique* who happen to have no idea how it ought to be used, so that that which is defined here does not even qualify as definition in the proper sense, following the homonymy or equivocacy of this word which is thus distinguished from others.[24]

Here, the author acknowledges that the word is newly used, locating this novelty in 'workshops' – which suggests use beyond the traditionally cited spheres of *politique* activity, the *Parlement* and courts: perhaps it was a reference to printing shops in particular. The word is particularly tricky because of its 'homonymy or equivocacy': a potential plurality of meaning, and of varied uses (and mis-uses). The previous year, the author of *La foy et religion des Politiques*, had made a similar statement in his dedicatory letter (to an unnamed 'great lord'):

> Those who here and there in private and public we call POLITIQUES are not yet manifest Huguenots, nor true and zealous Catholics: but a mixed merchandise, a boutique filled with all kinds of intoxicants intermingling together in confusion, and so it is very difficult and dangerous to write you a perfect definition of them.[25]

Here *politique* is something that people are called, rather than call themselves: the appearance of the term alongside the verb 'appeler' ('on appelle': 'we call') is characteristic of this material as well as of some earlier uses of the term (for example, the fragment in Goulart's *Mémoires*, 'commencement des Politiques qu'on appelle'). And this name indicates a liminal, or mixed state: between Huguenot and 'true Catholic'. The author uses commercial metaphors ('mixed merchandise', 'boutique') to create a sense of confusion, and also of abundance – this could be read as a reference to the frequent use of the term as well as to its variation. Words, phrases, and even entire speeches were often referred to as having magical or drug-like properties in sixteenth-century France; in the next chapter we see this

---

[24] 'Mais avant que j'entre plus avant en matiere, il ne sera pas impertinent de donner la definition de ce mot Politique nouvellement usité aux officines Françoises: car tel parle de Politique qui ne sçait paravanture pas comment il se doit usurper, d'autant qu'en ce lieu icy qui est Definy ne compete pas à ce que doit competer la Definition, suyvant l'homonymie ou equivocque de ce mot qui se doit distinguer en ceste sorte.' *Le karesme et mœurs du Politique où il est amplement discouru de sa manière de vivre, de son Estat & Religion* (Paris: Pierre-Des-Hayes, 1589), p. 5.

[25] 'Ceux que par deça & en privé & en public on appelle POLITIQUES, ne sont encore Huguenots manifestes, ne Catholiques vrais & zelez: mais une marchandise meslee, & boutique remplie de tant de sortes de drogueries confuses par ensemble, qu'il est fort difficile & dangereux de vous en escrire une parfaite diffinition.' *La foy et religion des Politiques de ce temps. Contenant la refutation de leurs heresies. Seconde edition* (Paris: Bichon, 1588), p. 3.

satirised in the *Satyre ménippée* whose subtitle is 'The Virtue of the Catholicon' ('Catholicon', a drug with declining efficacy, is a figure for radical Catholic polemic).[26] In this pamphlet, it is *politique* that is 'filled with all kinds of intoxicants' ('remplie de tant de sortes de drogueries'), which makes it difficult to define and its effects dangerous. The *politique* is then also dangerous precisely because [he] is 'mixed merchandise'.

As in the *Karesme*, this mixed state makes the word *politique* so difficult to define perfectly: as such, these opening statements more or less define the term by its mobility between opposing people, terms, and ideas. And, as we shall see, this mobility is at the core of the authors' critiques of *politique* thinking and behaviour. It also likely reflects a real paranoia on the part of Leaguer loyalists about the propensity of some of their supporters to turn against them.[27] But the mobility of the term also allows these authors to make of it what they will, and gives them the freedom to categorise as *politique* as any non-Huguenot supporter of Henri de Navarre, and thus as their ideological opponent. One way in which the term *politique* is 'mixed merchandise' is in the jumble of insults that mark the use of this term in late sixteenth-century polemic as operating in a vituperative mode, as early modern hate speech.

The 'Bad' *Politique*

In these texts, the term *politique* appears amidst a maelstrom of vituperative insults. Such language use can be described according to various theoretical schemes, either developed in Ancient Rome and received in Renaissance France (*vituperatio*, *calomnatio*, or slander), or by modern pragmatic linguists (illocutionary, or perlocutionary, speech acts).[28] This is conveyed first of all by the appearance of the word within a cluster of other nouns such as 'atheist', 'heretic', 'navarrist', etc. – or simply by the

---

[26] On sixteenth-century belief in the magical or drug-like power of words, see Butterworth, *Poisoned Words*, p. 24. The authors of the *Satyre ménippée* were strongly influenced by Rabelais; their 'Catholicon' is likely a nod to his 'Pantagruelion'.

[27] Greengrass describes Parisian paranoia about 'clandestine activities' and conspiracies in this period. Perhaps this paranoia was inspired in part by the pamphlets; there is also overlap between pamphlet authorship and paranoiac prosecution. See Mark Greengrass with Tom Hamilton, 'Lettres compromettantes. La Ligue et la clandestinité des "politiques"', unpublished conference paper, delivered at 'La clandestinité au XVIe siècle pendant les guerres de religion en France', Paris, 11 June 2019.

[28] On the conventions of slander, see Butterworth, *Poisoned Words*, esp. pp. 20 and 31. On speech acts, see John Searle, Ferenc Kiefer, and Manfred Bierwisch, *Speech Act Theory and Pragmatics* (Dordrecht and London: Reidel, 1980). On clusters of negative epithets in political writing *c.* 1588–89, see Jonathan Patterson, '"Diables incarnez, Machiavelistes, Heretiques": The Villains of Pierre Matthieu's La Guisiade Reconsidered', *French Studies*, LXX.1 (2015), 1–16.

identification of the *politique* as 'enemy', as in the pamphlet *La contrepoison contre les artifices et inventions des politiques et autres ennemis de la religion catholique* ('Antidote to the artifices and inventions of politiques and other enemies of the Catholic religion', 1589) which purports to be a textual remedy for *politique* poison. Another, *Les impostures et calomnies des Huguenots, Politiques & Atheistes pour colorer le massacre és personnes de Messeigneurs les Cardinal & Duc de Guyse par Henry de Valois* ('The lies and calumnies of Huguenots, Politiques and Atheists to justify the massacre of the persons of Messeigneurs the Cardinal and Duke of Guise by Henri de Valois', 1589), associates *politiques* with Huguenots and atheists in the title as well as in more than half of the fourteen uses of the term in the body of the text, in which the *politique* is described as 'atheist, idiot, insane', and then a few pages later as 'Politiques, or rather, Atheists'.[29]

An important part of the vilification of the *politique* is the divorce from ideas of 'good government', instead setting up the *politique* as a fundamental cause of social instability. In general, the anti-*politique* pamphlets paint a picture of the *politique* as irreligious, or, at least, as prioritising human affairs over religious responsibilities both individual and collective. This is summed up in one pamphlet in the following way:

> And insofar as some or other of them cry ceaselessly, The State, The State: The *Police*, The *Police*, without worrying about the holy religion as the first priority, even going as far as saying that the *Police* should be everything and the priority of all, they are rightly called *Politiques*.[30]

The author draws tight links between the terms *politique*, *estat*, and *police* that represents a marked change from the looser grouping of such terms in earlier texts. And the prioritisation of human affairs described here is portrayed as disastrous for the human realm as well as for the souls of those concerned, as demonstrated by a broadsheet in Pierre de L'Estoile's *Drolleries* (Figure 2), which shows 'The Upturned Cauldron of Huguenots, Politiques, Atheists, Espernonistes, Libertins, with the Lament of Ministers and Preachers of the French Kingdom' ('La marmitte renversée des huguenots, Politiques, Atheistes, Espernonistes, Libertins. Avec la Complainte des Ministres & predicans du Royaume de France').[31]

---

[29] *Les impostures et calomnies des Huguenots, politiques & atheistes pour colorer le massacre és personnes de Messeigneurs les Cardinal & Duc de Guyse par Henry de Valois* (1589), pp. 6 and 8.

[30] 'Et pour autant que les uns & les autres crient sans cesse: L'Estat, L'Estat: La Police, La Police, sans se soucier en premier lieu de la saincte religion: voire disent la Police luy devoir estre en tout & par tout preferee, ils sont justement appellez Politiques.' *La foy et religion des Politiques de ce temps*, p. 5.

[31] On the *Drolleries*, see Hamilton, and Gilbert Schrenck, 'Introduction', in Pierre de L'Estoile, *Les belles figures et drolleries de la Ligue*, ed. by Gilbert Schrenck (Geneva: Droz, 2016), pp. ix–xxxii.

Figure 2. Anon., 'La Marmitte renversée', woodcut on paper, in Pierre de L'Estoile, *Les belles figures et drolleries de la League* (c. 1589–98).
Bibliothèque nationale de France

The image of the upturned cauldron was a common one in woodcuts of the Wars of Religion, influenced by the 'world upside-down' topos prevalent in visual and written media of the sixteenth century (and especially in religious polemic).[32] The image shows a crowd of *politiques* and their cronies (marked by another list of negative epithets), including d'Espernon, Henri III's favourite, who is stoking the flames beneath a cauldron, which in this kind of image is considered to represent the state. A preacher kneels, remonstrating with the group: this represents the role that many Parisian preachers took upon themselves during the League

---

[32] On the image of the *Marmite renversée*, see Phillip Benedict, 'Of Marmites and Martyrs: Image and Polemics in the Wars of Religion', in *The French Renaissance in Prints from the Bibliothèque nationale de France* (Los Angeles, CA: Grunwald Centre for the Graphic Arts, University of California, 1994), pp. 109–37. On German popular propaganda, see Robert Scribner, *For the Sake of Simple Folk: Popular Propaganda for the German Reformation* (Cambridge: Cambridge University Press, 1981).

years, that is, trying to save the state from Henri de Navarre and other enemies of the true religion. The preacher holds a piece of paper, which might represent the texts that preachers were writing and printing in this period with the same purpose. The accompanying verse, in two stanzas, accuses Henri de Navarre of failing to right the *marmite*.[33]

The poem ventriloquises the figures who address Henri de Navarre and d'Espernon, complaining that they will never be able to right the cauldron. The verse thereby puts a satirical gloss on the image by implying (in the title) that the useless coalition of 'huguenots, Politiques, Atheists, Espernonistes, [and] Libertins' is trying to stabilise the state but is unable to do so. The Huguenots, *politiques* and their allies who voice the poem are increasingly giving up and deciding to make a break for Protestant England; d'Espernon is summarily banished. The poem is another attempt to exclude opponents of the League from Paris, and from France: the *politiques* are located among a set of groups deemed threatening and undesirable. This kind of redistribution of undesirable elements on a wider European map is a counter-move against the Huguenot polemicists discussed in the previous chapter, who attempt to convert all of Europe to the Reformed faith; this woodcut puts them back in their (English) box.

Pierre de L'Estoile records how associations between *Calviniste, politique, heretique, atheiste*, and *navarriste* were received and reinforced by the people of Paris, showing how they were formed in the world beyond the text. An example of this is his description of the execution of one Jean Guitel, from Angers, who was burnt at the stake in July 1588:

> The people believed, and cried out (according to what they had been led to believe and to cry out) that he was Calvinist. On the contrary, he was a true atheist, as was made evident on the scaffold, where he let forth execrable blasphemies against God, the holy trinity, and other articles of the Christian faith that are believed as much by Calvinists as by Roman Catholics. But the unhappiness of the time was such, and the minds of the simple folk so poisoned by the sorceries of the League, that all criminals were Calvinists, Heretics, *Politiques*, or Navarrists.[34]

---

[33] Pierre de L'Estoile, *Les belles figures et drolleries de la Ligue* http://gallica.bnf.fr/ark:/12148.

[34] 'Le peuple croioit et crioit (selon qu'on le faisoit croire et crier) qu'il estoit Calviniste; mais, au contraire, c'estoit un vrai atheiste, comme il montra evidemment au supplice, où il prononça execrables blasphemes contre Dieu, la S.e Trinité et autres articles de la foi chrestienne, que croient unanimement tant les Calvinistes que les Catholiques Rommains. Mais le malheur du temps estoit tel, et les esprits du simple peuple tellement empoisonnés des sorceleries de la League, que tous criminels estoient Calvinistes, Heretiques, Politiques ou Navarristes.' L'Estoile, *Mémoires-Journaux*, III, pp. 171–72. See also Hamilton, *Pierre de L'Estoile and his World*, p. 142 on Parisian crowds crying for the extermination of *politiques* and Huguenots.

In his use of the verbs 'believe and cry out' ('croire et crier', emphasised by being in parenthesis), L'Estoile implies a strong link between belief and speech, while suggesting that this link is forged and manipulated from above (by preachers).[35] The excerpt shows the low view that Pierre de L'Estoile had of the Parisian populace, the 'simple folk' whose minds had been poisoned by League propaganda and who thus considered all criminals Calvinists, heretics, *Politiques*, or supporters of Henri de Navarre. The implication is that the boundaries between all these were blurred to the extent that true atheists such as Guitel were mistaken for any of the other groups considered criminal by the League. The frequent use of various insulting epithets together seems to have reinforced the condemnatory power of each of them, and their ability to convince the people of Paris, at least temporarily, that anyone designated as such was a criminal.

Popular cries of *politique* were not only recorded in Paris or in Pierre de L'Estoile's reports. The term as a slur in legal cases is also found in *arrêts* concerning libel and in at least one concerning violent crime, in the case of the murderer Jehan Pyot in Lyon, who told the court in 1591 that his adversary had called him 'bigarré politicque' and caused the ruin of his reputation and family.[36] This usage echoes the titles of pamphlets published in Lyon in the preceding two years, and demonstrates, along with the Guitel case recorded by L'Estoile, that during the League period concern over being identified (or not) as *politique* was a widespread phenomenon with impact beyond the relatively narrow sphere of the *noblesse de robe*. Jehan Pyot's occupation is listed as 'labourer and winegrower'; another slightly later case in Auxerre involving a cobbler records an exchange of insults in which one cry of *politique* is answered with another of *putain* ('whore').[37] The associations here with terms like *bigarré* and *putain* show a degree of absorption both of the specific language of mixedness associated with *politiques* and the tendency of this term to act with negative force in a fashion similar to more established insults.

The anti-*politique* pamphlets are negative not only in the sense that they share a pessimistic vision of the world, but in that their purpose is destructive: to oppose alternatives, as a means of defending League politics and ideology. What does *politique* actually mean, if anything, when used as a destructive force of opposition and reversal? Jan Miernowski has argued

---

[35] On rumour and the 'public voice' in early modern France, and the role of the Wars of Religion in shaping them, see Butterworth, *The Unbridled Tongue*, esp. pp. 102–04.

[36] MS AN X2B 165 1591-09-03. Many thanks to Tom Hamilton for this reference. On a similar case in Amiens, see Crouzet, *Guerriers de Dieu*, p. 249.

[37] MS AN X2A 1397 1594-01-08. Again, thanks to Tom Hamilton.

that the term should be understood primarily, if not exclusively, as an insult in this period: this was the primary rhetorical strategy of the pamphleteers, who deliberately turned more positive associations of the term *politique* on their head in order to describe and circumscribe the abstract, indefinite 'evil' that they seek to persuade their readers is present in their enemies.[38] He suggests that in such pamphlet literature the term *politique* is effectively content-free: not describing reality, or providing information, but an expression of pure antagonism.[39] Perhaps this is what authors of pamphlets like the *Karesme* were referring to without realising it when they described the difficulties and confusion in the definition of the word *politique* – because it is 'only' a speech act, designating criminality, and lacks a 'real' referent. This is what characterises 'hate speech', which Miernowski describes as being anti-discourse, anti-rhetoric, or anti-poetic (the latter, for example, in his analysis of Etienne Jodelle): polemical uses of the term *politique* fit this taxonomy.[40]

One of the best examples of anti-*politique* hate speech might be the apostrophe to the *politiques* in one pamphlet which characterises them at the end of a list of insulting adjectives, as wretched, damned, a heretic, idolatrous, villain, enemy of sanctity, religion and conscience, treacherous, feigning good conduct, but at best tricked or enchanted, and at worst, worse than a Huguenot.[41] Hate speech as negation, and as anti-content, seems to characterise uses of *politique* here, in which the best *politiques* have simply been bewitched (sorcery is often used to explain both *politique* devilishness and the errors of those who mistakenly trust them); the anonymous pamphleteers are attempting to break the spell.[42] This 'mixed bag' of toxic associations operates as a whirl of insults that create a kind of inferential interference, so that what is revealed about the term *politique* is that its meaning is negative both in the sense of it referring to a 'bad' element, and in the sense that it simply means 'not Leaguer Catholic'. What seems to have happened, then, is that a dynamic element in early modern political writing – *politique* as specialised form of knowledge and its powerful agent – has been overturned and emptied of semantic content. And yet, the 'mixedness' and ambiguity proper to the word *politique* in

---

[38] Miernowski, '"Politique" comme injure', pp. 349–50.   [39] Ibid., p. 349.

[40] Miernowski, *La beauté de la haine: Essais de misologie littéraire* (Geneva: Droz, 2014). For his analysis of sixteenth-century hate speech, from Jodelle to the *Ligueur* pamphlets, see Chapter 1, pp. 21–74.

[41] *Les impostures et calomnies*, p. 23.

[42] Another example of this is *La contrepoison contre les artifices et inventions des politiques et autres ennemis de la religion catholique* (Paris: J. Le Riche, 1589).

polemical pamphlets still refers to a particular person who is distinct from *libertins, atheistes,* and so on, even as distinctions between such categories are blurred. This particular person is a subject, as well as an object, behaves and thinks in certain ways that also relate to flexibility and ambivalence, and can be recognised as such.

Mixed Messages

The pamphlets I discuss in this chapter are not only anti-*politique*, but in some ways could be described as 'anti-texts' to the extent that their avowed purpose is generally more refutation than proposition. However, to do this they have to have some kind of content to resist, or refute. To this end, people called *politiques* are described as having certain qualities, or doing certain things. In the title of the *Antidote* pamphlet, for example, they are shown as engaging in insulting and slanderous language themselves ('artifices et inventions'); the *politiques* are, meanwhile explicitly figured as calumniators in the title of the pamphlet *The Lies and Calumnies of Politiques.* These pamphlets refute particular works belonging to the longer sequence of political writings discussed across this book. The 'mixed' quality of the term *politique* thus also refers to its retention of other, earlier associations that a 'slower' inferential reading reveals as existing underneath the 'white noise' of insulting hate speech.

The pamphlet authors show awareness of the changes that the term has experienced, and a sense that the term could carry both positive and negative associations.[43] One pamphleteer, cited at the opening of Chapter 1, laments the transition of the term *politique* from being honorific, 'un nom d'honneur' (as it was in the writings of Bodin and Le Roy published in the 1560s and 70s) to horrific ('un nom d'horreur').[44] In this verse the term is brought into relief by references to acts of naming that accompany it each time. This signals the potential of *politique* to be different each time it is uttered, depending on when and where it is used, and who uses it. Negative connotations of the word are established as recent, a corruption of a previously positive, powerful word, by those who have abused its power. The contingency of this manifestation of *politique* is further highlighted in all the titles that refer to its belonging to the contemporary moment: today's *politique,* not yesterday's, is the problem.

---

[43] Jan Miernowski, '"Politique" comme injure', pp. 341–42.
[44] *Description de l'homme politique de ce temps avec sa foy et religion qui est un catalogue de plusieurs heresies et athéismes, où tombent ceux qui préfèrent l'estat humain à la religion catholique* (Paris: Bichon, 1588), p. 3.

Another pamphlet praises Scipio as a great *politique* of times past, then rails against contemporary *politiques*, suggesting that these bad characters are numerous and potentially surrounding the reader, causing them to lose sleep:

> It is these *Politique* libertines ['ces libertins Politiques'], these Machiavellian factionalists, these seditious Bourbonists, these Navarrist firebrands, these royal partisans, these hidden atheists, against whom you must carefully guard yourself, by whom you must always expect to be surprised, whose designs are long in the making, their secret and covert machinations are those which should keep you awake at night.[45]

Rather than just appearing out of nowhere, the bad *politique* of today is the product of the reception of a number of texts. It is not by chance that the *politiques* here are *libertins* or that the *libertins* are *politiques*; *libertin* might evoke the Huguenot texts discussed in the previous chapter, which make use of the term *politique* to argue for liberty in the sense of freedom of worship. The texts the League pamphlets are most obviously responding to, though, are the translations of Machiavelli, and the *Contre-Machiavel*, which I have demonstrated were already part of the increasingly complex and contested history of the term *politique*. Numerous pamphlets refer to Machiavelli in relation to the *politiques;* the *Contrepoison* describes him, for example, as 'the evangelist of the Politiques', echoing *La foy et religion des politiques* ('The Faith and Religion of Politiques'), which decries 'the damnable advice of Court Evangelist, Machiavelli', and blames his influence for the readiness with which princes and courtiers renege on their oaths.[46]

  This latter pamphlet, *La foy et religion des Politiques*, goes on to name texts as *politiques*, as well as people: 'Belloy, the *Antiguisart*, *discours Politiques*, *Apologie du Roy de Navarre*, *Brutum fulmen etc.*, and others' ('tels que sont Belloy, Antiguisart, discours Politiques, Apologie du Roy de Navarre, Brutum fulmen &c. & autres'). In fact, the main body of the text is a step-by-step refutation, described in the subtitle as a 'catalogue', of all the errors made in these texts, complete with page references.[47] The

---

[45] 'Ce sont ces libertins Politiques, ces factieux Machiavelistes, ces séditieux Borbonnistes, ces boutesfeux Navarristes, ces Partisans Royaux, ces dissimulez atheystes, contre lesquels tu te dois soigneusement parer, les surprises desquels tu dois redouter, leurs desseings de long temps projettez, leurs machinations couvertes & secrets, sont celles qui te doivent empescher le sommeil.' *Avis a l'irresolu de Limoges*, p. 46.

[46] *Contrepoison*, p. 13; *La foy et religion des Politiques*, p. 54.

[47] This animadversion seems to be an example of what Butterworth calls the 'practice' of slander, a conventional approach of which was 'close attention to the target text, reproduced and answered point by point'; Butterworth, *Poisoned Words* p. 4. There is one use of the term *politique* attached to the title of one of these texts: 'Politic antiguizardé' – referring, presumably, to Hotman's *Le tigre*,

primary source of the errors catalogued in this text is Pierre de Belloy's *De l'authorité du roy et crimes de leze majesté, qui se commettent par Leagues, designation de successeur, & libelles escrits contre la personne & dignité du Prince* ('On the Authority of the King and Crimes of Lèse-Majesté Committed by Leagues, on the Designation of a Successor, and on Pamphlets Written against the Person and Dignity of the Prince', 1587). Belloy attacked the League, arguing for obedience to the monarch in all circumstances, and that the king and Church were so fundamentally connected that defying monarchic authority in the name of the Catholic Church was a logical impossibility. Belloy's text itself was self-consciously part of a long-running textual quarrel, with the author stating that the intention is to correct the errors of the prolific Catholic pamphleteer Artus Desiré, and those of his associates.[48] *La foy et religion* was not the only pamphlet to link de Belloy with *politiques*: another pamphlet describes *politiques*, assisted by Machiavelli and de Belloy, as responsible for the corruption of Henri III and his decision to assassinate the Guise brothers.[49]

In sum, the bad *politique* of Leaguer polemic c. 1588–93 did not appear overnight, no matter what alarming impression some polemicists wished to give the Parisian populace. Rather, this dramatic turn in the history of the word emerged from a conflict-ridden textual genealogy, which led League sympathisers to use the term to attack their opponents, with recourse to well-practised mechanisms of slander, rather than, say, instrumentalising it for their own cause in a more positive way as the Huguenot polemicists had done in the previous decade. Their works should be considered not only as literary texts (for all their sometimes dubious quality) but also as part of the intellectual history of the period.[50]

Politique Manners

Politique not only refers to a set of texts and their political ideas, but also to certain ways of thinking and behaving that are also 'mixed'; these qualities

which was subtitled 'anti-guisard', *La foy et religion des Politiques*, p. 27. See [Hotman] *Le Tigre* (1560), facsimile ed. by Charles Read (Paris: Académie des bibliophiles, 1970).

[48] [Pierre de Belloy], *De l'authorité du roy et crimes de Leze Majesté, qui se commettent par ligues, designation de successeur, & libelles escrits contre la personne & dignité du Prince* (1587). Désiré was involved in a wide web of angry readings; he wrote his own *Contrepoison* against Clément Marot's sonnets in 1561.

[49] *Les impostures et calomnies des Huguenots, politiques & atheistes pour colorer le massacre ès personnes de Messeigneurs les Cardinal & Duc de Guyse par Henry de Valois* (Paris, 1589), p. 23

[50] On League political thought, see Baumgartner, Crouzet, *Guerriers de Dieu*, Nicholls, and Zwierlein, *The Political Thought of the Catholic League*.

also work to define the *politique* as 'bad' in the moral framework of these pamphlets. Pamphlets such as *La vie et condition des politiques* ('The Life and Condition of the *Politiques*'), and *Le karesme et mœurs du politique*, both printed in 1589, demonstrate in their titles a wish to describe and identify *politique* behaviours. I have already shown that the word *politique* was considered singularly difficult to define, among all other words. The aspects of these texts dealing with the 'life', 'condition', and 'way of life' ('maniere de vivre') of so-called *politiques* also set the word apart from the cacophony of insults hurled in print, on the streets, and from the pulpit, at anyone doubting the League. The 'manners' and 'condition' of the *politique* generally imply being two-faced, both willing and likely to change one's mind. In the *Karesme*, the author makes it his mission to establish that the *politiques* are not trustworthy, complaining at the beginning that the *politiques* are skilful manipulators, able to take in even the most astute: 'Let nobody trust them who should not wish to be tricked, for the cleverest are taken in. They seem habitually to show a plain and open face, and underneath that they slither through your fields like vipers.'[51] Here, the verb 'monstrer' describes the *politique*'s ability to conceal his 'viper-like' true qualities – the sense is that the *politique* is a monster hiding in plain sight. The author of *La vie et condition* echoes this anxiety:

> This Kingdom, which I have figured as a sick body ravaged by extreme illness and close to death, has been sharply assailed by heretics, enemies of God's honour and holiness, Atheists, and *politiques* who are hidden, covert people, two-sided in their hearts and their mouths.[52]

In this example, the *politiques* come at the end of the list of enemies, specifically described as hidden and covert ('gens cachés couverts doubles en cœur & en bouche'). The avowed aim of the pamphlet is to expose this double-ness, and to unveil what is hidden: 'The aim, then, of this little notice, is to represent to you the reasons why you must guard yourself against the guiles, the treason, the all too clear fraud [fraude trop

---

[51] 'Qui ne s'y fie qui ne voudra, car les plus habilles y sont pris. Ceux la vous semblent coustumierement monstrer un plain & rond visage, ce pendant ils rampent soubs vos prés comme vipereaux.' *Karesme*, p. 2.

[52] 'Ce Royaume, ce que j'ay figuré estre un corps mallade d'extreme maladie et prest de sa ruine, a esté vivement assailly par les heretiques, ennemys de l'honneur de Dieu, & de sainteté, Atheistes, & politiques gens cachés couverts doubles en cœur & en bouche.' *La vie et condition des politiques, et atheistes de ce temps avec un advertisement pour se garder d'eux & de n'admettre indiscretement & indifferement tous ceux qui s'offriront au party de la Saincte union* (Paris: Fizelier, 1589), p. 9.

descouverte'], of those evil atheist *Politiques*.'[53] The participle 'descouverte' recalls the 'cachés couverts' in the previous excerpt, underlining the author's faith in the revelatory powers of his own text. And what they particularly seek to warn against, as well as the generally treasonous dual nature of this *politique* figure, is their 'guile' (*cautelle* – defined by Cotgrave as a 'wile', a 'sleight', a 'guileful devise or endeavour'), suggesting that *politique* deceit is not only that they appear as normal humans when in fact they are monstrous vipers: it is what they say, and how they say it.[54]

The *politiques* are associated with ways of talking – and, indeed, of arguing – in many pamphlets, though especially in the *Karesme* and *Vie et condition*. In *Les impostures et calomnies*, the author dares the *politiques* to try and have their way with words: 'Let these good people the *Politiques* come forth with their pretty reasonings, and they will not lack pretty answers.'[55] A sense of quarrelling, debating, and exchanging of views (alongside insults), is present throughout this body of texts, with the *politique* figure an active participant in the quarrelling. Some of the texts, indeed, are exclusively in dialogue form, such as *Deux devis, d'un Catholique et d'un Politique, sur l'exhortation faicte au peuple de Nantes*, and *La dispute d'un catholique de Paris, contre un Politique de la ville de Tours* ('Two Speeches, of a Catholic and a Politique, on the Exhortation Made to the People of Nantes', and 'The Dispute between a Catholic of Paris and a Politique from the Town of Tours', 1591). The figure of the *politique* conveyed when these texts are considered together (as well as quite frequently in each individual reading) is a dynamic subject, as well as the object of hate. And what the *politique* subject is doing is talking and arguing, and doing so in a manner that effectively embodies the mobility we have already noted in the word itself: they are about to change positions, or hold two positions at once, and it is this which makes them monstrously bad.

The centrepiece of the *Karesme* pamphlet is a reported argument over-heard by the author, between a *politique* and a devoted Leaguer, which exemplifies exactly what the author thinks is wrong with the *politiques*. The altercation is introduced with a general description of how the

---

[53] 'Le but donc auquel tend ce petit advertissement est de vous representer les causes pour lesquelles vous vous devez garder de la cautelle, de la trahison, de la fraude trop descouverte, de ses meschans Atheistes Pollitiques.' Ibid., p. 14.

[54] 'Cautelle', in Cotgrave, *Dictionarie* www.pbm.com/~lindahl/cotgrave/search/166l.html [accessed 3 August 2020].

[55] 'Apportent donc ces bonnes gens tes Politiques leurs belles raisons, & ils ne manqueront pas de bonnes rescponces.' *Impostures et calomnies*, p. 36.

politiques 'let themselves drift, now here, now there' ('se laissent aller, tantost cy, tantost là'), and the author asks, sardonically, 'But is it not a beautiful perfection in man to accommodate himself to all things?' ('Mais n'est-ce pas une belle perfection à un homme de s'accomoder à toutes choses?')[56] This is followed by a description of a supposedly recent meeting between a faithful follower of the League with one who doubts them:

> Although he thought he was dealing with some idiot who would agree with everything put to him (as is it the custom of such people to denigrate the union [the League] among those whom they believe are of the same view), he was forced to sing the opposite tune in the very same instant, for the man listening to him had more blood on his hands than he did, however he may have wanted things to appear; this other then reproached him for having disdained and spoken against the Catholic Apostolic and Roman Religion. So the first fellow quite incontinently began to soften matters as much as possible, saying that he was a very good Catholic and had only made such propositions and arguments as a manner of speaking ['maniere de devis']. Well, is that an acceptable excuse? Now, see if you trust the *Politique*.[57]

The speaker who criticised the League assumes he has a sympathetic audience, but is forced to change his tune ('chanter la Palinodie'). His about-turn is apparently brought on by a perceived threat of violence (his opponent has 'more blood on his hands'), and his own failure to match the threat. The marginal gloss of this episode reads: 'the infamy of the Politique'. The cardinal crime here, though, seems less the anti-League opinion than the speaker's protestations that what he was saying was only a way of talking, a figure of speech: that he had only made such propositions as 'a manner of speaking'. The problem is the false tune, the *palinodie*, so that the author's quarrel is really with the figure of speech, the manner of expression.[58] And this, in fact, is the prime identifying feature of a *politique*: a 'maniere de devis' (way of speaking), hiding within the 'maniere de vie' (way of life) in the full title of the pamphlet. A similar critique is expressed in *La vie et condition*, in which the *politique* is a false friend,

---

[56] *Karesme*, p. 15.

[57] 'Mais combien qu'il pensast avoir affaire à quelque niez qui luy accorderoit tout ce qui mettoit en avant, comme c'est la coustume de telles gens de detracter de l'union entre ceux qu'ilz pensent estre de leur farine, il fut contraint au mesme instant de chanter la Palinodie, car celuy qui l'escoutoit ayant plus de sang aux ongles que luy quelque semblant qu'il n'en feit, l'accuse & le reprent d'avoir mespris & parlé contre la Religion Catholique, Apostolique & Romaine. Il commença tout incontinent à filer le plus doux qui fut possible, qu'il estoit fort bon Catholique, qu'il n'avoit mis en ieu ces propos & altercations qu'en maniere de devis. Vrayment voila une excuse fort pertinente? Fiez-vous maintenant au Politique.' Ibid., p. 16.

[58] On the figure of Palinodus in polemic, see Scribner, p. 233.

'servant of the times' ('serviteur du temps') who should be recognisable from his 'jargon':

> Don't you know that he's a servant of the times? Don't you recognise a *Politique* and a heretic from his jargon? Don't you realise that the wolf and the dog look alike? And as an ancient Sage says, won't a flatterer, a Politique, a coward, an adulterer, a parasitic peddler of tall tales, pretend very hard to be your friend?[59]

In these works, the properties of the word seem almost indistinguishable from the properties of the referents to which the authors are trying to attach it in order to create an enemy and police the boundaries of society as they think it ought to function. Since the enemy is, to an extent, a way of using language, and 'simply' a word itself rather than real and identifiable people, it almost seems as though they are creating an enemy – a viper-like monster – from thin air, through their use of a particularly mobile term. The aggressive uses of the term *politique* in these texts, then, are 'agonistic' in their antagonism, as well as being insulting and condemnatory.[60]

But this is not just a closed discursive circle in which the word and its referent are interchangeable. There are broader implications here for the political and aesthetic modes of the period. A key principle of Loys Le Roy's theory of change in *De la vicissitude* is that different times call for different practices, and perhaps even different truths; in Le Roy's view, mortal man is inescapably a 'servant of the times', although on a grander scale than in the vituperative pamphlet above. Mutability is also a central theme of Montaigne's *Essais*, for instance in the passage in 'On Cannibals' where he observes the literally shifting sands of the banks of the Dordogne near his home (p. 183/p. 209). For Le Roy and especially for Montaigne, alteration and instability are poetic and philosophical keys. Their works read differently following a consideration of the pamphlet literature discussed in this chapter. The language of the *Karesme* pamphlet's critique of those who 'let themselves drift' ('se laissent aller') recalls the description in II.6 of Montaigne's near death experience: 'I took pleasure in growing languid and letting myself go' (p.327).[61] This passage has been read, among other

---

[59] 'Sçavez-vous pas qu'il est serviteur du temps? Cognoissez vous point un Pollitique & un heretique à son jargon? Vous representez-vous point que le loup et le chien sont semblables? Et comme dit un ancien Sage, qu'un flateur, un Pollitique, un paillard, un adultaire, un escornifleur, contrefaict de fort pres l'amy?' *La vie et condition*, p. 25.

[60] 'Agonistic' in the sense that they fulfil Viala's conceptualisation of an 'agonistic' or 'quarrelsome' discursive mode in which quarrels have creative as well as destructive functions. See Alain Viala, 'Un temps de querelles', p. 18.

[61] '[je] prenois plaisir à m'alanguir et à me laisser aller', p. 392.

things, as a tacit comment on living (and nearly dying, accidentally) in the civil wars.[62] The author of the *Karesme* pamphlet repeats the verb construction 'se laisser aller' when despairing of the airy inconstancy of the *politiques*: 'More inconstant than a weather vane, they let themselves be carried by any wind' ('Qui plus inconstans que des giroüettes se laissent aller à tout vent').[63] Montaigne, who wrote in III.6 ('On Coaches') of the potential multiplicity and vicissitude of all forms, declared in 'On Experience' (III.13) that after all, when he examined life he found 'virtually nothing but wind. But what of it? We are all wind' (p. 1035).[64]

These are, as I have said, aesthetic, poetic, and philosophical principles in Montaigne. They can also be understood as political. Criticism of such flexibility in contemporary writing that uses, at times, identical phrasing, politicises these principles. Montaigne is not necessarily the *politique* target of these pamphlets, nor – as I hope is clear by this point – do I think that he fulfils all the criteria attached to being properly or improperly *politique* suggested by contemporaries at various points in his lifetime. His defence of La Boétie is similar to the self-defence of the anonymous *politique* in the *Karesme* (that the *Discours* was a purely intellectual exercise), but his apparent fury at the way Protestant readers changed his friend's work and mixed it up with their political writings makes it clear that he was himself alert to the dangers of 'mixed merchandise' in textual form. My point is not, in this chapter on recognitions, to suddenly unveil Montaigne as *politique*, but to demonstrate the overlap, and perhaps mutual influence, between politics and aesthetics, and between discursive quarrelling and the actions and creations of real people.

For all that *politique* appears to refer back to itself, and to a kind of aporia wherein its true definition is evasive, these uses of the term *politique* are ineluctably attached to the prizing or decrying of various kinds of political activity in the real world. L'Estoile, with his Protestant associates, who avoided sectarian conflict even as it raged in Paris and threatened to engulf him, certainly seems to have been ambivalent about the merits of the respective confessional causes.[65] Montaigne was connected to Henri de Navarre (he held the honorific title of 'Gentleman of the Chamber'), and occupied the role of a go-between in various political transactions: a 'useful

---

[62] Wes Williams, *Monsters and Their Meanings*, p. 151.   [63] *Karesme*, p. 12.
[64] 'à peu près que du vent. Mais quoy nous sommes par tout vent', p. 1157.
[65] Hamilton, *Pierre de L'Estoile and his World*, pp. 125–34. Hamilton makes a clear case for L'Estoile's devout Catholic faith despite his aversion to the League.

mediator'.[66] He could therefore have been diagnosed as *politique* as defined by these pamphlets. Jean Bodin, for his part, perhaps earned the epithet 'a dangerous *politicque*' (cited at the start of the chapter), owing to his sharing some of these characteristics; equally, criticisms of Bodin could have informed the pamphlets – the description of Bodin's ignominy in a later section of Richart's *Mémoires* conveys the close connections between real and written lives.

Richart details Bodin's long enmity with the Jesuit preacher Antoine Tholozam, who ordered a search of Bodin's house in June 1589 and deliberated for some time before allowing his life to be spared, after the discovery of a document in the house detailing Henri de Navarre's lineage and his descent from the house of Bourbon (thus making him legitimate heir to the French throne). Richart suggests that Bodin was wrong to attempt to stay in the town:

> It would have been better for his honour to leave town at the start of these wars as many others of his kind did, without swimming between two streams as he thought to do, by which attempt he lost all the honour and the reputation he had spent so long acquiring for himself.[67]

This description of Bodin as swimming between two streams and consequently losing all honour and good reputation evokes the doubleness consistently associated with the *politique* in the pamphlet material.[68] His attempt to be in two camps exiled Bodin in effect if not in fact, and represents the failure of his attempts to talk, or write, his way out of the problem.

---

[66] See Hoffmann, *Montaigne's Career*, p. 145. See also Mark Greengrass, 'Montaigne and the Wars of Religion', in *The Oxford Handbook of Montaigne*, ed. by Philippe Desan (Oxford: Oxford University Press, 2016), pp. 138–57 (pp. 156–57). Jouanna also shows how Montaigne had to 'act on all fronts' ('agir sur tous les fronts') in the 1580s and suggests that his actions flirted with double agency. See Jouanna, *Montaigne*, pp. 238–94, esp. pp. 260–62. See also Daniel Ménager, 'La diplomatie de Montaigne', in *Montaigne politique*, pp. 139–54. Montaigne's role as intermediary, though complex, should not be exaggerated. Greengrass describes Montaigne as a 'bit player' in regional and national politics.

[67] 'Il lui eust ésté mieux pour son honneur sortir la ville au commencement de ces guerres comme feirent beaucoup daultres de sa qualité sans nager entre deux eaues comme il penssoit faire ou il a perdu tout l'honneur et la reputation quil sestoit acquis de longtemps.' Richart, p. 230.

[68] On the image of 'swimming between two streams' as a descriptor of Michel de l'Hospital, see Marie Seong-Hak Kim, 'Nager entre deux eaux'. This phrase was commonly used in the period to denote ambiguity, and 'trying to have it both ways'. On the phrase as a descriptor of Protestants who wished to remain loyal to the French crown, see Stuart Carroll, '"Nager entre deux eaux": The Princes and the Ambiguity of French Protestantism', *Sixteenth-Century Journal*, 44.4 (2013), 985–1020.

The *Politique* Body

The story of *politique* in pamphlets from *c.* 1588–93 is one in which words are used to conjure up phantoms and monsters, and to exclude ideological opponents. The word was used negatively, but also creatively, to argue in favour of intransigence and against flexibility, mixing, and ambivalence. This is inextricable from the way that the word itself is used, and the meaning attributed to it, as the mobility of the word and the mobility of the person called *politique* have a symbiotic function both within specific texts, and also in the broader world that the critic can imagine with the help of chroniclers like L'Estoile and Richart. But the term *politique*, at the same time as referring to imaginary creatures, to ways of talking and speaking, and even – at its core – to the changeable potential of language itself, must also be thought of as attached to bodies, both general and particular. The author of *La vie et conditions* makes this point:

> But those qualities which are invisible, hidden, and impenetrable by the eyes of the body, which can only be known as fallacious ratiocination and purely conjectural discourse, are very hard to cure, and most often must go to the grave with the body that they have besieged and irremediably weakened.[69]

This passage echoes others in this and other pamphlets in which the author expresses frustration at *politique* qualities being hidden, or invisible, not immediately obvious to the eye – but rather recognisable from his way of speaking: his 'fallacious ratiocination' and 'conjectural discourse'. But here the author suggests that this way of talking is often accompanied by a weak and corrupted body, and that the cure is all the more difficult owing to the metaphysical – rather than purely physical – nature of the problem. The sense that the *politique*'s weakness of mind would be associated with weakness of body is perhaps behind the dismissive description of the *politique*'s 'mincing gestures' ('gestes mignardes') in the *Karesme*.[70] In this period, mind and body were thought to be engaged in exchanges of mutual influence in much the same way as we have seen the 'real' and the 'textual' influence each other.[71] Moreover, the sense of the 'body politic' suffering the illness of discord and civil war is a recurrent trope in these and other

---

[69] 'Mais les autres qui sont invisibles, cachés & impenetrables par les yeux corporels qui ne se peuvent cognoistre que par fallacieuse ratiocination & discours seulement conjectural sont de bien plus difficile guarison & le plus souvent accompagnent le corps assiegé & affailli d'elles irremediablement jusqu'au cerceuil.' *Vie et condition*, p. 8.

[70] *Karesme*, p. 10.

[71] On contemporary ideas about the body, see, for example, Lisa Silverman, *Tortured Subjects: Pain, Truth, and the Body in Early Modern France* (Chicago, IL and London: Chicago University Press, 2001), and Banks, 'Interpretations of the Body Politic'.

political writings, as is the metaphor of 'good' political action as medicine (Bodin uses this image frequently).[72]

The 'bad' *politiques* figure in these pamphlets as a corrupted part of the body politic, as well as being described as having corrupted bodies of their own. The author of *La vie et condition* points to the connection between the two kinds of corruption by figuring the kingdom as a body ravaged by sickness.[73] Besides this, there are examples of *politiques* being described as having particular physical predilections, notably where their stomachs are concerned.[74] In the *Karesme* pamphlet, the *politique* is described as not observing Lenten strictures, but instead selecting the finest and softest livers to eat: *politique* softness ('douceur') is mirrored in their diet.[75] This is part of a lengthy section in the pamphlet in which the *politique* is described as complaining about the ill effects of fish, and water, on his mind and stomach (further underlining a mind–body connection, as well as associations with fish, and with water).

The fact that the *politique* emerges from these pamphlets as a figure for, indeed the embodiment of, discursive mobility gives a sense of the *politique* as more imaginary than real, especially given the lack of directly self-identifying *politiques* in this period. But for the authors of these pamphlets, there was no doubt that there were real *politiques* out there in the world, with vulnerable and indulged bodies. The image of the pampered, liver-eating *politique* was informed by a material context of deprivation, nigh on starvation: supplies were generally disrupted by the civil war, and during the siege laid by Henri IV in 1590, thousands of Parisians starved to death, with preachers praising the dead as martyrs to the true faith.[76] Huchard also points out that the period of Lent was a very active one for pamphlet production, often influenced by the Lenten sermons that attracted huge crowds (this is borne out by the *Karesme* ['Lent'] pamphlet, which emphasises the failure of *politique* piety during the period of fasting, and is likely to have been one such sermon).[77]

The context of deprivation must be taken into account when considering depictions of comfortable *politiques*, and the rage against them that

[72] See also John O'Brien, 'Intestinal Disorders', in *Writers in Conflict in Sixteenth-Century France: Essays in Honour of Malcolm Quainton*, ed. by Elizabeth Vinestock and David Foster (Durham, NC: Durham University Press, 2008), pp. 239–60.
[73] *Vie et condition*, p. 9.
[74] O'Brien discusses metaphors of digestion and indigestion in relation to the body politic in 'Intestinal Disorders'.
[75] *Karesme*, p. 18.   [76] See Huchard, 'Echos des prédicateurs parisiens', p. 184.
[77] Ibid., pp. 187–89.

preachers tried to inspire in their hungry audiences (both listeners in church and readers of their written tracts). And the material context serves to remind us that the term also had a material reality in terms of it being spoken by preachers as well as appearing in large letters as part of the title of pamphlets and broadsheets that were sold and passed around all over Paris at this time. Moreover, the term became attached to real bodies in the sense that actual people – not least Bodin – were condemned as *politique*: *La foy et religion* names texts and authors, and some pamphlets, such as *La trahison descouverte des Politiques de la ville de Troyes en Champaigne*, contain the kinds of lists of *politiques* that L'Estoile describes as circulating in Paris at the same time.[78] The pamphlet reports that eighteen *politiques* were taken prisoner and put to death – an example for any others who might be reading:

> As for their persons, they are daily put to death, as their crime merits. They serve a very necessary example to you other *Politique* messieurs, who trouble the affairs of the kingdom according to your appetite, and who try each day through your secret and covert conceits to return us to servitude and deliver us into the hands of our enemy: it does not please God to permit this.[79]

The reference to the *politique* appetite and 'secret conceits' ('imaginations dissimulees') makes a further link between mind and body – and, more generally, this passage reminds readers that the identification of *politique* people could and did lead to dead bodies labelled as *politique*: Bodin was threatened with this fate, but seems to have escaped (he is recorded as dying in or around 1596, probably of the plague). Pierre de L'Estoile, who was placed on a list of *politiques* to be assassinated but also survived, gives one very striking description of a group of notable *politiques* who did not escape: the leaders of the Paris *Parlement*, Brisson, Larcher, and Tardif, who were lynched in 1591. Brisson had had a lengthy career as a lawyer and *parlementaire*, and is connected to the longer textual history of

---

[78] The term *politique* was also pivotal in the case against François Brigard, discussed by Greengrass with Tom Hamilton, and separately by Hamilton in 'Political Crime in the Wars of Religion: François Brigard's Sedition', in *Sedition: The Spread of Controversial Literature and Ideas in France and Scotland, c. 1550–1610*, ed. by John O'Brien and Marc Schachter (Turnhout: Brepols, forthcoming).

[79] 'Quant à leur personnes l'on procede journellement à la mort ainsi que le crime le merite. Exemple certes tres necessaire pour vous autres messieurs les Politiques, qui troublez les affaires de ce royaume à vostre appetit, & qui taschez de jour à autre par vos imaginations dissimulees, & couvertes nous remettre en servitude, & nous livrer entre les mains de nostre ennemy ce qu'il ne plaise à Dieu de permettre.' *La trahison descouverte des Politiques de la ville de Troyes en Champaigne, Avec les noms des Capitaines & Politiques, qui avoient conspiré contre la Saincte Union des Catholiques* (Paris: D. Binet and A. Brueil, [n. d., 1589?]), p. 11.

politiques: he was the author of a summary of French law that was updated and expanded by Louis Le Caron in 1601, and he knew and worked with Jean Bodin over three decades.[80] Brisson stayed in Paris when many moderates left, and had been an uneasy ally to the League; that members of the *Seize* took this murderous action was the product of their increasing frustration with the failure of *parlementaire* colleagues such as Brisson to punish the *politiques* they felt were thwarting them – his sorry fate shows the meeting of conspiracy, conspiracy theories, and political manoeuvring around uses of *politique*.[81] It also shows the *Seize* turning against established forms of governance in a more radical sense, since an attack on the *Président* of the *Parlement* was, as Barnavi and Descimon comment, akin to an attack on the *Parlement* itself.[82]

In his journal, L'Estoile frequently describes executions and goes into considerable detail when the unfortunate people concerned are notables of the city. He describes how Brisson attempted to avoid his execution by making a long speech, which L'Estoile interprets as partly an attempt at filibustering, as well as an attempt to persuade his captors, and his audience, that he ought to be spared: he also described Brisson's bodily reaction to the charges against him: how, in his terror upon seeing that his filibustering had failed, he became very pale and drenched in sweat.[83] Like Bodin in Laon, with deadlier consequences, Brisson's address to the gathered crowd failed to avert violence. After their deaths, the bodies of Brisson, Larcher, and Tardif were displayed to the crowd with labels on them: Larcher's read 'fauteur des Politiques' ('Enabler of *Politiques*').[84] These facts, alongside the details recounted by L'Estoile, serves to reinforce the point that use of the word *politique* had an active and deadly impact in the world beyond the text.[85]

The *Politique* Monster

In this chapter, we have seen the term *politique* in an urgent context, used as a spur to the kind of social panic that led Greengrass to call this mass of

---

[80] Barnabé Brisson and Louis Le Caron, *Le code du roy Henry III, rédigé en ordre par B. Brisson, augmenté et illustré par L. Le Caron* (Paris, 1601). Lloyd, *Jean Bodin*, p. 197.

[81] See Barnavi and Descimon for a full account of this targeted assassination. They describe how closely Brisson worked with his future murderers, referring to a '*politique* strain' ('un courant *politique*') at the heart of the Parisian League; clearly there was overlap between Leaguers and *politiques* even as polemicists attempted to enact clear delineation, pp. 177–78. For an account of the court cases and failed attacks on *politiques* that ultimately led to the lynching, see pp. 178–200.

[82] Ibid., pp. 204–05.   [83] L'Estoile, *Mémoires-Journaux*, v, pp. 124–26.

[84] L'Estoile, *Mémoires-Journaux*, v, p. 126.

[85] This said, the extent of its deadly impact is not exactly what the *Seize* may have desired; some suggest that, like the assassination of Coligny in 1572, this lynching was meant to trigger a new Saint Bartholomew's Day. See Huchard, 'Echos des prédicateurs parisiens', p. 187.

pamphlets 'panic literature'. The word operates as a deadly insult, and comes to refer to a monstrous figure of vaguely all-encompassing evil, in order to give readers the impression that the enemies of the League were an organised opposing force and not simply an increasing majority of French citizens. But the 'bad' *politique* was by no means fixed as one kind of speech act: rather, the pamphlets consistently and repeatedly refer to the mobility of the word: a mobility which becomes a fundamental characteristic of these monstrous figures the writers are attempting to create and to pin down. This urgent moment of unusual focus on the word itself, as well as on the character called *politique*, may have been something of a sudden flurry, but was also a product of a broader context of political writing, from Machiavelli to Belloy – as well as being connected to the wider literary production of the time. Part of the work here has been to connect this moment in which the term *politique* is especially key to the longer story of its use across the period of the Wars of Religion. Throughout the chapter, I have emphasised the fraught, interrelated connections between the real and the textual, in which real people like Bodin and Brisson experience a failure to persuade people with language, and to win respect on the basis of their writings, and in which writers of pamphlets tussle with the arguments and 'fallacious ratiocination' of imaginary *politiques*. When the word *politique* is particularly 'key', then, it refers to several different but connected linguistic and rhetorical functions, and in so doing becomes the focal point of conflicts being fought in the socio-political landscape beyond the text.

These different, but connected, linguistic and rhetorical functions all come together in the final source I will discuss here: an image of a grotesque body, a monster, named *Politique*. There are hardly any visual depictions of the *politique*, but two are found in L'Estoile's *Drolleries* collection. The first, discussed above, is the 'Upturned Cauldron'; the second is this depiction of the *politique* as monster, one of the first broadsheets in the collection, with the title 'Le pourtraict & description du Politique de ce temps. Extraict de l'escriture saincte' ('Portrait and Description of the Politique of this time with an extract from Holy Scripture', Figure 3).

The pamphlets I discuss in this chapter attempt to stage a moment of recognition, in which the *politique* is re-cognised and so recognised as malign. As Cave points out, the thing that is suddenly discovered in such a moment is 'marvellous: the truth of fabulous myth or legend'.[86] In this image from L'Estoile's *Drolleries*, the full mythological and 'fabulous' potential of these moves is realised: the *politique* is revealed as a monster

---

[86] Cave, *Recognitions*, p. 2.

Figure 3.   Anon, 'Le Pourtraict et description du Politique de ce temps' (detail), woodcut on paper (Paris: Le Bouc and Chevillot, 1589), in Pierre de L'Estoile, *Les belles figures et drolleries de la Ligue* (*c*. 1589–98). Bibliothèque nationale de France

who is an amalgam of mythological creatures – part Siren, part Dagon, and, in the image, Medusa-like with snakes for hair (though this isn't referenced in the accompanying ekphrastic poem, the 'description' referenced in the title).[87] The *politique* here may then be an amalgam of the endless factionalised quarrelling of contemporary discourse, figured as a 'Syrene' (whose clarion call will direct the ship of state to its doom) but also tied to the mast like Odysseus attempting to resist the Siren. The *Politique*, both subject and object, launches its own apparently injurious speech at the same time as receiving marks of opprobrium in the same text, and in this case in the same image. In the longer story of this book, this

[87] Pierre de L'Estoile had a vast collection of *canards* describing sightings of monsters, monstrous births, and so on. Wilson suggests that there was a particular spate of monster prints *c*. 1560–80, connected to the millenarianism of the epoch and anxieties stoked by the violence of the wars. See Dudley Wilson, *Signs and Portents: Monstrous Births from the Middle Ages to the Enlightenment* (London and New York, NY: Routledge, 1993), pp. 32–36. See also Williams, *Monsters and Their Meanings*, and *Monstrous Bodies/ Political Monstrosities in Early Modern Europe*, ed. by Laura Knoppers and Joan B. Landes (Ithaca, NY and London: Cornell University Press, 2014).

image also offers a kind of anchor, or moment of 'recognition', in which the essential mobility of the term *politique* is 'revealed', thus demonstrating the fundamental problem of meaning, and of knowledge, posed by this shifting, flexible term across decades of conceptual and actual strife. But as I suggested at the opening, this moment of 'recognition' is not one of resolution, but rather refers back to an endless ongoing discussion of what politics could and should be.

The full page (Figure 4) shows the layering technique that L'Estoile frequently employed in the composition of his *Drolleries*: beneath the *Pourtraict et description* there is a vague and threatening announcement printed in Troyes and 'published at the crossroads to be cried and proclaimed'. The announcement deplores the Estates at Blois where the Guise brothers were killed, exhorts local Catholics to stay zealous and true and to condemn anyone wavering in their zeal, and ominously asks 'anyone who hears anything' to report it. To the side, the 'Chant rial' (which could be translated as 'mocking song') is a comic dialogue in popular dialect between two men discussing whether to believe rumours from the Palais; their speech is reminiscent of some of the servant characters in Molière's farcical scenes (such as Alain and Georgette's exchanges in *L'école des femmes*). The overall effect here is a kind of reconstruction of the voices and views of the moment in the city: the composition invites the reader to imagine town criers, popular discussion, and polemical verse.

The broadsheet itself is composed of the image, the ekphrastic verse directly beneath it, and around that the 'extract from Scripture' which is actually another vituperative poem with each verse following a Bible quotation – it reads like a pastiche of a sermon. Although its religious intent was likely sincere, it could almost be a satire of Leaguer attacks against *politiques,* bringing together all the pamphlet tropes explored in this chapter. This longer poem is a repetitive attack on the 'Dagon' figure as duplicitous: as like a mole, a leech, a crow, and a leopard, one who prioritises 'la chose humaine' (the mortal world) over their duty to God. It makes brief reference to some of the figures in the image itself, for instance explaining that the children reaching for bubbles are 'governors of the Republic' who chase honour instead of serving God: bubbles are a common symbol of vanity.

More of the ekphrastic poem is devoted to explaining the various objects surrounding the central *politique* figure. For example, the poem explains

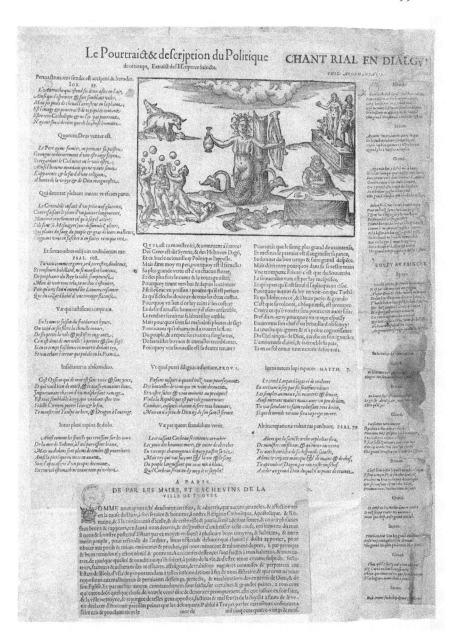

Figure 4. Anon, 'Le Pourtraict et description du Politique de ce temps' (full page), in
Pierre de L'Estoile, *Les belles figures et drolleries de la Ligue* (c. 1589–98).
Bibliothèque nationale de France

that the *Politique* monster has a bottle in his/her hand, because its stomach
is its chief concern, reprising other references to the *politique* as fonder of
fine foods than of moral goods. The turbans in the foreground, which
could be a vague reference to Ottoman habits of dress, are presented as
evidence that the *politique* will shamelessly believe anything. However, the
defining features of the *politique* monster are expressed in the first ten lines
of the accompanying verse:

> What is this monster, and what is its name?
> The Greeks called it Siren and the Hebrews Dagon,
> And in this Century, today it is called Politique,
> But tell me: why is he female?
> Her great virtue is to flatter every person
> And undermine the heart and spirit of the strongest men.
> Why, beneath the belt, towards the ground,
> Is he like a fish? Because he is a perjurer
> And limps doubtfully on both sides.[88]

The verse here has many of the features characteristic of anti-*politique*
polemic: an emphasis on naming, and on the temporary, time-specific
nature of this naming ('ce siecle' in the poem, and 'de ce temps' in the
title). It is also typical to see an association between *politiques* and animals,
and specifically with fish, as we saw earlier. That this *politique* is a fish
below the belt recalls the opening of Horace's *Ars poetica*, in which the
image of someone who is a 'lovely woman' on top and an 'ugly fish' below
is evoked as the unavoidably comic product of a poetic imagination that
has transgressed appropriate boundaries; Montaigne cites this image at the
opening of I.28, 'Of Friendship', as part of his representation of his *Essais*
as monstrous bodies (p. 164).[89] The implicit reference to Horace emphasises that to be *politique* is to embody a kind of failure of language and
imagination, as well as offering a further connection between Montaigne's
writing and contemporary representations of *politiques*. The association
would further affirm the erudition of the creator of this broadsheet, and
the transfer of poetic culture to political print. This is further borne out by

[88] 'Quel est ce monstre ici, et comment a-t-il nom? / Des Grecs est dit Syrene, & des Hebrieux Dagon, / Et ce Siecle aujourdhuy Politique l'appelle, / Mais dites moy un peu, pourquoy est il femelle? / Sa plus grande vertue est d'un chacun flatter, / Et des plus fors le cueur & le courage oster. / Pourquoy tirant vers bas & depuis la ceinture / Est il comme un poisson? Pource qu'il est perjure / Et qu'il cloche douteux de tous les deux costez.' Here, I've mixed the gender of the subject pronouns to reflect the emphasis on ambiguous gender; possessives in French agree with the object, not the subject as in English, so a direct translation is impossible.
[89] Horace, *Ars poetica*, in *Satires, Epistles, The Art of Poetry*, tr. by H. Rushton Fairclough (Cambridge, MA: Harvard University Press, 1926), pp. 442–90 (p. 451).

the similarities between the *politique* and some of Andrea Alciato's emblems. The emblem with the title 'The Wisdom of Man is Folly to God' in the collection printed at Paris in 1584 – depicting a figure who is half man, half snake – was also accompanied by an verse that begins very similarly to the *politique* poem: 'Mais quoy? Quel monstre icy? Quel nom peust-il avoir?' (What? What monster is here? What name can it have?).[90] Placed in this context, the *politique* is clearly 'emblematic' of the literary-political problems of the period.

Beyond this, and more unusually, the verse emphasises the 'femaleness' of the *politique* figure here, mobilising long-standing associations between deceit and femininity, and also evoking what I discussed at the end of Chapter 3, namely that there are good and bad ways of being *politique*, that women cannot be good *politiques*, and that they lead potentially good (male) *politiques* astray. The presence of Venus and Mars on the *cassone* (marriage chest) in the top right underlines this gendered aspect, recalling the significance of marriage as a political analogy in the period. Female agency is certainly figured as destructive for a potential male audience here, where the feminised *politique* flatters and effectively 'unmans' the strongest men; this would, then, be a travestied marriage. But the monster's gender is itself flexible; the repetitions of the masculine subject pronoun 'il' in the French, which refer to 'ce monstre' (this monster), imply mixed gender as well as all the other mixed qualities at play here: a mix of myths, a mix of genders, and, perhaps most crucially of all, mixed opinions: 'he limps doubtfully on both sides'. This monster, then, is a figure for indecision and ceaseless shifting of position: an embodiment of doubt or of its more ethically dubious relative, duplicity.

The monstrous *politique* could be considered anti-human, anti-society, or anti-morality, but this image also expresses anxieties about certain modes or behaviours, and thus carries content as well as being an act of aggression and condemnation. To suggest that the insulting function of the term *politique* is its only function would undermine what is particular to it, as opposed to the cluster of other terms that vilify supporters of Henri de Navarre (himself, of course, a mobile and ambiguous figure): that is, its mobility and irrepressible ambiguity. Wes Williams writes that in the

---

[90] Andrea Alciato, 'Sapienta humana stultitia est apud Deum', in *Emblemata/Emblemes* (Paris, 1584) www.emblems.arts.gla.ac.uk/alciato/ emblem.php?id=FALc005 [accessed 15 January 2021]. The *politique* also resembles the emblem representing literary fame as a sea monster encircled by a snake in Andrea Alciato, 'Ex literarium studiis immortalitatem acquiri', in *Emblematum libellus* (Paris, 1534) www.emblems.arts.gla.ac.uk/ alciato/dual. php? type1=1&id1=A34b041&type2=2& id2=sm53_C7r [accessed 15 January 2021].

sixteenth century, monsters were migrating from the realm of the real to the metaphorical; focus shifted from fantastical figures from uncharted territory, to the monster within the community, or even within the individual subject – and that the Wars of Religion were at the crucible of this change, as monsters came to represent 'a whole brood of anxieties concerning hybridity, novelty, and change'.[91] The *politique* monster seems a typical example of this, down to its hybrid gender and double tail.[92] Indeed, the *politique* monster is both *an* amalgam, and amalgam itself. Neither one thing nor the other, the term *politique* in these texts refers to all manner of evils, in which the central evil is how it resists being pinned down even as polemicists seek to do so; in the following, final chapter, we will see how, as the wars draw to a close, writers attempt to put an end to this increasingly circular conversation.

---

[91] Williams, *Monsters and Their Meanings*, p. 4.

[92] It may have been a stock image, but I have not found it elsewhere, e.g. in Ripa's *Iconologia*. See Cesare Ripa, *Iconologia*, ed. by Piero Buscaroli and Mario Praz (Milan: TEO, 1992).

CHAPTER 6

Strange Meeting
The Dialogue d'entre le Maheustre et le Manant, *and the* Satyre ménippée

The *Dialogue d'entre le Maheustre et le Manant, contenant les raisons de leurs debats et questions en ses presens troubles au royaume de France* ('Dialogue between the Maheustre and the Manant Containing the Reasons of their Debates and Questions in their Present Troubles in the Kingdom of France') was printed in 1593. It became the unlikely survivor of Henri IV's campaign of censorship in the years following the Wars of Religion; only a rewritten royalist version was known until the original was discovered in the nineteenth century.[1] The opening of the *Dialogue* stages the meeting of two characters as yet unknown to one another, somewhere outside Paris:

MAHEUSTRE: Who goes there?
MANANT: What does that mean, 'Who goes there'? I don't understand this language.
MAHEUSTRE: Respond to what I ask you: Who goes there, to whose party do you belong?
MANANT: I am Catholic.
MAHEUSTRE: As am I, but are you of the party of the King, or of the Princes of Lorraine?
MANANT: You ask for too much qualification. I am able to tell you nothing other than that I am Catholic, living by the Religion of my fathers.
MAHEUSTRE: Yet you must speak French, and I must know which party you favour.[2]

---

[1] See Baumgartner, p. 219, and Hamilton, *Pierre de L'Estoile and his World*, p. 160.
[2] 'MAHEUSTRE: Qui vive? MANANT: Qu'est-ce à dire: "qui vive", je n'entends point ce langage. MAHEUSTRE: Responds à ce que je te demande: Qui vive, de quel party es-tu? MANANT: Je suis catholique. MAHEUSTRE: Et moy aussi, mais es-tu du party du Roy, ou des Princes de Lorraine? MANANT: Vous me demandez trop de qualitez. Je ne vous sçaurois dire autre chose, sinon que je suis catholique, vivant en la Religion de mes peres. MAHEUSTRE: Si faut-il que tu parles françois, et que je sçache quel party tu tiens.' *Dialogue d'entre le Maheustre et le Manant*, ed. by Peter Ascoli (Geneva: Droz, 1977), p. 43. All further quotations from the *Dialogue* will be from this edition.

The mutual incomprehension is marked at the opening and close of this excerpt ('I don't understand this language'; 'Yet you must speak French'). The opening watchword, in French, is 'qui vive?', which translates literally as 'who lives?': the expected answer might be 'vive le Roi!' ('Long live the King!') which would make their allegiance clear. Instead, a setting of conflict and mistrust is established: two men meet in an unknown place and time, and struggle to discover whether they are allies or enemies.

The trope of strange meetings is a rich one in sixteenth-century literature. The meeting of Pantagruel and Panurge in Rabelais's *Pantagruel* (Chapter 9: 'How Pantagruel found Panurge who he loved all his life') is ultimately successful, but initially marked by incomprehension and linguistic difficulty, Panurge cycling through a series of languages that Pantagruel cannot understand.[3] Montaigne describes two tense meetings with strangers in times of war towards the end of III.11 ('Of Phisiognomy'): in the second, he is attacked by robbers during 'some truce or other' and spared owing to his 'face and the freedom and firmness of [his] speech' (pp. 990–91).[4] The tension born of the Manant's refusal to engage with the watchword and reveal himself as friend or foe in the *Dialogue* particularly anticipates another literary meeting that opens a play written within the same decade, set in the Danish kingdom of Elsinore:

BERNARDO: Who's there?
FRANCISCO: Nay, answer me: stand, and unfold yourself.
BERNARDO: Long live the king![5]

Both the *Dialogue* and *Hamlet* open with a meeting on the boundary of a kingdom, and an attempt to establish allegiances. Each opening also raises the broader question of who is, or should be, king: a question posed throughout both texts, but barely answered. In *Hamlet*, the implicit 'qui vive' is answered more quickly, but there is a strikingly similar sense of equivocation, of incomplete communication, and frustrated recognition. These opening lines of *Hamlet* have been much commented upon; Francisco's 'curious resistance to answering the question' has been viewed as laying a rhetorical pattern for the play of '[a] distortion of the relation

---

[3] Rabelais, ed. by Huchon, pp. 246–50; Rabelais, tr. Frame, pp. 170–72.
[4] 'Je ne sçay quelle treve'; 'mon visage, liberté, et fermeté de mes parolles', pp. 1108–10.
[5] 'The Tragedy of Hamlet, Prince of Denmark', in William Shakespeare, *Complete Works*, ed. by Jonathan Bate and Eric Rasmussen (London: Macmillan, 2007), pp. 1924–2003 (p. 1924).

between words and things'.[6] His response sets the expected pattern of words askew, in an exchange that evokes farce but where 'a sense of fear is much stronger than any intuition of the ridiculous'.[7] Two recent editors of Shakespeare concur that this opening establishes the mood of a play in which no character 'unfolds themselves'.[8] Such uncertainty is also crucial to the *Dialogue d'entre le Maheustre et le Manant*, a text in which epistemological and political problems are as bound together as they are in *Hamlet*.

Taken together, these examples – *Hamlet*, on the one hand, among the best-known texts of Western literature; on the other, the *Dialogue*, which languished in a forgotten archive and today receives little critical attention – both express existential anxiety about identity and strangers in late sixteenth-century Europe, associated with concerns about shifting political alliances and uncertain royal succession, heightened by confessional conflict. In this chapter, I explore the ways in which the word *politique* occupies a fault line in attempts to resolve such generalised and particular anxieties, in texts that, both as consequence and as remedy, put pressure on the relation between words and things.

Dialogue and Satire

In 1593, the Wars of Religion were drawing to a close. Following a series of military successes, Henri de Navarre was encamped outside Paris but unable to enter the city because its staunchly Catholic inhabitants would not tolerate a Protestant monarch. In January of that year, a meeting of the Estates General was called in Paris by Leaguers and their allies, without the participation of Henri de Navarre, in order to elect an alternative king. This was a failure. The following year, having (re)converted to Catholicism, Henri de Navarre made his entry into Paris. Although the resentments and injuries caused by the wars would take far longer to subside or be forgotten, that moment in 1594 marked the defeat of the League, clearing the way for Henri IV.

The *Dialogue d'entre le Maheustre et le Manant* was written by a diehard, and – in the circumstances – bitterly disappointed, opponent of Henri IV.

---

[6] Andrew Zurcher, *Shakespeare and Law* (London: Methuen, 2010), pp. 229–30. See also A. D. Nuttall, 'Hamlet: Conversations with the Dead', *Proceedings of the British Academy*, LXXIV (1988), 53–69.
[7] Nuttall, p. 54.
[8] Jonathan Bate and Eric Rasmussen, 'The Tragedy of Hamlet, Prince of Denmark: Introduction', in Shakespeare, *Complete Works*, pp. 1918–23 (p. 1918).

The title recalls those of the pamphlets discussed in the previous chapter, some of which are dialogues and many of which recount conversational conflicts. However, this is a much longer work. It gives a detailed account of Parisian history in the years 1590–93, and demonstrates insider knowledge of the rise and fall of the hard-line Catholic council which ruled Paris with the support of the city's clerics and theologians, after Henri III left the city on the *Journée des Barricades* in 1588. This knowledge has led critics to assume that the author must have been a member of this council, known as the *Seize*. The likeliest candidate is François Morin de Cromé, who has already appeared once in this book, though unnamed: Pierre de L'Estoile says he is the orchestrator of the lynching of Brisson, Larcher, and Tardif.[9]

The dialogue is between the Manant (a burgher of Paris and supporter of the Catholic League) and the Maheustre (a supporter of Henri de Navarre); their meeting is a kind of truce, a pause in the fighting as these characters attempt to address their differences in words rather than with violence. Their – albeit short-lived – laying down of arms in favour of discussion recalls Montaigne's survival of his own strange encounter during 'some truce or other'. The term *Maheustre* refers to the clothes worn by the future King's foot soldiers and was already associated with the term *politique*, such as in the title of the pamphlet *L'aveuglement et grande inconsideration des Politiques, dicts Maheustres, lesquels veulent introduire Henry de Bourbon, jadis Roy de Navarre, à la Couronne de France, à cause de sa pretendüe succession* ('The Blindness and Imprudence of the Politiques, Called Maheustres, Who Want to Introduce Henry de Bourbon, Formerly King of Navarre, to the Throne of France, Due to His Pretended Succession'), published in 1592 by a Sorbonne theologian.[10] The terms *politique* and *maheustre* seem to have converged with the approach of Henri de Navarre's armies (populated by *maheustres*) and increasing support for Henri among non-military citizens who were known as *politiques*. The Manant refers throughout the *Dialogue* to *politiques* who are the friends ('amis') of the Maheustre.

The two characters agree to a proposition made by the Manant: 'Let us honestly and without insult discuss what we are' ('devisons honnestement et sans injure ce que nous sommes', p. 43).[11] The injunction to proceed

---

[9] See L'Estoile, *Mémoires-Journaux*, p. 132; Ascoli, pp. 24–26.

[10] On potential origins of the term *Maheustre*, see Baumgartner, pp. 211–12. See *L'aveuglement et grande inconsideration des Politiques, dicts Maheustres, lesquels veulent introduire Henry de Bourbon, jadis Roy de Navarre, à la Couronne de France, à cause de sa pretendüe succession* (Paris: Rollin, 1592).

[11] This proposition evokes a minimalist kind of compassionate toleration that Katherine Ibbett describes emerging from religious difference in *Compassion's Edge: Fellow-Feeling and Its Limits in*

'without insult' points to the shift in this text away from the rapid-fire vituperation of the works discussed in the previous chapter. Here, I discuss longer texts that rework the uses of *politique* that were so prevalent around the crisis of 1589. In some ways these reworkings could be read as attempts to settle once and for all the long-running ideological conflicts of the civil wars; but this does not mean, in the case of the *Dialogue*, reconciliation between the Maheustre and the Manant. Their conversation is encapsulated in the following excerpt:

MAHEUSTRE: It is not reasonable that those who desire peace must suffer the stubbornness of others.

MANANT: It is less reasonable to lose one's religion to recognise a heretic [as king]. (p. 125)[12]

In this fight over the lesser of two reasons there is little, if any, consensus: it is a *dialogue de sourds*. Daniel Ménager argues that the Maheustre and the Manant are speaking at cross purposes throughout the *Dialogue* due to a fundamental opposition between theology, represented by the Manant, and civil law, or politics, represented by the Maheustre: the text stages a refusal, to a certain extent, of the possibility of secular and religious authority joining forces in government.[13] The core of this position is a refusal to accept that Catholics and Protestants can coexist within the same state; the Manant predicts perpetual civil war if people persist in trying to make this happen (p. 56). And yet, what is striking about the work is that it nonetheless mounts such a devastating critique of the League that Henri de Navarre was delighted with it and commissioned a royalist revision that was printed with a pro-Navarre text that proved far more popular with contemporaries: the *Satyre ménippée*.[14]

The first version of the *Satyre ménippée* ('Menippean Satire'), like the *Dialogue*, was written in 1593, during the uneasy period of truce before

<hr />

Early Modern France (Pennsylvania, PA: University of Pennsylvania Press, 2017); it also recalls the mereness of Roger Williams's version of tolerant discourse discussed in Bejan's *Mere Civility*.

[12] 'MAHEUSTRE: Il n'est pas raisonnable que ceux qui desirent la paix souffrent pour les opinionastres. MANANT: Il est moins raisonnable perdre sa religion pour recognoistre un heretique.'

[13] Daniel Ménager, 'Le *Dialogue entre le Maheustre et le Manant*: Mystique ou politique?', in *Histoire et littérature au siècle de Montaigne: Mélanges offerts à Claude-Gilbert Dubois*, ed. by Françoise Argod-Dutard (Geneva: Droz 2001), pp. 97–108 (p. 105).

[14] A royalist version of the *Dialogue* (thought to have been edited by none other than supposed editor of the *Satyre*, Pierre Pithou) was first included as an appendix to the *Satyre ménippée* in an edition falsely dated 1593, but compiled no earlier than the beginning of 1595. An extract from the *Dialogue* is also included under the title *Abrégé* in a 1599 edition of the *Satyre*. Thus the original *Dialogue* was co-opted to serve the purposes of propaganda for Henri IV: a hint that the opposition between the texts may not be so stark.

Henri IV's coronation. The conceit is that it is the record of the 1593 Estates General, kept by an Italian diplomat. It was expanded greatly between 1593 and 1595: here I am primarily looking at the text that corresponds to the edition printed in Tours in 1594, because of the near-simultaneity with the composition and dissemination of the *Dialogue*. The 1594 prologue, 'L'imprimeur au lecteur' ('The Printer to the Reader'), explains the picaresque adventures of the manuscript that took it to its Parisian printer: the original writer had intended to send it to his Florentine master, but on his prolonged journey home – via Amiens, and Flanders – he was robbed of all his possessions by a servant, who was then robbed by some monks, who then could not read the Italian and gave it to another monk who could, who was then himself robbed by a group of 'Gentilhommes' ('Gentlemen') – likely a comic reference to the group who composed the *Satyre* – who translated it into French and gave it to the anonymous printer.

'L'imprimeur au lecteur' is followed by a series of further prefatory pieces: *La vertu du Catholicon* ('The Virtue of the Catholicon'), in which charlatans attempt to sell a bogus wonder-drug called 'Le Catholicon', a figure for empty Leaguer rhetoric, to Parisians under its 'Spanish' name, 'higuero d'inferno' ('hell-fig'). This is followed by *La procession des Ligueurs* (a description of a kind of 'opening ceremony' of the League's Estates General), then by *Tapisseries*: ekphrastic descriptions of tapestries depicting absurd images of episodes in the histories of the wars, including one of the Battle of Ivry in 1590, depicting 'Leaguers showing their arses to the Maheustres' ('les Ligueurs qui montrent leur cul aux maheustres').[15] The main body of the text is composed of supposed transcriptions of the speeches made at the meeting. Leaguer speeches are answered, and opposed, by that of Colonel d'Aubray, 'for the third estate' (in life, d'Aubray was *Prévôt des Marchands*). All were real historical figures, but the Leaguers are given a grotesque makeover: the Duc de Mayenne (Lieutenant of Paris, and now the only surviving Guise brother) is extremely bloodthirsty, Cardinal Pellevé and the papal legate Sega give barely coherent speeches in Latin, Italian, and French, and Bishop Roze (in life, rector of the Sorbonne) has all the eloquence and learning of Rabelais's absurd cleric, Maistre Janotus.

The final and by far the longest text of the *Satyre ménippée* is d'Aubray's long *harangue*. This is a restrained but passionate plea for an end to war,

---

[15] *Satyre ménippée*, ed. by Martial Martin (Lyon: Presses universitaires de Lyon, 2010), p. 47. All further quotations from the *Satyre* will be from this edition unless otherwise stated.

and a robust defence of the legitimacy of Henri de Navarre. D'Aubray's overall position can be summed up in his own words: 'Ultimately everyone is tired of this war which we well understand is no longer a question of our religion, but of our servitude' (p. 177).[16] Here, he makes the argument for peace, minimising the theological controversy by suggesting that the question is fundamentally a civil one: 'concerning our servitude'.[17] D'Aubray has been taken as a *politique* spokesman largely because of this position.

In contrast to the stark quality of the prose in the *Dialogue*, the *Satyre*, which is clearly influenced by Rabelais and cites this influence in the 1595 preface, abounds with imagery, neologisms, and scatological humour; the work has, like Rabelais's *œuvre*, been categorised as carnavalesque.[18] It is thought to have been compiled by a group of men belonging to what Martin describes as 'a learned elite' ('une élite savante'), who favoured the accession of Henri de Navarre, and were led by Pierre Pithou.[19] The profiles of Pithou and other potential authors are similar to those of most others referenced in this book. That the *Satyre* was composed and circulated through the collected efforts of an elite group especially evokes the Huguenot authors discussed in Chapter 4; attempts to define political communities around the term *politique* were often communal. The comparison between these two groups also demonstrates that – for all the emphasis placed on lawyers and the *noblesse de robe* in the construction of the royalist *politiques*, apt in the case of the *Satyre* – groups of elite men with shared educational backgrounds and common literary and theoretical references came up, at different times, with rather different visions of the political community.

[16] 'Enfin chascun est laz de la guerre en laquelle nous voyons bien qu'il n'est plus question de nostre religion, mais de nostre servitude.' The reference to *servitude* also evokes the discussions of *liberté* and *servitude* explored in Chapter 4.

[17] The freedom that the authors of the *Satyre* may have been seeking may have been that of a liberated French (or Gallican) church; see n. 19.

[18] *Satyre ménippée* (2007), p. 161; Mikhail Bakhtin, *Rabelais and His World*, tr. by Hélène Iswolsky (Bloomington, IN: Indiana University Press, 1984), pp. 60, 63, 186–87; Martial Martin, 'Préface', in *La Satyre ménippée* (2007), pp. xv–clxxiii (p. liv).

[19] Pierre Pithou, a Protestant who narrowly escaped death in the Saint Bartholomew's Day massacres, reverted to Catholicism in 1573. He is described by Kelley as a 'patriotic philologist'. In 1576 he wrote a pamphlet entitled *Les libertez de l'eglise gallicane*. Kelley sees his role in the *Satyre ménippée* two decades later as evidence of his commitment to Gallican ideals; that is, to the religious independence of France. See Kelley, *The Foundations of Modern Historical Scholarship*, pp. 242–56. See also Parsons, pp. 124–29. For more on Pithou, see *Pithou, les lettres, et la paix du royaume*, ed. by Marie-Madeleine Fragonard (Paris: Champion, 2003). For an account, with biographical details, of probable contributors to the *Satyre ménippée*, see Martin, 'Préface', pp. xlvii–lvi.

There is a European scope to the *Satyre ménippée*: its picaresque journey to print; the Spanish and Italian characters; its various translations and numerous references to England. This transnational frame and the text's mobility across Europe recalls that of many of the texts discussed in this book. In the *Satyre* in particular this also functions as a means to define, and defend, what the authors consider to be France, or Frenchness. As part of this, various categories are problematised and challenged in the text: *catholique, françois, ligueur, politique*. Where the *Dialogue* seeks to confirm for posterity that the *politiques* were enemies of the true faith, the *Satyre ménippée* seeks to rehabilitate them as decent French citizens, and in so doing to normalise their support for Henri IV. In making a case for peace, and for Henri, the *Satyre* has also been viewed by critics and historians as the expression of the *politique* sentiment that won out at the end of the wars; this in strong contrast to the *Dialogue*, considered the final *cri de cœur* of their defeated opponents.[20]

The dialogue form had been crucial in writing and rewriting *politiques* and politics since before the outbreak of war. The word itself became a location of encounter and debate, its meaning constructed dialogically. In this final chapter, the texts are failed dialogues and, in the case of the *Satyre ménippée*, grotesque, parodied speech. Among the polemical works of the late sixteenth century, the *Dialogue* has received more literary attention than most (notably from Ménager in 2001).[21] Its peculiar form has also been noted, with several critics observing its departure from, and innovation in, the conventions of dialogue.[22] The *Satyre ménippée*, meanwhile, has long been held as a monument of the French literary canon, and as much a literary event as a political one.[23] It sold very well, and has been

---

[20] *Etudes sur la Satyre ménippée*, ed. by Frank Lestringant and Daniel Ménager (Geneva: Droz, 1987), p. 17. Elsewhere, Ménager details the three principal readings of the *Dialogue*: as 'l'expression passionnée d'une conviction catholique'; as a source used by 'Politique' historians to document the downfall of the League; as 'le manifeste d'une pensée politique radicale'. See Ménager, 'Le *Dialogue entre le Maheustre et le Manant*: Mystique ou Politique?', p. 98.

[21] Aside from Ménager, Demonet has also looked at the *Dialogue*, notably in M.-L. Demonet, 'Le politique "necessaire" de Montaigne', pp. 31–32.

[22] Ménager comments on the remarkable modifications of form within the *Dialogue*, see Ménager, 'Le *Dialogue entre le Maheustre et le Manant*', p. 100; Ascoli writes that new, more balanced kinds of dialogue (in comparison with the highly partisan pamphlet dialogues) were emerging at this moment in the civil wars, see Ascoli pp. 14–15; Baranova writes that in fact among such dialogues, Cromé's is unique, see Baranova, *A coup de libelles*, pp. 424–25.

[23] I am indebted to the comprehensive list of secondary criticism provided by the editor of the 2007 edition of the *Satyre ménippée*, Martial Martin. See 'Bibliographie' in *Satyre ménippée: Le libelle roi*, ed. M. Martin, www.satyremenippee.fr/bibliographie_menippee [accessed 3 August 2020]. The *Satyre* also represents an innovation in literary form; something the authors make clear in their 1595 preface, where they discuss at length their reasons for calling the text a *Satyre*

viewed as a kind of textual salve that healed discord in France as the wars ended; Kenny writes that even if its impact has been exaggerated, it was 'perhaps the most effective textual intervention of all in the Wars of Religion'.[24] It was quickly translated, for example into English in 1595 as *A Pleasant Satyre, or Poesie*.[25] The extent of its practical impact after the pivotal events of 1593 has, however, been called into question, as Henri IV's victory was more or less assured from late 1593, facilitated by his reconversion and secured by a lack of any convincing opponent.[26] In light of this, some see the *Satyre* and the *Dialogue* as 'reified' texts (in a sub-Marxist sense) in which previously live debates and struggles are shrouded in irony, and in 'literariness'; this argument emerges particularly in studies of the *Satyre* that argue for its genesis being contingent on a brief political necessity, and its continued production and development being a more 'literary' process.[27] This not only minimises the continuing tensions of the period 1594–1610, but draws too stark a line between political action and literary effect.[28] The texts in question employ literary strategies to intervene in politics, and in political thought. Both work to imagine and engineer new kinds of communities from the public that they describe and are writing for: the *Dialogue* clearly differentiates between the *politiques* and the Catholic people of Paris; the *Satyre* gestures to a broader public of reasonable citizens as a foil to the grotesque, babbling Leaguers.[29]

---

ménippée. See *Satyre ménippée* (2007), pp. 160–62. On the history of the Menippean satire, see Ingrid de Smet, *Menippean Satire and the Republic of Letters* (Geneva: Droz, 1996), esp. pp. 42–45, for her assessment of how the *Satyre ménippée* fits into the broader tradition. On satire more generally, see e.g. Pauline M. Smith, *Continuity and Change in Renaissance Satire* (Hull: University of Hull Press, 1993). On language and the meaning of words in the text, see Marie-Luce Demonet, 'Un aspect du discours polémique avant les *Provinciales*: du bon sens des mots dans la *Satyre Ménippée*', *Courrier du Centre international Blaise Pascal*, 18 (1996), 43–50.

[24] Neil Kenny, 'Introduction', in *Writers in Conflict in Sixteenth-Century France*, pp. 1–14 (p. 12).
[25] *A Pleasant Satyre or Poesie: Wherein Is Discovered the Catholicon of Spayne, and the Chiefe Leaders of the League. Finelie Fetcht Over, and Laide Open in Their Colours. New Turned Out of French into English*, tr. by Thomas Wilcox (London, 1595).
[26] This narrative is persuasively contested by Jean-Paul Barbier-Mueller, see 'Pour une chronologie des premières éditions de la *Satyre ménippée*', *Bibliothèque d'Humanisme et Renaissance*, 67.2 (2005), 373–93 (p. 392).
[27] This is certainly Turchetti's view; see 'Une Question mal-posée', p. 385.
[28] When Henri was assassinated in 1610, Pierre de L'Estoile feared that the wars would begin again, as if 1598–1610 had just been an usually long period of truce. See Hamilton, p. 195.
[29] On the question of emerging regional and national identities formed through the manipulation, and participation, of a reading public, see Benedict Anderson, *Imagined Communities: Reflections on the Origins and Spread of Nationalism* (London: Verso, 1983). Anderson's starting point is in the eighteenth century, but his observations apply to earlier contexts, with the caveat that the communities constructed by the imaginative efforts of authors and readers in the eighteenth century are not 'nation states' in the modern sense. See Timothy Hampton, *Literature and Nation in the Sixteenth Century*.

In modern criticism, *politique*, when used to refer to groups or ideas in the Wars of Religion, generally appears in inverted commas, or with the tag so-called (as in the so-called *politiques*), making use of the word a conspicuous kind of textual speech act. This echoes the language of the period, from Goulart onwards. In the *Satyre ménippée* and the *Dialogue d'entre le Maheustre et le Manant*, the term is almost always accompanied by discourse verbs and verbs of naming ('baptiser', 'appeller'), demonstrating the authors' awareness of the way the term has been used in earlier polemical writing, and their consciousness of its potency as an insulting speech act. Rather than reading either text as the manifesto of a particular *politique* or Leaguer position, it is productive to look at how the authors test and reorient these categories in order to make arguments about recent history, and to intervene in the political future of their communities. Both works occupy a threshold position in a putative *politique* canon – between Valois and Bourbon, between civil war and uneasy truce. The *Satyre* is an attempt to broker peace, and the *Dialogue* is a call to endless war, or to martyrdom; both are staged conversations of a kind. In both texts – appropriately enough, given that this chapter marks a final stage in the present narrative about the history of the term *politique* – the authors offer, and invite, a final reckoning.

Naming, Renaming, and Redescribing: 'Our Friends, Whom You Call *Politiques*'

Both the *Dialogue d'entre le Maheustre et le Manant* and the *Satyre ménippée* make considerable use of terms broadly designating the adversarial categories of this period: *ligueur, royaliste, heretique, gallican, politique*. The word *politique* occurs *c.* 30–35 times in each text.[30] It usually appears attached less to particular events or people, than alongside other terms (from *heretique* to *royaux*). Both texts, then, resonate with the insults fired from the Catholic presses of Paris in the preceding decade.

The Manant makes the first use of *politique* in the *Dialogue*, referring to 'all those of the opposing party, who are heretics, atheists, Politiques, covetous and ambitious' (p. 85).[31] These, broadly, are the words associated with *politique* in the his speeches throughout, sometimes with the addition

---

[30] See *Dialogue*, pp. 85, 92, 113, 116, 121, 122, 124, 130–32, 140, 148, 153, 168, 169–72, 184–85, 209, and 211; and *Satyre ménippée* (2010), pp. 27, 45, 55, 57, 59, 61, 63, 66, 67, 71, 80, 81, 92, 101, 105, 130, and 154.

[31] 'tous ceux du party contraire, tant heretiques, athees, Politiques, envieux qu'ambitieux'.

of 'fauteur', meaning co-conspirator, or accomplice (see pp. 113 and 121) – for example, in a discussion of the tactics of the self-appointed radical Catholic council (the *Seize*) *c.* 1591: 'they resisted by arms and counsel the enterprises and schemes of the heretics and accomplices of the Politiques' (p. 113).[32] This echoes the phrase 'Fauteur des Politiques' pinned to Claude Larcher's body in 1591; since Cromé was both the author of the *Dialogue* and the orchestrator of Larcher's lynching, this brings the potentially murderous consequences of these uses of *politique* into particular relief.[33] The term does not always appear with all the aforementioned tags, but does so in the first seven uses, and then again emphatically in the last two. It therefore seems that the author takes care to repeat the negative associations that would have been familiar to readers in the wake of the flurry of polemical pamphlets discussed in Chapter 5.

The Maheustre challenges these dangerous connotations, referring to the *politiques* as friends and allies. All but two of his uses of *politique* are constructed around the phrase 'our friends, whom you call Politiques' ('noz amis, que vous appelez Politiques': see, for example, pp. 132 and 153). The exceptions are: 'all those disposed to peace with the King, whom you call Politiques', and 'our friends and allies, whom you call Politiques' (pp. 161 and 168).[34] That the word nearly always appears introduced by the relative clause 'that/whom you call' in the speeches of the Maheustre serves to highlight this term in particular as contested, with the relative clause indicating implicit doubt of the appellation.

Much though the structure of the *Satyre ménippée* creates a sense of opposition similar to that established in the *Dialogue*, its uses of *politique* cannot be placed on either side of this opposition. Instead, a fairly coherent picture emerges across the whole of the text of *politique* as a favourite insult of the grotesque Leaguers, and people called *politique* actually being decent, loyal citizens. In the Leaguer speeches, negative associations are less strong than those in the *Dialogue*: the only instance of 'Politiques Heretiques' is from the Papal legate Sega; otherwise the *politiques* are simply 'bad' ('meschan', e.g. p. 59) or 'impudent' (p. 109). The most

---

[32] 'ils ont resistez par armes et conseil, aux entreprises et intelligences des heretiques et des fauteurs Politiques'.

[33] 'Fauteur' is one of a group of frequently used negative descriptors in the *Dialogue*; the frequency of this otherwise relatively unusual term perhaps strengthens the sense of connection between the pivotal murder of Brisson, Larcher, and Tardif, and the text. *Fauteur* often appears near the term *politique*; for example, at the close of the text when the Manant refers to the Maheustre and his associates disapprovingly, as 'Politiques et fauteurs d'heretiques' (p. 211).

[34] 'tous ceux qui estoient disposez à la paix avec le Roy, que vous appelez Politiques'/ 'noz amis et confederez, que vous appelez Politiques'.

frequent associated term is in fact 'royaux' ('royalists'), which occurs in roughly half the Leaguer uses. Thus the *Satyre* challenges anti-*politique* associations, establishing alternative connotations in the speeches of the Leaguers themselves. In Sega's *harangue*, the Leaguers are described as 'Spanishified Frenchmen' ('Français Espagnolisé'), who are the murderers of 'fathers, brothers, cousins, neighbours, Magistrates, Princes of the Blood, and Politique Heretics, in this most-Christian war' (p. 75).[35] The 'Politiques Hérétiques' are slipped in at the end of a list of increasingly controversial but theoretically ethically sound categories. 'Magistrates' and 'Princes of the blood' were only controversial in that magistrates were widely castigated by Leaguers for supporting Henri de Navarre and arguing for his legitimacy on the grounds that he was a 'Prince of the Blood'. The 'most-Christian war' is likely a reference here to the fact that the King of France had traditionally been referred to as the Most-Christian King (*le Roi trèschrétien*) since the medieval period. The heavily ironic approbation of a most-Christian war in which fathers, sons, and neighbours are murdered, implies that the 'Politiques Hérétiques' are perhaps unfairly targeted, the result of Spanish meddling rather than earthly administration of divine justice. Since the implication is that the war is the very opposite of 'most-Christian', the reader may infer that the grounds on which the *politiques* may be accused of being heretics are equally dubious.

There is a further move in the anti-*politique harangues* of the *Satyre* that reinforces the strength of Henri de Navarre's position via use of *politique*. In the first six *harangues* of the *Satyre*, the *Politiques* are established as the enemies of the Leaguer speakers, but crucially, they are repeatedly referred to as a large group: one of the opening descriptive passages, 'La vertu du Catholicon', emphasises that there are more *Politiques* than partisans of the *Seize* in Paris (p. 27). Mayenne also refers to 'a heap of Politiques among us' ('un taz de Politiques qui sont parmy nous', p. 63) and discusses the damaging impact of 'the Politique party' ('le party des Politiques', p. 68), while Pellevé complains that 'some Politiques are spreading I don't know what kind of rumour among the public' ('quelques Politiques répandent dans le public je ne sais quel bruit', p. 81). This sense of a threatening swarm of *Politiques* is in part a parody of paranoiac Leaguer sermons and pamphlets, but beneath the parody is the implication that the *Politiques*

---

[35] 'pères, frères, cousins, voisins, Magistrats, Princes du sang, Politiques Hérétiques, en cette guerre Très-Chrétienne'.

represent the greater part of popular opinion.[36] The strategy of lacing parody with an attempt to convey an impression of the 'true' situation in Paris also occurs in the Leaguer *harangues* in relation to the frequent association of the terms *royaux* ('royalist') and *politique*. It reinforces the status of Henri de Navarre as *Roi*, since his supporters are *royaux*, and group all opposition to the League into the camp of the future Henri IV.

In her discussion of the term *politique*, Demonet argues that *politique* and *royaliste* more or less collapse into one another across the period 1586–96.[37] This is partly staged in the *Satyre* (though not entirely, since d'Aubray does not make the association other than by implication), but it is not borne out in the *Dialogue*, and the appearance of the term alongside nominalist gestures such as 'whom you call' or 'whom you baptise' indicates rather the conflict present in its use. As such, it seems that any association of *politique* and *royaliste* results from a deliberate attempt to encourage the proximity of the two terms in the parodied speeches of the Leaguers themselves, converting the 'rumour' bemoaned by Pellevé into actual social harmony.

In fact, in the *Satyre* it is d'Aubray, alleged *politique*, who makes the same associations as the Manant in the *Dialogue* when, discussing the threats made by the *Seize* to 'the best of us' ('les meilleurs'), he says that the latter have been treated 'as ... heretics, or politiques' ('comme ... des heretiques, ou politiques') (p. 130). D'Aubray also complains of the treatment of 'citizens and gentlemen ... who are baptised with the name of *politique*, conspirator, and accomplice of heretics' (p. 154).[38] The implication is that a false baptism has taken place, a pointed critique of the preachers who accused *politiques* from the pulpit. This phrasing, like the 'que vous appelez' clause in the Maheustre's speeches, emphasises and problematises the very act of naming a *politique*. As well as contesting connotations and establishing alternative associations for *politique*, these texts engage intensely with the problems of meaning and communication

---

[36] For descriptions of anti-*politique* sermons, see, for example, L'Estoile, *Mémoires-Journaux*, v, pp. 141 and 281. This representation of the changing tide of Parisian opinion was at least partly accurate; previously obdurate League supporters were turning to Navarre in increasing numbers at this time. See, for instance the trial of former Leaguer François Brigard, arraigned in 1591 for, among other things, 'cryptoroyalist' conspiracy. See Greengrass with Hamilton, 'Lettres compromettantes. La Ligue et la clandestinité des "politiques"'.

[37] Demonet, 'Quelques avatars du mot "Politique"', p. 45.

[38] 'Des habitans et des gentilhomme ... lesquels on baptizoit du nom de politiques ou d'adherants, et fauteurs d'heretiques'. The term 'politique' is not capitalised in d'Aubray's *harangue* – unlike in the Leaguer *harangues*, and the *Dialogue*. Perhaps this was a deliberate move on the part of the authors to make the so-called *Politiques* appear less conspicuous, on the page as in reality.

that have haunted all the writers attempting to pin down *politique* and its referents in this period.

A sense that misnaming was a common political strategy in the period is present in many works of the 1590s, including one by a contemporary author who imagined the Leaguers boasting about the ways that they had used certain words to discredit their enemies (*politique, fauteurs d'hérétiques, bigarrez* ['motley, or of mixed colour': this is a frequently associated 'keyword', as we have seen in Chapters 2 and 5]). The author writes that, in order to shore up the strength of their 'Union', they betray the notion of unity itself:

> To support our Union we have withdrawn from union with our neigh-bours, brothers, our fellow citizens who are as Catholic as we are ... and to make our ambitions successful, we have imposed names on them such as Politiques, *Bigarrez*, accomplices of Heretics, and other names that we have rendered odious, through the mistreatment that we have put them through.[39]

In their consistent use of naming verbs that effectively work as speech marks around terms like *politique*, the *Satyre ménippée* and the *Dialogue* alert their readers to their own and other writers' strategies of naming, misnaming, and renaming. In this way, the meaning of terms, and of *politique* in particular, is brought to the fore. Uncertainty about the meaning and uses of words more generally is a feature of both the *Dialogue* and the *Satyre ménippée*. In the *Dialogue* this leads to anxiety and threatened violence; in the *Satyre*, mutability of meaning is often more a source of comedy than of melancholy.

In the *Dialogue*, following the opening, both speakers claim to be following 'the word of God': the crisis of legitimate interpretation that results from neither speaker being prepared to surrender this claim dominates the text. Later on, the Manant declares that 'at present we no longer believe in words' ('à present l'on ne croit plus en paroles', p. 90). Eventually, as the text draws to a close, attempts to resolve their differences in words dissolve into threats of physical violence (the Maheustre offers the following warning to the Manant: 'your babble will not save you from the strength of our cutlasses' ('vostre caquet ne vous sauvera de la force de nos

---

[39] 'Pour agrandir notre Union nous nous sommes désunis d'avec nos voisins, nos frères, nos concitoyens, Catholiques aussi bien que nous ... Et pour colorer les effects de nos ambitions, nous leur avons imposé des noms de Politiques, Bigarrez, fauteurs d'Hérétiques, et autres noms, que nous avons rendu odieux, par les mauvais traictemens, dont nous les avons fait remarquer.' *La guide des chemins pour les desvoyez de la saincte union* (Paris: Roger, 1590), quoted in Miernowski, '"Politique" comme injure', p. 339.

coustelas', p. 195). The *Satyre ménippée* presents the war of words as the effect of the *Catholicon* drug (hence the subtitle of the text, 'la vertu du Catholicon'). When taken by the Leaguer speakers, this drug makes them reveal themselves ('unfold themselves', perhaps) as their 'true' grotesque selves. The very name *Catholicon* was probably a kind of joke on the part of the author-editors, who would surely have been familiar with the *Catholicon* that was a large monolingual Latin dictionary originally compiled in the thirteenth century. This dictionary was printed many times in the early sixteenth century but was gradually being replaced as an authority on words and their meanings by Etienne Dolet's *Commentaria Latina linguae* and Henri Estienne's *Dictionarium* (both of these authors, one notes, were Protestants; Dolet was executed for heresy).[40] The *Catholicon* might then have been recognised by readers as an increasingly obsolete repository of words whose meanings were being updated and replaced.

The *Catholicon* of the *Satyre ménippée* confers the ability or inclination to establish relations between words and things (badly). One of the 'articles' of the *Catholicon* in the *Satyre ménippée* announces that 'as long as you have taken a grain of Higuero, whoever you taunt will be considered a Huguenot or the accomplice of heretics' (p. 30).[41] The corrosive effects of Leaguer language are satirised throughout the *harangues*. In the speech of the Rector Roze, where the satire of failed Leaguer eloquence reaches its peak, the speaker asserts that he has washed his judgements in *Catholicon* soap: 'Spanish Catholicon, a soap that removes everything' ('catholicon d'espagne, qui est ung savon qui efface tout', p. 104). The writers of the *Satyre* here test the boundary between the literal and the metaphorical by having Roze imply that he is actually foaming at the mouth. The presentation of radical Catholic speech as the product of a devilish drug recalls the description of the word *politique* in the *Karesme et mœurs du Politique* pamphlet as a 'shop full of all kinds of intoxicants' ('boutique remplie de tant de sortes de drogueries'), and therefore seems to refer to, and to satirise, a context in which words have alchemical potential.[42] D'Aubray's *harangue* is a foil to Leaguer frothing and foaming; in both main parts of the *Satyre*, the authors make use of the excessive, absurd

---

[40] Ann Moss, *Renaissance Truth and the Latin Language Turn* (Oxford: Oxford University Press, 2003), pp. 15–16, 27, and 34–35.

[41] 'pourveu qu'ayez pris dés le matin un grain de Higuiero, quiconque vous taxera sera estimé Huguenot ou fauteur d'heretique'.

[42] *Le karesme et mœurs du Politique*, p. 5. This emphasis on the alchemical power of language, with comic effect, is another way in which the authors of the *Satyre* echo Rabelais.

power of language to problematise and reconstruct the meaning of various socio-political categories, of which *politique* is one.

Overall, it is clear that the connotations of the word *politique* are not fixed in these texts. The word moves between *athee, ennemy, heretique, fauteur, amis, royaux,* and *bourgeois,* and its reframing has strong moral implications. *Politique* is never found in isolation, but always alongside other words that anchor it as 'good' or 'bad', or that disrupt previous associations through use of irony. In itself, the word is a cipher, representing either civic virtue *(amis, royaux, bourgeois)* or vices that straddle religious and civic spheres *(athee* and *heretique* as crimes against God; *fauteur* and *ennemy* as crimes against civil codes) – all depending on the description.

The titles of many of the polemical pamphlets of the late 1580s include the word *description,* announcing their attempts to describe, fix, or define the referents of *politique.* In the *Satyre ménippée* and the *Dialogue,* the term *politique* is subject to redescription as a means of tipping the moral balance and so rewriting the political landscape. A key rhetorical tool at their disposal in this process of engineering of meaning is, then, redescription. Skinner has shown how the act of reframing terms, through the rhetorical technique referred to variously as redescription, *distinctio,* and *paradiastole,* played into a debate that had been present in moral philosophy since Plato acknowledged that judgement was only possible within defined terms.[43] Following Skinner, my understanding of redescription here encompasses not only the polarising rhetorical move of repositioning vice as virtue, but also a broader rewriting of the terms of the conflict, staged in the very use of the word *politique.* Contemporary treatises on slander reflect a similarly comprehensive view of the operations of redescription.[44] Beyond the spheres of polemic and slander, sixteenth-century concern with redescription was a product of humanist reading practices and education. Indeed, Cave writes that due to commonplace-ordering techniques central to the schooling of most educated men in France by the end of the sixteenth century, 'the problematic of *paradiastole* had come to condition an entire period's way of thinking'.[45]

---

[43] Quentin Skinner, *Reason and Rhetoric in the Philosophy of Hobbes* (Cambridge: Cambridge University Press, 1996), p. 140.

[44] Butterworth, p. 33.

[45] 'la problématique de la paradiastole en vient à conditionner la manière de pensée de toute une époque'. Cave, *Pré-histoires,* p. 102. Cave relates *paradiastole* to the problem of *mediocritas* and the Aristotelian mean, so important to the ethical status of *politique* as a middle term referring to the middle ground, and to a person in the middle. See Chapter 1. See also Moss, *Printed Commonplace Books.*

Redescription and Resistance

The *Dialogue d'entre le Maheustre et le Manant* attempts to resist this kind of thought-conditioning. The Maheustre's redescriptions of *politique* give cause for suspicion rather than offering resolution. In his speeches, *politique* 'fauteurs' are consistently redescribed as 'amis' ('noz amis, que vous appelez politiques'), wherein the vice of collaboration becomes the virtue of friendship. In this case, however, the redescription is laced with irony: the author recasts this 'friendship' as a move of expediency. In the Manant's introductory passage to his history of the downfall of the *Seize*, he refers to 'their enemies the Politiques, who did so much and such careful work, with such authority and diligence, so as to leave left neither friend nor foe unquestioned in their search for the wrongdoings of the Seize' (p. 130).[46] This provides an ironic gloss on the Maheustre's refrain about 'noz amis, que vous appellez Politiques', if they were prepared to seek out 'amy ou ennemy' in order to establish their false 'intelligence'. The suggestion seems to be that *politique amitié*, and *intelligence*, are manipulated for reasons of expediency, or – as the Manant has it – hypocrisy. In this respect, *politique* emerges not only as a contested, mobile term, but the concept of mobility itself seems once again to be written into the term with negative ethical implications.[47]

The Manant's role, by contrast, is to overtly resist the redescriptive moves attempted by his opponent. His speeches are full of binary oppositions and he opposes all reconciliation between them. The Maheustre remonstrates: 'you argue as a theologian, and with rigour: let us speak as statespeople' ('vous argumentez en theologien, et à la rigueur; parlons en gens d'estat') – the implication being that discussing matters as men of state involves greater moral flexibility (p. 57). The Manant responds with a misogynistic rant about how the Maheustre's suggestions involve fundamentally sullying virtue by bringing it into contact with vice; the chaste girl ('fille pudique') in the analogy is Catholic France, incarnation of virtue, and the 'debauched man' is Henri de Navarre, incarnation of vice:

---

[46] 'les Politiques leurs ennemis, qui ont fait tant et si exactes recherches, et avec tant d'authorité et de diligence, qu'il n'y a eu amy ou ennemy qu'ils n'ay recherché pour sçavoir si les Seize leur avoient fait tort'.

[47] This reprises the theme of monstrous, destructive ambivalence central to the portrayal of *politiques* in the pamphlets of Chapter 5.

MANANT: I ask you, would you hand over a chaste girl who is honest, beautiful,
           virtuous, and modest, to a debauched man full of pox and given over
           to all vices, if he said he would amend his ways and no longer be so?
           If he came back to you as a married man, would you hand over your
           daughter? (p. 58)[48]

Once again weaponising female sexuality, and vulnerability, to serve a
political argument, like many other of the authors cited in this book, here
the author of the *Dialogue* stages what amounts to a diatribe against
paradiastole, itself redescribed as prostitution. The Manant utterly denies
the possibility that vice can be amended, repackaged, or *redescribed* as
virtue. His resistance to the Maheustre's attempts to persuade him to
change his perspective on events, actions, or ideas is what makes the
Dialogue so fundamentally a *dialogue de sourds*, with each character referring at various moments to the fact that each is essentially, if not speaking a
different language, then using language differently, with a very different
sense of the limitations and flexibility of the meaning of words. This is
clear in the opening with the Manant's deliberate incomprehension of the
watchword 'qui vive', and is still taking place over a hundred pages later.
Towards the end of the *Dialogue*, the Maheustre makes one last attempt to
get the Manant to shift, to be more flexible with language: 'you speak as if
you are resolved', he says, 'but you could well change your language' ('vous
parlez en resolu, mais vous pourra bien changer de langage', p. 178). The
Manant's refusal, once more, at this late juncture, triggers the final
aggressive spiral of the *Dialogue* in which both characters agree that their
disagreements can only be resolved on the battlefield.

It is the Maheustre who reopens hostilities, provoked by the Manant's
passive resistance:

MAHEUSTRE: Let us end our disputes! I hope to gain by the sword what cannot
            be gained by sweetness and reason.
MANANT: As long as you are all Politiques and accomplices of heretics,
            reason and sweetness will always elude you.[49]

From this, it is clear that the term *politique* is at the heart of the Manant's
refusal to engage in, or be persuaded by, redescriptive arguments. The

---

[48] 'Je vous demande, voudriez-vous bailler une fille pudique, honneste, belle, vertueuse, et modeste, à
   un homme desbauché, verollé et abandonné à tous vices, soubs umbre qu'il vous diroit qu'il
   s'amenderoit, et qu'il n'y retourneroit plus, et que s'il y retourneroit estant marié, que vous luy
   osteriez vostre fille?'
[49] 'MAHEUSTRE: Cessons nos disputes! J'espere de gaigner par l'espee ce qui ne se peut avoir par
   douceur et raison. MANANT: Tant que vous serez Politiques et fauteurs d'heretiques, vous n'aurez
   raison ny douceur.'

entire *Dialogue* can be seen as an unresolved meeting between opposites, which amount to flexibility (the Maheustre) and resolution (the Manant), in which the dangerous ethical flexibility of the term *politique* is critiqued as a means of resisting ambiguity, and the middle ground. By the end, the Manant simply repeats the same word, 'Dieu' ('God'), in response to the Maheustre's interrogations: a final explicit refusal to invest in the power play of *paradiastole*.

The authors of the *Satyre ménippée* both satirise and contest negative uses of the term *politique*, using redescription to settle the arguments staged between Leaguers and d'Aubray and, implicitly, the disputes of the wider reading public. The key moment at which *politique* is subject to redescription in the *Satyre ménippée* occurs in d'Aubray's *harangue* when he recites a poem that begins 'To know ['cognoistre'] the politiques' ('Pour cognoistre les politiques', pp. 154–57); the use of the verb 'cognoistre' here evokes earlier attempts to know, recognise, and re-cognise the *politique*. This poem parodies these earlier attempts and in doing so aims to defuse them.

The interruption of prose with verse marks the poem out within the text; although one definition of 'menippean' is that it is a mix of prose and poetry, this is only one of two such moments in d'Aubray's speech.[50] He introduces the verse at the end of a lengthy complaint about the way that Paris has been governed since the departure of Henri III and the deleterious impact on the 'good people' ('gens de bien') who have suffered 'a thousand concussions, extortions, and villainies' ('mille concussions, exactions, et vilenies', p. 154). Almost as a postscript, d'Aubray then employs *praeteritio* to suggest that he *will not* talk about the material devastation wrought on people named as *politiques*; in fact, he has a whole poem to recite on the subject:

> I leave aside the matter of the pillaging of the richest houses, the sale of precious furnishings, the imprisonment and ransoming of inhabitants and gentlemen who were known to be well off and to have money; such people were baptised with the name of politiques or factionalists, and accomplices of heretics. An amusing rhyme was composed about this at that time, which I consider worthy of being included in the register and record of our Estates. (p. 154)[51]

---

[50] De Smet, *Menippean Satire*, p. 23.

[51] 'Je laisse les pillages de plusieurs riches maisons, la vente des precieux meubles, les emprisonnemens, et ransonnemens des habitans et gentilshommes qu'on sçavoit estre pecunieux, et garnis d'argent lesquels on baptizoit du nom de politiques ou d'adherants, et fauteurs d'heretiques: et sur ce propos fut faicte de ce temps là, une plaisante rime, que j'estime digne d'estre inserée aux registres, et cayers de nos estats.'

The emphasis on people named as *politiques* simply being decent citizens with considerable personal wealth is a consistent theme. The negative associations with the term *politique*, characterised as an unjust baptism, are repeated in the opening lines:

> To really know the politiques,
> Factionalists, accomplices of heretics,
> Though they be hidden and covert
> You only have to read this verse.
>   (p. 154)[52]

These lines parody the language and approach of anti-*politique* pamphlets, not only in the repetition of terms like 'accomplice' ('fauteur'), but also in the indication that the poem will provide a way to really know a *politique*, and in the suggestion that they are hidden and covert, 'cachez et couverts' (recalling the lines of the pamphlet *La vie et condition des Politiques*, which lambasts 'politiques gens cachés couverts').[53] The whole poem is full of echoes of the pamphlets, announcing in line 36 (almost exactly halfway through) that somebody is an 'adhérant' (a factionalist) if they express a wish for peace. This is followed by a warning that satirises those pamphlets that told readers to be on guard against *politique* argumentative strategies: 'He will put such a good face on things / Be careful that he doesn't draw you in' ('Combien qu'il face bonne mine / Gardez qu'il ne vous enfarine' (p. 155). In line 4 ('you only have to read this verse'), the suggestion is that the poem will reverse all of this by revealing exactly what is hiding at the heart of all the name-calling and the insults. Suddenly, identifying a *Politique* will be easy.

    The primary purpose of the poem is to assert that *Politiques* are no more than decent citizens whose core characteristic, rather than *opposing* the League, is simply *not being part of it* (they are not a party themselves; they are just not part of another party). The poem describes the *Politiques* by means of their refusals: they refuse to donate all personal belongings for the use of the League; to take up arms; to participate in religious rituals associated with the League and the *Seize* ('devotions', 'processions', p. 155); to listen to radical preachers; to accept the authority of leaders of the *Seize*; to celebrate the assassination of Henri III; and to believe printed propaganda ('They are those who, when Bichon, or Nivelle / Have printed some *nouvelle* / Doubt its content, and enquire about the author'

---

[52] 'Pour cognoistre les politiques, / Adherants, fauteurs d'heretiques, / Tant soyent-ils cachez et couverts, / Il ne faut que lire ces vers.'
[53] *La vie et condition des politiques*, p. 9.

('Qui lorsque Bichon, ou Nivelle / Ont imprimé quelque nouvelle / En doute, et s'enquiert de l'auteur', pp. 156–57).[54] Here, a *Politique* instead recognises and praises Henri de Navarre and talks of peace (p. 155). The conclusion of the whole poem denies that this is in any way a result either of political allegiance or religious persuasion: They are that [*politique*], and why so? Because / They have some money in their purse' (Ils en sont, et pourquoy? Et pour ce / Qu'ils ont de l'argent dans leur bourse', p. 157). By the poem's conclusion, the *Politiques* are disassociated from vices both civil and theological, and the word emptied of its ideological charge and replaced with a purse. In this case, redescription is employed to eliminate associated vices and normalise the *politique* stance.

The *politiques* are presented as materially wealthy in d'Aubray's introduction, and both the beginning and end of the poem: 'they are those who don't wish to donate all their goods / to this cause which is no good' ('Qui ne veut donner tout son bien / A ceste cause ne vaut rien', p. 154).[55] The connection between 'goods' and the status of 'good people' reflects the porous boundary between material wealth and moral reputation. Emily Butterworth has shown that there was a strong equivalent between theft and slander in the early modern period, with good reputation often figured as a kind of 'bien', and defamation figured as theft.[56] In Chapter 3 we saw that Bodin gave *proprium* as a Latin translation of *politique*, thus linking the vernacular term to a set of associations with property and propriety. In the pamphlet literature analysed in Chapter 5, the *Politiques* were ferociously criticised for their prioritisation of the temporal over the spiritual, and of physical comfort over the privations endured by truly committed Catholics, putting a negative ethical charge on the connection between *politique*, property, and propriety. Throughout the wars, material desecration and the tearing down of physical symbols of opposition were hallmarks of the conflict; houses that had been abandoned by people fleeing Paris were often ransacked, and goods belonging to enemies of the League were systematically seized. Such devastation can also be understood metaphorically; the 'pillaging' of *Politique* houses lamented by d'Aubray in his introduction to the poem might also then be understood as an expression of the impact of the slanderous words of preachers who falsely baptised certain citizens as *politiques* from their pulpits. The end of the poem,

---

[54] Bichon and Nivelle produced several of the pamphlets discussed in Chapter 5; see Figure 1.
[55] On the material wealth of the *noblesse de robe* or 'fourth estate', see Patterson, *Representing Avarice*, pp. 160–200.
[56] Butterworth, *Poisoned Words*, pp. 38–39.

effectively replacing *politique* with *bourse*, enacts a kind of restitution of 'good' moral status as well as of literal 'goods', with the insult written out by means of redescription.

That the material wealth of so-called *politiques* was an important part of anti-*politique* propaganda and sermonising is supported by an anecdote from 1592 recounted by L'Estoile, in which he describes a sermon by Maistre Cœilli, *Curé* of Saint-Germain de l'Auxerrois (on the Place du Louvre), calling on the 'crocheteux de Paris' to ransack the houses of *politiques*: 'crocheteux' generally referred to occasional porters, with a secondary meaning of 'petty thief'.[57] According to L'Estoile, the *crocheteux* took offence at being singled out as best suited to thievery, and expressed this in letter pinned to the church doors and around the area. L'Estoile appears to quote the letter in full, but in fact says he is reporting the 'tenor' of the letter, so is actually composing it himself as a reporting of the apparently real version, in which the *crocheteux* assert that they will not attack honourable people, and that though they may be poor and simple folk, they know that the preacher's instructions go against God's commandments.[58] Perhaps this incident was the more-or-less straightforward reporting of a sermon and its response in the materially deprived context of Paris in 1592, but *crocheteur* was also used in sixteenth-century linguistic theory describing a kind of writing and translation that was more flexible and workaday than stiffly erudite texts (material described as *docte*, or learned). Norton describes the *crocheteurs* of Abel Mathieu's 1559 treatise on translation as nimble 'linguistic journeymen', with the activity of translation characterised as akin to lock-picking.[59] The *crocheteux* of L'Estoile's *Journal* might have been the upstanding poor refusing to take their rich neighbours' possessions; equally, the anecdote might recount a linguistic joke played on the preacher Cœilli by ideological opponents who sought to redirect, or to 'pick the locks' of his vituperative language. Material goods, moral goods, and linguistic change were inextricably linked in late sixteenth-century France.

Redescription/Conversion

The *Satyre ménippée*'s editorial collective was instrumental – or, at least, wanted to appear instrumental – in the wresting of power away from hard-

---

[57] L'Estoile, v, p. 177; 'Crocheteur' in Cotgrave, *Dictionarie* www.pbm.com/~lindahl/cotgrave/search/261l.html [accessed 3 August 2020].

[58] L'Estoile, v, p. 177.

[59] Glyn P. Norton, *The Ideology and Language of Translation in Renaissance France and Their Humanist Antecedents* (Geneva: Droz, 1984), pp. 303–07.

line Catholics in order to hand power to a monarch whose religious affiliation was as mobile, if not more so, than the meaning of *politique*. Redescription of *politique* by supporters of Henri de Navarre was part of a wider reorganisation of ethical and ideological categories as a response to the prospect, and then the fact, of Henri de Navarre's conversion to Catholicism, which enabled him to be renamed as 'roy', and as 'Henri IV'. D'Aubray's oratorical triumph in the *Satyre*, and by extension the success of Henri IV, depended greatly on acceptance of the king's conversion. In both the *Dialogue* and the *Satyre*, the term *politique* and the person or people to whom it referred are argumentative pivots in evaluations of the ethics of conversion. The conversion of Henri IV is the principal topic of roughly the first third of the *Dialogue*.[60] The conversion was widely discussed and criticised in Paris: in a contemporary Leaguer dialogue, the host informs his guests at the opening that the purpose is to 'make the King of Navarre's thoughts known, and the effects of this unhoped for and so sudden a conversion' ('faire recognoistre les pensées du Roy de Navarre, & les effets de ceste inesperee & si soudaine conversion').[61]

The author of the *Dialogue*, writing over the course of 1593, responded to new events as they occurred. At the moment at which he presumably heard the news of Navarre's delicately negotiated (re)conversion, the Manant launches into a lengthy analysis of why exactly this conversion is not persuasive. He starts with an account of Henri's conversion and subsequent relapse in the 1570s (pp. 62–63), refers to the discussion as a de facto 'trial' and calls the new conversion 'false and the nullest of nullities' ('feinte et nulle de toute nullité', p. 69). His view is that Henri's words alone are not enough: as a proof of the nullity of the conversion, the Manant points out that 'no tears have been shed by this new convert' ('on n'a veu aucunes larmes de ce nouveau converty', p. 64). He also criticises Henri for converting in Suresnes, where it is convenient, rather than making the trip to Rome: again, the lack of observed physical exertion (as well as the lack of commitment to the supranational Catholic community) operates as a proof of the nullity of words as confirmation of true faith.

More broadly, the text offers a lengthy critique of the flexibility of mind required to convert, or simply to change one's mind, of which the diatribe

---

[60] Ménager, 'Le *Dialogue entre le Maheustre et le Manant*', p. 99. On Henri IV's conversion, see Michael Wolfe, *The Conversion of Henri IV: Politics, Power and Religious Belief in Early Modern France* (Cambridge, MA: Harvard University Press, 1993).
[61] [Louis d'Orléans], *Le banquet et apres-dinee* (n.p.).

against redescription (discussed above) is part: the analogy between Paris as a pure young woman given over to a debauched man simply because he has got married is explicitly about the potential surrender of the city in the wake of the conversion. What constitutes a justified and believable conversion, and what motivates conversion, is a key point of discussion throughout. From the beginning, the Maheustre exhorts the Manant to accept the necessity of conversion in a general sense: 'Christian charity obliges you to use gentleness and remonstration rather than remaining obstinate, especially with the Kings and Princes of the world, in order to convert them' (p. 45).[62] The opposition between 'convert' ('convertir') and 'remain obstinate' ('opinionastrer') indeed, runs parallel to the Maheustre's insistence on the flexibility of words and their meanings, and the Manant's refusal to accept this. By the end of the *Dialogue*, the Maheustre announces with frustration that he has finally understood that 'only the sword can convert you' ('il n'y a que l'espee qui vous puisse convertir', p. 194).

In the *Satyre ménippée*, the legitimacy of Henri de Navarre is also at the heart of the argument. In the poem 'Pour cognoistre les politiques ...', *politiques* are identifiable because they call Henri de Navarre (soon to be officially renamed Henri IV) 'king' instead of 'the biarnois' (p. 155; this was a common epithet, and refers to Henri's home region, the Béarn). His conversion to Catholicism is not a major focus of the text, but when it is raised in d'Aubray's *harangue* it is presented as inviolate: conversion in order to be king is the fulfilment of moral duty rather than expediency (pp. 188–89). In this sense, d'Aubray's speech places royal duty above confessional conscience, but these different kinds of ethical obligation are not in conflict: they are shown to be interdependent.

Where the *Satyre* does discuss conversion at some length, it is to satirise Catholic zeal. The *Catholicon* drug that the speakers take at the beginning in order to force them to speak the truth leads to the exposure of the so-called *Saincte Ligue* as a dishonest conversion of troublemakers into supposedly pious zealots; this is explicitly stated in Monsieur de Lion's *harangue*, in his apostrophe to the *Catholicon* which echoes (and satirises) the opening of the paternoster:

> O holy Catholicon of Spain, who art the cause of the doubling of the cost of the mass, the overpriced sacred candles, the increase on offerings and multiplication of blessings, which in turn mean that there are no more

---

[62] 'La charité chrestienne vous oblige d'user de douceur et remonstrance, et specialement aux Roys et princes de la terre, afin de les convertir, et non pas opinionastrer.'

baddies, thieves, incendiary troublemakers, liars, cutthroats and brigands: for, by this holy conversion, they have all changed name, and taken the honorable title of zealous catholeaguers. (p. 91)[63]

There is an echo of contemporary economic concerns with all these references to overpriced religious services. Overall the Leaguers are reframed as the converts to a false Catholicism corrupted by ideology (hence the wordplay of 'catholeaguers' ['catholigues']). The crucial work done here is to introduce conversion as a constant, linguistic process, more about redescribing than about fundamentally altering one's religious stance. The writers of the *Satyre* are demonstrating that conversion in a broader sense is a process inherent to all political stances, and thus normalising the idea of conversion, which becomes one more move in an inherently mobile ideological terrain.

'The *Politiques* Who Distort Meaning'

So far, we have seen the authors of the *Dialogue* and the *Satyre* using rhetoric, or resisting it, to gain political ground. But there is more: in the *Satyre ménippée*, the *politiques* are found engaging in rhetorical strategies of their own. In d'Aubray's poem, key *politique* attributes ('they don't *say* Biarnois', ['qui ne *dict* point le Biarnois']; 'qui n'ayme point *ouyr* prescher'; 'they don't *speak* reverently' ['Qui ne *parle* reveremment'] pp. 154–55 [my italics]) are expressed by discourse verbs. In the opening descriptive passage of 'La vertu du Catholicon' where the attendees of the *États* are described, the *politiques* appear as 'les Politiques qui detorquoyent' ('the *Politiques* who distort', p. 27). For 'detorquoyer', Martin gives 'distort from the true meaning' ('détourner du sens véritable').[64] However, another potential translation would be 'redescribe'; here, the 'Politiques' are mocking cardinals' hats and redescribing their scalps as scabrous, rather than sacred, implying a lack of spiritual authority. Elsewhere, Mayenne refers to his campaign in Guyenne 'that the politiques call mere sabre-rattling' ('que les politiques appelent incagade'): here, the 'Politiques' appear redescribing Mayenne's military valour as aggressive posturing. The verb 'appeler' ('to name') appears once again, only this time, the *politiques* are the subjects of

---

[63] 'Ô saint Catholicon d'Espagne, qui es cause que le prix des messes est redoublé, les chandelles benistes rencheries, les offrandes augmentées, et les saluts multiplies, qui es cause qu'il n'y a plus de perfides, de voleurs, d'incendiaires, de faulsayres, de coupegorges et brigants: puisque par ceste saincte conversion, ils ont changé de nom, et ont pris cest honorable tiltre de catholigues zelez.'

[64] Martin, 'Glossaire', in *Satyre ménippée* (2010), pp. 220–34 (p. 224).

the verb: 'les politiques appelent'. Meanwhile, the chaotic Leaguer speeches are examples of poor rhetoric – exemplified by the fact that Roze's audience start talking amongst themselves before he has finished, so that he is unable to conclude (p. 115). He is thus staged as the epitome of an unsuccessful orator, having started with such enthusiasm, literally frothing with the *Catholicon* soap: 'I have been seized by an unspeakable ardour, such is my desire to set forth my rhetoric' ('je suis meu d'une indicible ardeur de mettre avant ma rhetorique', p. 101). The joke, as ever, is on him, since his words are unspeakable in quite another sense. The authors of the *Satyre* engage in a cruel ventriloquism, staging anti-eloquence in the Leaguer speeches through which references to the power of *politique* eloquence are scattered.

Critics have, indeed, read the *Satyre* as staging a 'crisis in eloquence'.[65] The broader sixteenth-century crisis of eloquence was also a question of the management of Classical inheritance, in which writers in the later sixteenth century moved towards a greater appreciation of Tacitus and a denigration of Cicero.[66] In the *Satyre*, not only does d'Aubray refer to Tacitus, but the failed rhetorician, Roze, refers to Cicero as a model. He opens his absurd speech by praising contemporary eloquence. He says that, formerly one had to study at length to be considered a man of letters (to be, as it were, an expert); but no more, with happy results: 'better than Cicero do they now dispute *inventione*' ('mieux que Ciceron maintenant ils disputent de *inventione*', p. 104). The editors of the *Satyre* use their knowledge of different rhetorical modes to mock their ideological opponents and put forward alternative models.

An investment in the power of rhetorical devices – not just redescription – to unseat powerful enemies is present throughout d'Aubray's speech, performing the *politique* work described by Mayenne and others in the preceding *harangues*. For example, in the part that argues in favour of the legitimacy of Henri de Navarre, the author introduces a critique of the way that the Duc de Mayenne exploited the power vacuum that developed after Henri III's death. D'Aubray argues that Mayenne's power is legally invalid, and that 'whoever invented this expediency failed both in terms of grammar and of state' ('quiconques inventa cet expedient, faillit aux termes de grammaire et d'estat', p. 163). Just as d'Aubray later suggests that royal power and faith are coterminous, here, 'grammar' and 'state' are

---

[65] See Ménager and Lestringant, 'Introduction', and also Ménager, 'La crise de l'éloquence', in *Etudes sur la Satyre ménippée*, pp. 19–38 (p. 16) and 121–47.

[66] Salmon, 'Cicero and Tacitus', p. 329.

interwoven. The rules of statecraft and of language combine here to imply that the state is a linguistic construct whose very stability lies in effective definition (and understanding) of its terms.

This critique is then followed by an example of one of these rhetorical strategies shown to be so crucial in establishing what the state actually is, and to whom power ought to belong – a striking repetition of the word 'Lieutenant' that constructs a kind of *reductio ad absurdum* in relation to Mayenne's lieutenancy, as well as developing 'lieutenant' as an extended metonym for the process of naming itself:

> Whoever is Lieutenant, is Lieutenant of another, for whom he holds [il tient] the place [lieu] … and a Lieutenant is Lieutenant of another man, but to say that a man is Lieutenant of an inanimate object, like the state, or a King's crown, is an absurd thing and cannot be upheld. (p. 163)[67]

Echoing, and partially inverting, Bodin's theory that abstract sovereignty finds its most appropriate embodiment in a relation between the monarch and the republic, d'Aubray argues that a Lieutenant cannot act directly on behalf of the state or the crown. The repetition of 'Lieutenant' creates a sense of the absurd before d'Aubray calls it that, and also emphasises the root – 'lieu' ('place') and 'tenant' ('holder'). It thus drives home d'Aubray's point, namely that Mayenne is a temporary placeholder, in the absence of 'another man' (who must be, d'Aubray hints, a King). It is also made clear from this moment in the speech that what makes a Lieutenant, and gives him power, is the naming itself; we shall see shortly how this argument is applied to other, more powerful categories, such as King.

The *politiques* of the *Dialogue* are also described as engaging in adversarial linguistic strategies, as the Maheustre reports:

> And you can be assured that the papers scattered in the streets against the *Seize* come either from our friends the Politiques, or at their instruction. They have composed these missives to stoke horror of the *Seize* among the people, and to make them lose their faith. (p. 153)[68]

This evokes Pierre de L'Estoile's circulation of a poem defending *politiques*, and a moment in Roze's speech in the *Satyre*, where he complains about 'these impudent *politiques*, who have caricatured you all on paper' ('ces

---

[67] 'Quiconques est Lieutenant, est Lieutenant, d'ung autre, duquel il tient le lieu … et Lieutenant est Lieutenant d'ung autre homme, mais de dire qu'ung homme soit Lieutenant d'une chose inanimée, comme l'estat, ou la couronne d'ung Roy, c'est chose absurde, et qui ne peut soustenir.'

[68] 'Et vous puis asseurer que les billets jettez parmy les rues contre les Seize procedent de ceste part et de l'instruction de noz amis, que vous appellez Politiques, qui ont composé lesdits billets pour mettre en horreur les Seize au peuple et leur faire perdre leur creance.'

impudents politiques, qui vous ont mis en figure en une belle feuille de papier': surely this is a self-referential wink from the creators of the *Satyre*); Roze advocates seeking out, and punishing 'their terrible politique printers' ('ses meschants imprimeurs politiques', p. 109). In the *Dialogue* the 'Politiques' are also portrayed as writers, but they are rarely quoted directly. Instead, *politique* wordplay is reduced to 'bruit' ('noise', or 'rumour') and 'brouillure' ('fog': also a term for rumour) and thus its efficacy at intervening in the 'real' is blocked, or called into question. In the rare instances where particular arguments are reported, the implication is that 'Politique' manipulation of language involves a dangerous manipulation of the truth. A quarter of all the uses of *politique* in the *Dialogue* occur within two pages (pp. 130–31) in which the Manant describes the downfall of the *Seize* and lays the blame squarely with 'their enemies the Politiques'. The history offered in this speech is that the *politiques* took advantage of their connections in the *Parlement* and the *Chambre des Comptes* in order to redescribe supporters of the *Seize* as petty criminals, and thus to persuade various magistrates to sign search and arrest warrants against members of the *Seize* and their supporters, despite all allegations being unsubstantiated and then proven false: 'And nonetheless the Politiques found no proof either' ('Et neantmoins les Politiques ne tireront non plus de preuve', p. 130).

The manipulation of language presented positively in the *Satyre* is thus written into the *Dialogue* as a more suspect flexibility in which little importance is afforded to what is actually true. Thus, *politique* is consistently emphasised as being subject to, and participating in, rhetorical manipulation. Moreover, the inherent mobility of the term works as a representation of these processes. The term *politique* is thus both subject to redescription, and figures as a subject who redescribes.

Redescribing Borders

The mobility of terms in these texts, and of *politique* in particular, is also connected to material contexts of deprivation and violence, as well as to shifting balances of power and belonging within individual parishes and in the wider Parisian community. The mobility of *politique* is also a means of negotiating boundaries of actual physical space, and of the communities who exist within and beyond those boundaries.[69] In this respect these

---

[69] On the connection between national identity and literary representations of communities and their borders, see Hampton, *Literature and Nation in the Sixteenth Century*; on sixteenth-century formulations of selfhood and identity through topographical writing, see Tom Conley, *The Self-*

works make similar moves to the Huguenot pamphlets of the 1570s, which attempt to negotiate new kinds of belonging across European space; these texts, by contrast, focus on France, and particularly on Paris, the contested city. Paris had always had a special role in the Wars of Religion, as Barbara Diefendorf explains:

> Most cities were too small to influence the larger course of the wars; they played out before a local audience their bloody dramas of persecution and revenge. Paris, by its size and political importance, was an exception to this rule. Had it not been for the fierce Catholicism of the people of Paris, the wars of religion would have taken a very different course. Perhaps they would not have taken place at all.[70]

The integrity of Paris's status as an exceptional and inviolable Catholic stronghold had been tested to the limit by the siege of 1590, but still in 1593 the people held out against the prospect of a Protestant king. At the moment of the composition of the *Dialogue* and the *Satyre*, Henri was encamped beyond the city perimeter, negotiating terms of entry. The flow of the wider population in and out of the city during the religious wars depending on who was in control was also a major feature of Parisian experience during the war years; Pierre de L'Estoile was one of the only people named by others as *politique* who remained in Paris in 1589–92.

In the *Dialogue*, the Manant claims to represent – and praises at length – the people of Paris. The term *politique* first appears in a long speech by the Manant bemoaning the present state of the city (pp. 84–85), in which – he claims – the people have been cruelly let down and abandoned by members of higher social classes: princes, the nobility, the clergy, the magistrature. It is one of the most striking political gestures of the *Dialogue*, arguing – albeit possibly disingenuously – for a degree of popular self-determination rarely given consideration in sixteenth-century France. This lament, along with the inclusion of magistrates as a class, could be read as an account of the sociological changes that occurred in French cities, and Paris in particular, across the sixteenth century: changes made at dramatic speed in the context of the upheaval of the wars. Robert Descimon in fact uses a spatial metaphor to describe the change in class structures and the rise of the magistrates and the associated *noblesse de robe*

Made Map: Cartographic Writing in Early Modern France (Minneapolis, MN: University of Minnesota Press, 1996).

[70] Barbara Diefendorf, *Beneath the Cross*, p. 180. On the importance of Paris, see also Robert Descimon, 'L'échevinage parisien sous Henri IV (1594–1609): Autonomie urbaine, conflits politiques et exclusives sociales', in *La ville, la bourgeoisie et la genèse de l'Etat moderne (XIIe–XVIIIe siècles)*, ed. by Neithard Bulst and Jean-Phillipe Genet (Paris: CNRS, 1988) pp. 113–50.

under Henri IV and into the seventeenth century: 'It therefore seems necessary, in considerations of politics between 1594 and 1661, to accept the principle that a complete reorientation ('dépaysement') occurred.'[71] The *Dialogue* recognises this reorientation in its early stages ('dépaysement' is a stronger word, suggesting disorientation and displacement as well as reorientation: it literally means loss of one's country). The people displacing the established population are none other than *politiques*. In the speeches of the Manant, 'the people' and 'the city' have a metonymic relation that is being undermined by an influx of *politiques*. He claims that the *Seize* is the only group that represents the interests of the people and the city:

> I have recognised as truth that our cause, the city, received great care thanks to their vigilance, and I'm not surprised that they are attacked, because they opposed all of the other party: [who are] heretics, atheists, Politiques, covetous, and ambitious. (p. 85)[72]

In the *Dialogue*, 'la ville' and the *Seize* are in one 'party' and the *politiques* are in the opposing 'party'; the author enacts the exclusion of *politiques* and their associates from the city on a lexical level, an exclusion that he could not achieve in real life (in fact, in real life, it was the reverse: Cromé supposedly wrote the *Dialogue* while holed up for his own safety in the house of a Spanish ambassador; Mayenne was furious with him for the *Dialogue*, and subsequently he was exiled and probably assassinated on Henri IV's orders after his accession).[73] The integrity of the city is constantly threatened in the *Dialogue*; the Manant concludes the section that I have just been quoting with a lamentation: 'Such great tragedies of plotting and treason have been staged in this city' ('Il s'est joué dans ceste ville des tragedies d'intelligence et trahison si grandes', p. 85).[74] Later on, the Maheustre raises the point that the houses of *politiques*, heretics, and absentees have been looted (pp. 184–85) – a critique of the Leaguer leadership is inserted into one of the Maheustre's speeches at this point,

---

[71] 'Il nous paraît ainsi nécessaire, pour évoquer la politique de 1594 à 1661, d'accepter le principe d'un vrai dépaysement', Robert Descimon and Christian Jouhaud, *La France du premier XVIIe siècle 1594–1661* (Paris: Belin, 1996), p. 7. The *Dialogue* laments what appears as a kind of pre-modern version of gentrification.

[72] 'J'ay recogneu par la verité que la cause, la ville, ont receu un grand secours de leur vigilance, et ne m'estonne s'ils sont enviez, parce qu'ils se sont opposez à tous ceux du party contraire, tant heretiques, athees, Politiques, envieux qu'ambitieux.'

[73] Ménager, 'Mystique ou politique', p. 97; Ascoli, p. 26.

[74] Cromé had attempted to counteract such conspiracies (as he perceived them to be) in his handling of the Brigard case and the murders of Brisson, Larcher, and Tardif. He defends these murders in the *Dialogue*, pp. 183–84. See Greengrass with Hamilton, and Hamilton, 'Political Crimes'.

when he accuses the high-born ringleaders of keeping all the seized goods for themselves and leaving the people deprived. The Manant's response (evoking the Pellevé character in the *Satyre*) is to accuse the *politiques* of spreading rumours ('bruit') and of colluding with magistrates to allow enemies to enter Paris under the cover of the truce (p. 185).

The Mayenne character in the *Satyre* also bemoans the presence of so many *politiques* in the city. The connection between the increased physical presence of *politiques* and enemies, a threatened *politique* takeover of Paris, and the rumours that they bring with them, underlines the link between language use and the occupation of physical space. Considering such representations of an influx of *politiques*, strangers, and enemies more laterally, we might see in them a perhaps unconscious illustration of what Annabel Brett has described as a crucial tension in early modern political thought, between *civitas* as city, and *civitas* as commonwealth: tellingly, Brett illustrates this point with reference to Paris, versus France.[75] Bodin attempted to resolve this tension, to an extent, through his practice of analogy: a marriage is to a city is to a republic. In the *Dialogue*, the Parisian populace and the very integrity of their city are threatened by a different vision of politics, embodied by actual people called *politiques*, who swarm into the space and attempt to absorb 'Paris' into a larger system. Like the Huguenot authors of the *Reveille-matin des françois*, the *Dialogue*'s author sought to balance a version of Frenchness with a vision of a state in which towns and cities might retain considerable autonomy. Without the symbiosis the author imagines between the city and its loyal Catholic populace, Paris, for him, is no longer Paris.

From the opening 'strange meeting' onwards, uncertainty about time and place pervades the *Dialogue*. We can infer only that the conversation takes place in or around Paris due to references to 'this city'; the conversation seems to take place in a kind of no man's land, and the actual city is not what it was, or has been betrayed, or is overrun by enemies to the extent that it is no longer recognisable. Illustrated copies of a shortened royalist version of the *Dialogue*, in verse, circulated under Henri IV, and show the meeting taking place outside the city walls (see Figure 5).[76] In this image, the personified League is attempting to win back a Manant who is now 'unleagued' '(de-ligué': marking another intervention in the history of the words *ligue* and *ligueur*) and is instead doffing his cap to the heroic-looking Maheustre, whose elevated position on horseback and correspondingly higher social status indicates the way in which the royalist version made the Maheustre the master of the rewritten *Dialogue*. Behind the

---

[75] Brett, *Changes of State*, p. 7.   [76] See Hamilton, p. 160.

Figure 5. Anon., 'Les entre-paroles du Manant de-ligué, & du Maheustre', woodcut on paper (Paris, Le Clerc), in Pierre de L'Estoile, *Les belles figures et drolleries de la League* (*c.* 1589–98.)
Bibliothèque nationale de France

Maheustre, corn is falling from the sky, as if from heaven, suggesting the material abundance that will bring succour to the starving and impoverished population behind the city walls. Behind the Manant, there is the League, personified as an aristocratic woman, walking with a stick and holding a mask: she might be a representation of Catherine de Montpensier, sister of Mayenne and the Guise brothers, satirised in the *Processions* at the opening of the *Satyre ménippée*. That she is holding a mask shows that negative political connotations of deceit and role-playing transfer easily across ideological categories. The verse accompanying the image is a rewriting of the opening of the original *Dialogue*, in which the Maheustre explains in a slightly more helpful way what he means by 'qui vive?' and what the Manant stands to gain by pledging allegiance to Henri IV in answering 'vive le roy'. The implication is that what is at stake is entry to the city, and thus the community, which has been so troubled and divided.

The *Satyre ménippée* is set more concretely in Paris. In his *harangue*, d'Aubray also laments the present state of the city, both in the opening of the speech (p. 127) and at another later point (p. 168) where he calls Paris a new Jerusalem beset by horrors (drawing on Josephus's history of the siege and subsequent destruction of Jerusalem in AD 70). In the first example, d'Aubray redescribes of Paris as a den of beasts, in the grip of a kind of frenzy, accompanied by the degradation of kingship represented by the attempts made by the Estates General to put forward all sorts of unsuitable candidates as potential kings of France ('roytelets', ['kinglets'], p. 27). As a result, Paris is not what it was, and is full of wild beasts (and foreigners). D'Aubray adds that Paris is in the grip of a new Spanish inquisition, 'harder to bear for people born free and frank, as the French are, than the cruellest deaths' ('plus dure à supporter aux esprits nez libres et francs, comme sont les François, que les plus cruelles morts', p. 127). The opposition between the 'true' dignity of Paris and its present state as 'den of beasts' is mirrored by an opposition between true 'Frenchness' and a France overrun by Spanish influence, with Paris as 'microcosm and summary of the world' ('microcosme, et abregé du monde', p. 167). In the *Dialogue*, the Manant expressly says that he would not care if the King were German, Spanish, or anything else, as long as he was a true Catholic; the Gallican leanings of the authors of the *Satyre ménippée* make the King's Frenchness his most important quality.[77] We also find here almost the

---

[77] On the clash between League and Gallican approaches, see Sophie Nicholls, 'Gallican Liberties and the Catholic League', in *Thinking about Intellectual History* (=*History of European* Ideas, 40.7 [2014]), 940–64.

diametric opposite of the claims made in the *Dialogue* for Parisian excep-
tionality and distinction; here, Paris is a microcosm of the state itself. The
description of Paris as 'summary' or *abregé*, somewhat awkward in English,
casts the city as a synopsis of the text that is the wider world, reinforcing
the close relation between world and text staged in the *Satyre*.

D'Aubray's speech is presented as an exemplar of a particularly French
form of eloquence, in contrast with the un-French babbling of the
Leaguers. In the 1595 *Discours de l'imprimeur*, the 'printer' notes the
following about the supposed authorship of the text:

> I have seen many learned men, and have judged myself from the style and
> language of this book, that an Italian could not have written a work that is
> so French and so polished, which shows such a perfect understand of all the
> affairs and the nature of all the foremost persons of France.[78]

The *Dialogue* and the *Satyre* both fight to claim Paris as an imaginary
centre, as well as an actual place, but on different grounds: these are made
clear in the authors' marshalling, redescribing, and undermining, of different terms. Both texts are thus full of references to, or evocations of,
different kinds of exile, invasion, occupation, and belonging; for instance,
at the end of d'Aubray's *harangue* (which will shortly be met by total
silence from his grotesque listeners) he laments that those calling for peace
will be exiled as heretics or *maheustres*. But the real purpose, and, indeed
(according to Szabarì) the effect of the *Satyre* was to force Navarre's
enemies into exile and to reclaim the contested territory for the new
Henri IV.[79] In making this argument, Szabarì particularly refers to the
journeys made by the printers in the supplementary text, but reclamation
of territory is also happening on a lexical level in d'Aubray's *harangue*. And
ultimately, the author-editors show faith in linguistic means to the end of
redrawing the boundaries of their communities; following his account of
supposed praise of the *Satyre* as 'French' and 'polished', the narrative 'je'
of the 'Discours de l'imprimeur' notes:

> I have also heard complaints about a bookseller who, either through avarice
> or jealousy, had this work printed in tiny lettering, most incorrect and
> unpleasant, and who had the temerity to leave out whatever he wished,

---

[78] 'J'ay veu plusieurs doctes hommes, et moy-mesmes ay bien aysément jugé par le stile et le langage
du livre, qu'un Italien ne peut avoir faict un ovrage si françois et si poly, qui monstre une parfaicte
cognoissance de toutes les affaires, et du naturel de toutes les personnes plus signalees en France.'
Discours de l'imprimeur, p. 157.
[79] Szabarì, p. 159.

which Justice should not endure. Nevertheless, the *argument* is public, and anyone can make additions that serve the subject.[80]

The *Argument* is something like the blurb of an early modern book, and offers a summary of content and often appears at the head of each individual chapter, as in Le Roy's translation of Aristotle, and the opening of the *Reveille-matin*. That the *argument* here is imagined as public suggests that supplements and paratexts are here imagined to be endless, and anyone might add to them. In this vision of a proto-Habermasian public sphere, readers, and writers, will thus negotiate in order to establish what exactly will be considered just – and in order to do so, they will have to agree upon, or redescribe, their terms.

In the *Dialogue d'entre le Maheustre et le Manant*, in one of the Manant's last long speeches, he concludes that one day there will be a good Catholic King who will 're-establish good and chase out evil' ('restablir le bien et chasser le mal') despite the machinations of Henri de Navarre, his heretic allies, *politiques*, schismatics, hypocrites, and all the ambitious tyrants, whoever they are, who threaten good people (p. 208). The expressed wish to 're-establish good and chase out evil' makes explicit the conflation of literal and ideological movement, and the sense that mobility of terms, people, goods, and rulers, occurs in a moral universe that is subject to catastrophic flux. The Manant (and by extension the disappointed author of the *Dialogue*) wishes to end this catastrophe by extinguishing the mobility that, as I have shown in this chapter, is incarnated in the term *politique*. The authors of the *Satyre ménippée* prefer, ultimately, to let their version of a public *argument* dictate the direction of movement, and in doing so engage in a new version of the ideal conversations staged by Pasquier and others in the 1560s which seemed to have been lost in the violent confrontations of the civil wars. One version of the emergence of the so-called public sphere, and of the struggle for membership and autonomy within or without it, in tandem with the establishment of what has come to be known as the modern state, is fought out in these two texts whose publication history was so intertwined and whose authors opposed one another so bitterly. These are not just abstract struggles but involve class conflict in a proto-Marxian sense, as well as a clash between nostalgic longing for united Catholicism against modernising proto-nationalist

---

[80] 'Aussi l'ay-je oüy plaindre d'un Libraire, qui par avarice ou jalousie des autres, a fait imprimer cet œuvre en petits characteres, mal corrects et mal plaisants, et a esté si temeraire, d'y oster ce qu'il a voulu: ce que la Justice, ne devroit pas endurer. Toutefois l'argument est public, où chacun peut faire des additions qui servent à la matière.' *Discours de l'imprimeur*, p. 157.

Gallicanism.[81] Within this, the term *politique*, *c.* 1593, with its unique status as both object of redescription and redescribing subject, can be understood as a kind of border, or marker of belonging, in itself.

The conflicts staged around the term in the *Satyre ménippée* and the *Dialogue* hinge on who has the upper hand in the writing, and which voices will therefore dictate the *Argument* evoked in the *Discours de l'imprimeur*. This is something that the author of the *Dialogue* bemoans, and which the *Satyre ménippée* accepts, and attempts to manipulate. L'Estoile furnishes us with a neat example of the impact of all the writing and rewriting of the term *politique* on a 'real' audience in 1593, describing an encounter with Senault, a leader of the *Seize* who was known for writing poisonous anti-*politique* tracts. On 15 June, Senault is seen writing in a corner of the *Chancellerie*, and L'Estoile records an unidentified person shouting 'We are all Politiques! Go ahead and boldly write against us on your paper!' ('Nous sommes tous Politiques! Ecris-nous hardiment sur ton papier!')[82] This challenge was being undertaken by the authors of the *Dialogue* and the *Satyre* perhaps even at the very moment of the anonymous challenge to Senault. Perhaps the success of the pro-*politique* stance offered by the *Satyre* is evident in the positive, stable definitions offered by Furetière a decade later: 'In the troubles of the League there were the *Politiques*, who were in the party of the King against the Leaguers.'[83] From *c.* 1572, the term *politique* had worked as a vector for ethical controversy. The *Satyre* attempts to influence the direction of popular discourse by undoing the word's power as a trigger for controversy and violence, while the *Dialogue* paradoxically attempts to deny the impact of the use and manipulation of language as represented by the word *politique*. It is the meaning of *politique* in the *Satyre*, however, that later readers seem to have retained, from Furetière to the present day. This remembering of the *politique* underlines the importance of acknowledging the role of rhetoric in the construction of reality. It is crucial to remember that the *politique* operates as a figure for the agents in this process, rather than simply its symptom, or its misleading ghost.

---

[81] On the politics of Gallicanism, see Parsons, pp. 185–226.

[82] L'Estoile, *Mémoires-Journaux*, VI, p. 29.

[83] 'Dans les troubles de la League il y avoit les *Politiques*, qui estoient du party du Roy contre les Ligueurs', 'Politique', in Furetière, *Dictionnaire Universel.*

Conclusion

This book has been an attempt to trace some of what Montaigne described as the 'fine field' of 'vacillation and dispute' characteristic of the language of politics (p. 603).[1] Language itself was a problem for sixteenth-century writers. The possibilities of communication were investigated and often found wanting, and the words, metaphors, and narrative forms that expressed different kinds of thought were used fluidly within a wider crisis in European culture that afforded creative opportunity as well as potential devastation. Within this, *politique* represents a particularly urgent problem of meaning in part because it is a pivot between theory and practice, used to imagine how the world could be, and how to implement those conditional possibilities. Louise Godard de Donville argues that the figure of the *libertin* was a textual creation ('a *literary* fact, the outcome of polemic') distinct from 'events' and 'reality'; my argument about *politique* is that, during the Wars of Religion, it *was* a kind of event, continuous with and influencing lived reality, and offering a means of exploring and negotiating collective and individual identities.[2]

Dialogue, including reported and/or narrated conversation, emerges as a crucial mode and field of enquiry for the crisis of meaning acted out in uses of the term *politique* in this period. Authors invent or borrow a character called *le politique* who participates in these dialogues and conversations: a fictional strategy to strengthen their arguments and to compel their reader to reconstitute their politics; to be loyal to the crown, or to the Huguenot or Catholic cause, or to nascent ideas of 'Frenchness'. These conversations take place within the field of vacillation and dispute: more often than not, the speakers do not resolve their differences. In both theory

---

[1] 'Notamment aux affaires politiques il y a un beau champ ouvert au bransle et à la contestation', p. 694.
[2] 'un fait *littéraire*, un procédé de polémique', Godard de Donville, pp. 116 and 405.

and polemic, the *politique* characters tend to absorb or embody the abstract qualities of dialogic argument, negotiation and flexibility.

Indeed, *politique* is an especially mobile word even within the shifting vocabularies of the period: it is an incarnation of changing ideologies, of pragmatic compromise, of a composite, fragmented body politic, and of negotiation itself. It is both a knowing subject and an object to be known and (re-)cognised. This is most obviously the case in polemical texts that exploit and/or condemn the amorphous flexibility of the political, especially against the rigidity of religious zeal. However, it is true, too, in texts that belong to the canon of political thought, such as Bodin's *République*, in which the author exploits the flexibility of politics as he understood it in order to invest power in an authoritarian *politique* figure who would bring order to civil chaos. Authors manipulate the mobility of *politique* (often with the expressed aim of reducing this mobility) as a means of representing, explaining, theorising and post-rationalising socio-political experience, and as a means of intervening in it. Uses of politics and *politiques* were part of a social world in which political power was shifting away from noble dynasties and towards courts and *Parlements*: towards a rising social class, the *noblesse de robe*. The mobility of *politique* was also social mobility. New ideas about politics and *politiques* emerged out of war; out of religious conflict – and also out of a class conflict that left space for the expansion of the figure of the *politique*, the semi-professional politician, in popular imagination and practical administration.

Politics rose as a discipline in sixteenth-century Europe. The French case shows its increased significance as an object of study and discussion in educational and intellectual contexts. Politics as an abstract notion (*la politique*) and the figure of the political actor or statesman (*le politique*) are intimately connected; at the heart of this connection is the sense that political ideas operate as a pivot between theory and action. Abstract 'politics' is always rooted in ideological motivation and contemporary context. Polemical characterisations of *politiques* are also – but not necessarily reciprocally – inflected by abstract thought. I have illustrated this connection between politics and *politiques* partly by thinking across genres, beyond the canon of political thought: an approach facilitated by a focus on language rather than on ideas in the strictest sense. I have sought the thought in polemical vituperation even if the politics of polemical pamphlets are at times highly unsubtle, not to say banal (although this is not true of, for instance, the *Dialogue d'entre le Maheustre et le Manant* or the *Reveille-matin des françois*). The genres most associated with the political are generally argumentative prose texts: treatises and tracts. But the generic contexts of *politique* are broad, ranging from poetry, to pamphlets, to Menippean satire. The sixteenth-century political conversation is best understood in this broader textual context. I make no claim to have studied all political activity or even all political texts in sixteenth-century France, and certainly not all instances of the word *politique*. I leave it to others to argue whether 'all writing is political' or 'all political writing is literary'; but if there has been a particular polemical thrust to this project, it has been this emphasis on the literary – not only the textual – in considerations of early modern politics.

The problematisation of politics as a category in the sixteenth century has sometimes been seen as a negative turn in the long history of this concept; this, in a broader context of doubt about the potential outcomes of intellectual and poetic endeavour. All sixteenth-century European writing can be categorised as 'late humanist'; late humanism is often qualified by pessimism about what language and literature can do, and so about what *humanism* can do. Sixteenth-century France was in some ways a microcosm of the shift from humanist optimism to doubt and anxiety, since François I's reign is characterised as one of cultural flourishing, and the civil wars a time of devastation, though clearly such broad narratives are destructive to the particular moments of faith, optimism, irony, and despair in each individual time and text: endings and origins necessarily blur. The survival of the dialogue form is one respect in which earlier and later humanisms merge.[3] Moreover, as Desan argues, and as texts as early in the century as Budé's *Institution du Prince* go some way to demonstrating, the worm was always in the apple; the garden always already fallen.[4] Redefinitions of the word *politique*, born of the humanist project, test the boundaries of any associated ideals. Struggles over what politics might mean thus operate as a case study serving a definition of humanist endeavour as an endless attempt to rethink the relation between ideal and real, often playfully, sometimes painfully.[5]

This study ends around the turn of the seventeenth century, but the first half of that century looked a lot like the end of the sixteenth. The king was

---

[3] Frisch, *The Invention of the Eye Witness*, pp. 181–87. Another potential continuity is the ongoing emphasis on the personal qualities of rulers and politicians, albeit a less idealistic emphasis than that described by Hankin in *Virtue Politics*.

[4] Desan, 'The Worm in the Apple', p. 13. Intriguingly, Desan assures his reader that the worm eventually turns into a butterfly, that is, the *Grand siècle*, p. 28.

[5] Here I disagree slightly with Jardine and Grafton, who define humanism as adherence to an ideal, and the humanities as the practical, educational application of such principles as can be drawn from the ideal. Grafton and Jardine, p. xvi.

assassinated by a radical Catholic in 1610, and in the 1640s dissatisfied nobles turned once again against the monarchy in the uprising known as the Fronde (1648–53).[6] Indeed, Mack Holt considers that confessional conflict in the period between 1610 and 1629 amount to a final 'war of religion', culminating in the siege of La Rochelle in 1627–28.[7] The assassination of Henri IV and its aftermath could be considered another ending to the story I tell in this book; an end to the phase in political writing (and censorship) that began with the *Satyre menippée* and was thoroughly concerned with Henri's image and programme. Further work on *politiques* could certainly consider in more detail histories of the civil war written in the late 1590s and early seventeenth century, in both prose and verse – not only by those who framed the end of the wars as a *politique* triumph, but also by more politically marginalised writers such as Agrippa d'Aubigné (whose *Tragiques* were partly composed during the wars but only printed for the first time in 1616) – all these enacted a process of (mis) remembering the conflict of previous decades.[8]

The relationships between religion, government, and citizenship remained fraught, then, after the assassination of Henri IV. Jotham Parsons ends his study of erudite Gallicanism with the failure of the movement *c.* 1615, a failure he considers to have been consolidated by the failure of the Fronde.[9] Confessional tensions could not be extinguished. In 1685 the Edict of Nantes was revoked. Issues that intersected in uses and contestations of *politique* persisted as the Catholic Reformation developed in France, amid continued arguments over true faith, conformity, and the possibility of socio-political unity.[10] Sixteenth-century uses of *politique* certainly did not sketch a smooth path to secularism, or to *laïcité*.[11] Moreover, connections between the literary and the political

---

[6] See Robin Briggs, *Early Modern France 1560–1715* (Oxford: Oxford University Press, 1977), pp. 128–65.

[7] Mack P. Holt, *The French Wars of Religion*, pp. 178–94.

[8] On remembering the wars of religion, see Andrea Frisch, *Forgetting Differences: Tragedy, Historiography and the French Wars of Religion* (Edinburgh: Edinburgh University Press, 2015).

[9] Parsons, p. 274.

[10] Richard Parish describes the long seventeenth century (between the end of the Wars of Religion and the beginning of the period known as the Enlightenment) as a high point of Catholic writing and spirituality. Richard Parish, *Catholic Particularity in Early Modern France: 'Christianity is Strange'* (Oxford: Oxford University Press, 2011), p. 4. On seventeenth-century accounts of religious difference, see Katherine Ibbett, *Compassion's Edge*, pp. 98–133. At the end of her discussion of compassion during the Wars of Religion, Ibbett comments that 'France's political communities continued to look out for pity long after the end of the wars, but more often took their cues from the partisans than the *politiques*', p. 59.

[11] If post-Reformation theology was fundamentally fractured, that did not prevent constant intersection between religion and politics. On political theology, see Kahn, *The Future of Illusion*,

continued, as they do in every era; the relation between politics and literary writing in the seventeenth century, and the continuing culture of political pamphlets, have been the object of much critical attention.[12] There have also been studies of factionalised discourse from the League to the Fronde, drawing out what these movements had in common.[13] By ending my book in the mid-1590s I do not mean to deny connections with the decades that followed. However, the vocabularies of the arguments changed. We have already seen (in Chapters 4 and 5) that *liberté* and *libertin* intersect with *politique* at different moments; Godard de Donville points out that descriptions of *libertinage* developed, in part, from portrayals of 'bad Catholics', who were usually portrayed as 'gallican, or "politique", or partial non-believer' (these associations have seen *libertins*, too, placed in the vanguard of secularism).[14] In this way – and without drawing any singular grand narrative stretching from *politique* and *ligueur* to *libertin* and *dévot*, to *liberté*, *égalité*, and *fraternité* – we see how certain keywords (differently key at different moments in history) bump into each other, and act on each other's meanings.

This study ends with the sixteenth century, then, because contestations of politics and *politiques* in themselves were especially dynamic – indeed, violent – during the civil wars. Although a few polemical pamphlets criticising *politiques* – or ways of doing or thinking about politics – were printed in the first decade or so of the next century, and formed part of the printed discussions that accompanied the Fronde, *politique* was not a keyword in the same way once the Wars of Religion had ended.[15] In political writing from c. 1593 onwards, following the effective victory of Henri IV, the term *politique* was rehabilitated and its opposing terms

esp. pp. 1–22. She writes of political theology as the 'haunting' of liberal modernity by religion (p. 4), and of the shared imaginary of religion and politics (p. 22). She discusses how twentieth-century theorists (Freud; Schmitt; Kantorowicz; Cassirer; Benjamin) turned to the early modern period in the context of crises of liberalism and increasing preoccupation with theological-political conflict.

[12] Three of the most influential studies in French are Hélène Merlin-Kajman, *Public et littérature en France au XVII siècle* (Paris: Belles Lettres, 2004); and Christian Jouhaud, *Mazarinades: La Fronde des mots* (Paris: Aubier, 1985 and *Les pouvoirs de la littérature* (Paris: Gallimard, 2000). See also Katherine Ibbett, *The Style of the State in Neoclassical Theatre, 1630–1660* (Aldershot: Ashgate, 2009), and *Compassion's Edge*.

[13] *Littérature et politique: Factions et dissidences de la Ligue à la Fronde*, ed. by Malina Stefanovska and Adrien Paschoud (Paris: Garnier, 2015).

[14] Godard de Donville, p. 407.

[15] Ibbett, *The Style of the State*, pp. 4–9. For a late example of an explicitly anti-*politique* pamphlet, see Hercule de Cherbeyt, *Apologie contre les Politiques ennemis de la Religion et de l'État* (Paris: Bertault, 1618).

denigrated, particularly *ligueur*; we saw this process occurring in the final chapter of this book.

In a print included towards the end of L'Estoile's *Drolleries* collection, 'The Poverty and Lamentation of the League' (likely printed after Henri IV's coronation), a poem and an accompanying image personify the League as a figure in rags (Figure 6), reinforcing links between material and reputational damage discussed in Chapters 5 and 6.[16] The League defeated is depicted as an elderly female figure, her palace burning behind her, holding a frayed rope labelled 'Ambition' that is gradually losing its hold on the crown. The poem, a first-person lamentation in the voice of the defeated League, suggests that this degradation is the result of public realisation of what the word *ligue* actually means. In keeping with this reversal of fortunes, there are echoes of the poem *Description du Politique* (quoted in the Introduction and Chapter 4) that are so strong as to surely be deliberate. *La description du politique* describes *politique* as 'a name filled with rubbish' ('un nom rempli d'ordures') and 'disdained': in the lamentation it is *Ligueur* which has become a disdained dirty word, so that the League figure is stripped of riches and living in a rubbish heap ('I have only a heap of filth', 'je n'ay qu'un tas d'ordures'). *Ligueur*, then, is effectively redescribed, replacing *politique* as the ultimate insult:

> They have finally recognised that the name 'Saincte ligue'
> Is nothing but a pitfall, a nasty trap.
> Now all persons great and small mock me,
> And chase me away where they once paid me honour.
> They would rather bear all kinds of insults
> Than be called *Ligueurs*, so much am I disdained:
> I have no more palace, I have only a heap of filth
> In which I abide, languishing, in vile rags.[17]

This context had an impact even on writers who had supported, and continued to support, League principles. While the author of the *Dialogue d'entre le Maheustre et le Manant* attempts to resist new connotations of *Ligueur* and *Catholique*, in another text attributed to League political theorist Louis d'Orléans, a speaker redescribes a *Ligueur* as a sensible statesman, a true *politique*:

---

[16] See Hamilton, p. 160.

[17] 'Ils ont enfin cognu qu'un nom de Saincte ligue / N'estoit qu'un tresbuchet & un piege abuseur, / Les grands, & les petits ore me font la figue, / Et ceux me font chassant qui me faisoient honneur. / Ils souffriront plustot toutes sortes d'injures / Qu'estre nommez Ligueurs, tant je suis à mespris: / Je n'ay plus de palais, je n'ay qu'un tas d'ordures / Où je gis languissante avec de vils habits.'

Figure 6.   Anon., 'La pauvreté et lamentation de la Ligue', woodcut on paper (Paris, Le Clerc), in Pierre de L'Estoile, *Les belles figures et drolleries de la Ligue* (c. 1589–98). Bibliothèque nationale de France

> If the *police* is the constitution of a state, according to which every person
> lives, I conclude that a Leaguer who wants to live and die maintaining such
> a *police* established by our ancestors in France and continued by our Kings
> these eleven hundred years, is not only a true Politique, but an honourable
> and commendable Politique.[18]

Here, Orléans reclaims politics and *politiques* for his own side. There may
be bitter humour behind the apparent rehabilitation of the name *politique*
in a Leaguer text, and the implication remains that there have been some
mistakes about what a true *politique* should stand for. Still, on the surface
at least, in this text *politique* ends the century as a name of honour,
divorced from formerly negative and highly contested associations. Even
a 'slower' reading that acknowledges the latent troubling of these problematised categories allows for the survival of an ideal version of a *politique*
person. This is not, however, a neatly symmetrical end to the story in
which the *politique* is restored to former glory. The end of one kind of
polemical use of *politique* wasn't even quite that, as later pamphlets show.
Not only were there continuities in French writing, but it also seems clear
that changes that occurred in sixteenth-century France had a long-term
impact in European literature and thought.

The influence of the French Civil Wars on the English political imaginary offers an especially rich case in point. The name of the group of
dissatisfied nobles known as 'les malcontents' (literally, 'the unhappy
ones') was popularised as the title of John Marston's 1603 play *The
Malcontent*, and is now used to refer to a character in a play who is
disaffected and prone to rebellion. It has been commented upon that the
malcontents who populate the early modern English theatrical canon, of
whom the most well-known is surely Hamlet, transcend borders, are
mobile in European space (the Danish Hamlet for instance is educated
in Luther's town, Wittenberg) and display a 'worrisome linguistic facility',
rather like the fictional *politiques* of late sixteenth-century French
polemic.[19] George Chapman's play, *Bussy d'Ambois* (1603/04) is set at
the court of Henri III; even earlier than this, Christopher Marlowe's
Massacre at Paris (1593) dramatised the Saint Bartholomew's Day

---

[18] 'Si police est la constitution d'un estat, selon laquelle chacun doit vivre, je conclus que le Ligueur
qui veut vivre & mourir en la manutention de ceste police establie en France par nos Majeurs, et
continuée par nos Rois unze cens ans, est non seulement un vray Politique, mais un honorable &
recommendable Politique.' [Louis d'Orléans], *Le banquet et apresdinee* (n.p.).
[19] Mark Thornton Burnett, 'Staging the Malcontent in Early Modern England', in *A Companion to
Renaissance Drama*, ed. by Arthur F. Kinney (Oxford: Blackwell, 2004), pp. 336–52 (p. 336).

massacre.[20] In Chapter 2 I looked briefly at a dialogue by Thomas More which shows that the word 'polytyke' was ambiguous in English long before the French Wars of Religion; still, some of Shakespeare's uses of the word surely bear the mark of struggles that took place on the continent in the intervening years. In his pastoral comedy, *The Merry Wives of Windsor,* the host asks, mockingly, 'Am I politic, am I subtle, am I a Machiavel?'[21] This play, which features a Frenchman struggling to communicate with the English, seems to lightly satirise the echoes of disputes from mainland Europe in rural England.

Of all the English writers active at the turn of the seventeenth century, the one who seems to engage most closely with the French drama around politics and *politiques* is Francis Bacon. In his youth (in the late 1570s) Bacon spent three years in the service of the ambassador to France, Amyas Paulet, and there has been some speculation about the impact of this stay in France on Bacon's intellectual development.[22] Twenty or so years later, Bacon's *Essays* (clearly marked by his reading of Montaigne) contained many uses of the word 'politic' and a few of 'politique', both adjectival and substantive: most refer either to a type of political person, or to the 'body politic'. For example, in 'Of Seditions and Troubles', Bacon describes how troubles are natural in the body politic, and says that 'the politic and artificial nourishing and entertaining of hopes' is 'one of the best antidotes against the poison of discontentments'.[23] That politic is aligned with artifice – that is, with creative acts – is an interesting modulation on negative associations in French between political action and the telling of tall tales. In the previous chapter, 'Of Goodness and Goodness of Nature', Bacon turns to the character of the political man, writing that unhappy ('malignant', or perhaps 'malcontent') types are best suited to politics:

> Such dispositions are the very errours of human nature; and yet they are the fittest timber to make great politiques of; like to knee timber, that is good for ships, that are ordained to be tossed; but not for building houses, that shall stand firm.[24]

[20] On French influence on English drama, see Richard Hillman, *Shakespeare, Marlowe and the Politics of France* (Basingstoke: Palgrave, 2002).

[21] William Shakespeare, 'The Merry Wives of Windsor', in *Complete Works*, pp. 102–55 (p. 127).

[22] Markku Peltonen, 'Introduction', in *The Cambridge Companion to Bacon*, ed. by Markku Peltonen (Cambridge: Cambridge University Press, 1996), pp. 1–22 (p. 2). See also Boutcher, Vol 1.

[23] Francis Bacon, 'Essays', in *Collected Works, VI, Part II: Literary Works*, ed. by James Spedding, Robert Leslie Ellis, Douglas Heath, 15 vols. (London: Routledge/Thoemmes, 1996), VI, pp. 409–11.

[24] Ibid., p. 404.

Here, Bacon uses the French spelling for a kind of *politique* who is flexible and stoical, and not particularly good. One wonders if both Bacon and Hobbes (who also spent time in France) used the –que suffix when they were feeling a French influence particularly strongly. In any case, the fact that both writers use both spellings suggests that in some ways, *politique* was an indelibly French sort of word in seventeenth-century England.[25]

Bacon was deeply familiar, too, with the wrangling over the term *politique* in French writing: he must have been, because a late unfinished dialogue, *An Advertisement Touching an Holy Warre* (*c.* 1622) is set in Paris, and features the following characters: Eusebius (who 'beareth the character of a Moderate Divine'), Gamaliel ('a Protestant Zelant'), Zebedaeus ('a Romish Catholic Zelant'), Martius ('a Military Man'), Pollio ('a Courtier') and Eupolis ('a Politique').[26] The presence of 'courtier', 'zelant', and 'politique' evokes early dialogues by Le Caron and Pasquier as well as much later fictional conversations between Leaguers and their opponents, sometimes called *politiques*; 'Eusebius' was also, we recall, the pseudonym of the author of the *Reveille-matin*.

Bacon began this dialogue in a period of retirement from politics after he was brought down by scandal, and he abandoned it for similarly contingent reasons, but valued it sufficiently to have it translated into Latin and included in his *Opera moralia et civilia*. Eupolis's name, which means 'happy polis', seems a nod to More's Eu/U-topia, and also a kind of inverted version of an unhappy 'malcontent'. Like the character in *The Merry Wives of Windsor* who asks if he is 'politic', 'subtle', or 'a Machiavel', Eupolis is a host, who – similar, too, to Pasquier's *politic* figure in *Le pourparler du prince* – facilitates the discussion and sets the topic. This is to be a debate as to which conditions justify 'holy war'. Eupolis makes the stakes horribly clear by asking whether, if a cause for holy war is established, it should be pursued to the point of the 'displanting and extermination of people'.[27] With its critique of Spanish colonialism and references

---

[25] The -que ending is common in Hobbes. One example is a description of Thucydides as the 'most *politique* historiographer', quoted in Robin Sowerby, 'Thomas Hobbes's Translation of Thucydides', *Translation and Literature*, 7.2 (1998) 147–69 (p. 147). See also Kinch Hoekstra, 'Hobbes's Thucydides' in *The Oxford Handbook of Hobbes*, ed. by Al P. Martinich and Kinch Hoekstra (Oxford: Oxford University Press: 2016), pp. 547–74. Hoekstra cites a contemporary of Hobbes, Thomas Barnes, who referred to 'politique affaires' in 1624 (p. 556). It may be that Hobbes and his contemporaries used the -que ending more in the earlier part of the seventeenth century, and in Hobbes's case during his 'humanist phase' that ended in 1630 (Hoekstra, p. 548).

[26] Francis Bacon, 'Advertisement Touching an Holy Warre', in *Collected Works, VII, Part I: Literary and Professional Works*, ed. Spedding et al. (London: Routledge/Thoemmes, 1996), VII, pp. 17–36.

[27] Bacon, 'Advertisement', p. 26.

to the cruelties of warfare, Bacon's dialogue fragment brings together the connected threads of conquest and religious conflict that wrought such havoc in the early modern world – or rather, it is the *politique* character in the dialogue who brings these threads together.

The status of Bacon's *politique* character as host of a varied discussion and mediator of a number of ideological positions seems to bear the influences of French uses and critiques of so-called *politique* people and what they (didn't) stand for. Indeed, in different and perhaps quite accidental ways, Shakespeare and Bacon reveal much about the word politic/*politique* by making it a 'host': the word was an invaluable carrier, even if it was often treated as a parasite. Bacon's *politique* has a further characteristic that is striking. Eupolis describes how the dialogue ought to go, and says that although Pollio will esteem the discussion to be 'but impossibilities and eagles in the clouds', he shall 'do [his] best to prove the enterprise possible, and to show how all impediments may be ever removed or overcomen'.[28] He is promising, in short, that the question can be resolved: this, indeed, seems a recipe for a happy polis. It is therefore both ironic and apt that the discussion never takes place, and is only introduced (at some length). Still, here we see Bacon's character promising to blend the preferable with the possible: a desirable function of politics that some have seen as having become diminished in the heat of the urgent early modern attention to the political.

The dialogic, conversational sixteenth-century modes of political writing informed theatre in both England and France, and in seventeenth-century France theatre was a primary cultural and political mode, in which personas and character types were self-consciously explored. Interest in the role of the political actor is evident from the treatise-memoirs written by agents of the seventeenth-century state in France; Katherine Ibbett has argued for the proximity of political and theatrical action in her readings of Richelieu's *Political Testament* and Corneille's plays.[29] Louis Marin writes that for Gabriel Naudé, who introduced the concept of the 'coup d'état' to political theory, politics is a kind of theatrical performance in which the person imbued with political knowledge takes centre stage.[30] In England, Hobbes's concern with 'personation' and the person of the state, and

[28] Ibid., p. 24.   [29] Ibbett, *Style of the State*, pp. 123–45.
[30] Louis Marin, 'Pour une théorie baroque de l'action politique': Lecture des *Considérations politiques sur les coups d'Etat* de Gabriel Naudé', in Gabriel Naudé, *Considérations politiques sur les Coups d'Etat, précédé de 'Pour une théorie baroque de l'action politique' par Louis Marin*, ed. by Frédérique Marin and Marie-Odile Perulli (Paris: Editions de Paris, 1988), pp. 5–66. Marin writes that politics as knowledge in action is 'a *theatrical* turn in which the subject of political knowledge is the

indeed the image of Leviathan as the one and the many, surely bears the influence of contemporary concerns with politics as a person and as a character in a drama or a narrative.[31]

Both actors and politicians were mistrusted in early modern France. Concerns about political action as dissimulation, masking both truth and true identity, were common to sixteenth- and seventeenth-century examinations of the political.[32] The question of politics as role-play and the ethical consequences thereof seems still unresolved; the modern philosopher who seems most optimistic about politics as performative, conducted by 'persons' (that is by personas) is Hannah Arendt, for whom 'persons' could be people constituted as active citizens.[33] Montaigne, like many early modern French writers, seems to have been more cautious about the relationship between political roles and human singularity. With its 'vacillation' between optimism and pessimism about the performativity of politics and the duplicity of the performers, the sixteenth-century political conversation demonstrates the legacy of humanist attention to the human in its multiple refigurings of the role of the actor.

Early modern conceptions of politics and *politiques* involved considerable anxiety about the ethical status of political characters and categories, and increasing focus on what I have referred to as the bad *politique*, even if *politiques* were subsequently credited for bringing an end to the devastation of the wars. For Viroli, increasing anxiety about the possibility of good politics represents a loss, a kind of ethical drainage: the end of confidence in politics with any kind of higher goal than the preservation of state power by whatever means necessary. He further argues that the end of the sixteenth century marked the end of politics as civil philosophy and the beginning of politics as reason of state, inaugurated by Botero's *Reason of State* ('Della ragion di stato'), published in 1589 and translated into French for the first time in 1599; Viroli's focus is European but primarily Italian.[34]

---

principal character' ('le statut de cette connaissance-action est celui d'un *coup de théâtre* dont le sujet du savoir politique serait le protagoniste') [my italics], p. 44.

[31] Quentin Skinner, 'Hobbes and the Purely Artificial Person of the State', *Journal of Political Philosophy*, 7.1 (1999), 1–29.

[32] Marin, p. 32. Marin also argues that Naudé's conception of politics functioned according to a masking-unmasking dialectic (in which what was being 'unmasked' by politics was power itself), p. 35.

[33] Hannah Arendt, *The Promise of Politics*, ed. by Jerome Kohn (New York, NY: Schoken, 2005), p. 52. Craig Calhoun and John McGowan, 'Introduction', in *Hannah Arendt and the Meaning of Politics*, ed. by Craig Calhoun and John McGowan (Minneapolis, MN and London: University of Minnesota Press, 1997), pp. 1–26 (pp. 7–9).

[34] Viroli, *From Politics to Reason of State*, p. 280. Italian influences on French political thought and representations are another common feature between sixteenth- and seventeenth-century France, as

Skinner has shown that emergence of the state as the idea that dominated European political thought in the later part of the early modern period dates to around the same moment, though he seems to regret this less than Viroli, considering it more a fundamental characteristic of modernity, for better or worse.[35]

The key political texts of seventeenth-century France are certainly more focused on the state than on what politics and *politiques* are or should be, at least in terms of vocabulary and definitions. Gabriel Naudé's *Considérations politiques sur un coup d'état* ('Political Reflections on the Coup d'État', 1639) and Cardinal Richelieu's *Testament politique* ('Political Testament', published in 1688, though Richelieu died in 1642), reflect this change, though their framing of their treatises as *politique* demonstrates the enduring power of the term as a generic marker. Both authors mostly use *politique* adjectivally, or as a collective noun to refer to experts in what would now be called political theory; in Richelieu, those who might have also been called *politiques* in the previous century are now referred to as 'men of state' or 'state counsellors'.[36] Naudé explicitly frames himself as an inheritor of a sixteenth-century literary and political tradition, citing Montaigne and Charron as stylistic inspirations and Bodin as the only previous thinker who recognised that the *coup d'état* was a new, highly significant aspect of politics beyond the common assumptions of most *politiques*.[37] Naudé also echoes earlier critiques of *politiques* most strikingly in his acknowledgement that, while justice is important in all political endeavours, a counsellor ('conseiller') has less recourse to noble, universal justice and more to that which is 'artificial, particular, *politique*' since this kind is 'soft enough to accommodate ... common human weakness, unexpected turns, and differences of time, person, issue'. This, says Naudé, obliges us often to undertake actions that natural justice would reject and condemn absolutely.[38] It is a reformulation of the classic juxtaposition of the useful and the honest, interesting for how much that which is *politique* has been arrogated to the former realm, and also for the relation between the political and the creative (the artificial). Richelieu, though considered a master of flexibility and manipulation, nonetheless presents 'true philosophy, Christian law, and politics' as united in the

was the presence of an influential Medici queen (Marie de' Medici, second wife of Henri IV, ruled as regent between 1610 and 1617).
[35] Skinner, *Foundations*, II, pp. 353–58.
[36] Armand Jean Duplessis, duc de Richelieu, *Testament politique*, ed. by François Hildeheimer (Paris: Champion, 1995), e.g. pp. 215, 221, and 223.
[37] Marin, p. 32; Naudé, p. 84.   [38] Naudé, p. 164.

service of a core argument of his text, that is the need to subordinate private concerns to public interest.[39] At least on the surface, in person and in writing Cardinal Richelieu incarnates an enduring connection in the seventeenth century between church and state. These contrasting instances, though anecdotal, suggest that questions of the theologico-moral status of politics, and of its ability to transcend what would eventually be called realpolitik, were evidently not resolved. Neither a sense of 'politics as dirty work' nor of 'politics as striving for a better community' was firmly established.

One might make something of the difference between adjective and noun in these two cases: *political* justice being lax enough to accommodate both change and moral evil; *politics* as a rigorous standard. A lasting legacy of sixteenth-century attention to political language might well be concern with the different modes that the differing abstract and concrete nouns and correlating adjectives in the word group of 'politics' imply, and particularly the different possibilities offered by the distinction between *le politique* and *la politique*.[40] Four and a half centuries after Loys Le Roy's inaugural address at the *Collège royal*, Pierre Rosanvallon took up a chair that Le Roy would surely have envied, in *Histoire contemporaine et moderne du politique* ('modern and contemporary political history') at the same institution, now called the *Collège de France*. In his inaugural lecture Rosanvallon defined a more flexible masculine substantive against a more authoritative feminine in his opening lecture, preferring to focus on the 'modality' of the former: 'Referring substantively to *the political* ['en parlant *du* politique'], I thus refer as much to a modality of existence in shared life, as to a form of collective action that is implicitly distinct from the deployment of *politics*'.[41] Rosanvallon's distinction between the lived modality of *le politique*, and *la politique* as something to enact or impose, seems to plausibly be a traceable inheritor of early modern distinctions between *le politique* as live agent and *la politique* as discipline or doctrine (although a longer word history would be required to test this hypothesis). Rosanvallon goes on to justify this distinction by defining *politics* as a matter of institutional norms

---

[39] Richelieu, p. 249.

[40] Philippe Raynaud, 'Politique (le), Politique (la)' in *Dictionnaire des intraduisibles*, pp. 964–65.

[41] 'En parlant substantivement *du* politique, je qualifie ainsi tant une modalité d'existence de la vie commune qu'une forme de l'action collective qui se distingue implicitement de l'exercice de *la* politique', Pierre Rosanvallon, *Pour une histoire conceptuelle du politique* (Paris: Seuil, 2002), p. 14. The first chair with the term *politique* actually in the title was that of 'Economie politique': see Abel Lefranc, *Histoire du Collège de France depuis ses origines jusqu'à la fin du premier empire* (Paris: Hachette, 1893), p. 388.

and competition for power, and *the political* as 'everything that constitutes a society [*cité*]' beyond the immediacy of governmental action.[42] Framing *la politique* as rule and *le politique* as 'everything else', a kind of endless *au-delà*, certainly evokes the struggle between politics as normative structure and politics as fundamentally flexible and impossible to define that marked the texts I have analysed in this book.

Rosanvallon's juxtaposition of politics and the political reproduces a central preoccupation of twentieth-century French political theory.[43] These preoccupations developed partially out of the (often critical) reception of Carl Schmitt, who conceived of 'the political' as a challenge to what he saw as the state's monopoly on 'politics'; he explained in an early version of the highly influential work that became *The Concept of the Political* that this monopoly of the state on politics originated with Machiavelli and Bodin.[44] Schmitt's own preoccupation with the decline of the Weimar state and subsequent support for the Nazi regime demonstrates the limitations of his own position in practice. Still, his assertion about his early modern forebears confirms a Franco-Italian genealogy for what politics is thought to have become as it entered modernity, and suggests a peculiarly (early) modern dynamic between politics and the political. What is missing from this account of the legacy of early modern political writing, however, is the person, the *politique*, the character acting out the drama of politics with and against the political.

I end this book, then, by observing that the theatrical and character-oriented question of who a political person might be is another important legacy of sixteenth-century French political writing. It is a legacy too often overlooked by those attempting to associate a group of people called *politiques* with particular ideas and governmental forms. My closing emphasis on the fictionality of the *politique* person, when all things are considered, is in no way an argument against the existence of a group of tolerant pragmatists. Rather, it is an argument that the fictional aspects of both the group and of the singular character, *le politique*, are important and influential in the genealogy of the figure of the politician, and in the history of European political imagination. This character must be understood as playing his role in the construction of a vision of masculinity, within and beyond governmental politics. My emphases throughout this

---

[42] Rosanvallon, p. 14, pp. 46–47. Rosanvallon's focus on the *cité* has a semi-idealist civic aspect that Viroli identified with civil philosophy and regretted as having been displaced by reason of state.

[43] Apter, pp. 22–36.

[44] Carl Schmitt, *The Concept of the Political: Expanded Edition*, tr. by George Schwab (Chicago, IL and London: University of Chicago Press, 2007), p. 6.

book on the irreducibly plural languages of politics and on the word *politique* itself, are connected to the theatrically oriented development of a *politique* character by the idea of performance and performativity, as well as by the negative charge of hypocrisy sometimes attached to political language, and political action.[45] Arendt wrote that 'action and speech' might be the two 'outstanding political activities'.[46] In sixteenth-century France, *acting* and speech are outstanding political preoccupations. Absorbing the lessons of the humanist project and the wars of words of the previous century, seventeenth-century dramatic theory held that speech *was* action: 'parler, c'est agir'.[47] The textual acts of self-fashioning and character assassination undertaken by political agents acting temporarily on the sixteenth-century political stage demonstrate the integration of written politics and *politiques* into the real world of life, death, and the events in between.

* * *

What does it mean to write about past politics and the political, now? If certain Catholic Leaguers of then are akin to the politico-theological fundamentalists of now, what does it mean to recuperate their writings as politics? If the fictional centre ground of sixteenth-century politics is as mobile and illusory as today's so-called centrism, does that justify an all-out abandonment of middleness as a desirable location? In the case of the former, I would say that recuperating the political thought in hate speech should not sanitise that discourse, but should show that it is not so 'other' as to be content-free; that the boundaries between murderous screeds and high political thought are lightly drawn, and cannot be reduced to the difference between euphemism and direct assertion, nor to situated-ness within or without boundaries of law and state power. In terms of 'being in the middle', certainly I would advocate – as would many contemporary writers and political philosophers – an abandonment of the idea that the centre has a fixed location, or any inherent value. I think that my analysis shows, however, that although 'the centre cannot hold', its changeability is powerful, and worth arguing over. The middleness of politics and *politiques* might be constructed, but it is not arbitrary: it is the result of different kinds of reading processes and rhetorical acts.

---

[45] Runciman, pp. 6–7.   [46] Arendt, p. 62.
[47] Abbé d'Aubignac, *La pratique du théâtre* [1657], ed. by Hélène Baby (Paris: Champion, 2011), p. 407. See Michael Hawcroft, *Word as Action: Racine, Rhetoric, and Theatrical Language* (Oxford: Oxford University Press, 1992), esp. pp. 12–60.

The mobility of politics and *politiques* in the sixteenth century were a function of language use, and of the plurality of those who used and abused political language. The meanings of words, and of the word group including 'politics', 'political', and 'politician', are slippery, often indistinct. To this extent it seems that politics and *politiques* are essentially elusive. Any meaning is negotiated, and partial: an imperfect translation. In some ways, this might be disappointing. In some ways, the whole book has been about disappointment: political failures, unrealised ideals, texts taken out of context, meanings distorted. There are no *politique* heroes. From Bodin and Le Roy to the frustrated author of the *Dialogue d'entre le Maheustre et le Manant*, nobody really got what they wanted, and definitions of politics and *politiques* were frequently partial, unsatisfying, or ridiculed. All this has echoes in the present, where large-scale political projects fail, and populations dissatisfied with the inauthenticity of politics and with politicians turn to leaders who promise something more 'real' (while hyperbolically exploiting the flexibility of politics), and who might prefer to be princes more than *politiques*. But the book has also been about the pleasures and possibilities of contesting, unsettling – even distorting – meaning. Scepticism about authenticity should not mean giving up on evidence, or integrity. Seeing the world in terms of fiction and poetics does not necessitate abandoning truth claims or settling for constant deferral of meaning or of ethical judgement. It poses the question of the impact of art, and acting, on real lives. Perhaps part of an answer to the affective aspect of the *politique* problem is to reconsider the unstable, performative nature of language and of political action, to see it as art, rather than as failure in itself.

Bibliography

MANUSCRIPT PRIMARY SOURCES

Archives nationales de France (AN)

AN X2A 1397, 1594-01-08
AN X2B 165, 1591-07-19

Bibliothèque nationale de France (BNF)

BNF MS Fr 3186
BNF MS Fr 12247

PRINTED PRIMARY SOURCES

Anon., *A Pleasant Satyre or Poesie: Wherein Is Discovered the Catholicon of Spayne, and the Chiefe Leaders of the League. Finelie Fetcht Over, and Laide Open in Their Colours. New Turned Out of French into English*, trans. by Thomas Wilcox (London: Orwin, 1595).

Coppie de la responce faite par un polytique de ceste ville de Paris, aux precedens Memoires secrets, qu'un sien Amy lu avoit envoyés de Bloys, en forme de Missive ([Lyon]: [J. Pillehotte], 1589).

Coppie d'une lettre escripte par un Catholique à un Politique, sur l'arrest prononcé en la Synagogue de Tours le cinquiesme d'aoust dernier (Lyon: [n. pub.], 1591).

Declaration de Monseigneur Francois fils & frere de Roy, Duc d'Alençon, &c. Contenant les raisons de sa sortie de la Court (Paris: [n. pub.], 1575).

Description de l'homme politique de ce temps avec sa foy et religion qui est un catalogue de plusieurs heresies et athéismes, où tombent ceux qui préfèrent l'estat humain à la religion catholique (Paris: G. Bichon, 1588).

Dialogue d'entre le Maheustre et le Manant, ed. by P. Ascoli (Geneva: Droz, 1977).

Discours des trahisons, perfidies et desloyautez des politiques de Paris (Lyon: L. Tantillon, 1589).

Discours veritable de la deffaite obtenue sur les trouppes des politiques et hérétiques, du pays et duché de Berry (Paris: D. Millot, 1589).

L'arpocratie, ou Rabais du caquet des politiques et jebusiens de nostre aage (Lyon: J. Pattrason, 1589).

La contrepoison contre les artifices et inventions des politiques et autres ennemis de la religion Catholique (Paris: A. Le Riche, 1589).

La dispute d'un catholique de Paris, contre un Politique de la ville de Tours (Paris: R. Nivelle and R. Thierry, 1591).

La foy et religion des Politiques de ce temps. Contenant la refutation de leurs heresies Les impostures et calomnies des Huguenots, politiques & atheistes pour colorer le massacre és personnes de Messeigneurs les Cardinal & Duc de Guyse par Henry de Valois (Paris: G. Bichon, 1588).

La TRAHISON descouverte des politiques de la ville de Rouen (Paris: [n. pub.], 1589).

La TRAHISON descouverte des politiques de la ville de Troyes en Champaigne, Avec les noms des Capitaines & Politiques, qui avoient conspiré contre la Saincte Union des Catholiques (Paris: D. Binet and A. Du Breuil, [1589?]).

Le discours merveilleux de la vie, actions, et déportements de Cathérine de Médicis, royne mere, ed. by N. Cazauran (Geneva: Droz, 1995).

Le karesme et mœurs du Politique où il est amplement discouru de sa manière de vivre, de son Estat & Religion (Paris: P. Des Hayes, 1589).

Le reveille-matin des françois, ed. by J.-R. Fanlo, M. Lambiase, and P.-A. Mellet (Paris: Garnier, 2016).

Mémoires semez par quelques politics aux Estats, qui se tiennent, en la ville de Bloys. Avec la response Catholique à iceux (Paris: [n. pub.], 1588).

Responce au cartel d'un politique bigarré qui ne s'est osé nommer (Lyon: L. Tantillon, 1591).

Satyre ménippée, ed. by M. Martin (Paris: Champion, 2007).

Satyre ménippée, ed. by M. Martin (Lyon: Presses universitaires de Lyon, 2010).

Aristotle, *Politics*, ed. by R. F. Stalley, tr. by Ernest Barker (Oxford: Oxford University Press, 1998).

d'Aubignac, *La pratique du théâtre* [1657], ed. by H. Baby (Paris: Champion, 2011).

Bacon, F., *Collected Works*, ed. by J. Spedding, R. L. Ellis, and D. Heath, 15 vols. (London: Routledge/Thoemmes, 1996).

Barnaud, N., *Le miroir des françois* (Paris: [n. pub.], 1582).

Du Bellay, J., *Les regrets* (Paris: Gallimard, 1967).

Belloy, P. de, *De l'authorité du roy et crimes de Leze Majesté, qui se commettent par ligues, designation de successeur, & libelles escrits contre la personne & dignité du Prince* ([n.p.]: [n. pub.], 1587).

Bodin, J., *Lettre de Monsieur Bodin* (Lyon: J. Pillehotte, 1590).

'Methodus ad facilem historiarum cognitionem', in *Œuvres philosophiques de Jean Bodin*, ed. by P. Mesnard (Paris: Presses universitaires de France, 1951), pp. 105–277.

Les six livres de la République, ed. by C. Frémont, M.-D. Couzinet, and H. Rochais, 6 vols. (Paris: Fayard, 1986).

Les six livres de la république: De republica libri sex / livre premier, liber 1, ed. by M. Turchetti and N. de Araujo (Paris: Classiques Garnier, 2013).

La Boétie, E. de, *Discours de la servitude volontaire, ou contr'un*, ed. by M. Smith (Geneva: Droz, 1987).

Botero, G., *The Reason of State*, ed. and tr. by R. Bireley (Cambridge: Cambridge University Press, 2017).

Brisson, B., and L. Le Caron, *Le code du roy Henry III, rédigé en ordre par B. Brisson, augmenté et illustré par L. Le Caron* (Paris: J. Mettayer and P. L'Huillier, 1601).

Budé, G., *Le livre de l'institution du Prince, au Roy de France treschrestien Francoys premier de ce nom* (Paris: Foucher, 1547).

De l'institution du prince (Paris: Larrivour, 1547) [facsimile ed., Farnborough: Gregg Press, 1966].

'De l'institution du prince', in C. Bontems, L.-P. Raybaud, and J.-P. Brancourt, *Le Prince dans la France des XVIe et XVIIe siècles* (Paris: Presses Universitaires de France, 1965), pp. 77–140.

Philologie/De philologia, ed. and tr. by M.-M. de la Garanderie (Paris: Belles lettres, 2001).

Calvin, J., *Institution de la religion chrétienne (1541)*, ed. by O. Millet (Geneva: Droz, 2008).

Three French Treatises, ed. by F. M. Higman (London: Athlone Press, 1970).

Cherbeyt, H. de, *Apologie contre les Politiques ennemis de la religion et de l'État* (Paris: Bertault, 1618).

[de Coras, J.], *Question politique: S'il est licite aux subjects de capitular avec leur prince*, ed. by R. M. Kingdon (Geneva: Droz, 1989).

Estienne, H., *Traicté de la conformité du langage françois avec le Grec* (Paris: Robert Estienne, 1569).

Traité preparatif à l'apologie pour Herodote, ed. by B. Boudou, 2 vols. (Geneva: Droz, 2007).

Furetière, A., *Dictionnaire universel* (The Hague and Rotterdam: Leers, 1690).

Gentillet, I., *Anti-Machiavel, Edition de 1576*, ed. by C. Edward Rathé (Geneva: Droz, 1968).

Goulart, S., *Mémoires de l'Estat de France, sous Charles Neufiesme. Troisième volume. Seconde Edition, reveue, corrigee & augmentee* ([n.p.]: [n. pub.], 1579).

Horace, *Ars poetica*, in *Satires, Epistles, The Art of Poetry*, tr. by H. R. Fairclough (Cambridge, MA: Harvard University Press, 1926), pp. 442–90.

[Hotman, F.], *Le tigre* (1560), ed. by C. Read (Paris: Académie des bibliophiles, 1970).

Le Bossu, J., *Deux devis, d'un Catholique et d'un Politique, sur l'exhortation faicte au peuple de Nantes [...] le huitième jour de Juin, mil cinq cens quatre vingts et neuf* (Nantes: N. Desmarestz and F. Faverye, 1589).

Le Caron, L., *Dialogues*, ed. by J. A. Buhlmann and D. Gilman (Geneva: Droz, 1996).

L'Estoile, P. de, *Mémoires-Journaux*, ed. by G. Brunet et al., 11 vols. (Paris: Libraire des bibliophiles, 1975–83).

Les belles figures et drolleries de la Ligue, ed. by G. Schrenck (Geneva: Droz, 2016).

L'Hospital, M. de, *Discours et correspondance: La plume et la tribune II*, ed. by L. Petris (Geneva: Droz, 2013).

Le Roy, L., *Consideration sur l'histoire françoise, et l'universelle de ce Temps, dont les merveilles sont succinctement recitées* (Paris: F. Morel, 1567).

De la vicissitude (Paris: F. Morel, 1575).

Prolegomena politica. Oratio ab eo habita Parisiis inito professionis Regiae, in ennaratione Politicorum Aristoteles (Paris: F. Morel, 1575).

Les Politiques d'Aristote, tr. en fr., avec expositions (Paris: M. Vascovan, 1576).

De la vicissitude ou variété des choses en l'univers: La traduzione italiana di Ercole Cato, ed. by M. E. Severini (Paris: Classiques Garnier, 2014).

Littré, E., *Dictionnaire de la langue française*, 4 vols. (Paris: Hachette, 1872–77).

Machiavelli, N., *Le Prince de Nicolas Machiavelle secrétaire et citoien de Florence. Traduit d'Italien en Françoys par Guillaume Cappel* (Paris: C. Estienne, 1553).

Opere, ed. by C. Vivanti, 3 vols. (Turin: Einaudi-Gallimard, 1997).

The Prince, tr. by G. Bull (London: Penguin, 2004).

Montaigne, M., *The Complete Works*, tr. by D. Frame (London: Everyman, 2003).

Essais, ed. by J. Balsamo, M. Magnien, and C. Magnien-Simonin (Paris: Gallimard, 2007).

More, T., *The Complete Works*, ed. by J. B. Trapp, 15 vols. (London and New Haven, NJ: Yale University Press, 1963–97).

Naudé, G., *Considérations politiques sur les coups d'Etat, précédé de 'Pour une théorie baroque de l'action politique' par Louis Marin*, ed. by F. Marin and M.-O. Perulli (Paris: Editions de Paris, 1988).

La Noue, F. de, *Discours politiques et militaires* (Geneva: Droz, 1967).

[Orléans, L. d'], *Banquet et apresdinee du Comte d'Arête* (Paris: G. Bichon, 1594).

Pasquier, E., *Pourparlers*, ed. by B. Sayhi-Périgot (Paris: Champion, 1995).

Les recherches de la France, ed. by M.-M. Fragonard and F. Roudaut, 3 vols. (Paris: Champion, 1996).

[Pigenat, J.], *L'aveuglement et grande inconsideration des Politiques, dicts Maheustres, lesquels veulent introduire Henry de Bourbon, jadis Roy de Navarre, à la Couronne de France, à cause de sa pretenduë succession, par Fr. I. P. D. en Theologie* (Paris: R. Thierry, 1592).

Plato, *Republic*, ed. and tr. by R. Waterfield (Oxford: Oxford University Press, 1998).

Plutarch, *Moralia*, tr. by H. N. Fowler, 15 vols. (Cambridge, MA: Harvard University Press, 1936).

De la Popelinière, L., *L'histoire de France, t. II 1558–60*, ed. by J.-C. Laborie, B. Pierre, and P.-J. Souriac, under the direction of D. Turrel (Geneva: Droz, 2016).

Rabelais, F., *Œuvres complètes*, ed. by M. Huchon (Paris: Gallimard, 1994).
Complete Works, tr. by D. Frame (Berkeley, Los Angeles, CA and Oxford: California University Press, 1992).
Richart, A., *Mémoires sur la ligue dans le laonnais* (Laon: Libraries de la Société; Paris: Didron-Neveu, 1869).
Richelet, P., *Dictionnaire françois [1680]* (Geneva: Widerhold, 2007).
Richelieu, A. J. D., duc de, *Testament politique*, ed. by F. Hildeheimer (Paris: Champion, 1995).
Ripa, C., *Iconologia*, ed. by P. Buscaroli and M. Praz (Milan: TEO, 1992).
Ronsard, P., *La Franciade*, ed. by P. Laumonier, R. Lebègue, and G. Demerson (Paris: Nizet, 1983).
Seyssel, C. de, *La monarchie de France, et deux autres Fragments politiques*, ed. by J. Poujol (Paris: Libraire d'Argences, 1961).
Shakespeare, W., *Complete Works*, ed. by J. Bate and E. Rasmussen (London: Macmillan, 2007).
Sorbin, A., *Le vray resveille-matin des calvinistes, et publicains françois: Où est amplement discouru de l'auctorité des princes, & du devoir des sujets envers iceux. Par M. Arnault Sorbin, dit de Saincte foy, Predicateur du Roy, & Docteur Theologal de Tholous* (Paris: G. Chaudière, 1576).
Tory, G., *Le champ fleury, ou l'art et science de la proportion des lettres* (Paris: Bosse, 1529).
Touchard, J., *Allegresse chrestienne de l'heureux succès des guerres de ce royaume, et de la justice de Dieu contre les rebelles au Roy, & comme de droit divin, est licite à Sa Majesté punir ses sujets, pour la religion violée* (Paris: M. de Roigny, 1572).
Voltaire, *Voltaire's Correspondence*, ed. by T. Besterman, 107 vols. (Geneva: Institut et musée Voltaire, 1953–65).

SECONDARY SOURCES

Akkerman, N., and Houben, B., eds., *The Politics of Female Households: Ladies-in-Waiting across Early Modern Europe* (Leiden and Boston, MA: Brill, 2014).
Althusser, L., *Machiavel et nous* (Paris: Tallandier, 2009).
Anderson, B., *Imagined Communities: Reflections on the Origins and Spread of Nationalism* (London: Verso, 1983).
Angelo, V., *Les Curés de Paris au XVIᵉ siècle* (Paris: Editions du Cerf, 2005).
Anglo, S., *Machiavelli – The First Century: Studies in Enthusiasm, Hostility, and Irrelevance* (Oxford: Oxford University Press, 2005).
Antony, R., Carroll, S., and Dodds Pennock, C., eds., *The Cambridge World History of Violence, Volume III* (Cambridge: Cambridge University Press, 2020).
Appelbaum, R., *Terrorism before the Letter: Mythography and Political Violence in England, Scotland, and France 1559–1642* (Oxford: Oxford University Press, 2015).
Apter, E., *Unexceptional Politics: On Obstruction, Impasse, and the Impolitic* (London: Verso, 2018).

Arendt, H., 'Walter Benjamin: 1892–1940', in W. Benjamin, *Illuminations*, tr. by H. Zorn (London: Random House, 1999), pp. 7–61.

The Promise of Politics, ed. by J. Kohn (New York, NY: Schoken, 2005).

Armitage, D., *Civil Wars: A History in Ideas* (New Haven, CT: Yale University Press, 2017).

Austin, J. L., *How to Do Things with Words* (Oxford: Clarendon Press, 1962).

Baker, P., *Italian Renaissance Humanism in the Mirror* (Cambridge: Cambridge University Press, 2015).

Bakhtin, M., *Rabelais and His World*, tr. by H. Iswolsky (Bloomington, IN: Indiana University Press, 1984).

Baldini, A. E., ed., *Bodin a 400 anni dalla morte: Bilancio storiografico e prospettive di ricerca* (Florence: Olschki, 1997).

Baranova, T. D., *A coups de libelles: Une culture politique au temps des guerres de religion (1562–1598)* (Geneva: Droz, 2012).

Barbier-Mueller, J.-P., 'Pour une chronologie des premières éditions de la Satyre ménippée', *Bibliothèque d'Humanisme et Renaissance*, 67.2 (2005), 373–93.

Barnavi, E., *Le Parti de Dieu: Etude sociale et politique des chefs de la Ligue parisienne, 1585–1594* (Brussels: Nauwelaerts, 1980)

Barnavi, E., and R. Descimon, *La Sainte Ligue, le juge et la potence: L'assassinat du président Brisson (15 novembre 1591)* (Paris: Hachette, 1985).

Baron, H., *The Crisis of the Early Italian Renaissance: Civic Humanism and Republican Liberty in an Age of Classicism and Tyranny*, 2 vols. (Princeton, NJ: Princeton University Press, 1955).

Baumgartner, F., *Radical Reactionaries: The Political Thought of the French Catholic League* (Geneva: Droz, 1976).

Beame, E., 'The Politique and the Historians', *Journal of the History of Ideas*, 54.3 (1993), 355–79.

Beaune, C., *Naissance de la nation France* (Paris: Gallimard, 1985).

Becker, Abraham, *Un humaniste au XVIe siècle: Loys le Roy (Ludovicus regius) de Coutances* (Paris: Lecène, Oudin et Cie, 1896).

Becker, Anna, 'Gender in the History of Early Modern Political Thought', *The Historical Journal* (2017), 843–63.

Gendering the Renaissance Commonwealth (Cambridge: Cambridge University Press, 2019).

Bejan, T. M., *Mere Civility: Disagreement and the Limits of Toleration* (Cambridge, MA and London: Harvard University Press, 2017).

Benedict, P., 'Of Marmites and Martyrs: Image and Polemics in the Wars of Religion', in *The French Renaissance in Prints from the Bibliothèque nationale de France* (Los Angeles, CA: Grunwald Centre for the Graphic Arts, University of California), pp. 109–37.

Bénévent, C., and Walsby, M., 'Lost Issues and Self-Censorship: Rethinking the Publishing History of Guillaume Budé's *De l'institution du Prince*', in *Lost Books: Reconstructing the Print World of Pre-Industrial Europe*, ed. by F. Bruni and A. Pettegree (Leiden and Boston, MA: Brill, 2016), pp. 239–75.

Bergin, J. *The Politics of Religion in Early Modern France* (New Haven, CT: Yale University Press, 2014).

Bernard, M., C. Biet, and M.-M. Fragonard, *Tragédies et récits de martyres en France (fin XVIe–début XVIIe siècle)* (Paris: Garnier, 2009).

Berlin, I., *Selected Writings: Against the Current, Essays in the History of Ideas*, ed. by H. Hardy (Oxford: Clarendon Press, 1991).

Blair, A., *The Theater of Nature: Bodin and Renaissance Science* (Princeton, NJ: Princeton University Press, 1997).

Too Much to Know: Managing Scholarly Information Before the Modern Age (New Haven, CT: Yale University Press, 2010).

Bloch, M., *Apologie pour l'histoire: Ou, métier de l'historien* (Paris: Colin, 1949).

Bom, E. de, ed., *(Un)masking the Realities of Power: Justus Lipsius and the Dynamics of Political Writing in Early Modern Europe* (Leiden: Brill, 2011).

Boone, R. A., *War, Domination, and the Monarchy of France: Claude de Seyssel and the Language of Politics in the Renaissance* (Leiden and Boston, MA: Brill, 2007).

Boutcher, W., *The School of Montaigne in Europe Volume 1: The Patron-Author* (Oxford: Oxford University Press, 2017).

The School of Montaigne in Early Modern Europe: Volume II: The Reader Writer (Oxford: Oxford University Press, 2017).

Brady, A., and Butterworth, E., eds., *The Uses of the Future in Early Modern Europe* (London: Routledge, 2009).

Brett, A., 'What Is Intellectual History Now?', in *What Is History Now?*, ed. by D. Cannadine (London: Palgrave Macmillan, 2002), pp. 113–31.

Changes of State: Nature and the Limits of the City in Early Modern Natural Law (Princeton, NJ, and Oxford: Princeton University Press, 2011).

Broch, J., *L'école des "Politiques" (1559–98): La contribution des juristes et publicistes français à la construction de l'Etat royal* (Marseille: Presses universitaires d'Aix-Marseille, 2012).

Brooks, J. *Courtly Song in Late Sixteenth-Century France* (Chicago, IL and London: University of Chicago Press, 2000).

Briggs, R., *Early Modern France 1560–1715* (Oxford: Oxford University Press, 1977).

Communities of Belief: Cultural and Social Tensions in Early Modern France (Oxford: Clarendon, 1989).

Burke, M. J., and M. Richter, *Why Concepts Matter: Translating Social and Political Thought* (Leiden: Brill, 2012).

Burke, P., *The Fortunes of the Courtier: The European Reception of Castiglione's Corteggiano* (Cambridge: Polity, 1995).

Burke, P., Harrison, B., and Slack, P., eds., *Civil Histories: Essays Presented to Keith Thomas* (Oxford: Oxford University Press, 2000).

Burnett, M. T., 'Staging the Malcontent in Early Modern England', in *A Companion to Renaissance Drama*, ed. by A. F. Kinney (Oxford: Blackwell, 2004), pp. 336–52.

Burns, J. H., ed., *The Cambridge History of Political Thought* (Cambridge: Cambridge University Press, 1992).

Butterworth, E., *Poisoned Words: Slander and Satire in Early Modern France* (London: Legenda, 2006).

The Unbridled Tongue: Babble and Gossip in Renaissance France (Oxford: Oxford University Press, 2016).

Calhoun, C., and McGowan, J., *Hannah Arendt and the Meaning of Politics* (Minneapolis, MN and London: University of Minnesota Press, 1997).

Cameron, K., ed., *From Valois to Bourbon: Dynasty, State, and Society in Early Modern France* (Exeter: University of Exeter Press, 1989).

Carroll, S. *Blood and Violence in Early Modern France* (Oxford: Oxford University Press, 2006).

'"Nager entre deux eaux": The Princes and the Ambiguity of French Protestantism', *Sixteenth-Century Journal*, 44.4 (2013), 985–1020.

'Political Justice and the Outbreak of the Wars of Religion', *French History*, 33.2 (2019), 177–98.

Cassin, B., ed., *Vocabulaire européen des philosophes: Dictionnaire des intraduisibles* (Paris: Seuil, 2004).

Cave, T., *Recognitions: A Study in Poetics* (Oxford: Clarendon, 1988).

Pré-histoires: Textes troublés au seuil de la modernité (Geneva: Droz, 1999).

'Locating the Early Modern', *Paragraph* 29.1 (2006), 12–26.

Retrospectives: Essays in Literature, Poetics, and Cultural History, ed. by N. Kenny and W. Williams (London: Legenda, 2009).

Thomas More's Utopia in Early Modern Europe: Paratexts and Contexts (Manchester: Manchester University Press, 2012).

Thinking with Literature: Towards a Cognitive Criticism (Oxford: Oxford University Press, 2016).

Cave, T., and Wilson, D. eds., *Reading Beyond the Code: Literature and Relevance Theory* (Oxford: Oxford University Press, 2018).

Cazaux, C. *La musique à la cour de François Ier* (Paris: Ecole nationale de Chartres, 2002).

Chiron, P., and Radi, L., eds., *Valeur des lettres à la Renaissance. Débats et réflexions sur la vertu de la littérature* (Paris: Champion, 2016).

Clark, S., 'The "Gendering" of Witchcraft in Early Modern French Demonology: Misogyny of Polarity', *French History*, 5.4 (1990), 426–37.

Thinking with Demons: Witchcraft in Early Modern Europe (Oxford: Oxford University Press, 1999).

Condren, C., Gaukroger, S., and Hunter, I., eds., *The Philosopher in Early Modern Europe: The Nature of a Contested Identity* (Cambridge: Cambridge University Press, 2006).

Conley, T., *The Self-Made Map: Cartographic Writing in Early Modern France* (Minneapolis, MN: University of Minnesota Press, 1996).

Constant, J.-M., *La Ligue* (Paris: Fayard, 1996).

Cosandey F., and Descimon, R., eds., *L'absolutisme en France* (Paris: Seuil, 2002).

Couzinet, M.-D., *Histoire et méthode à la Renaissance: Une lecture de la Methodus de Jean Bodin* (Paris: Vrin, 1996).
Jean Bodin (Paris: Menini, 2001).
Crouzet, D., *Les guerriers de Dieu. La violence au temps des troubles de religion (vers 1525–vers 1610)*, 2 vols. (Paris: Champ Vallon, 1990).
La sagesse et le malheur: Michel de L'Hospital, chancelier de France (Paris: Champ Vallon, 2002).
Crue, F. de, *Le Parti des Politiques au lendemain de la Saint-Barthélemy: La Molle et Coconat* (Paris: Plon, 1892).
Cummings, B., *The Literary Culture of the Reformation: Grammar and Grace*, 2nd ed. (Oxford: Oxford University Press, 2007).
Curtius, E., *European Literature and the Latin Middle Ages*, tr. by Willard Trask (London: Routledge, 1953).
Dahlinger, J. H., *Etienne Pasquier on Ethics and History* (New York, NY and Oxford: Peter Lang, 2007).
Saving France in the 1580s: Writings of Etienne Pasquier (New York, NY: Peter Lang, 2014).
Daubresse, S., *Le Parlement de Paris ou la voix de la raison (1559–1589)* (Geneva: Droz, 2005).
Daubresse, S., and Haan, B., eds., *La Ligue et ses frontières: Engagements catholiques à distance du radicalisme à la fin des guerres de religion* (Rennes: Presses universitaires de Rennes, 2015).
Davies, S. F., and Fletcher, P., eds., *News in Early Modern Europe: Currents and Connections* (Leiden: Brill, 2014).
Demerson, G., *Rabelais* (Paris: Balland, 1986).
Demonet, M.-L., 'Quelques avatars du mot "politique" (XIVe–XVIIe siècles)', *Langage et société*, 113.3 (2005), 33–62.
Desan, P., *Naissance de la méthode: Machiavel, La Ramée, Bodin, Montaigne, Descartes* (Paris: Nizet, 1987).
Desan, P., ed., *Humanism in Crisis: The Decline of the French Renaissance* (Ann Arbor, MI: University of Michigan Press, 1991).
Montaigne politique (Paris: Champion, 2006).
Montaigne: Une biographie politique (Paris: Jacob, 2014).
Montaigne: A Life, tr. by Steven Rendall and Lisa Neal (Newark, NJ: Princeton University Press, 2017).
The Oxford Handbook of Montaigne (Oxford: Oxford University Press, 2016).
Descimon, R., 'L'échevinage parisien sous Henri IV (1594–1609): Autonomie urbaine, conflits politiques et exclusives sociales', in *La ville, la bourgeoisie et la genèse de l'Etat moderne (XIIᵉ–XVIIIᵉ siècles)*, ed. by N. Bulst and J.-Ph. Genet (Paris: CNRS, 1988), pp. 113–50.
'L'Invention de la noblesse de robe. La jurisprudence du Parlement de Paris aux XVIe et XVIIe siècles', in *Les Parlements de Province: Pouvoirs, justice et société du XVe au XVIIIe siècle*, ed. by J. Poumarède and J. Thomas (Toulouse: fraMespa, 1996), pp. 677–90.

Descimon, R., and E. Haddad, *Epreuves de noblesse. L'expérience nobiliaire de la haute robe parisienne (XVIe–XVIIIe siècles)* (Paris: Les Belles Lettres, 2010).

Descimon, R., and C. Jouhaud, *La France du premier XVIIe siècle 1594–1661* (Paris: Belin, 1996).

Diefendorf, B., *Beneath the Cross: Catholics and Huguenots in Sixteenth-Century Paris* (Oxford: Oxford University Press, 1991).

Blood Wedding: The Saint Bartholomew's Day Massacre in History and Memory (Boston, MA: Boston University Press, 2006).

Dionne, V., *Montaigne, écrivain de la conciliation* (Paris: Garnier, 2014).

Duport, D., ed., *Loys Le Roy: Renaissance et vicissitude du monde* (Caen: Presses universitaires de Caen, 2011).

Duport, D., *Le jardin et la nature: Ordre et variété dans la littérature de la Renaissance* (Geneva: Droz, 2002).

Eden, K., *The Renaissance Rediscovery of Intimacy* (Chicago, IL: Chicago University Press, 2012).

Eisenstein, E., *The Printing Press as an Agent of Change* (Cambridge: Cambridge University Press, 1980).

Etienne Pasquier et ses Recherches de la France = Cahiers V. L. Saulnier, 8 (Paris: Presses de l'École normale supérieure, 1991).

Fanlo, J.-R., *Tracés, ruptures: La composition instable des Tragiques* (Paris: Champion, 1990).

Felman, S., *The Scandal of the Speaking Body: Dom Juan with J. L. Austin, or Seduction in Two Languages* (Stanford: CA, Stanford University Press, 2002).

Felski, R., *The Uses of Literature* (Oxford: Blackwell, 2008).

Flaz, J., 'Political Philosophy and the Patriarchal Unconscious: A Psychoanalytic Perspective on Epistemology and Metaphysics', in *Discovering Reality: Feminist Perspectives on Epistemology, Metaphysics, Methodology, and Philosophy of Science*, ed. by Sandra Harding and Merrill B. Hintikka, 2nd ed. (Dordrecht: Kluwer, 2003) pp. 245–82.

Foa, J., *Le tombeau de la paix. Une histoire des édits de pacification (1560–1572)* (Limoges: Pulim, 2015).

Foisneau, L., ed., *Politique, droit et théologie chez Bodin, Grotius et Hobbes* (Paris: Kimé, 1997).

Fontana, B., *Montaigne's Politics: Authority and Governance in the Essais* (Princeton, NJ: Princeton University Press, 2008).

Ford, P., *The Judgment of Palaemon: The Contest between Neo-Latin and Vernacular Poetry in Renaissance France* (Leiden: Brill, 2013).

Forrestal, A., and Nelson, E., eds., *Politics and Religion in Early Bourbon France* (Basingstoke: Palgrave Macmillan, 2009).

Foucault, M., *Dits et écrits 1954–1988*, ed. by D. Defert and F. Ewald, 4 vols. (Paris: Gallimard, 1994).

Fragonard, M.-M., ed., *Pithou, les Lettres, et la paix du royaume* (Paris: Champion, 2003).

Franklin, J. H., *Jean Bodin and the Sixteenth-Century Revolution in the Methodology of Law and History* (New York, NY: Columbia University Press, 1963).

Jean Bodin (Aldershot: Ashgate, 2006).

Frisch, A., *The Invention of the Eyewitness: Witness and Testimony in Early Modern France* (Chapel Hill, NC: University of North Carolina Press, 2004).

Forgetting Differences: Tragedy, Historiography and the French Wars of Religion (Edinburgh: Edinburgh University Press, 2015).

Garanderie, M.-M. de la, *Guillaume Budé, philosophe de la culture*, ed. by Luigi-Alberto Sanchi (Paris: Garnier, 2010).

Garin, E., *Italian Humanism: Philosophy and the Civic Life in the Renaissance* (Oxford: Blackwell, 1965).

Genette, G., *Seuils* (Paris: Seuil, 1987).

Giavarini, L., ed., *L'Écriture des juristes. XVIe–XVIIIe siècle* (Paris: Champion, 2010).

Godard, A., *Le dialogue à la Renaissance* (Paris, Presses Universitaires de France, 2001).

Godard de Donville, L, *Le libertin des origins à 1665: Un produit des apologètes* (Paris: Biblio 17, 1989).

Goyard-Fabre, S., *Jean Bodin et le droit de La République* (Paris: Presses Universitaires de Ffance, 1990).

Goyet, F., *Le sublime du 'lieu commun': L'invention rhétorique dans l'Antiquité et à la Renaissance* (Paris: Champion, 1996).

Les audaces de la prudence: Littérature et politique aux XVIe et XVIIe siècles (Paris: Classiques Garnier, 2009).

Grafton, A., *What Was History?* (Cambridge: Cambridge University Press, 2007, repr. 2012).

Grafton A., and L. Jardine, *From Humanism to the Humanities: Education and the Liberal Arts in Fifteenth- and Sixteenth-Century Europe* (London: Duckworth, 1986).

Graves-Monroe, A., *Post tenebras lex: Preuves et propagande dans l'historiographie engagée de Simon Goulart (1543–1628)* (Geneva: Droz, 2012).

Greenblatt, S., *Renaissance Self-Fashioning from More to Shakespeare* (Chicago, IL: University of Chicago Press, 1980).

Greene, R., *Five Words: Critical Semantics in the Age of Shakespeare and Cervantes* (Chicago, IL: University of Chicago Press, 2013).

Greene, T. M., *The Light in Troy: Imitation and Discovery in Renaissance* (New Haven, NJ: Yale University Press, 1982).

Greengrass, M., *France in the Age of Henri IV: The Struggle for Stability*, 2nd ed. (London: Longman, 1995).

Governing Passions: Peace and Reform in the French Kingdom, 1576–1585 (Oxford: Oxford University Press, 2007).

Greengrass, M., with Tom Hamilton, 'Lettres compromettantes. La Ligue et la clandestinité des "politiques"', unpublished conference paper, delivered at 'La clandestinité au XVIe siècle pendant les guerres de religion en France', Paris, 11 June 2019.

Greffe, F., and J. Lothe, *La vie, les livres et les lectures de Pierre de L'Estoile: Nouvelles recherches* (Paris: Champion, 2004).

Gundersheimer, W. L., *The Life and Works of Louis Le Roy* (Geneva: Droz, 1966).

Habermas, J., *Postmetaphysical Thinking: Philosophical Essays* (Cambridge: Polity, 1992).

Hackett, H., *Early Modern Exchanges: Dialogues between Nations and Cultures, 1550–1750* (Farnham: Ashgate, 2015).

Hamilton, T., *Pierre de L'Estoile and His World in the Wars of Religion* (Oxford: Oxford University Press, 2017).

'Political Crime in the Wars of Religion: François Brigard's Sedition', in *Sedition: The Spread of Controversial Literature and Ideas in France and Scotland, c. 1550–1610,* ed. by J. O'Brien and M. Schachter (Turnhout: Brepols, forthcoming).

Hampton, T., *Literature and Nation in the Sixteenth Century: Inventing Renaissance France* (Ithaca, NY: Cornell University Press, 2009).

Hancock, R. C., *Calvin and the Foundations of Modern Politics* (Ithaca, NY and London: Cornell University Press, 1989).

Hankins, J., ed., *Renaissance Civic Humanism: Reappraisals and Reflections* (Cambridge: Cambridge University Press, 1995).

Hankins, J., *Virtue Politics: Soulcraft and Statecraft in Renaissance Italy* (Cambridge, MA: Harvard University Press, 2020).

Hardwick, J., *The Practice of Patriarchy: Gender and the Politics of Household Authority in Early Modern France* (Pennsylvania, PA: Pennsylvania State University Press, 1998).

Harrigan, M., *Frontiers of Servitude: Slavery in Narratives of the Early French Atlantic* (Manchester: Manchester University Press, 2018).

Hawcroft, M., *Word as Action: Racine, Rhetoric, and Theatrical Language* (Oxford: Oxford University Press, 1992).

Heidegger, M., 'The Origin of the Work of Art', in *Poetry, Language, Thought,* tr. by Albert Hofstadter (New York, NY: Harper and Row, 1967), pp. 15–89.

Being and Time, tr. by Joan Stambaugh (Albany, NY: SUNY Press, 2010).

Heitsch, D., and J.-F. Vallée, eds., *Printed Voices: The Renaissance Culture of Dialogue* (Toronto: University of Toronto Press, 2004).

Hillis Miller, J., 'The Critic as Host', *Critical Inquiry,* 3 (1977), 439–77.

Hillman, R., *Shakespeare, Marlowe and the Politics of France* (Basingstoke: Palgrave, 2002).

Hoffmann, G., *Montaigne's Career* (Oxford: Clarendon Press, 1998).

'Anatomy of the Mass: Montaigne's Cannibals', *PMLA,* 117.2 (2002), 207–21.

Reforming French Culture: Satire, Spiritual Alienation, and Connection to Strangers (Oxford: Oxford University Press, 2017).

Holland, A., and Scholar, R., eds., *Pre-Histories and Afterlives: Studies in Critical Method* (London: Legenda, 2009).

Holt, M. P., *The Duke of Anjou and the Politique Struggle during the Wars of Religion* (Cambridge: Cambridge University Press, 1986).

The French Wars of Religion 1562–1629 (Cambridge: Cambridge University Press, 2005).

Horn, L. R., and G. Ward, *Handbook of Pragmatics* (Oxford: Blackwell, 2004).

Hostiou, J.-M., and Viala, A., eds., *Le temps des querelles* (=*Littératures classiques,* 81, 2013).

Huchard, C., *D'encre et de sang. Simon Goulart et la Saint-Barthélemy* (Paris: Champion, 2007).

Huchon, M., 'Rabelais, les universités et la mobilité: Les phantasmes du Pantagruel à des fins de propagande', in *Les échanges entre les universités européennes à la Renaissance. Colloque international organisé par la Société française d'Étude du Seizième Siècle*, ed. by M. Bideaux and M.-M. Fragonard (Geneva: Droz, 2003), pp. 143–58.

Huppert, G., *The Idea of Perfect History: Historical Erudition and Historical Philosophy in Renaissance France* (Urbana, IL: University of Illinois Press, 1970).

Huseman, W., *La personnalité littérare de François de la Noue, 1531–91* (Paris: Nizet, 1986).

Ibbett, K., *The Style of the State in Neoclassical Theatre, 1630–1660* (Aldershot: Ashgate, 2009).

Compassion's Edge: Fellow Feeling and Its Limits in Early Modern France (Pennsylvania, PA: University of Pennsylvania Press, 2017).

Iagolnitzer, M., 'La publication du "Discours de la servitude volontaire" dans les "Dialogi" ou le "Reveille-matin des Français"', *Bulletin de la société des amis de Montaigne*, 18–19 (1976), 99–108.

Jameson, F., *The Political Unconscious: Narrative as a Socially Symbolic Act* (London: Methuen, 1981).

Jehasse, J., 'Loys Le Roy, maître et émule de Jean Bodin', in *Etudes sur Etienne Dolet: Le théâtre au XVIe siècle: Le Forez, Le Lyonnais et L'Histoire du Livre, publiées à la mémoire de Claude Longeon*, ed. by G.-A. Pérouse (Geneva: Droz, 1993), pp. 251–64.

Jouanna, A., *Le devoir de révolte: La noblesse française et la gestation de l'état moderne, 1559–1661* (Paris: Fayard, 1989).

Le pouvoir absolu: Naissance de l'imaginaire politique de la royauté (Paris: Gallimard, 2013). *Montaigne* (Paris: Gallimard, 2017).

Jouanna, A., Boucher, J., Biloghi, D., and Le Thiec, G., *Histoire et dictionnaire des Guerres de Religion* (Paris: Laffont, 1998).

Jouhaud, C., *Mazarinades: La Fronde des mots* (Paris: Aubier, 1985).

Les pouvoirs de la littérature (Paris: Gallimard, 2000).

Kahn, V., *Rhetoric, Prudence, and Skepticism in the Renaissance* (Ithaca, NY: Cornell University Press, 1985).

The Future of Illusion: Political Theology and Early Modern Texts (Chicago, IL: University of Chicago Press, 2014).

The Trouble with Literature (Oxford: Oxford University Press, 2020).

Kantorowicz, E., *The King's Two Bodies: Studies in Medieval Political Theology* (Princeton, NJ: Princeton University Press, 1997).

Kelley, D. R., *Foundations of Modern Historical Scholarship: Language, Law, and History in the French Renaissance* (New York, NY: Columbia University Press, 1970).

The Beginnings of Ideology: Consciousness and Society in the French Reformation (Cambridge: Cambridge University Press, 1981).

Kenny, N., *Curiosity in Early Modern Europe: Word Histories* (Wiesbaden: Harrassowitz, 1998).

The Uses of Curiosity in Early Modern France and Germany (Oxford: Oxford University Press, 2004).

Death and Tenses: Posthumous Presence in Early Modern France (Oxford: Oxford University Press, 2015).

Keohane, O., 'Bodin on Sovereignty: Taking Exception to Translation?', *Paragraph*, 38.2 (2015), 245–60.

Kessler, E., Kraye, J., Schmitt, C., and Skinner, Q., eds., *The Cambridge History of Renaissance Philosophy* (Cambridge: Cambridge University Press, 1998).

Kingdon, R. M., *Myths about the St Bartholomew's Day Massacres 1572–1576* (Cambridge, MA: Harvard University Press, 1988).

Geneva and the Coming of the Wars of Religion in France 1555–1563 (Geneva: Droz, 1956, repr. 2007).

Knecht, R. J., *Catherine De' Medici* (London: Longman, 1998).

The Rise and Fall of Renaissance France (Oxford: Oxford University Press, 2001).

Knoppers, L., and Landes, B., eds., *Monstrous Bodies/ Political Monstrosities in Early Modern Europe* (Ithaca, NY and London: Cornell University Press, 2014).

Koselleck, R., *Futures Past: On the Semantics of Historical Time* (New York, NY: Columbia University Press, 2004).

Kraye, J., ed., *The Cambridge Companion to Renaissance Humanism* (Cambridge: Cambridge University Press, 1996).

Kushner, E., *Le dialogue à la Renaissance: Histoire et poétique* (Geneva: Droz, 2004).

Labitte, *De la démocratie chez les prédicateurs de la Ligue*, 2nd ed. (Paris: Durand, 1865).

Lane, M., *Greek and Roman Political Ideas* (London: Pelican, 2014).

Langer, U., *Vertu du discours, discours de la vertu: Littérature et philosophie morale au XVIe siècle en France* (Geneva: Droz, 1999).

Langer, U., ed., *Au-delà de la Poétique: Aristote et la littérature de la Renaissance / Beyond the Poetics: Aristotle and Early Modern Literature* (Geneva: Droz, 2002).

ed., *The Cambridge Companion to Montaigne* (Cambridge: Cambridge University Press, 2005).

Le Clech-Charton, S., *Guillaume Budé, l'humaniste et le prince* (Paris: Rive neuve, 2008).

Lecoq, A.-M., *François Ier imaginaire. Symbolique et politique à l'aube de la Renaissance française* (Paris: Macula, 1987).

Lefranc, A., *Histoire du Collège de France depuis ses origines jusqu'à la fin du premier empire* (Paris: Hachette, 1893).

Leopold, D., and M. Steers, *Political Theory: Methods and Approaches* (Oxford: Oxford University Press, 2008).

Lestringant, F., and Ménager, D., eds., *Etudes sur la Satyre ménippée* (Geneva: Droz, 1987).

Lines, D., 'Lefèvre and French Aristotelianism on the Eve of the Sixteenth Century', in *Der Aristotelismus in der Frühen Neuzeit – Kontinuität oder Wiederaneignung?*, ed. by G. Frank and A. Speer (Harrassowitz: Wiesbaden, 2007), pp. 273–89.

Lloyd, H. A., ed., *The Reception of Bodin* (Leiden: Brill, 2013).

Lloyd, H. A., Jean Bodin, *'This Pre-eminent Man of France'* (Oxford: Oxford University Press, 2017).

Lipscomb, S., *The Voices of Nîmes: Women, Sex and Marriage in Reformation Languedoc* (Oxford: Oxford University Press, 2019).

Long, K. P., *High Anxiety: Masculinity in Crisis in Early Modern France* (Kirksville, MO: Truman State University Press, 2002).

Mac Carthy, I., ed., *Renaissance Keywords* (Oxford: Legenda, 2013).

Mac Carthy, I., *The Grace of the Italian Renaissance* (Princeton, NJ: Princeton University Press, 2020).

Macdonald, K., *Biography in Early Modern France* (London: Legenda, 2007)

Machielsen, J., 'The Lion, the Witch, and the King: Thomas Stapleton's "Apologia pro Rege Catholico Philippo II" (1592)', *English Historical Review*, 129 (2014), 19–46.

Mackenzie, L., *The Poetry of Place: Lyric, Landscape and Ideology in Renaissance France* (Toronto: Toronto University Press).

Maclean, I., *Interpretation and Meaning in the Renaissance: The Case of Law* (Cambridge: Cambridge University Press, 1992).

'From Prudence to Policy: Some Notes on the Pre-History of Policy Science', in *Guest Lectures* (Nijmegen: Katholieke universiteit, 1993), pp. 5–27.

Scholarship, Commerce, Religion: The Learned Book in the Age of Confessions 1560-1630 (Boston, MA: Harvard University Press, 2012).

Malcolm, N., 'Positive Views of Islam and Ottoman Rule in the Sixteenth Century: The Case of Jean Bodin', in *The Renaissance and the Ottoman World*, ed. by Anna Contadini and Claire Norton (Aldershot: Ashgate, 2013).

Useful Enemies: Islam and the Ottoman Empire in Western Political Thought, 1450–1750 (Oxford: Oxford University Press, 2018).

Marr, A., Garrod, R., Marcaida, J. R., and Oosterhoff, R. J., *Logodaedalus: Word Histories of Ingenuity in Early Modern Europe* (Pittsburgh, PA: Pittsburgh University Press, 2018).

Martin, H.J., Chartier, R., and Vivet, J. P., eds., *Histoire de l'édition française tome 1. Le livre conquérant du Moyen-Âge au milieu du XVIIe siècle* (Paris: Promodis, 1982).

Martinich, A., and K. Hoekstra, eds., *The Oxford Handbook of Hobbes* (Oxford: Oxford University Press: 2016).

McIlvenna, U., *Scandal and Reputation at the Court of Catherine de Medici* (London: Routledge, 2016).

Mellet, P.-A., *Les traités monarchomaques: Confusion des temps, résistance armée, et monarchie parfaite* (Geneva: Droz, 2007).

Ménager, D., 'Le *Dialogue entre le Maheustre et le Manant:* Mystique ou Politique?', in *Histoire et littérature au siècle de Montaigne: Mélanges offerts à Claude-Gilbert Dubois*, ed. by F. Argod-Dutard (Geneva: Droz, 2001), pp. 97–108.

Mentzer, R. A., and Spicer, A., eds., *Society and Culture in the Huguenot World 1559-1685* (Cambridge: Cambridge University Press, 2002).

Merlin-Kajman, H., *Public et littérature en France au XVII siècle* (Paris: Belles Lettres, 2004).

Miernowski, J., *La beauté de la haine: Essais de misologie littéraire* (Geneva: Droz, 2014).

Miglietti, S., 'Sovereignty, Territory, and Population in Jean Bodin's *République*', *French Studies*, 72.1 (2018), 17–34.

Moriarty, M., *Disguised Vices: Theories of Virtue in Early Modern French Thought* (Oxford: Oxford University Press, 2011).

Moss, A. *Printed Commonplace Books and the Structuring of Renaissance Thought* (Oxford: Clarendon Press, 1996)
Renaissance Truth and the Latin Language Turn (Oxford: Oxford University Press, 2003).

Mouffe, C., *The Democratic Paradox* (London: Verso, 2000).

Murdock, G., Roberts, P., and Spicer, A., eds., *Ritual and Violence: Natalie Zemon Davis and Early Modern France* (Oxford: Oxford University Press, 2012).

Murphy, K., and Traninger, A., eds., *The Emergence of Impartiality* (Leiden: Brill, 2014).

Musolff, A., and Zink, J., eds., *Metaphor and Discourse* (New York, NY: Palgrave Macmillan, 2009).

Najemy, J. M., 'Machiavelli and History', *Renaissance Quarterly*, 67.4 (2014), 1131–64.

Nakam, G., *Montaigne et son temps. Les événements et les essais. L'histoire, la vie, le livre* (Paris: Gallimard, 1993).

Nicholls, S., 'Gallican Liberties and the Catholic League', in *Thinking about Intellectual History (=History of European Ideas*, 40.7, 2014), 940–64.
'Political and Legal Thought', in *The Cambridge History of French Thought*, ed. by M. Moriarty and J. Jennings (Cambridge: Cambridge University Press, 2019), pp. 90–96.
Political Thought in the French Wars of Religion (Cambridge: Cambridge University Press, forthcoming).

Norman, L., *The Shock of the Ancient: Literature and History in Early Modern France* (Chicago, IL: University of Chicago Press, 2011).

Norton, G. P., *The Ideology and Language of Translation in Renaissance France and Their Humanist Antecedents* (Geneva: Droz, 1984).

Nuttall, A. D., 'Hamlet: Conversations with the Dead', *Proceedings of the British Academy*, 74 (1988), 53–69.

O'Brien, J., '"Le propre de l'homme": Reading Montaigne's Cannibals in Context', *Forum for Modern Language Studies*, 53.2 (2016), 220–34.

O'Brien, J, and Schachter, M., eds., *La première circulation de la Servitude volontaire en France et au-delà* (Paris: Champion, 2019).

Oliver, J. H., *Shipwreck in French Renaissance Writing: The Direful Spectacle* (Oxford: Oxford University Press, 2019).

Ong, W. J., *Ramus, Method, and the Decay of Dialogue: From the Art of Discourse to the Art of Reason* (Cambridge, MA: Harvard University Press, 1958).

Orwell, G., *Politics and the English Language* (London: Penguin, 2013).

Pagden, A., ed., *The Languages of Political Theory in Early Modern Europe* (Cambridge: Cambridge University Press, 1987).

Pallier, D., *Recherches sur l'imprimerie à Paris pendant la Ligue (1585–1594)* (Geneva: Droz, 1976).

Palonen, K., *Politics and Conceptual Histories: Rhetorical and Temporal Perspectives* (Baden-Baden: Nomos Verlagsgesellschaft, 2014).

Papin, P., 'Duplicité et traîtrise: L'image des "Politiques" durant la Ligue', *Revue d'histoire moderne et contemporaine*, 38.1 (1991), 3–21.

Parish, R., *Catholic Particularity in Early Modern France: 'Christianity Is Strange'* (Oxford: Oxford University Press, 2011).

Parsons, J. *The Church in the Republic: Gallicanism and Political Ideology in Renaissance France* (Washington, DC: Catholic University of America Press, 2004).

Patterson, J., '"Diables incarnez, Machiavelistes, Heretiques": The Villains of Pierre Matthieu's La Guisiade Reconsidered', *French Studies*, 70.1 (2015), 1–16.

Representing Avarice in Late Renaissance France (Oxford: Oxford University Press, 2015).

Peltonen, M., ed., *The Cambridge Companion to Bacon* (Cambridge: Cambridge University Press, 1996).

Petris, L., *La plume et la tribune: Michel de L'Hospital et ses discours (1559–1562)* (Geneva: Droz, 2002).

Pettegree, A., *Reformation and the Culture of Persuasion* (Cambridge: Cambridge University Press, 2005).

Pintard, R., *Libertins érudits* (Paris: Jammes, 1970).

Pitkin, *Fortune Is a Woman: Gender and Politics in the Thought of Niccolò Machiavelli* (Berkeley, CA: University of California Press, 1984).

Pocock, J. G. A., *The Machiavellian Moment: Florentine Political Thought and the Atlantic Republican Tradition* (Princeton, NJ: Princeton University Press, 1975).

Popkin, R., ed., *The Columbia History of Western Philosophy* (New York, NY: Columbia University Press, 1999).

Pot, O., ed., *Simon Goulart: Un pasteur aux intérêts vastes comme le monde* (Geneva: Droz, 2013).

Prendergast, C., *The Order of Mimesis: Balzac, Stendhal, Flaubert, Nerval* (Cambridge: Cambridge University Press, 1986).

Quint, D., *Montaigne and the Quality of Mercy: Ethical and Political Themes in the Essais* (Princeton, NJ: Princeton University Press, 1998).

Racaut, L., *Hatred in Print: Catholic Propaganda and Protestant Identity during the French Wars of Religion* (Aldershot: Ashgate, 2002).

Rancière, J., *Le partage du sensible. Esthétique et politique* (Paris: La Fabrique, 2000).

The Politics of Aesthetics, tr. by Gabriel Rockill (Paris: La Fabrique, 2000).

Roberts, P., *Peace and Authority during the French Religious Wars c. 1560–1600* (Basingstoke: Palgrave Macmillan, 2013).

Robin, C., *The Reactionary Mind: Conservatism from Edmund Burke to Sarah Palin* (Oxford: Oxford University Press, 2011).

Rosanvallon, P., *Pour une histoire conceptuelle du politique* (Paris: Seuil, 2002).

Rouget, F., ed., *François Ier et la vie littéraire de son temps (1515–47)* (Paris: Garnier, 2017).

Runciman, D., *Political Hypocrisy: The Mask of Power, from Hobbes to Orwell and Beyond* (Princeton, NJ and Oxford: Princeton University Press, 2008).

Ryan, A., *On Politics: A History of Political Thought from Herodotus to the Present* (London: Penguin, 2013).

Salmon, J. M. H., *Society in Crisis: France in the Sixteenth Century* (London: Methuen, 1979).

'Cicero and Tacitus in Sixteenth-Century France', *The American Historical Review*, 85.2 (1980), 307–31.

Said, E. W., *Humanism and Democratic Criticism* (Basingstoke: Palgrave Macmillan, 2004).

Santoro, M., *Fortuna, ragione e prudenza nella civiltà letteraria del Cinquecento* (Naples: Liguori, 1966).

Schaefer, D. L., *The Political Philosophy of Montaigne* (Ithaca, NY: Cornell University Press, 1990).

Schmitt, C., *The Concept of the Political: Expanded Edition*, tr. by George Schwab (Chicago, IL and London: University of Chicago Press, 2007).

Schmitt, C. B., *Aristotle and the Renaissance* (Cambridge, MA: Harvard University Press, 1983).

Scholar, R., *The Je-Ne-Sais-Quoi in Early Modern Europe: Encounters with a Certain Something* (Oxford: Oxford University Press, 2005).

Montaigne and the Art of Free-Thinking (Oxford: Peter Lang, 2010).

'Montaigne et la "vanité" des utopies', *Revue de synthèse*, 137.3–4 (2016), 321–43.

Sciacca, E., *Umanesimo e scienza politica nella Francia del XVI secolo: Loys Le Roy* (Florence: Olschki, 2007).

Scribner, R., *For the Sake of Simple Folk: Popular Propaganda for the German Reformation* (Cambridge: Cambridge University Press, 1981).

Searle, J., F. Kiefer, and M. Bierwisch, *Speech Act Theory and Pragmatics* (Dordrecht: Reidel, 1980).

Silverman, L., *Tortured Subjects: Pain, Truth, and the Body in Early Modern France* (Chicago, IL: Chicago University Press, 2001).

Simiz, S., ed., *La parole publique en ville des Réformes à la Révolution* (Villeneuve-d'Ascq: Presses universitaires du Septentrion, 2012).

Skinner, Q., *The Foundations of Modern Political Thought*, 2 vols. (Cambridge: Cambridge University Press, 1978).

'The Idea of a Cultural Lexicon', *Essays in Criticism*, 29 (1979), 207–24.

Reason and Rhetoric in the Philosophy of Hobbes (Cambridge: Cambridge University Press, 1996).

'Hobbes and the Purely Artificial Person of the State', *Journal of Political Philosophy*, 7.1 (1999), 1–29.

Visions of Politics, 3 vols. (Cambridge: Cambridge University Press, 2002).

Hobbes and Republican Liberty (Cambridge: Cambridge University Press, 2008).

From Humanism to Hobbes (Cambridge: Cambridge University Press, 2018).

Smet, I. de, *Menippean Satire and the Republic of Letters* (Geneva: Droz, 1996).

Thuanus: The Making of Jacques-Auguste de Thou (1553–1617) (Geneva: Droz, 2006).

Smith, P. M., *Continuity and Change in Renaissance Satire* (Hull: University of Hull Press, 1993).

Smith, S., 'Democracy and the Body Politic from Aristotle to Hobbes', *Political Theory*, 46 (2018), 167–96.

'The Language of Political Science in Early Modern Europe', *Journal of the History of Ideas* (2019), 203–26.

Snyder, J. R., *Writing the Scene of Speaking: Theories of Dialogue in the Late Italian Renaissance* (Stanford, CA: Stanford University Press, 1989).

Sowerby, R., 'Thomas Hobbes's Translation of Thucydides', *Translation and Literature*, 7.2 (1998) 147–69.

Sperber, D., and D. Wilson, *Relevance: Communication and Cognition* (Oxford: Oxford University Press, 1986).

Meaning and Relevance (Cambridge: Cambridge University Press, 2012).

Spitz, J.-F., *Bodin et la souveraineté* (Paris: Presses Universitaires de France, 1998).

Stanton, D., *The Dynamics of Gender in Early Modern France: Women Writ, Women Writing* (Farnham: Ashgate, 2014).

Starobinski, J., *Montaigne en mouvement* (Paris: Gallimard, 1982, repr. 1993).

Stawarz-Luginbühl, R., *Un théâtre de l'épreuve: Tragédies huguenotes en marge des guerres de religion* (Geneva: Droz, 2012).

Stefanovska M., and Paschoud, A., eds., *Littérature et politique: Factions et dissidences de la Ligue à la Fronde* (Paris: Garnier, 2015).

Stierle, K., 'Translatio studii and Renaissance: From Vertical to Horizontal Translation', in *The Translatability of Cultures: Figurations of the Space Between*, ed. by S. Budick and W. Iser (Stanford, CA: Stanford University Press, 1996), pp. 55–67.

Szabarì, A., *Less Rightly Said: Scandals and Readers in Sixteenth-Century France* (Stanford, CA: Stanford University Press, 2010).

Taboureau, J., *Un moraliste militaire du XVIe siècle: François de la Noue (1531–91)* (Paris: Lavauzelle, 1909).

Taylor, C., *The Language Animal: The Full Shape of the Human Linguistic Capacity* (Cambridge, MA, and London: Harvard University Press, 2016).

Todorov, *Le jardin imparfait: La pensée humaniste en France* (Paris: Grasset, 1998).

Tuck, R., *Philosophy and Government 1572–1651* (Cambridge: Cambridge University Press, 1993).

Van Orden, K. *Music, Discipline, and Arms in Early Modern France* (Chicago, IL: University of Chicago Press, 2005).

Vasoli, C., *Armonia e giustizia: Studi sulle idee filosofiche di Jean Bodin* (Florence: Olschki, 2008).

Vignes, J., 'Dialogue', in *Dictionnaire du littéraire,* ed. by A. Viala and P. Aron (Paris: PUF, 2002), pp. 147–49.

Vinestock, E., and D. Foster, *Writers in Conflict in Sixteenth-Century France: Essays in Honour of Malcolm Quainton* (Durham: Durham University Press, 2008).

Viroli, M., 'The Revolution in the Concept of Politics', *Political Theory*, 20 (1992), 473–95.

    From Politics to Reason of State: The Acquisition and Transformation of The Language of Politics, 1250–600 (Cambridge: Cambridge University Press, 1992).

Voss, P. J., *Elizabethan News Pamphlets: Shakespeare, Spenser, Marlowe, and the Birth of Journalism* (Pittsburgh, PA: Duquesne University Press, 2001).

Wanegffelen, T., ed., *De Michel de L'Hospital à L'Edit de Nantes: Politique et religion face aux Eglises* (Clermont-Ferrand: Presses universitaires Blaise Pascal, 2002).

Wanegffelen, T., *Cathérine de Médicis. Le pouvoir au féminin* (Paris: Payot, 2005).

    Le pouvoir contesté: Souveraines d'Europe à la Renaissance (Paris: Payot, 2008).

Williams, R., *Keywords: A Vocabulary of Society and Culture* (London: Fontana, 1988).

Williams, W., *Monsters and Their Meanings in Early Modern Culture: Mighty Magic* (Oxford: Oxford University Press, 2011).

Wilson, D., *Signs and Portents: Monstrous Births from the Middle Ages to the Enlightenment* (London: Routledge, 1993).

Winn, C. K., *The Dialogue in Early Modern France, 1547–1630: Art and Argument* (Washington, DC: Catholic University of America Press, 1993).

Wolfe, M., *The Conversion of Henri IV: Politics, Power, and Religious Belief in Early Modern France* (Cambridge, MA: Harvard University Press, 1993).

Xenophontos, S., *Ethical Education in Plutarch: Moralising Agents and Contexts* (Berlin: De Gruyter, 2016).

Zemon Davis, N., 'The Rites of Violence: Religious Riot in Sixteenth-Century France', *Past and Present*, 59 (1973), 51–91.

    Society and Culture in Early Modern France. Eight Essays (Stanford, CA: Stanford University Press, 1975).

Zurcher, A., *Shakespeare and Law* (London: Methuen, 2010).

Zwierlein, *Discorso und Lex. Die Enstehung neur Denkrahmen im 16, Jarhundert und die Wahrnehmung der französischen Religionskreige in Italien und*

Deutschland, Schriftenreihe der Historischen Kommision bei der Bayerischen Akademie der Wissenschaften (Munich: Vendoeck and Reprecht, 2006).
The Political Thought of the French League and Rome (Geneva: Droz, 2016).

INTERNET SOURCES

Alciato, A., 'Ex literarium studiis immortalitatem acquiri', in *Emblematum libellus* (Paris, 1534) www.emblems.arts.gla.ac.uk/alciato/dual.php?type1=1&id1=A34b041&type2=2&id2=sm53_C7r [accessed 15 January 2021].

'Sapientia humana stultitia est apud Deum', in *Embelamta/Emblemes* (Paris, 1584) www.emblems.arts.gla.ac.uk/alciato/emblem.php?id=FALc005 [accessed 15 January 2021].

'Bibliographie', in *Satyre ménippée: le libelle roi*, ed. by M. Martin www .satyremenippee.fr/bibliographie_menippee [accessed 3 August 2020].

'Cautelle', in R. Cotgrave, *Dictionarie of the French and English Tongues* (London: Islip, 1611), compiled by G. Lindhal, www.pbm.com/~lindahl/cotgrave/search/166l.html [accessed 3 August 2020].

'Crocheteur', in R. Cotgrave, *Dictionarie of the French and English Tongues* (London: Islip, 1611), compiled by G. Lindhal, www.pbm.com/~lindahl/cotgrave/search/261l.html [accessed 3 August 2020].

Gilmont, J. F., with Graves-Monroe, A., 'Les Mémoires de l'estat de France sous Charles IX (1576–1579) de Simon Goulart: bilan bibiliographique', *Etudes d'histoire du livre*, 11 (2015) https://revues.droz.org/index.php/HCL/ article/view/2326/3890 [accessed 15 January 2021].

Kuhn, H., 'Aristotelianism in the Renaissance', in *Stanford Encyclopedia of Philosophy* https://plato.stanford.edu/entries/aristotelianism-renaissance [accessed 3 August 2020].

L'Estoile, P. de, ed., *Les belles figures et drolleries de la Ligue* http://gallicadossiers .bnf.fr/Anthologie/ [accessed 3 August 2020].

'Pamphlet, n.', in *The Oxford English Dictionary* www.oed.com/search? searchType=dictionary&q=pamphlet&_searchBtn=Search [accessed 3 August 2020].

'Politique', in D. Diderot, J. d'Alembert, et al., *Encyclopédie ou Dictionnaire raisonné des sciences, des arts et des métiers, par une Société de gens de lettres* (1751–72), ed. by R. Morrissey and G. Roe http://artflx.uchicago. edu/ cgi-bin/philologic/getobject.pl?c.11:2093. encyclopedie0113 [accessed 31 July 2020].

'Politique', in A. Furetière, *Dictionnaire universel* (La Haye and Rotterdam, 1690) www.classiques-garnier.com/numerique-bases/index.php?module= App&action=FrameMain [accessed 28 July 2020].

'Politique', in P. Richelet, *Dictionnaire françois* [1680] (Geneva: Widerhold, 2007) http://ezproxy-prd.bodleian.ox.ac.uk:2242/numerique-bases/index .php?module=App&action=FrameMain [accessed 3 August 2018].

Turchetti, M., 'Jean Bodin', in *Stanford Encyclopedia of Philosophy* http://plato .stanford.edu/entries/bodin/ [accessed 3 August 2020].

LECTURES

Lane, M., 'Office and Anarchy', in *Constitutions before Constitutionalism: Classical Greek Ideas of Office and Rule*, The Carlyle Lectures, Oxford, 16 January 2018.

Smith, S., 'Making the State: Poetry and the Origins of Political Theory', Quentin Skinner Lecture 2017, University of Cambridge, 7 June 2017.

Index

Lightning Source UK Ltd.
Milton Keynes UK
UKHW021455020821
388116UK00004B/29